Life &
Money

Columbia Studies in Political Thought / Political History

Columbia Studies in Political Thought / Political History

Dick Howard, General Editor

Columbia Studies in Political Thought / Political History is a series dedicated to exploring the possibilities for democratic initiative and the revitalization of politics in the wake of the exhaustion of twentieth-century ideological "isms." By taking a historical approach to the politics of ideas about power, governance, and the just society, this series seeks to foster and illuminate new political spaces for human action and choice.

Pierre Rosanvallon, *Democracy Past and Future*, edited by Samuel Moyn (2006)

Claude Lefort, *Complications: Communism and the Dilemmas of Democracy*, translated by Julian Bourg (2007)

Benjamin R. Barber, *The Truth of Power: Intellectual Affairs in the Clinton White House* (2008)

Andrew Arato, *Constitution Making Under Occupation: The Politics of Imposed Revolution in Iraq* (2009)

Dick Howard, *The Primacy of the Political: A History of Political Thought from the Greeks to the French and American Revolution* (2010)

Paul W. Kahn, *Political Theology: Four New Chapters on the Concept of Sovereignty* (2011)

Stephen Eric Bronner, *Socialism Unbound: Principles, Practices, and Prospects* (2011)

David William Bates, *States of War: Enlightenment Origins of the Political* (2011)

Warren Breckman, *Adventures of the Symbolic: Post-Marxism and Radical Democracy* (2013)

Martin Breaugh, *The Plebeian Experience: A Discontinuous History of Political Freedom*, translated by Lazer Lederhendler (2013)

Dieter Grimm, *Sovereignty: The Origin and Future of a Political and Legal Concept*, translated by Belinda Cooper (2015)

Frank Palmeri, *State of Nature, Stages of Society: Enlightenment Conjectural History and Modern Social Discourse* (2016)

Elías José Palti, *An Archaeology of the Political: Regimes of Power from the Seventeenth Century to the Present* (2017)

Zvi Ben-Dor Benite, Stefanos Geroulanos, and Nicole Jerr, eds., *The Scaffolding of Sovereignty: Global and Aesthetic Perspectives on the History of a Concept* (2017)

Life & Money

THE GENEALOGY OF
THE LIBERAL ECONOMY
AND THE DISPLACEMENT
OF POLITICS

Ute Tellmann

Columbia University Press

New York

Columbia University Press
Publishers Since 1893
New York   Chichester, West Sussex
cup.columbia.edu

Library of Congress Cataloging-in-Publication Data
Names: Tellmann, Ute Astrid, author.
Title: Life and money : the genealogy of the liberal economy and the
    displacement of politics / Ute Astrid Tellmann.
Description: New York : Columbia University Press, [2017] | Includes
    bibliographical references and index.
Identifiers: LCCN 2017008227 | ISBN 978-0-231-18226-3 (cloth : alk. paper) |
    ISBN 978-0-231-54407-8 (e-book)
Subjects: LCSH: Economics—Political aspects. | Liberalism—Economic
    aspects.
Classification: LCC HB74.P65 T45 2017 | DDC 330—dc23
LC record available at https://lccn.loc.gov/2017008227

Cover image: (*top*) John Maynard Keynes © Sueddeutsche Zeitung Photo/
Alamy Stock Photo. (*bottom*) Thomas Robert Malthus © GL Archive/Alamy
Stock Photo

Cover design: Lisa Hamm

Contents

Foreword

DICK HOWARD

The slash in the series title "Political Thought/Political History" expresses the idea that neither pole can be analyzed and understood without the other; they are a unity in difference. The volumes published thus far in the series propose interpretations of this structural interdependence of political thought and political history. Each volume avoids the twin temptations either to unite the two poles in a Hegelian-Marxist type of philosophy of history, or to treat them as wholly independent and external to one another, related only by empirical causation. The relation that at once links and distinguishes these two faces is often called "the political." Although an implicit or explicit understanding of the political is presupposed by political thought, it becomes manifest only in specific political or historical contexts. The singularity of an event should not be reduced to an a posteriori expression of a circular logic that presupposes what it wants to prove; on the contrary, the momentary unity of political history with political thought is the reason that this book series is concerned with political *thought* rather than with the normative logic of political philosophy.

Ute Tellmann's *Life and Money* illustrates the way in which an interpretive history of the political encourages a critical perspective on contemporary political life. She explains in her preface that this project resulted from her "dissatisfaction with the disciplinary bounds of political theory" (vii). The two poles that her concise title binds together express the theoretical presuppositions of the two economic thinkers whose work she examines: Robert Thomas Malthus and John Maynard Keynes. Her knowledge of the economic literature, its context, as well as the political debates from which it emerged is wide and her eye for the singular is perceptive. Her research aims to understand what she calls the "quasi-ontological" difference between the economic and the economy itself (5). The economic, she explains, "forms the very condition of possibility of [an author's] argumentation" (165). The study of its particular historical expression "makes one wonder how else one could have negotiated and debated this 'critical space' of the economic" (192). This difference, to which she refers frequently, gives rise to Tellmann's repeated references to the "malleability" of the economic.

Although she also refers to the existence of a "political difference" and discusses "the political dimension of economics" (27), which is based on the interdependence of the political and the economic, Tellmann does not develop this part of her interpretation, perhaps because her book is "largely inspired by and indebted to Foucault's work" (31). Yet her subtitle, "The Genealogy of the Liberal Economy and the Displacement of Politics," suggests the need to explain how the economic came to exist as a challenge to political thought after the exhaustion of what had been called political economy in the eighteenth century. This is the genealogical question addressed in Part I, which illustrates the way that "life" came to define the economic. Malthus is crucial to Tellmann's reconstruction even though his work was less important for the discipline of economics proper than that of Ricardo, for example. Malthus's insistence on the power of necessity, the immanence of scarcity, and the search for future security can be said to mark the "displacement of politics."

Part I illustrates the breadth of Tellmann's analysis. Its goal is to show that, despite its own claims, classical liberalism is not based simply on economic considerations. The three chapters that demonstrate this thesis are summarized here briefly. The first edition of Malthus's *Essay on the Principle of Population* was published in 1798, when the political upheavals of the French revolution were still felt; by the time its sixth edition appeared in 1826, the economic had acquired its autonomy, delimiting the sphere of necessity that politics could not violate. Perhaps the most telling expression of the shift is Malthus's insistence, during the debates on the abolition of the Poor Laws, that there is no "right to live." Such a right, he argues, would return people to a savage state in which they are caught in the immediacy of the desire for consumption, unable to conceive the need to prepare for the future; as a result, they multiply too rapidly, lives of plenty give way to conditions of scarcity, and eventually natural death must follow. Civilization entails the ability to put off desire, and its maintenance depends on fear of a future that has no guarantee. Malthus's argument makes clear that "liberalism" is not based on principles of laissez-faire or property rights.[1] The recognition of necessity becomes the key to a prosperous future that preserves the lives of the living (by means of colonial expansion if necessary). As a result, the unit of economic evaluation must be the "population" whose ways and needs liberal government must take into account. In this way, government of the economic leaves no place for the political.

Part II focuses on the centrality of "money" to the definition of the economic in Keynes's thought. Its three chapters are inversely symmetrical to Part I. There is a critical movement away from austere surrender to the forces of necessity, followed by the liberation of what Keynes called the "vital spirits" of economic and monetary speculation. These spirits are tamed in turn by a macroeconomic neoliberal "anti-political economy" (167), which recaptures the liberal idea that population offers a national bounded space in which experts define the measure of (and therefore the allocation of) wealth. The parallels between the two parts of Tellmann's genealogical reconstruction are of course not exact; she is writing a work of political thought. But that is precisely the reason that these parallels are so thought-provoking.

The critique of the liberal culture of austerity in the late nineteenth century called into question classical economic logic based on scarcity, necessity, and the promise of future stability. Keynes was part of the movement of cultural modernism;[2] he also wrote the critical *Treatise on Probability* (1921). The centrality of money to his theory of the economic reflects these influences. Just as modernity turns around the perception of the individual subject who experiences a reality that is fragmented and in which fixity, certainty, and totality are impossible, so too Keynes replaced the classical theory of money, in which money is a mere representation of real values, with a dynamic and openly pluralist conception. Keynes takes account of what Tellmann calls the "material temporalities of money," which permit, for example, the invention of new forms of credit and debt. As she points out, there was good reason to call Keynes the "Einstein of economics" (23). The modern vision of the economic, Keynes predicted, was the prelude to the "slow death of the rentier." Could it also be seen as an invitation to the democratization of the stock market's chaotic wisdom of anonymous choices? If values are conventional, open to change, and ultimately pragmatic, then what is now the task of government?

Tellmann's reading of Keynes is carefully nuanced: she distinguishes between the economist and his followers, and even more importantly, she recognizes Keynes's own inconsistencies and uncertainties.[3] She insists on the difference between the economic and the empirically existent economy that opens the space for choice. Nonetheless, her final chapter, "The Archipolitics of Macroeconomics," concludes that the role of government in the Keynesian scheme closes off the "malleability" that she has stressed throughout her study. Applying Jacques Rancière's concept of an "archipolitics," Tellmann writes that "whenever there is a vision of 'the economy' or 'the global market' as a unified entity whose laws one can only avoid if one is willing to invite calamities of a higher order, one can suspect that we are dealing with a masterpiece of archipolitics in the clothes of economic thought that has displaced the malleable economic."[4] The critical implication of Tellmann's reconstruction is that Keynesianism has come to represent a sort of "hydraulic" vision of government that recreates in modified form the antipolitical vision of nineteenth-century classical liberalism. Just as government then was expected to maintain an economic equilibrium in order to preserve the life of the population, so today's economists must make use of the varieties and velocities of money in order to do the same.

Tellmann's use of the concept of archipolitics recalls—but is not identical to—the concept of antipolitics as I have used it in my own writings.[5] For her, archipolitics calls attention to the elimination of the "malleability" produced by the distinction of the economic from the real economy. This economic difference implies that the same principles that articulate the economic (i.e., "life" and "money") could be given a different empirical form. How that could occur is not clear. Insofar as Tellmann's subtitle associates the liberal economy with the displacement of politics, the only possibility appears to be a reassertion of the difference between the economic and the economy—perhaps, as in Rancière's writings, through a type of social rebellion or perhaps in a Foucaldian figure that remains to be defined. What seems to be missing is an account of the relation between the political and the economic—i.e., a *political* difference—that could restore the unity and the difference of the economic and the economy. In the place of the liberal project of governmentality, perhaps a twenty-first century republican politics could take on this new challenge?

In the meantime, critical analyses of "Political Thought/Political History" continue to be needed. Ute Tellmann's creative use of Michel Foucault's work is a significant contribution to the ongoing dialogue.

Preface

This book took a long time to come into being. Between its early inception and its final version are many years during which I changed disciplines, continents, and academic cultures. These interdisciplinary and geographic travels were not just circumstantial to this project but mirror its very subject matter. The project crosses over academic disciplines and debates: It interlaces political and sociological theory, history, economic thought, and cultural theory as well as insights from postcolonial thought and feminist theory for rendering understandable what has turned liberal economy into a domain of technocratic management and necessity—and in order to divest our notion of liberal economy from such assumptions by recovering the contentious history of the economic.

The starting point of this work was the dissatisfaction with the disciplinary bounds of political theory. Political theory has extensively elaborated on the political nature of setting limits to the sphere of politics, but it faces difficulties in portraying what politics means beyond these limits. In order to address the political nature of the broader material-social order, political theory needs an account of its very object of contention, its *res*, so to speak, in a particular way: such an account must neither ignore the recalcitrance, inner density, and specificity of what it deals with, nor must it made to succumb to an image of unyielding laws of necessity. Looking politically at things requires both trying to find a name for "what is" and enlarging the sense of possibility for shaping it. It is not sufficient to highlight the general historical contingency of this or that social construction; one needs accounts of reality that are specific and yet malleable.

Many of the accounts of economy lack these qualities. They are depicted as laws of the market or of capitalism, as realism of scarcity, or they are presented in the form of highly technical expert knowledge that makes it very difficult to understand how far they are already embodiments of political choices that have alternatives. Is there a way that political theory can be part of opening up and multiplying the ways to rethink the specificity and malleability of economy? This book is an attempt to open up accounts of liberal economy to such a political perspective. It looks at economic thought from the stance of political theory, meaning that it searches for the specificity and malleability of the economic in systems of thought that are dedicated to this subject matter and yet do much to displace it.

The book is born out of a keen awareness that new possibilities for thought belong to particular historical constellations. It is therefore a historical book that deals with how particular crisis in the history of liberalism have opened up the notion of liberal economy from within. At the same time, it is not about merely about the past. Historical constellations have a life beyond themselves. Reading and rereading them from the present can recover what they hold in store. Sometimes it is easier to see novelty in the past than it is to understand what the present is ripe with and what it opens up to. This is especially the case when the contemporary appears to be lacking belief in political possibility and is full of fear of what is to come.

Exploring the middle ground, where "the economic" and "the political" can meet, was not without difficulties. Inhabiting this zone turns oneself into a strange species: one reads the canon but the wrong one; one deals with history but is not a historian; one learns the trade of the economist but does not share their self-confidence and certainty; one reads the anthropologist and sociologist, who aim at shedding a new light on economic practices, but one does not follow their steps; one sees connections between the distant past and the most actual debates and events but in such mediated way that it takes some time to explain. Sitting in this middle ground is at the same time uncomfortable and incredibly rewarding. It sets the task to explicate the crossings that one witnesses from this spot.

It took time to do this work of explication and framing more than anything else. While parts of the argument presented in this book have stayed the same since its beginning, it was a work of constant writing and rewriting to explicate what this in-between consists of. To bring this project to fruition, I needed two responses at once: those who would encourage me to venture into this rich and uncomfortable thought-space and those who would relentlessly push me to clarify, explicate, specify, and discipline myself in deciding which connection to follow, how, and why. I was fortunate to be blessed with both. In this way, many mentors, colleagues, and friends have helped me to write this book.

The beginnings of this project go back to my time at graduate school at Cornell University. I want to thank Susan Buck-Morss for encouraging me to take up this project, for inspiration, guidance, and support in how to inhabit this thought-space. I thank Jonathan Kirshner for asking the right questions; Anna Marie Smith, for making sure I took up not five projects but one; Isaac Kramnick, for planting the love of British radicalism into me; Jason Frank, for seeing the connections to contemporary political theory; and, last but not least, Geoffrey Waite, for unforgettable demonstrations of what it means to read a text.

The intellectual community at Cornell is a wonderful combination of intellectual endeavor and friendship. I have enormously benefited from being part of it. I thank Banu Bargu and Leila Ibrahim, Torben Lohmüller and John Kim, Kathrin Gordy and Sandrine Poisson, Adelheid Voskuhl, Dorian Stuber and Marianne Tettlebaum, Craig Ewasiuk, Mindy Peden, Shannon Mariotti, Megan Thomas, and K-Sue Park. My gratitude goes to Irene Mittelberg for wonderful kitchen talks, coffee, poems, and art. Out of sharing a beautiful house grew a beautiful friendship.

The project received institutional and financial support, without which it could not have been accomplished. A Luigi Einaudi Fellowship awarded by the Institute for European Studies at Cornell University enabled the archival research at King's College Archive, Cambridge. A Mellon Fellowship and a grant by the Studienstiftung des deutschen Volkes supported the research that culminated in the final version of this project. I very much thank the archivists at King's College Archive for helping me to sort out the connections between Keynes and Nietzsche.

I continued with this project upon my return to Europe and to the discipline of sociology at the University of Basel and the University of Hamburg. I thank Urs Stäheli, who belongs to the few sociologists who are open to political theory and historical research and who favor an intellectual inspiration over the certainties of the canon. To him I owe the time and space to follow this project through. An academic community of friends and colleagues supported me during this time in Basel and Hamburg, among whom are Lea Bühlmann and Stefan Nellen, Dirk Verdicchio and Silke Berlanger, Franziska Dahlmeier, Eike Marten, Anke Siebold and Doris Deiglmayr, Jörg Ebrecht, Hans-Joachim Rieckman, Carolin Wiedeman, Katharina Braun, Vassilis Tsianos, and Marianne Pieper. Mathias Leese, Jannek Schweer, Jessica Mijnssen were of wonderful help for putting the manuscript together and for making sure everything is in right order. Some parts of this research have appeared in different versions, and I acknowledge kind permissions: "Historical Ontologies of Uncertainty and Money: Rethinking the Current Critique of Finance," *Journal of Cultural Economy* 9, no. 1 (2016): 63–85; "Catastrophic Populations and the Fear of the Future: Malthus and the Genealogy of Liberal Economy," *Theory, Culture & Society* 30, no. 1 (2013): 135–55.

The intellectual companionship that nourished me during these years did not belong to one place. It came from different researchers that share kindred intellectual sensibilities even though they follow them in so many different ways and places. One constant companionship and support comes from Marieke de Goede, for which I am very grateful. I thank Nina Boy for putting us all together into a research network and for her intellectual passions in our discussions. I have benefited from the discussions with Paul Langley, Andreas Langenohl, Samin Amin, Anthony Amicelle, Emily Gilbert, and Oliver Kessler.

I was very happy to taste something of the great intellectual community at the University of Sydney upon an invitation to participate at the "Rethinking Money Workshop" from the Social Studies of Finance Research Group, where I had the chance to discuss parts of this work with Michael Rafferty, Dough Holmes, Brett Neilson, Dick Bryan, Leigh Claire la Berge, Lana Swartz, Fiona Allen, and Miguel Vatter, among others. Special thanks go to Melinda Cooper and Martijn Konings for being kindred spirits and interlocutors for rethinking economy and for offering institutional support to get this work published.

I have presented and discussed many of the thoughts that went into this book in various occasions and received helpful comments from Mitchell Dean, Thomas Lemke, Andreas Folkers, Ulrich Bröckling, Susanne

Krassman, Luis Lobo-Guerrero, and Martin Saar. I was very lucky that my work was closely read and extensively discussed at the colloquium of political theory at the University of Bremen by Frieder Vogelmann, Martin Nonhoff, and Anna Hollendung. It was a great pleasure to discuss the concept of scarcity and budgets with the research group Low Budget Urbanity at the Hafen City University of Hamburg, notably Heike Derwanz and Alexa Färber.

I want to thank Bill Maurer and Lotta Björklund Larsen for closely reading and commenting on parts of the manuscript. They posed challenging, very important questions and gave wonderful encouragement to the project, which was both much appreciated.

Above all, it is my pleasure to thank Stephen Collier for his unfailing and immense support for this book. His close readings and perspicacious comments on various stages of the manuscript were much needed and much appreciated. He was of invaluable help, and this book owes enormously to his generosity in giving time and thought to this project. I am very grateful for having had him as an interlocutor throughout this time.

I also want to thank Wendy Lochner at Columbia University Press for taking this project on and for her determination and kindness in seeing this project through the publication process. The team at Columbia University Press was wonderful to work with; special thanks go to Lisa Hamm for the beautiful design of the cover. I benefitted enormously from the patience and diligence of Patti Bower and Cecilia Cancellaro for polishing the text; thanks also go to Kara Pekar for helping to put together the index. I want to thank the reviewers both for what they saw in this project and for their insightful criticisms that helped me to improve the manuscript tremendously for the final draft.

I owe the most to my loved ones. My parents have always encouraged me to venture outside of what I already knew. I thank them for having been so supportive, loving, and fun throughout. I dedicate the work to my mother and the memory of my father, who died too early, with so much love for life left unlived. I would have accomplished nothing without the love of my sister, Karin. Her energy and support are unrivaled, and I want to thank her for all she has done for me. My gratitude goes, last but not least, to Sven, my husband and intellectual partner, who has been there for me throughout all this time, listening, reading, discussing, and rereading patiently what I presented to him, while our son, Paul, offered delightful distractions, insisting to look at trees rather than to write on them. The book would not be there without my companion's support. His intellectual companionship, humor, and love make life so much richer and brighter. With him, even the most tedious part of academic life turns into an occasion for having a good conversation and, above all, a good laugh.

Life &
Money

Introduction

The Economic and the Genealogy of Liberalism

I n the wake of the financial crisis of 2008 a short moment occurred in which deep-seated beliefs about liberal economy and its relation to politics were subject to profound puzzlement and fundamental questioning. The fact that financial values had simply disappeared, that risk calculations seemed to have no basis, and that billions of taxpayer dollars had to be used to save those who appeared to be the culprits of this drama has challenged assumptions of economic efficiency, rationality, and reality. The Financial Crisis Inquiry Commission, established to study the causes of this meltdown, uttered fascination, surprise, and shock about the willful blindness, ignorance, and lack of judgment of the side of financial actors and institutions before the crisis.[1] The reactions of this commission stood for many others. Were financial markets not the harbingers of efficiency and necessary discipline in a world of scarce resources?[2] On which grounds were these markets granted the authority to decide about and represent what should count as hard facts in the world of economy? What counts as economic reality, and who accounts for it? The crisis opened up what sociologist William Davies described as a "critical space . . . in which standard methodologies, moral principles and anthropological presuppositions can be thrown into doubt."[3]

The effects of such critical questioning turned out to be rather limited. As profound and pressing as this evaluative chaos was, it was overlaid by something else: an imperative of saving the system and a rather narrowed debate about how to fix what had led the financial system astray. The first emergency measures sought to inject liquidity into the system, to restore confidence, and to ensure that no cascade of credit failures would bring the system to a halt. These emergency measures were followed by a set of "crisis narratives" designed to correct the putative "fictions" and "delusions" that reigned before the crisis.[4] Of course, there were many different expert opinions about how to ensure the "realism" of financial markets after all the delusions. Different strands of established economic theory were applied to provide answers. Old authorities were called upon. Policy proposals were presented regarding risk management, capital requirements, and clearance mechanisms for financial markets. In other words, the debate about what counts as economic objectivity, and who accounts for it, shifted. It retreated into a highly technical discussion of regulatory proposals meant to set financial markets back on track while it simultaneously became increasingly difficult to understand the politics at stake.

The quickness with which the open space for political reflection was closed was surprising given how dramatic and scandalous this crisis had appeared. The hope that this event could have been an occasion for rethinking critique, regulation, and the meaning of liberal economy in a more fundamental sense was not fulfilled.[5] The political ramifications of the crisis appear to be lopsided: it favored resettling rather than delving into the foundation on which we debate and understand liberal economy and its relation to politics. How would the debates about liberal economy and its relation to politics change if such "critical space" persisted? Can one retrieve such moments of conceptual openness from other crises of liberalism that did allow for a more thorough rethinking of liberalism? Is it possible to revisit and enlarge the "critical spaces" of liberalism in order to recover economic difference?

This book engages in such undertaking. It restages and reconstructs specific crises in the history of liberalism that transformed the way the economic problem was posed. The story told here magnifies the "critical space" that emerged at specific historical junctures and excavates how the economy was open to debate. It focuses on the disagreements about the most fundamental kernel of economic reality and its relation to political reason. At the same time, it accounts for how this "critical space" was closed and how a new boundary between economy and politics was reestablished. In other words, the book offers an analysis of historical junctures in the history of liberalism that unraveled and reassembled the political and economic imagination of liberalism. The story told here is what I call a genealogy of the economic in liberalism. The conceptual novelty of this approach is explained further below. Stated in most general terms, it is an act of recuperating a sense of the malleability of the economic in liberalism while offering an account of how it gets displaced. Ignoring the boundaries between political theory and economic thought, the book shows how these disciplines are entangled for closing the critical space of debate and for declaring what should be regarded as economically necessary.

The first scene that this book focuses on occurs at the turn of the nineteenth century. It is marked by a novel demarcation between economy and politics in liberalism: economic necessity was invented for liberalism. Liberal economy turned into a domain of unyielding laws that override issues of justice or political demands for equality. These conceptual shifts emerged in an environment of heated political contestation: democratic radicalism, revolutionary upheaval, and the turn to empire characterized this situation. The question of life, corporeal existence, subsistence, and reproduction stood at the heart of these political contestations and conceptual changes. Thomas Robert Malthus's writings on population, economy, and politics captured that mélange of political uncertainties and the turn toward necessity in a paradigmatic way. The first part of the book revisits this scene of contestation: I distill from it the open question of the economic, and I lay bare the political and cultural arguments that turn economy into a question of necessity.

The second scene that moves to center stage in the second part of the book takes place roughly one hundred years later, when liberalism was challenged by another moment of contestation. The first decades of the twentieth century saw, again, a constellation of revolutionary upheavals, political struggles, imperial uncertainty, and cultural and social change, which led to a profound questioning of the foundations and bounds of the body politic. The question of what constitutes economic reality was embroiled in its midst. The rise of Keynesianism is most emblematic of the internal re-articulation and challenge of liberal economy at that time. Today Keynesianism is mostly known and often derided as a postwar orthodoxy of macroeconomics that champions public spending beyond budgetary restrictions and a belief in technocratic state-management of the economy. But at first, Keynesianism constituted an internal critique of the liberal economic. Money proved to be the main lever for this fundamental critique of the ontology of the economic in liberalism. Before a new orthodoxy of Keynesianism emerged, a moment of inner contestation and indeterminacy ripe with economic difference emerged.

By focusing on particular moments of contestation and closure, of challenging and resettling the understanding of the economic and of economic necessity vis-à-vis politics, this book offers an original conceptual history of the economic and political in liberalism. It does not tell a tale about how the influence of the state or markets grew or shrank. It does not restrict itself to outlining the governmental regulations or political rationalities that always "embed" the market or "govern" the economy. Such accounts rely on an established notion of the market or the state that take specific notions of liberal economy or policies as given. In contrast, I focus on the historical making and unmaking of the conceptual division between the political and the economic in liberalism at moments when the kernel of economic reality stood in question. What happened in these situations is not simply a redrawing of the boundary between economy and politics in an unchanged landscape, so to speak, but an alteration of the very ground on which this boundary is drawn. The argument ventures deep into the historical archive in order to demonstrate that dominant tenets in the history of liberal economics have a shadow—a critical space where the "malleable economic" appears—that gets displaced and disfigured by the act of closing this space for debating what liberalism could mean.

On the Economic

Recording the double movement between the opening and closing of the space for negotiating liberal economy requires a specific type of conceptual history. I call this history a genealogy of the economic. The notion of "the economic" shifts attention away from "the economy" in order to provoke an interrogative stance toward deep-seated assumptions about what renders things economic as opposed to political, religious, or aesthetic. For example, are things economic because they are scarce? Or are they economic because they are tied to monetary calculation or exchange? How do these key attributes define a realm of economic necessity; how do they challenge it? I use the notion of the economic in order to focus on a quality or an attribute. This enables a fresh perspective on debates about liberal economy. Our conceptual languages that favor accounts of entities, institutions, and structures make us imagine the economy as a domain or as a field, growing larger or smaller vis-à-vis politics, religion, or art.[6] We are used to talking about processes of economization in terms of the dangerous intrusion of economic reasoning into realms hitherto shielded from it. But what exactly is meant by rendering things more or less economic? What conceptual language is available for understanding different intensities, degrees, and modes of economization? The territorial metaphor of "the economy" is not helpful for answering this question.

The economic is a conceptual coinage that is modeled in parallel fashion to the notion of the political. The notion of the political has been widely discussed within contemporary political theory without having an unequivocal definition.[7] Very broadly defined, it relates to contested processes of constitution, meaning here the processes of fixating and institutionalizing principles of order. The notion of "the political" or "the economic" bracket the institutionalized and fixated meanings that have become associated with politics or the economy respectively. These conceptual coinages open up a quasi-ontological level of inquiry about the type of reality that we are dealing with.[8] I want to look at the historical articulation of the specific yet malleable quality of the economic and render visible how it is constrained and fixed into a given notion of economy. While the notion of the political preoccupies contemporary political and social theory, the economic has—unfortunately—never been granted the same scholarly attention.[9]

Highlighting the parallelism between "the economic" and "the political" is not accidental in this context. It draws attention to the fact that the conceptualization of economy is not independent from the conceptualization of politics. As the political theorist Robert Walker recently suggested, these concepts have "equally complicated and consequential histories of mutual implication and antagonism."[10] A parallel conceptualization of the economic and the political allows us to study this co-constitution. One of the central claims of this book is that the division between politics and economy in liberalism denotes more than a difference between domains. Sociologists and economists are quick to address this division as belonging to a process of modern differentiation, which accords different sets of functional demands and values to different subsystems in society. But the conceptual division between economy and politics in liberalism is more than that. As will be argued, in the history of liberalism this conceptual separation has been used to grant the notion of economy a foundational role vis-à-vis politics. It bestows the epistemic privilege to the economic side for defining what is most irredeemable, unavoidable, and real in the making of social order.

Modern liberalism has a long history of granting the notion of economy the function of defining a limit to politics. As Sheldon Wolin put it in his seminal history of political thought, since the beginning of the nineteenth century, liberalism gives economics the privilege to fashion the "knowledge of society," thereby taking over a "territory originally held by political philosophy: that of possessing the sovereign knowledge to the welfare of the community as a whole." This limitation of politics and political philosophy went hand in hand with a "desperate long[ing] to transcend the political." The precedence given to economic categories did influence the Western tradition of thought as a whole and left its mark even on Karl Marx's critique of political economy. Taking economic dynamics as a basis for the explanation of societal order and political dynamics deeply influenced Marxism as a theoretical and political strategy. In this sense, "the anti-political impulses nurtured by classical liberalism" that Wolin diagnosed left their mark on its adversaries. Such impulses "took on a depth and pervasiveness unmatched in previous centuries."[11]

I argue that this aspiration to delimit politics disfigures our notion of economy: it has to be thought of as more unyielding, more pure and efficient than necessary. This disfiguration results from the fact that having to provide a foundation for politics puts certain requirements on our understanding of economy. While our sense of politics is closely connected to concerns about the dangers of wrong judgments, the proper distribution of power, and the misuse of resources, *inter alia*, our sense of economy seems to exclude the complexity of these dangers. Because the economic realm is conceptualized as a limit to and foundation of politics, this domain appears to be purified from these issues. The well-known arguments about the putative realism of the market bespeak this foundational role of economic beliefs. But how would the notion of liberal economy look if it were allowed to be as uncertain, power-ridden, and groundless as politics? To answer this question one must disentangle the economic from the notion of economy. One has to trace how the malleable economic gets displaced in the process of constitution.

This book is the result of something that political theorists rarely do—and sociologists never do: engage with the canon of economic thought as if it belonged to one's own discipline, subjecting it to the same strategies of analysis and critique used in political and social theory. Economists are as much political theorists as they are economists, but they rarely read in parallel. When tracing the mutual imbrication of the notion of economy and politics, one cannot privilege one side over the other or reduce one to the other. Borrowing the words of Bruno Latour, one has to "outline the symmetrical space and thereby reestablish the common understanding that organizes the separation" of these notions.[12] By establishing this common ground, one can study the irreducible intermingling of political and economic arguments and yet retain a sense of their difference.

Themes and Scenes of the Liberal Economic

As indicated earlier, this book looks at the double movement of the opening and closing of the economic through the lenses of two figures in the history of economic thought: Thomas Robert Malthus and John Maynard Keynes. These figures function as points of crystallization around which this book organizes the story about the contested meaning of economy in liberalism and its relation to politics. Given that this book revolves around two specific scenes and figures, its argument is largely historical—but not solely so. The argument that I present is as much conceptual as it is historical—both dimensions are inextricably tied; they inform and define each other. Even though the conceptual frames and findings therefore cannot and should not be entirely severed from these historical scenes, it is possible to tease them out in a more systematic and comparative way, helping the reader to better understand the broader conceptual significance that this historical argument entails.

The book has two parts, each dedicated to one scene of contestation. The two parts of the book mirror each other in how I reconstruct this double movement of opening and closing the critical space in liberalism. Both parts of the book commence with a historical account of the politics of contention that rendered the boundary between economy and politics porous and uncertain. What turns these scenes of intense political debate and protest into instances of "the political" is the way that they are tied to an epistemological uncertainty about how to understand the very object of conflict. For tracing the dimension of "the political" within the historical material, I look at how this indeterminacy manifested itself in the main terms of critique and debate at that particular time.

At the turn of the nineteenth century, the terms of contestation and critique consisted of a mélange of the notion of rights, an account of social order in terms of corporeal and social sentiments, and a belief in "social mathematics" designed to help the project of generating social and political equality. None of these elements were yet reducible to a notion of a single social or economic system, and a sense of search and experimentation animated all elements. Mingled with political passions and increased debate, this situation generated a "critical space" that allowed negotiation of how politics could address corporeal vulnerability and need in novel ways. Liberalism was torn open to a sense of political experimentation regarding the question of how to politicize the economy of life. The contemporary debates in political theory about the advent of modern biopolitics in this period barely capture this "critical space" that I bring to light in the first chapter. As I argue, the political possibility of a "wide sea of experiments" without restraint eventually motivated the novel conception of economy as a firmly bound domain with its own laws of necessity. Political arguments favored the notion of economic laws. They had the advantage of being clear, irrefutable, simple, and, hence, easily understood even by the illiterate masses who could not be trusted with matters as complex as economy (see chapter 1).

At the beginning of the twentieth century, there is a parallel emergence of such "critical space" within the liberal tradition. This time a rising tide of political contention mingled with a profound "modernist" questioning of notions of objectivity. The term "culture" stood at the heart of the languages of critique at that time. Cultural critique furnished the means for undoing the belief in the truth-value of economic rationality. Cast in this light, the economic subject appeared as prone to misjudgment as the political subject; both were guilty of conformism, and both were unable to maintain judgment against the masses. This language of critique had its own pitfalls. It employed tropes of degeneration and gendered stereotypes. But it also made the boundaries between economy and politics porous. The economic subject and the market no longer embodied the "reality principle" vis-à-vis the political world (see chapter 4).

From this historical scene of "the political," I turn toward the parallel reconstruction of "the economic" for each period. Unpacking the economic is a largely conceptual operation that requires engaging very closely with the economic writings of Malthus and Keynes. In each case I focus on a particular economic notion, such as scarcity or money, in order to disentangle the malleable economic that is connected to it. Searching for the contours of the economic means to accentuate the quality, specificity, and malleability of this attribute that we take largely for granted when we speak about scarcity or money. Instead of pondering the naturalizations within economic discourses, or instead of looking at how economic facts get modeled, quantified, and fixated, this strategy of reading takes the opposite route: it disentangles what makes up the composite of scarcity or money; it looks at the stories about their origins and asks what malleability they contain if read against the grain or if extrapolated from what the texts assert. Interestingly and unexpectedly, the historical ontology of the economic that I distill from these writings come to revolve in both cases around the notions of temporality and futurity—but they do so in a radically different way and with different implications.

In the case of Malthus's writings, this strategy of unpacking the economic focuses on the link between population and scarcity. The principle of population enshrined, dramatized, and rendered palpable a new sense of all-pervasive and quasi-ontological scarcity for liberal economic thought. I take this scene of emergence that links up the question of population with the dictum of scarcity as an opportunity to undo the black box of scarcity. I reveal that it is not population per se but a particular conception of "savage life" that is responsible for this link between scarcity and life. The principle of population is at bottom a fear of so-called savage life, which squanders resources without thinking about the future. Scarcity appears in turn as a regulatory "as-if" that should counter the propensity of "savage life" to get lost in the impression of today's plenty. In other words, scarcity appears as a technical and epistemological device for engendering economic futurity. Disentangling the fear of the cultural other from the question of economic futurity brings the malleability of the economic to the fore—it allows asking who and what do we trust or mistrust in turning the given abundance into economic futures. Detecting how fundamentally the question of economic futurity is tied to colonial notions of civilization in Malthus's texts also tells us about the importance of developing a postcolonial perspective on liberal economic thought (see chapter 2).

While it might be unanticipated to think about scarcity as epistemic virtue that ensures futurity, it seems more commonplace to understand Keynes's account of money in temporal terms. The financial crisis of 2008 brought about a revival of Keynes as an economist who knew about the fundamental role of eradicable uncertainty for economic life and capitalism. The importance of the notion of temporality for Keynesian critique of classical liberalism is widely established. But the analysis of the economic that I offer in the second part of the book diverges from this understanding of temporality as uncertainty. I contend instead that the Keynesian notion of money belongs to an elaboration of the economic not in terms of uncertainty but in terms of material temporality, measurement, and convention. For this reason, money appears to Keynes no longer as a medium of representation but as a material time machine with its own measures, due dates, and returns that are fixed by conventions. Money is but one plane of material temporality among others in this historical ontology of the economic. As I show, Keynes's writings contain an unbound liberal economic: a specific attribute that is malleable and open to impure processes of constitution (see chapter 5).

These acts of closure or settlement of "the economic" and "the political" are the subject matter of the final chapters in each part of the book. Eventually, the economic and the political must be transformed into institutionalized settings and practices that give form to what counts as economic objectivity and that delimit and shape the role of politics. The language of boundaries and domains that we are so familiar with belongs to such settlement of a "double constitution" of political-economic liberalism. This term "double constitution" is borrowed from the philosopher and anthropologist Bruno Latour, who coined it to shed a new light on the boundary between society and nature. He argues that we should understand the alleged purity of distinct spheres as a misleading, albeit politically versatile account of the hybrid entanglements between nature and society.[13] In a similar vein, I demonstrate how the boundary between the domain of economy and politics is an instrument effect of a hybrid institutionalization of economic objectivity and political forms of governing. As I will explain later, I understand this closure and settlement in terms of a specific "archipolitics" that displaces the malleability of the economic by political means.

The boundary that Malthus announced between economy and politics made him infamous: it consisted of a declaration of the rights that man does not have—that is, the "right to live." Malthus's arguments about the "right to live" belonged to the debates surrounding the abolition of the Poor Laws and the economic feasibility of public relief. Behind the concrete policy question stood the broader issues of equality and subsistence in a liberal polity. As can be shown, such declaration of the nonrights of man belongs to a specific settlement or closure of liberalism, which locates the stronghold of economic objectivity solely in the desires and aspirations of the subject. The types of political interventions regarded as appropriate by Malthus coalesce around the aim of turning savage life into economic *man*. Due to the fear of "savage life" that pervades Malthus's liberalism (and much of the liberalisms that were to come), he assumes that man cannot behave economically while being certain about his future: in this case, man would always remain mired in destructive immediacy of consumption and reproduction. Hence, with Malthus, liberalism turns toward policies that cultivate the fears and hopes of economic man (and his wife) in order to create civilization and economic futurity at once. Arguing against public support for single mothers, Malthus assumes that man should not be relieved from caring for his offspring, for otherwise he would not entertain such long views of futurity. A gendered and hierarchized politics of affects that targets economic man nested within social and conjugal relations results from this nexus of scarcity and population, containing yet displacing the more malleable economic (see chapter 3).

I tell a parallel but very different story about how in twentieth-century liberalism the economic is displaced and domesticated by a novel settlement in the case of Keynes. How does the economic understood as multiple planes of material temporalities turn into a managerial politics of macroeconomic management? As I will argue, this settlement is founded on a biopolitical yet culturalized notion of a national population. Moreover, a Burkean type of political conservatism and a belief in the superiority of singular persons in the art of judgment were conjoined in shaping the contours of Keynesian economic government. Chapter 6 unfolds the specific type of liberal governmentality that befits this newly bounded domain of "the economy." It is characterized by how it uses money as a tool of governing. Again, one can find a politics of affect targeting the desires of economic man—but this time the creation of a steady and well-tempered hope in those who invest money for future wealth became its main lever. Again, this governmental rationality would be impossible without novel understanding of the economic on which it rests but that also delimits and displaces (see chapter 6).

Is there a way to take up that "critical space" of the economic again and use this openness of imagining, designing, and experimenting with what liberal economy might mean? The epilogue takes up this question.

The scenes of contestation that this book restages lie a hundred years apart—they are in many ways entirely incomparable and unique, yet they can be made part of one story about the economic in liberalism. Having emphasized the similarity of approaching these two scenes of contestation and closure so far, I want to alert the reader to a main difference between these parts of the book. Malthus and Keynes played rather different roles for this double movement that I record: Whereas Malthus reacted to a radical questioning of liberal politics and economy that had emanated elsewhere, Keynes partook in both the opening and closing of this critical space. This results in a slightly different strategy of reading their texts. In the case of Malthus, I retrieve the "malleable economic" from within the assertion of economic necessity and scarcity that pervades his writings. Accordingly, the aspects of opening and closure cannot be divided as neatly among different chapters in the first part of the book as they work constantly against each other and remain tightly aligned. In the case of Keynes, the malleability of the economic can be excavated by following parts of his writings to their implicit conclusion and by exploring and explicating the critique that he mounted against classical liberalism. The juxtaposition of the movements of opening and closure can be better divided between different chapters. But for both parts of the book, the common structure that commences with the political languages of critique turns to the historical ontology of the economy and ends with an account of the settlement into novel boundaries, realms, and recipes for governing economic life retains its hold.

Using these two specific historical scenes for this account of economic difference and this analysis of its displacement necessarily implies the omission of many other scenes of contestation and languages of critique vis-à-vis economic and political liberalism. The historical and conceptual breadth of Marxist analysis and critique of liberal economy probably constitutes the most conspicuous absence in this narrative, together with countless other minoritarian scenes and modes of contention. There are two reasons to focus on the liberal tradition of economic thought and its main canonical twists and turns, which leads to such absences. One stems from the firm belief that one needs to target what has become the dominant horizon for thinking about economy and politics today in order to understand the boundaries of this horizon and to develop a sense of its inner possibilities and openings. This seems even more important as many tenets of liberal economic thought, especially those regarding scarcity and economic necessity, have a purchase beyond this tradition, informing, for example, much of the contemporary ecological criticism of economic growth and the outlook of the catastrophic future of shortages that we learn to expect. The other reason, especially for the conspicuous absence of Marx in this narrative, is that most political theorists and critical sociologists find Marx' analysis and terms of critique more accessible than other economists—accordingly, there is not just a huge wealth of literature and debate about it but also a self-imposed restriction on the side of the humanities for engaging with economic thought. In this situation, it seemed advisable to multiply the possibilities for traversing the disciplinary boundaries between political theory and economic thought and to look elsewhere for broadening the economic imagination that is lacking today. Broadly following the intellectual intuition of the philosopher Henri Bergson, one might say that it is from the past of what is given today that we can derive the sources of futurity. Which leaves the question of why Malthus and Keynes are the main figures in this "history of the present," or should I say in this "history of futurity"?

The following sections answer this question. They delve deeper into the historical and conceptual breaks in the history of liberal economic thought that occurred at the beginning of the nineteenth and twentieth centuries respectively, introducing the two historical protagonists of this genealogy of the economic—Malthus and Keynes—and explaining their importance and role for this story. A theoretical and methodological section rounds this introduction, which situates the books' theoretical and empirical contribution regarding the imbrication between the economic and the political dimensions of liberalism with respect to the current debates in political and social theory on "economics as culture."

Life and the Invention of Economic Necessity

At the beginning of the nineteenth century the liberal discourse on economy underwent a profound change. Karl Polanyi has famously described this change in terms of a novel "naturalism" that entered liberal economic thought. Questions of life and the resources necessary for survival assumed an important role for newly posing the economic problem in terms of an "ineluctable necessity."[14] The body, the threat of death, and the demands of corporeal existence became an "absolute social problem" and occupied the center of social and economic discourse.[15] According to Michel Foucault, the "naturalism" in economic thought signaled the emergence of a biopolitical horizon that accompanied liberalism since then.[16] He regarded political economy as the "major form of knowledge" that problematizes the government of collective life for liberalism. Neither Foucault nor Polanyi left any doubt about the importance of this historical conjuncture for understanding what modern liberalism became, political and economically.

Within the emerging discipline of economics, the advent of naturalism led to a changing notion of scarcity. Scarcity had already been an important concept for liberal thought during the eighteenth century, but it did not have the same quality, centrality, and generality for framing the economic problem.[17] Nowhere in the work of Adam Smith can one find generalized understandings of scarcity: "Scarcity is only a local circumstance, not a general situation."[18] In contrast, liberal economics since the nineteenth century assumed scarcity as a fundamental insufficiency that determined the condition of human existence. The limitation of the soil, the pressure of population growth, and the nourishment of the body are the themes that rendered the facts of scarcity palpable and predominant: economic man is a bodily creature governed by his finitude. He is cast as a human being who "who spends, wears out, and wastes his life in evading the imminence of death."[19]

The notion of scarcity remains central to liberal economics until today. But today the conception of scarcity is no longer explicitly based on a substantivist but rather a formalist understanding of the economic problem. Such a formalist account of the economic problem appears to eschew themes of livelihood, environmental limits, or corporeality.[20] It articulates the economic problem in terms of a choice between scarce resources, but no assumption needs to be made about the type of limits encountered or the terms in which enjoyment, utility, or gain is defined: "The need for aesthetic beauty or religious inspiration is no less potentially subject to scarcity of means than bread and butter."[21] But even though a formalist, "denaturalized" definition of scarcity gained precedence, the "naturalizing" moment at the beginning of the nineteenth century is still significant today.[22] One could say that arguments about "bioeconomic" necessity never entirely disappeared from arguments about the liberal market and have gained new importance in the context of ecological crisis.[23] But more importantly in this context is the fact that the reference to life and its limits has been central for turning scarcity into central concept for liberal economics. The notions of life, survival, and subsistence are the themes that structured the negotiation, changing, and resettling of the meaning of economy in liberalism at that time. By going back to that moment of emergence, we can learn something about the role of scarcity for liberal economic thought that is otherwise not apparent.

At the same time that the question of life and corporeal existence assumed such a formative role for liberal political economy, the conceptual boundary between economy and politics was subject to re-articulation.[24] A fundamental break divided the eighteenth-century world of Adam Smith from the nineteenth-century classical political economy.[25] With Smith, political economy was still part of the "science of the legislator." While eighteenth-century liberalism had unquestionably posited the economy as a distinct domain of social-economic relations, which comprised the rules of politeness, tastes, and exchange, it was not yet a dominion free of political consideration. Political categories of jurisprudence and liberty, the social logics of recognition, and of propriety and sympathy mingled with the economic bond, making it impure, fuzzy, and answerable to different orders of thought.[26] Hence, the closing decades of the eighteenth century had a markedly different understanding of the economy, its grounds, and its bounds: "When laissez-faire was new the frontier between political and economic, judgment was still shifting." The "politics of late eighteenth-century economic thought" did not yet frame state and market as "competing dominions."[27]

Both of the conceptual changes that occurred at the beginning of the nineteenth century—that is, the novel importance of issues of life and corporeality for liberal economics and the deepening of the boundary between politics and economy—took place in a moment of heated contestation. The French Revolution and the Haitian Revolution threatened to interlace issues of political constitutionalism and economy. British radical-ism probed the democratic side of liberalism and threatened to extend its political demands to the issues of subsistence and provision. Bread and constitution, poverty and liberty, life and politics intermingled in hitherto unprecedented ways. These violent disruptions no longer fit the world projected by the Scottish Enlightenment that had imagined progress as the piecemeal and peaceful process of human improvement, politeness, and exchange. The social question appeared for the first time and pre-sented itself to liberalism as a conundrum, as Robert Castel has elucidated in depth.[28] How this question was to be answered and what liberalism should and could mean at that moment were issues surrounded by high hopes and deep fears.

But, as is well known, these explorations did not push liberal economy and politics into a domain of further experimentation. Instead, it ended up with a "restoration of, above all, unquestionable and unquestioned ways of thinking."[29] The historian Emma Rothschild reminds us that the postrevolutionary "coalition of laissez-faire economic policy and political conservatism" was forged at that moment of passed upheaval. The out-come of this moment is still with us. "We still live, at the outset of the twenty-first century, in a world which is defined, in important respect, by [these] events."[30] This historical moment remains puzzling for the history of liberalism. In the words of J. G. A. Pocock, one needs to ask, "how did the complex synthesis [between political and economic arguments] evolve or degenerate into the science of classical economics"?[31]

The economist who is taken as an exemplary case for studying this his-torical moment from the vantage point of a genealogy of the economic is Thomas Robert Malthus. Today Malthus is remembered mostly as a theo-rist of population, but at that time he was the foremost economic thinker, influential in public and scientific debates.[32] He had one of the first chairs instituted in political economy, teaching the employees of the East Indian Company. But, most famously, he wrote an immediate bestseller that demonstrated the reality of scarcity to his contemporaries. The publica-tion of *Essay on the Principle of Population* in 1798 stands for the dramatiza-tion of biological finitude at the beginning of the nineteenth century. It effectively changed the political language in which the issue of economy was debated: from the language of rights to the facts of necessity. Malthus announced to the radical and revolutionary liberals of his time that there could not be a right to live. A powerful and famous allegory conveyed this message: "A man who is born into a world already possessed . . . has no claim of right to the smallest portion of food, and, in fact, has no business to be where he is. At nature's mighty feast there is no vacant cover for him. She tells him to be gone, and will quickly execute her own orders. . . . If these guests get up and make room for him . . . the order and harmony of the feat is disturbed, the plenty that before reigned is changed into scarcity."[33] This allegory that claimed the need to "let die" since there cannot be a right to food was so contentious that it had to be removed from subsequent editions. But its basic contention of the dangers of political artifice remained: Malthus asserts that the right to live would put scarce resources in the wrong hands to the detriment of all.

There are many reasons to look at Malthus as an important and influential representative of what economic liberalism was to become. Malthus' dramatization of scarcity turned liberal economy into a domain tied to the laws of necessity that were impossible to mitigate by political artifice. His arguments greatly influenced the debate that eventually led to the abolition of the Poor Laws. These laws had ordered the form of public relief in England since the end of the seventeenth century. The new type of public assistance that followed excluded not only single mothers but also the able-bodied poor from the possibility of accessing means of subsistence other than wages. The Malthusian fear that the poor would not cease to reproduce once given subsistence favored these novel restrictions on public relief.

While Malthus's writings paradigmatically encapsulate crucial tenets of nineteenth-century liberalism, he does not fully belong to this novel orthodoxy.[34] Malthus is a figure of transition in the history of economic thought. His interlocutors were still the "savants of the eighteenth century," and the political and moral discourses of that time remained important points of reference for Malthus. For this reason, many scholars look at Malthus not as a representative for what liberal political economy was to become but as a moral economist of his own right. They refer to the fact that Malthus embraced the need for political interventionism in some cases and did not subscribe to the dictum of laissez-faire wholeheartedly. Being in favor of national protectionism regarding agriculture and being cognizant of the possibility that capital could be overabundant, Malthus called upon politics for regulation. Furthermore, he is seen as espousing a "theology of scarcity" that cloaks essentially religious arguments with a veil of economic reasoning.[35] His economic thought has been identified as belonging to a distinct type of "Christian political economy."[36] For these reasons, many scholars find David Ricardo rather than Malthus to be the economist who has turned economics into a more formal and systematic science that is truly secular in its outlook and that should be regarded a milestone of liberal political economy in the nineteenth century. Malthus appears as wavering between the epistemologies of the eighteenth and the nineteenth century, belonging to neither: a curious relic in the large intellectual history of liberalism.

The difficulties of locating Malthus in the history of economics stem from trying to classify him according to established categories of economic thought. His writings on economy are judged according to what he said about specific economic concepts, such as rent, profit, supply, and demand. He is viewed in respect to how he allows the state to intervene or not into the domain of economy. Considering Malthus from such established sets of classification makes it difficult to fit him into any of the categories in which he might be placed. Scholars in the intellectual history of liberalism and the history of economic thought are therefore divided on what to make of Malthus and only unequivocal about this equivocal position: "Then as now, when the debate was joined, Malthus was required to carry a twin burden."[37]

But if seen from the perspective of a genealogy of the economic, the difficulty of locating Malthus disappears. As indicated before, this perspective does not focus on specific models or doctrines of economics that allow for a comparison between Malthus and his predecessors or followers regarding some established tenets of economic thought. From the vantage point of such a genealogy, the central question is not if some type of political interventionism is called for by an economist or not—since even the liberal "laissez-faire" is politically instituted and regulated as Karl Polanyi famously illustrated a long time ago. At stake for the current argument is the "historical ontology" of what constitutes economic reality vis-à-vis politics.[38] In respect to this aim, Malthus is a decisive figure in the history of liberal economic thought.

In this book, Malthus is presented as an economist and political theorist who answered to a "critical space" that had emerged in a moment of crisis by closing it. The genealogy of the economic therefore reads Malthus against the grain: it unpacks his allegation of economic necessity and scarcity by disentangling political and cultural fears from his account of the economic. Reading him as a political theorist and economist alike does not have to force his position into a coherence that does not exist. It unfolds the imbrication of political and economic arguments that established a familiar constellation of liberal economics and politics until today: the reference to scarcity as a kernel of market rationality and the belief that the markets are the best testing ground for what is feasible, necessary, possible, and imaginary in matters of material social order.

Money and the Invention of the Managed Economy

The second part of the book looks at a moment of crisis in the history of liberalism that occurs roughly one hundred years later. This moment functions like an inverted mirror to the first one. It questioned necessity and scarcity as exclusive *differentia specifica* of things economic. This time the question of money and the irreducible uncertainty regarding the future moved to center stage. The monetary realm was granted a role of its own in the determination of economic facts and turned into a paradigmatic case for rethinking liberal economy.

Seen from the history of economic thought, this turn to money challenged the assumption of money's neutrality that classical liberalism had entertained. This assumed neutrality rests on a definition of money as "nothing but . . . representation."[39] For classical liberalism, money is only a "veil" on economic values determined elsewhere.[40] Money can therefore appear to liberal discourse as neither adding nor taking, neither qualifying nor constituting the economic order of things: "The long-run money neutrality is a crucial property of the classical model."[41] But as soon as one ceases to accord money the role of being a neutral medium of representation, money turns into a Pandora's box. Money confounds issues of representation, discourse, politics, and economic valuation in an intricate knot.[42] Whenever money enters the picture as a force of its own, the edges of liberal economy become blurry, inviting "ubiquitous politics" into the economic realm.[43] As Karl Polanyi has put it, "the separation of the political and economic spheres had never been complete, and it was precisely in the matter of currency that is was necessarily incomplete."[44]

The turn of the conceptual focus toward money had its backdrop in the monetary disorder of the first decades of the twentieth century, which intensified the idea that the old models of economic theorizing had become obsolete: "The fluctuations in the value of money since 1914 have been on a scale so great as to constitute, with all that they involve, one of the most significant events in the economic history of the modern world."[45] The confidence that the economy could be regarded as a "fixed entity, sanctified by free trade and expressive of the genius of the greatest industrial society in the world," was shattered in the course of a general experience of change and crisis.[46] Economic beliefs were not the only ones that were shaken. Multiple sites of contention had eroded the certainties of the nineteenth century: the social question, the democratic franchise, the shifting gender roles, and the status of empire resurfaced and were simultaneous issues of struggle and debate. In the wake of these fundamental changes, the question of political economy returned as a contentious and disorderly subject, which it had been a hundred years before: "Between 1890 and 1920, Liberalism represented the English to themselves and to others in ways that were increasingly regarded as inadequate for a nation facing serious social 'issues' within, and carrying a large and growing empire without."[47]

A familiar historical narrative accounts for this moment of crisis and the resettlement it gave way to after World War II. It tells the story of the shift from laissez-faire economics to the welfare state. This story is about a rising politicization of economic issues as the involvement of political institutions with national economies grew. The argument presented here does not so much contest this narrative as complicate it. By attending more closely to the fundamental contingency that opened between the old orthodoxy and the new, it retrieves the critical space in which the liberal economic was recast. The economist whose texts can serve as the crystallization point for this change will not come as a surprise. John Maynard Keynes is a liberal economist who offered the most far-reaching and powerful critique of classical liberalism at that time. The models of market equilibrium appeared to him like "pretty, polite techniques, made for a well-paneled board oak room" that had only little to do with reality anymore.[48] The price of a cup of tea that neoclassical economics could determine with precision was no longer a pressing question—as Joan Robinson dryly remarked in the face of an economic machine that had gone haywire.[49] Keynes observed a shift in "our philosophy of economic life, our notions of what is reasonable and what is tolerable" that occurred "without changing our techniques or our copybook maxims."[50] Hence the "theory of the economic juggernaut," which holds

> that wages should be settled by economic pressure, otherwise called "hard facts," and that our vast machine should crash along, with regard only to its equilibrium as a whole, and without attention to the chance consequences of the journey to individual groups . . . [can no longer be applied] to a society which is rapidly abandoning these hypotheses.[51]

Keynes very explicitly conceived of himself as inaugurating a different view of economy. He pictured himself as someone who worked himself out of the "tunnel of economic orthodoxy," writing a book that would "revolutionize the way the world thinks about economic problems." The tradition of nineteenth century economics looked to him unified, built, as it were, on Ricardian foundations which he sought to "knock away."[52] At the same time, his macroeconomics became a blueprint for the management of the economy in the postwar years. It was the cornerstone of a new orthodoxy called the "grand neoclassical synthesis" that presented an account of the economic system suitable to a managerial politics.[53]

In order to retrieve Keynes for a genealogy of the economic, one has to grant as much attention to this grand synthesis as to the fact that Keynes's writings belonged to a broader discourse of cultural and modernist critique in the first decades of the twentieth century. As a member of both the Bloomsbury Group and a secret society called the Apostles, Keynes was part of the modernist avant-garde of his time. These illustrious groups counted Bertrand Russell, G. E. Moore, Virginia and Leonard Woolf, Clive Bell, Lytton Strachey, Roger Fry, and Duncan Grant, among others, as their members. These circles exercised—borrowing the words of Bertrand Russell—the art of "questioning . . . the familiar and imagining the unfamiliar." They were writers, artists, and editors "out to construct something new." As Leonard Woolf puts it: "We were the builders of a new society which should be free, rational, civilized, pursuing truth and beauty."[54] Raymond Williams describes their attitudes as "appealing to the supreme value of the civilized individuals, whose pluralisation, as more and more civilized individuals, was itself the only acceptable social form." The group was "in its personal instances and in its public interventions . . . as serious, as dedicated and as inventive as this position has ever, in the twentieth century, been."[55] Bloomsbury can stand as a concrete placeholder for a historical discursive shift that simultaneously encompassed politics, literature, economics, and the arts. Keynes's work crystallizes the modernist challenge against liberal economics.

At this time, the question of "what constitutes reality" was not only a concern to a specialized branch of philosophical inquiry. It was a "modernist" preoccupation that challenged the meaning of economy.[56] Placing Keynes within the context of modernism highlights the different understandings of representation, subjectivity, and objectivity that separated Keynesian discourse from its nineteenth-century predecessors. Through style and rhetoric, Keynes underwrites a "very particular and innovative analytic method which is not different in kind from, but is point-for-point opposed to, the method of what he calls 'classical' theory."[57] Keynesian economics share a modernist epistemology that revolves around a subject caught in fragmentary experiences and irreducible perspectivism.[58] Reality becomes a complex refraction of these intersecting perspectives, which no longer add up into an equilibrating totality. The whole that could possibly emerge out of these inchoate fragments not only exceeded the parts but required novel literary and representation techniques.[59] In Keynes's words: "We are faced at every turn with the problems . . . of discreteness, of discontinuity—the whole is not equal to the sum of the parts, comparisons of quantity fail us, small changes produce large effects, the assumptions of a uniform and homogeneous continuum are not satisfied."[60]

A profound difference between Keynesian economics and the nineteenth-century systems of thought also lies in the epistemology of uncertainty and probability that Keynes took as fundamental. As Keynes elaborated upon in his early *Treatise on Probability*, acquiring knowledge of reality is a precarious aspiration, especially when it concerns events of the future. There is, as Keynes famously announced, no "scientific basis on which to form any calculable probability whatever. We simply do not know."[61] With respect to the classical tradition, this understanding undermines the assumption of complete knowledge and rationality of the *homo oeconomicus*, thus ushering economic action onto a different plane where decisions "are based on guess work or on convention."[62] These challenges to classical economics take place parallel to the scientific revolution in physics at the beginning of the twentieth century. Keynes is sometimes referred to as the "Einstein of economics" as he replaced the a-temporality of classical economics in a move that also characterized Einstein's challenge to classical physics.[63]

The extent to which Keynes's "struggle of escape from habitual modes of thought" brought about an economics that is radically different from the classical tradition of economics led to a notorious discussion about what Keynes "really meant." Those who concur with Keynes' self-portrait as a heretic of sorts, emphasize the modernist aspects of his thought in order to salvage Keynesian discourse from the disenchantment with the "'hydraulic' Keynesianism of the 1950s and 1960s."[64] Keynes's pupils had fashioned a "machine of hydraulic pipes, with different colored liquids sloshing around a 'national economy'" designed to illustrate and predict the behavior of the macroeconomy.[65] This model of a national economy paradigmatically stands for the "containment" of Keynesian economics into the procrustean bed of classical economics after the Second World War, bespeaking the hope of making Keynesian policies "completely 'scientific' or 'automatic.'"[66] Eventually, Keynesianism was taken to be nothing but a refinement of the classical theories on equilibrium, only adding a specific case. Fundamentalist Keynesians or post-Keynesians hope to disclaim such proximity to neoclassical orthodoxy.[67] But they nevertheless have to reckon with the fact that Keynes himself "never once repudiated" such interpretation. On the contrary, "he endorsed it warmly"[68]—although he never conceded to a form of scientific reasoning that applied models irrespective of the circumstance either.[69]

The following analysis circumvents taking sides in this conversation. Keynes's position as an author is a lesser concern than the discursive shifts in the languages of contestation and the rearticulation of the boundaries of liberal economy that can be found in his texts. The oeuvre of Keynes is interesting in this context precisely because it encapsulates, in paradigmatic ways, both a critique and a reconstruction of a new conception of liberal economy and its boundaries. The historical-theoretical reading offered here attends to both aspects of this discourse: The fundamental challenges to the inherited discourse on economics and the founding of a novel orthodoxy form equal parts of the story. As I will show, the question of money assumes a central role for both parts. If Malthus is seen as an economist who answered to a situation of conceptual contestation by closing it, Keynes takes on a more complicated role. He partook in the unraveling of the beliefs in economic necessity, but at the same time he devised a new understanding of economic laws. This time it was an expert-governed "economic machine" that preformatted particular types of political intervention. Whereas Malthus closed the "critical space" generated elsewhere, Keynes's writings contain the double movement of opening and closing at the same time. The relevance of Keynes for a history of the present might be more obvious to the reader than the relevance of Malthus. The recent financial crisis has induced a short revival of Keynes as an economic thinker, and Keynesian monetary recipes still belong to the repertoire of central banks. Today he is heralded for his account of irreducible uncertainty and instability in financial markets. As will become clear in the course of my argument, reading Keynes from the vantage point of a genealogy of the economic introduces a different angle on this figure: not as an old master whose teachings can be revived as ready-mades but as an example for how liberal economy has been opened up toward the thinking of "the economic," which became displaced through the politics of the managed economy.

Rethinking Economy and the Question of Politics

For over a decade, it was not political theory but cultural sociology, anthropology, and science studies that pushed the agenda of "rethinking" economy. Designating economy and economics as part of culture helped to question the naturalization of this sphere and to understand it as a domain of "production, power and signification." The conceptualization of the market and capitalism in terms of a monolithic law of value, of necessity and functional coherence, has been queried as a particular image of the economy that hides its multiple fault lines, inner contingency, and cultural underpinnings. A lively scholarly debate attempts to furnish an interpretation of economic order that avoids the reification of the capitalist system and the market. The notion of "economics as culture" captures this effort: "[The] task of cultural critique must begin with the clear recognition that economics is a discourse that constructs a particular picture of the economy."[70] The first to push for such a cultural critique of economy were scholars trained in anthropology and postcolonial thought who started to scrutinize the concept of economic development that played an important role in the making of the postwar global order. The authority and proclaimed neutrality of expert knowledge on development, as used in international organizations such as the International Monetary Fund and the World Bank, stood at the center of their concerns. The analysis laid bare the premises of this knowledge, the relations of power to which it was tied, and the deceptive beliefs in "technological fixes" at work in these expert discourses. Culture, in other words, functioned as a strategic inroad for questioning the premises of economics.[71]

As a whole, the scholarly work on the naturalizations implicit in economics very much uses the methods and insights of social studies of science, historical epistemology, and the history of science in general. It aligns itself with numerous projects in the history of economic thought that seek to understand the trajectory of modern economics outside and beyond the teleology of progress. These histories recount the unsuccessful attempt of economics to emulate the natural sciences, the struggles about the "soul of economics" between the world wars, and the implication of military research with the development of economics and the rise of neoliberalism. This work shatters the claim of economics to be a form of knowledge that can dispense with understanding its own historical, social, or cultural conditions of existence. What counts as "economic fact" has a history itself.[72]

Over the recent decades, the debate has shifted more and more toward the analysis of contemporary forms of economic knowledge that have practical relevance in markets, central banks, or governmental agencies. The field of "cultural economy," as it is now called, hopes to show that "economy is an achievement rather than a starting point or a pre-existing reality that can simply be revealed and acted upon."[73] Our knowledge of the economy is not a neutral "camera" taking photographs of these processes but an "engine" driving it. Modes of counting, modeling, and calculating have been looked at in terms of how they render economy manageable, visible, and controllable in the hands of those who are "doing" the economy—be it in administrative units, the stock market, the banks, or the legal offices.[74] Studying economic calculations and models as part of creating the economic world has been called the "performativity thesis." Such an approach eschews the need to define the subject matter of economy but studies how such definitions are part of making a particular type of economy real.

This debate about the performativity of economics has invited a discussion about the political dimension of economics. If economics partakes in the making of economic worlds and facts, how can one differentiate and evaluate these forms of world-making? If economics cannot claim a status of neutral objectivity, what kind of implicit and explicit political dimension is involved in these practices of knowledge? Michel Callon, who is one of the main proponents of the "performativity thesis," surmises that the "politics and the economy are produced jointly in the same performation process" but does not elaborate how this insight can be used for analyzing economic difference.[75] This book takes up these questions regarding on the politics of economics. I argue that the question of politics is crucial for the project of "rethinking economy." Given that concepts of economy and politics are entangled in processes of co-constitution, juxtaposition, and mutual exclusion, studying the political dimension of economics can function as a privileged entry point for "rethinking economy."[76] As I demonstrate in this book, studying the political dimension of economics enables one to unpack the hybrid combinations of political arguments with economic ones and thus distills the malleability of the economic contained in these mixtures.

In order to specify the political dimension of economics, it is not sufficient to highlight the general contingency of performing the economic world through economics. Even if the understanding that one mode of performing the economy hides other possibilities seems to put the "consideration of politics . . . at the centre of . . . concern," the mere gesture toward contingency remains too abstract.[77] Claiming the universal contingency of economic knowledge as its implicit political element implies a very general notion of politics. Furthermore, it also harbors the danger of emptying the notion of contingency from any specificity. Instead of claiming an overgeneralized notion of contingency as a political element of economics per se, I find it important to specify the form that this contingency takes within the domain of economy. This specification would allow addressing the malleability of the liberal economic. By this I mean the particular and concrete ways in which a historical framing of liberal economy exposes its internal openness to political artifice and cultural determination. This allows me to pinpoint the hybrid constitution of liberal economy without rendering politics and economics indistinguishable and without subsuming one to the other.

The conceptual framework developed here does not fit neatly into the major strands of the debate that currently elaborates on the role of political concepts for economic thought. For this reason, it is helpful to provide a short account of the different ways the political element of economics has been identified in contemporary social theory and political theory. The purpose of this cursory and selective discussion is not to rehearse or debate these theorizations in any great detail but rather to situate the argument for the reader and to clarify the notion of politics and the political dimension that I have employed in this genealogy of the economic.

The Political Dimension of Economics

Max Weber has famously argued that the emergence of modern, occidental capitalism depended on cultural-political legitimation. According to him, the purely formal and procedural understanding of means and ends typical for economic actions fails to offer the motivation and legitimation that is necessary for stabilizing economic order. As is well known, Weber developed his argument mainly in respect to the role of religion in buttressing the obligation to work and sustaining the accumulation of riches with promises of salvation.[78] But he also addressed the political content of economics when he diagnosed an unrecognized interference of political values with scientific concepts. Weber argued for the clear distinction between what can be scientifically established and what should be explicitly announced an act of political choice. Especially in regard to the discipline of economics, he found it impossible to tolerate that a question of highest political importance would be turned into a "technical-economic" question of productivity.[79]

Gunnar Myrdal used this Weberian framework for his seminal discussion of the *Political Element in the Development of Economic Theory*. He contends that economics as a science entails an implicit normative and political basis insofar as it represents "the economy as a personified society which tries to make the best of the available resources, thus working towards a common goal."[80] Myrdal was deeply informed by Max Weber's understanding of politics defined as being tied to ultimate values (and the struggle about these values) and economics as being tied to formal rationalities. Hence, detecting a political element was to him equivocal to detecting value-commitments smuggled into an analytical model. According to Myrdal, the obfuscated notion of a collective and common standpoint inherent in the epistemological choices of economics becomes the entry point for political conclusions that do not follow explicitly from political premises.

A branch of scholarship called convention theory has recently updated the Weberian model for studying the entwinement between economic acts of valuation and political models of the common. The premise of this work is that there is no type of calculation, valuation, rationality, or equivalence that does not rest on a shared understanding of the common, which distributes worth and reward to its members and offers justification for the current order. Capitalism, understood as an amoral system of exploitation, requires legitimation that allows for claims of justice and fairness. A limited number of models of the common that offer such "justification" have been extrapolated from the history of political philosophy and economic thought. They provide the frameworks for negotiating the orders of reward and worth that members of the economic polity can claim.[81]

The approach taken here resonates in one respect with these elaborations of the political: it shares the presupposition that the political element consists, *inter alia*, in the act of envisioning the common. Economics has a long trajectory in claiming "common standpoint" for society as a whole, as Myrdal showed. But my conceptual framework also departs from this account of politics in two ways. First, I do not approach the political-economic visions of the common in terms of legitimation. Framing the political in terms of legitimation presumes a division between a set of normative arguments, on the one hand, and a factual account of the object to be legitimized, on the other.[82] The notion of legitimation thus has to adopt a given theoretical perspective on the economic order that needs to be justified. It fails to draw attention to the politics involved in defining the economic problem itself—for example, the delimitation of field of perception, the drawing of the line that parcels out what counts as economic necessity, and the boundaries to the political sphere that are assumed.

Second, I am interested in excavating the malleable economic that is implicit in such economic-cum-political accounts of the common. I am not so much concerned with the question of how a limited number of models are employed in organizations for negotiating the distribution of worth but in a double movement between the internal openness of such politico-economic accounts of the common and their fixation. For this reason, I have introduced the notion of the economic. It designates internal openness to political choice and cultural determination that a particular articulation of liberal economy harbors but displaces at the same time.

I loosely borrow from the philosopher Jacques Rancière to frame the dynamic of this double movement. Rancière has coined the notion "archi-politics" in order to address an envisioning of the common that renders the critical spaces of its contestability invisible. Archipolitics projects an order in which each position and each part is defined, resulting in a functional coherence and a unity. I use this notion to refer to what Myrdal called the "standpoint of society" implicit in economics. In the words of Rancière, one can say that economics thus contains a hidden "political philosophy, [which] by its desire to give to the community a single foundation, is fated to . . . cancel out politics through the gesture of founding it."[83] This means that the aspiration to depict "the economy" or "the market" as a functional totality always entails an importation of political—and, for that matter, religious, aesthetic, and cultural—determinations into economic reasoning.

Whereas the perspective on "the economic" signals the specificity and malleability of an economic relation, the determination and totalization of "the economy" tends to hide the political and cultural stabilization on which it rests. As Bonnie Honig has put it: "Every system is secured by placeholders that are irrevocably, structurally arbitrary. . . . They enable the system but are illegitimate from its vantage point."[84] Hence, even though liberal economics claims a clear division between the realms of politics and economy, this division only betrays the implicit and hybrid articulation of the "the economy." The conceptual divisions between politics and economy are therefore always permeable and inexact. They bear the traces of their hybrid foundation. As far as these conceptual divisions are made to serve as a foundation for politics or "archipolitics," they have to displace these impurities. My aim is to divest economic thought from such "archipolitics" in order to explicate and render negotiable the simultaneous and hybrid delineation of a politico-economic constitution.

Rancière juxtaposes this "archipolitics" with what is here called "the political."[85] "The political" refers to a moment of fundamental "disagreement" that unravels the established "system of self-evident facts" regarding the shared common, its parts, and its boundaries.[86] "Politics revolves around what is seen and what can be said about it, around who has the ability to see and the talent to speak, around the properties of spaces and the possibilities of time."[87] While Rancière has greatly elaborated on how such a political moment unravels the given regimes of political subjectivity, participation, and inclusion, he does not address the question of how the domain of economy changes its appearance when embroiled in this kind of political moment. But without specifying what economy becomes when it is *not* tied to "archipolitics," this moment of disagreement is

one-legged. Adding the notion of the economic to the notion of the political rectifies this asymmetry. It enables one to specify how the question of
economy appears when it is made to exhibit its own malleability. In this
way, it produces a more symmetrical account of a moment of political and
economic contestation.

To sum up, the discussion so far has led to a specification of the political
element in economics in a twofold sense: first, as an envisioning of the
common that is obfuscated within economic thought. It lends unity and
determination to the notion of "the economy." On this level we find a
hybrid arrangement of arguments, logics, and discourses, which accords
stability to the articulation of "the economy," while this impure constitution is ignored by claims to purity and foundation. Second, the political
element is defined as an act of essential contestation regarding the articulation of the economic body politic. It unravels the established articulation
of "economic facts." As such, it is accompanied by the notion of "the
economic," which exposes the malleability that this articulation of economy contains.

In this book, I want to combine this understanding of the political
element—and its accompanying notion of the economic—with Foucault's
framework for conceptualizing the entanglement between politics and
economics. Foucault has gone very far in studying the mutual imbrication
of politics and economics in liberalism. To him, liberalism itself is neither
an economic nor a political theory but rather "a specific art of government
oriented toward the population as a new political figure and disposing
over the political economy as a technique of intervention."[88] He takes
the emergence of the modern economy as a "level of reality" to be an "episode in the mutation of technologies of power and an episode in the install-
ment of this technique of apparatuses of security that seems to me to be one
of the typical features of modern societies."[89] The *homo oeconomicus* is seen as
"the partner, the vis-à-vis, the basic element of the new governmental reason formulated in the eighteenth century."[90]

Foucault pinpoints the political dimension of economics in terms of the
"technology" and a "dispositif" of power that it elaborates and to which it
belongs. The advantage of this approach lies in how it is able to tie the
intellectual history of liberal economic thought to the practical domain of
the exercise of power. The disadvantage consists in the relative neglect of
the dimension of "contestation and containment of contestation" as part

of politics. As the sociologist Andrew Barry contends: "Foucauldian analyses of technologies of government seem to fall in the trap [of rendering politics into a technical matter]."[91] Foucault remains tethered to a political-administrative perspective from which he takes up the question of economy. He looks at economic discourse only as far as it serves the aims of governing. His notion of governmentality is therefore a powerful tool for analyzing economics in terms of the strategies of power that it enables and elaborates. But it also implies a narrowing to a governmental perspective from the beginning. Adopting it, one cannot address the making of the shared horizon for articulating the economic problem that a governmental strategy does not exhaust or circumscribe. As Eve Chiapello and Nicolas Berland point out in a similar vein, governmentality needs an "additional reflective analysis of the origins of political rationalities and programmes of government, and the way in which they are constructed."[92] I am interested in the making and unmaking of such broader horizons that enable, exceed, and restrict governmental strategies at the same time.[93]

The conceptual architecture that juxtaposes the notions of "the economic" and "the political" with the archipolitical and governmentalized notion of "the economy" serves a twofold aim: to address the historically specific malleability of the liberal economic and to study the imbrication of political and economic categories in the moment of its fixation. The project of writing a genealogy of the economic does not imply that any analytical distinction between political and economic relations should be dispensed with or that any attempt to understand the complexity and materiality of economic life is to be denounced as politics. It does not hold out the hope that finally, both sides can be purified. But it promises to render visible the mixtures that we are dealing with and explores the possibilities for other ones.

Foucault's notion of governmentality is only one element in the broader conceptual architecture presented here. But the book as a whole is still largely inspired by and indebted to Foucault's work. While selectively adopting and including elements of Foucault's perspicacious analysis regarding liberalism, it takes Foucault's writings on genealogy and archaeology as its methodological vantage point for writing a genealogy of the economic that focuses on specific scenes, figures, and themes in the history of liberalism.

Methodological Queries: Reading Economists as Political Philosophers

By addressing the political and economic dimension in a more symmetrical fashion and by linking it to a double movement of conceptual opening and closure, this book offers a genealogy of liberal economy that argues with and against Foucault. It uses his method of genealogy to highlight the "contingent genesis" of liberal economy, but it uses it for writing a different history of liberalism than Foucault has done.[94] Foucault has defined genealogy as a method of doing historiography that eschews the continuity in the history of thought. In his words, it foregrounds "its jolts, its surprises, its unsteady victories and unpalatable defeats," showing that the essence of things was "fabricated in a piecemeal fashion from alien forms." A genealogical analysis concerns itself with temporal processes of emergence. Such emergence is described in terms of the "myriad events through which—thanks to which, against which—[a concept . . .] was formed." A genealogical analysis is therefore interested in the moments of apparition and the struggles that belong to it. It seeks to account for change and discontinuity by turning to the "substitutions, displacements, disguised conquests" that shape the making of a novel configuration of order.[95]

Foucault explicitly links a genealogical analysis to the "isolat[ion] of different scenes" of emergence. He talks about the "place of confrontation" that occurs in the interstice of orders where the "common space" is not yet defined. In terms of a history of a concept, the role of genealogy is to pluralize their multiple uses: "They must be made to appear as events on the stage of a historical process." Staging such scenes of apparition or emergence is done in view of the present: it aims to be critically relevant for the current situation.[96] For the current analysis, I adapt and modify Foucault's genealogical method in three ways: I put a heightened emphasis on the scenes of emergence, I argue for inclusion of the archaeological analysis of a space of possibility into the genealogical account of liberalism, and I add a focus on the effects of the conceptual oppositions and displacement between the economic and the political. As a whole, this means employing a strategy of parallel reading in which economists are also read as political theorists.

The book singles out exemplary scenes in order to magnify the moments of contestation and containment in the history of liberalism. I employ the notion of the "scene" in a twofold sense. First, the scene refers to specific historical moments that have critical relevance for today since the questions that were posed and answered regarding liberal economy remain present. These moments are widely known as "crises" within the history of liberalism. They can be reconstructed as historical situations that were characterized by an intensity of conflict and doubt about the meaning of liberalism. But the historical scenes that I reconstruct should not be viewed as a mere historical context. They are more and less than that: less, because I do not offer an exhaustive and historicist account of context; more, because they have been chosen to serve a particular theoretical interest. A "scene" is always a "mise en scene."[97] It is an artificial construction of a stage that concretizes, dramatizes, and intensifies an encounter. As a theoretical artifice, the scene goes beyond the notion of historical context. It entails the acts of crystallizing and localizing a conceptual change that is more ambiguous, less clear cut, and more drawn out than a single scene and its main figure could ever encompass. If it is done successfully, it both accommodates the historical account and renders them intelligible in a novel way.

Second, by addressing the level of "the economic," the genealogical analysis is broadened to include an elucidation of those aspects of a conceptual architecture and discursive order that harbor more possibilities than are actualized. To do so, it has to broaden the archaeological dimension of a genealogy, which helps to "define even those instances where they are absent, the moment when they remained unrealized."[98] Whereas the latter emphasizes the scenes of emergence, the former elucidates the discursive space beyond the strategic choices and battles. Foucault once signaled that his methods for studying discourse aimed at understanding the "historical unconscious."[99] This "unconscious" is not a hidden realm. It should rather be understood as a level of analysis that renders visible the formation as well as the space of possibility that a particular discourse offers. Foucault describes this in his *Archaeology of Knowledge* in following words: "But all the possible alternatives are not in fact realized: there are a good many partial groups, regional compatibilities, and coherent architectures that might have emerged, yet did not do so."[100] While Foucault drew attention to these different aspects of analysis, they were not followed up to the same extent in all of his writings. Studying "the economic" as a level of particular historical formation of economic thought means to address the discursive field from which strategies are chosen but which they do not encompass.

Third, the strategy of reading employed in this book emphasizes the formative dynamics of conceptual opposition and exclusion that determines a field of thought. This strategy of analysis demands close attention to a textual corpus: it searches for its inner divisions and for the double valences of its arguments. Incorporating such close reading into a genealogical analysis introduces an alien element since it focuses on particular authors and texts—something that a genealogical analysis usually eschews as belonging to a classical history of ideas. The intention is not to revert to a classical type of historiography but to push the genealogical method to address the history of a conceptual division, which is produced over and against the mixtures and impurities that make it possible in the first place.

As I have already said, I suggest reading Keynes and Malthus as economists and political theorists in order to address the double valences and displacements present in economic discourse.[101] I read them as political theorists in three ways, which correspond to the three modifications of the genealogical method suggested here. First, I look at how these texts belong to a scene of contestation. In this scene, the economist speaks as political theorist: he or she shapes the political language of debate and articulates the economy as a matter of public concern. Second, I turn toward an analysis of the economic. I read the economists on their home turf, but in approaching their texts I seek to outline and disentangle the economic from their economics. Third, I switch from this parallel reading of their political and economic side to a simultaneous account of their envisioning of an "economic body politic." This entails the settlement and stabilization of the boundary between the two realms. Reading economists as political theorists and vice versa means demonstrating how both realms are co-constituted and how this co-constitution involves the displacement of the economic into a stabilized, governmentalized and hybrid arrangement of "the economy" vis-à-vis politics. Taken together, these three steps allow us to study the imbrication of economic and political arguments and yet retain a sense of their difference. This method helps us understand the hybrid arrangements that make "the economy" articulable, governable, and effective. But it also opens up a conversation about "the economic" that exposes its malleability.

The general motivation to disentangle "the economic" from "the economy" stems from a sense of dissatisfaction with and astonishment about the conceptual impoverishment that characterizes the political and intellectual debates about economic matters today. Foucault once diagnosed an "impoverished political imagination."[102] To this diagnosis one certainly needs to add that of an "impoverished economic imagination." The financial crisis and the ensuing debt crisis have made this impoverishment palpably visibly. We live on a meager diet of conceptual tools for problematizing and reframing the question of economy and politics. While the exasperation with the old ways of organizing things are mounting and the end of crisis is not in sight, the debates about what regulation should mean, what liberal economy could mean, and how one should think about the politics involved are stale. Providing an historical account of the liberal economic, which foregrounds the struggle about the very terms of debate, seems advisable for widening the economic imagination or at least for understanding its impoverishment. As a whole, this work is critical. In Rancière's words: "Engaging in critique of the instituted divisions, then, paves the way for renewing our interrogations into what we are able to think and to do."[103] Taking up and modifying a phrase that Spinoza once coined for the notion of the body, one might say, we don't know yet what liberal economy can be.

Part I. Life

CHAPTER 1

The Invention of Economic Necessity

I n the last decade of the eighteenth century, the question of life
and subsistence entered the political stage. It did so more dramatically in the case of France, and more hesitantly and indeci-
sively in the case of Britain. The event that paradigmatically encapsulated
the looming threat of an unprecedented intermingling of life and politics
occurred on October 5, 1789. On that day six thousand women were
marching to Versailles, demanding bread and commanding the return of
the monarch back to the city. A longstanding despair about the inade-
quacy of bread supplies and its continuing high price had mingled with
dissatisfaction about the reluctance of the king to accept the declaration of
the rights of man. After besieging the place, they succeeded in forcing the
king back to the city. On October 6 the carriages with the king and a
crowd of people were returning to Paris, with wagons containing flour
following them.[1]

In his *Reflections on the Revolution in France*, Edmund Burke put his exasperation about these events into words, famous for the rhetoric and the
political debate that they ignited.[2] His despair about the lack of veneration
for tradition and the "swinish multitude" received a powerful reply
from the hands of Thomas Paine, who declared *Rights of Man*, including
those to subsistence. Both of these texts stood at the beginning of the
"most turbulent period in modern British history."[3] This period was
characterized by unprecedented popular mobilization, widening political

participation, and the proliferation of new political languages that expanded the notion of politics. Society, regarded as a material–social entity, turned into an object of experimentation in a context of political and epistemological uncertainty. Languages of rights, utility, sentiment, and probability mingled in this attempt to link the political revolution to a social one. But within a couple of years all of this was forgotten; it had faltered under the pressure of political opposition, bad harvests, terror, and war.[4]

Modern political theory has ascertained the politicization of life that occurred around this time in sober terms. In respect to the French Revolution, Hannah Arendt has famously argued that the social question invited the necessity of life onto the political stage, thereby abandoning the foundation of freedom to the "rights of the Sans-Culottes," which were "dress, food and the reproduction of the species."[5] It was "under the dictate" of the needs of the body that the "multitude of the poor" "appeared on the scene of politics": "Necessity appeared with them . . . and the new republic was stillborn; freedom had to be surrendered to necessity, to the urgency of the life process itself."[6] In her view, the political stage cannot accommodate the natural being, whose needs are uniform and who is governed by immediacy and want.

Michel Foucault has suggested a very different but equally disillusioned take on the politicization of life in this period. Side-stepping altogether this short-lived political spectacle and the terror that followed, he focused instead on the much more lasting innovation of the techniques of governing the living that emerged in this period. He diagnosed that political modernity crossed the biopolitical threshold at that time, meaning that the question of how to govern the living turned into a major administrative concern: health, longevity, circulation of goods, and the milieu of life became the objects of governmental care. For Foucault, this inclusion of life into politics was a correlate of new technique of power. The naturalism of life in the domain of politics unblocked the "problem of government" from the "juridical framework of sovereignty" and resulted in the extension of relations of power.[7]

But the politicization of life was not just about the refashioning of governmental strategies regarding the living. It was neither just a road to terror—if it was that at all. Instead, the politics of life was an open question, containing both a promise and a threat. The emergence of economic subsistence and life as a political question belonged to a scene of heated contestation. The intermingling of political passions, the appearance of novel political subjects on the stage and the impending politicization of economic life gave this decade its specific quality as a moment of "dissensus" in the sense that Jacques Rancière has defined this term: as a situation in which the "object or stage of discussion itself" is in question.[8] Different political languages, proposals, and demands overlapped while political passions and revolutionary hopes ran high.

On this scene of contestation, political economy emerged as a scientific discipline: "The transformation of political economy into a universal science, in the early decades of the nineteenth century was a repudiation of these revolutionary and counter-revolutionary disputes."[9] This new science changed the idiom of public debate as it confronted the heated political demands and experiments with the assessment of the inner workings of the economic system that determined the wealth and poverty of a nation. "The scientific analysis of the economic workings of society" became more and more a touchstone for the political promises of revolution and reform. Political economy counted as the "most highly developed and useful branch of the scientific study of society as a whole."[10] From the beginning of the nineteenth century onward, the "abstract propositions of economic science were invoked in practical politics"; they became constantly recurring "tropes and figures" in the "speeches, writings and conversations of all social classes."[11]

The book that prompted the public importance of political economy at the very moment of heated political contestation was the *Essay on the Principle of Population, as It Affects the Future Improvement of Society, with Remarks on the Speculations of Mr. Godwin, M. Condorcet, and Other Writers.* The essay furnished an argument about the harsh realities of economic scarcity that cannot be mitigated through political programs of reform.[12] It was a great success. Even though it "rained refutations," as one biographer of Malthus puts it, Malthus was never ignored, and within the following decades the book changed the terms of public debate.[13] The essay went through six editions by 1826 and "immediately became the centre of heated political debate."[14] "No contemporary volume," commented the *Edinburgh Review* two years after Malthus's death in 1838, "produced so powerful an effect upon the age in which it was written as the Essay on Population."[15] Malthus's doctrines of population and his political economy were popularized through a children's book, novels, journals, debating clubs, and public lectures.[16] It informed the reform of the Poor Laws in 1834 that was believed at the time to be "the first piece of legislation based on scientific or economical principles."[17] Malthus's political adversaries hoped in vain to "restore the old principles of political science" against the new language of population and economy in order to counter the success of the principle of population.[18] Malthus himself, referring to the "increasing attention paid to the science of political economy" found it "particularly gratifying, at the end of the year 1825, to see that what I stated as so desirable twenty years ago, seems to be now on its eve of accomplishment."[19] The success of his work on population earned him the chair of political economy, among the first one's ever instituted at the East India College in 1805, subsequently named Haileybury College.[20] Other universities and colleges followed suit.[21] By mid-nineteenth century, the laws of economy had become a world of its own, and the science of political economy an "innocuous, unpolitical subject."[22]

This chapter argues that the invention of economic laws of necessity, which the *Essay on Population* became famous for, was a response to the political uncertainty. The essay appeared in a context, in which the meaning of liberalism and the relation between economy and politics in liberalism had become ambiguous. Against this background, I read Malthus as a political theorist who is concerned with the virtues and dangers of the unlimited exercise of political reason. To Malthus, the widening of the political sphere appears to require epistemic foundations as a counterweight: the envisioning of the economy in terms of laws and scarcity that created undisputable facts. Just as Immanuel Kant fears that pure reason lacked proper limits and needed to be brought back to the shore of experience, Malthus seeks to bring political reason back to the recognition of unchangeable laws that would limit the amount of experimentation and change. But a notion of economy that is born out of a fear of politics is shaped by this apprehension. As a consequence, the economic realm appears as more immutable than it needs to be.

The remainder of this chapter proceeds as follows: The first section unfolds the situation of political contestation in England at that time. It substantiates the claim that politics was out of bounds. The second section addresses the "languages" that were dominant in the politicization of the question of life and subsistence. I focus on the epistemic uncertainty and indeterminacy surrounding these issues at the time. The third section traces how a politico-epistemological *problematique* of lacking foundations is a dominant theme in the *Essay on Population*. Posited against the "shoreless sea" of political reason, economic discourse turned into a project of foundation. The last section unfolds how—pace Foucault—the entrance of naturalism into liberal politics was about more than an administrative concern of a biopolitical governing of population. It was caught up and shaped by a search for epistemological and political certainty. Malthus feared, just like Arendt, the dominance of the social question in the arena of politics. But the object of this fear is not the politicization of life per se but the potential failure of political judgment in respect to questions that are not wholly political and not wholly economic either, but both at once.

Liberal Dissensus

It was not only Kant who famously contemplated the events of the French Revolution and their impact on the political fate of enlightenment from afar. Malthus was another spectator—albeit a more frightened than elated one. To him "the forcing manure" that brought about the French Revolution "has burst the calyx of humanity, the restraining bond of all society; and, however large the separate petals have grown, however strongly, or even beautifully a few of them have been marked; the whole is at present a loose, deformed, disjointed mass, without union, symmetry, or harmony of colouring."[23] For Kant, the French Revolution was despite of all "misery and atrocities" an event to be more greeted than feared, and he maintained that it could only arouse in the "hearts and desires of all spectators . . . a sympathy which borders almost on enthusiasm."[24] To Malthus, it looked like a spectacle that debased the human mind in "the most enlightened nations of the world . . . by such fermentation of disgusting passions, of fear, cruelty, malice, revenge, ambition, madness and folly, as would have disgraced the most savage nations in the most barbarous age."[25]

Malthus was alarmed by such revolutionary fervor that, in the words of his contemporary and adversary Marquis de Condorcet, "embrace[s] the entire economy of society, change[s] every social relation and find[s] its way down to the furthest link of the political chain."[26] But he did not have to look across the channel to feel alarmed about such a widening degree of political contestation that challenged the inherited precepts of order. Contentious English politics had started much earlier than the revolutionary upheavals in France. The 1760s had already been a decade of reform politics, characterized by an increasing critique of government.[27] But the French Revolution stimulated anew an "intense political debate within Britain and deeply polarized public opinion."[28] The British domestic confrontation gained "a momentum it would otherwise have lacked." Burke's *Reflections on the Revolution* and Paine's *Rights of Man*, appearing in 1790 and 1791, respectively, framed the "course of this momentum."[29] After this initial spark, the political debate evolved in response to the unfolding of the political events, but it lacked clear contours. "Reformism or radicalism in the 1790s is protean stuff," as it does not offer a "single program" and resists "a simple definite classification."[30]

Characteristic of this period was a novel "burgeoning political culture": Clubs and societies were formed, which brought together debates, mutual support, political information, and agitation. This widening of the spaces of expression of public opinion outside of parliament into the coffee houses and discussion clubs changed the political climate.[31] It is impossible to overestimate the impact of this change. Pamphlets, writings, and poems circulated through the clubs and radical societies in London and the provinces during the1790s. The "pamphlet had become a weapon, the debate [had become] a struggle over popular mobilization and political ascendancy."[32] The expansion and quickening of channels of communication—such as the postal service, newspapers, and cheap prints—were fostering a new interest in politics, "beyond the narrow oligarchy at Westminster."[33] The radical societies "put a high premium of the production and dissemination of printed propaganda." Political literature was cheap and consciously aiming at a mass audience. Its aim was to instruct the people "in their political rights . . . in a cheap and easily digested form."[34]

A new type of political language consciously written as part of this struggle about reform emerged more "rhetorical, explicit, bold, and accessible than ever before."[35] The publication of Paine's *Rights of Man* became the most visible example of this new type of political communication. The "success of the second part of the Rights of Man" was "in a true sense, phenomenal," as Edward Thompson puts it. It went "immediately into a 6d. edition" and "Paine's publications were said to be in almost every hand." At Paine's trial, it "was clearly stated that the cheapness of the abridged editions was an aggravation of the offence."[36] As Olivia

Smith details in her *Politics of Language,* "new readers were brought into the reading public" with the publication of the *Rights of Man*: "'Our peasantry now read the Rights of Man on mountains, and on moors, and by the wayside.'" It is estimated that the first part sold fifty thousand copies, the second one between 1791 and 1793, two hundred thousand. Abridged versions were distributed by the democratic clubs at cheap prices. She concludes that the political activity of the 1790s was entangled until at least 1795 with the publication of the *Rights of Man.* "To say that Thomas Paine animated his audience would be something of an understatement."[37]

The dominant subject of these democractic agitations were parliamentary reform, annual suffrage, and the rights of religious dissenters. But more and more these constitutional issues mingled or threatened to mingle with the politicization of economic life. The writings of Paine are a good example for how political demands became linked to economic ones.[38] While the "extension of manhood suffrage . . . [was] the first and principle aim of most democrats in this period," the attainment of the franchise was also widely regarded as means to achieve social and economic change.[39] Especially during this turbulent decade, the democratic radicalism was "transformed by a novel, sharp focus on the condition and means of livelihood of the laboring classes."[40] This occurred against the background of a series of bad harvests between 1794 and 1800. The years 1795 and 1796 as well as the years 1801 and 1802 saw large outbreaks of food disturbances and an increase in general popular discontent.

Historians are divided about the question how far these traditional economic grievances crossed the threshold to a more fundamental political critique.[41] But the conjunction among a great "passive disaffection" of the masses, an important change in the "sub-political attitudes," and a high level of politicization and agitation offered conduits of translating one into the other, especially since the French Revolution was a "watershed" and tended to "inject a political content to such disturbances where it did not exist or hardly existed before."[42] Hence, as the historian of this period, Harry Thomas Dickinson, summarized, it is "probably a mistake to regard economic protests and demands for political reform as two entirely separate phenomena."[43]

Regardless of whether, indeed, such intermingling of economic and political demands in a context of revolutionary passions occurred on a mass basis, one fact is historically undisputed: There was a great fear about this possibility. "The government was convinced that a real threat of revolution existed."[44] It assumed that "extraordinary measures were required to counter the success of the reform associations."[45] Especially the distribution of Paine's work was associated with the possibility of "profound and dangerous change."[46] Repressive measures instigated by William Pitt in 1794 and 1795—comprising the suspension of habeas corpus, the prohibition of political assemblies, and the extension of the verdict of high treason to any criticism of the constitution or the government—followed suit and brought this "radical surge, floods of lectures, meetings, conventions, book and pamphlets" to an end.[47] The crudest kind of repression: prosecution and imprisonment drove this movement underground, and a "strident apostasy" almost "obliterated the British enlightenment."[48]

Malthus wrote in the immediate wake of these protests. To him, the string of protests *and* the despotic reactions to it, the proliferation of literacy and political debate, and the language of rights mingling with economic distress appeared ignore all bounds and limits: there was excess on all sides. The meaning of liberalism was at stake. It is important to note that at that time liberalism was not a uniform body of thought or practice—in fact, the term "liberal" had not yet achieved any "recognizable political status, though many of the concepts often associated with it were in use."[49] This indeterminacy of liberalism, amplified by political upheavals, correlated with an epistemic uncertainty regarding the object of reform and contention: the nascent conceptions of society as a collective unit. The embryonic social sciences aspired to discover the "exact nature of human desires and needs" and their "social effects." But there was no "consensus . . . on either the meaning of 'social' or the methods of its 'science(s).'" There was only an "often unspoken agreement about the relationship of social science to politics: *la science social* would provide the master plan for a new political order."[50]

Sentiments, Society, and the Languages of Critique

Classical liberalism had always assumed a domain outside politics in which "spontaneous cooperation, the peaceful satisfaction of needs, and the absence of central control" produced a natural order.[51] But the notions of natural rights, property, and self-preservation ceased to capture this order of complex interrelations at the end of the eighteenth century. Karl Polanyi famously argued that the "very existence" of the "laws governing a complex society" came to "consciousness" at that time.[52] Likewise, Foucault suggested understanding this period in terms of the birth of the social. He contended that society should be seen as a prominent political figure for "calculating, rationalizing, and regulating the art of government" in the second half of the eighteenth century:[53] "We see a domain opening up of collective and political units constituted by social relations and bonds between individuals which go beyond the purely economic bond, yet without being purely juridical: society is characterized by bonds . . . which cannot be superimposed on the structures of the contract and the game of rights."[54]

The discursive space for debating this "collective and political unit" at that time was very much shaped by a constitutive linkage of the corporeal and the social. The sentient and corporeal being was the starting point, from which thinkers like David Hume, Adam Smith, Paine, William Godwin, or Condorcet developed their respective reasoning about sociability. The recourse to the "sentient being" provided utilitarian philosophy with its two "authorities" of "pain and pleasure." Furthermore, it formed the basis "for all knowledge of the interrelations of the physical and the moral," which the rise of physiology in the "science of man" promised to further. "Human beings were more or less irrevocably molded by the complex and interlinked impressions—internal and external—that acted on sensibility."[55] The body and the social mingled in the study of sensibility. But starting with the sentient being did not necessarily imply reducing the logic of sensibility into any simple calculus of pleasure and pain. Rather, the logics of sensibility linked with social affections, and bodily needs linked with accounts of political collectivity. The Scottish Enlightenment had made "sympathy the great cement of human society."[56] Thus, the social bond tied bodily needs and dependence, social affection, and economic calculations into a single connectivity. The "mutual relations, restrictions and connections of body and mind in the individual human being become indistinguishable from the questions of the structure of the collective body politic." In contrast, the separation between body and mind was seen as a sign of absolutist statecraft that "reduces the individual body to a cog in the rational-mechanical political body, while removing the individual mind from the realm of politics proper."[57]

The languages within which this new collective unit of society was debated centered on both the idioms of utility and right. In its broadest meaning, utilitarianism questions the authority of moral precepts derived from some natural law or given authority. It refers those obligations to the consequences and degrees of "utility" or "happiness" they bring and assumes those benefits as the only normative measure. In this period, especially in Britain, the language of utility was ubiquitous, ingrained in the "public feeling": Everyone was "speaking the language of utility" and those wanting their claims to be heard had to accommodate this language.[58] But everything could be claimed and done in this political language: natural rights were justified by their utility or refuted on the basis of utilitarian reasoning; the conservative case of Burke relied on this language, as did the anarchism of Godwin; Paine mingled his declaration of the *Rights of Man* with utilitarian reasoning about interests, will, and happiness.

Parallel to the ubiquitous use of the language of utility, the language of rights became predominant at the beginning of the decade following the events in France. For the British radicals, the language of rights promised to be the most potent weapon to press their aims, convinced "that the only practicable means of ameliorating the condition of mankind is to restore them to the full possession of their just and inalienable rights."[59] It is important to note that the language of rights was at that time as much a tool in a political struggle as it was linked to an epistemological hope to provide foundations for a new order: the simplicity and generality of such declaration of rights was tied to an epistemological promise: it would guarantee a "public knowledge of the rational principles of social order."[60] At the beginning of the period, the languages of utility and right were not exclusive of the other, and over the course of the political struggle they were used, adapted, and developed in response to events and adversaries. It was only by the middle of the decade that the vocabulary of natural rights had vanished as an important idiom of debate and the language of utility gained the upper hand.[61] The radicalizing "trajectory of the revolution" made many "uneasy about their earlier embrace of revolutionary slogans" that were couched in the language of rights.

Over the course of the following decades, understanding of social science became more closely tied to social utility, "divorcing the ideal of social science from the notion of natural right with which it had been conflated."[62] But the recourse to the calculation of the interested, willing, and desiring subject had initially not offered much certainty—for doing so, it had to be equipped with an infallible starting point to measure pleasures and pains. As the historian of utilitarianism Elie Halévy put it, utility could only become an object of scientific rigor when linked to necessity: economic man "must appear as a necessitous being." Only if somewhere someone exerts the maximum of effort and bears the maximum of pain, in order to secure the enjoyment of an object, a standard to measure utility can be offered.[63] The corporeal and sentient being had to become a naked body surrounded by the "chilling breath of want," as Malthus put it, in order such certainty could be offered.[64] Utility became tied more and more to a notion of "vital laws, functional coherence and physiology."[65]

But before utilitarian reasoning assumed such more definite vantage point, before it was untied from the language of rights, and before it became the sole guide of the social sciences in general and economics in particular, the aspiration of knowing and reforming society was fraught with much more uncertainty, politically and epistemologically. The writings of Condorcet, one of the adversaries against whom Malthus made his case, provide a window into a liberal socioeconomic science that lacks this certainty, that is not yet wedded to utility as a single and firm foundation of reasoning, and that has retained its ties to the political promise the true "social art," which had to achieve the end of "poverty, humiliation or dependence."[66] For the sake of the current argument, a cursory account of Condorcet's arguments paradigmatically shows how the impure domain of economy and society was an uncertain epistemic object of knowledge and political aspiration. It provides the canvas against which one can assess Malthus's fear of the indeterminacy in the social science and the political promises that it was tied to. The invention of economic laws and the reference to necessity was opposed to this openness. No "proper calculation" and "no application of knowledge and ingenuity" and "no effort" would mitigate necessity, as Malthus maintained against Condorcet.[67]

Condorcet's liberal envisioning of society did not assume any transparent visibility of the socioeconomic domain. The "frightening complexity of conflicting interests that link the survival and well-being of one individual to the general organizations of societies" was impossible to remedy, according to Condorcet.[68] Economy and society appeared as an incomplete system caught in a protracted process of transition. No single rule, no single machine, no rule of interest was offered as a regulative foundation that could be relied on. The economy was regarded as "an inexact and uncertain condition. It has lost the determined orderliness of exact regimes, or of laws of order. Its uncertainty is in turn closely inter-twined with the elusive condition of the disposition of enlightenment."[69] Endless calculation and probability were for Condorcet the means to address this uncertainty. It provided the basis for his "social mathematics" that was meant to be in the service of political reform.[70] Calculation was not mechanical endeavor but was linked to sensationalist inquiries into the minds.[71] One objective of the social mathematics was to "protect the truth of society amidst a mass of uncertain and changing opinions."[72] The "calculus of probability" would ensure that one dealt properly with the "different degrees of certainty" that pertained to social life. Much of his theoretical energies were caught with the question of how to determine facts not linked to general laws.[73]

Condorcet showed caution and circumspection in respect to proposing any "truth of society": "The process of public choice, a sort of political tatonnement, in which every benefit of a project is compared to every costs, was dauntingly complex," but it could not be avoided, since there was no "hydraulic machine" running by itself. Economic judgment was caught by whims and fears, logics of recognition, and custom, just as were political judgments. Its prospect of enlightenment had no other founda-tion than slowly acquired public sentiments and endless loops of reflection and discussion. In the words of Lorraine Daston, "to calculate was for Condorcet an education in both epistemology and civics, a way of analyzing ideas in order to fix the boundary between the known and the unknown as well as an exercise in political autonomy, an assertion of independence against priestcraft and tyranny" that rests not so much on "violence but on fear."[74]

In her study of the history of the economic fact, Mary Poovey described the epistemology of the science of society and wealth at the end of the eighteenth century in terms of the inner paradoxes that it entailed: The skepticism of the eighteenth century had no method for asserting and grounding the view of the social and economic totality.[75] But this impos-sibility to conceive of the socioeconomic whole as an ordered system as such did not simultaneously imply an injunction against envisioning eco-nomic order as an artifice of political experimentation. Thinkers like Condorcet, Paine, or Godwin linked this indeterminate account of the economic totality to the domain of political judgment.[76] In this respect, these thinkers diverged from the Scottish Enlightenment, which had entertained a deep skepticism both against the "men of systems," devising from above, but also against the prospects of political judgment by the many. For Smith, "politics is the 'folly of man,' while economic progress is like Candide's garden, which can be cultivated with success."[77] A "moral fragmentation of humanity" can be found in Smith between those able to enter the conversation about moral and political order and the "mob of mankind [that] can at best hope to live a merely decent life according to given rules."[78] In contrast, thinkers such as Paine, Condorcet, or Godwin linked their account of society—thought of as an evolving yet unfinished material–social connectivity—with a prominent role for political subjectivity. The radical democratic understanding of political judgment in Paine or the endless political discussions about the intertwining orders of exchange, liberty, and justice in Condorcet crossed over the divide between politics and economy without assuming them to be alike. They were deeply concerned about the question of how to ensure the subject's capacity to partake in political debate and decision.[79]

The type of liberalism that these thinkers articulated was neither uniform nor unproblematic. Godwin, for example, linked the sanctity of individual judgment to a utilitarian calculation of the value of one's life as it contributes to "general happiness." The outcomes of this calculation did not respect the rules of property or self-preservation: augmenting general happiness might imply the giving away of belongings or even one's own life, as demonstrated by the famous example of the chambermaid who would prefer that the bishop would be rescued from a fire instead of herself. While Condorcet dethroned utility, finding it to be a "vague principles and a fertile source of bad laws," Godwin wholeheartedly embraced it.[80]

Going back to this moment in liberalism does not mean to champion these thinkers as better versions of a liberal politico-economic imagination. But it is interesting to remember how these forms of liberalism at the close of the eighteenth century allowed for a different relation between the political and the economic: it tied a conception of a "fatherless" and hybrid economic world—as the historian Emma Rothschild puts it—with a "fatherless" political world. Economic reality was, in this sense, an open question of "what is given, of what is visible, and therefore of what can be said about it and done with respect to it."[81] Highlighting this moment of openness and experimentation in the account economy itself should not imply that there were no limits to indeterminacy and to the opening up of liberal economic order to political questioning and experimentation.[82]

Nevertheless, it is important to recall this political-epistemological inde-terminacy in regard to what "economic facts" were about. As I trace in the next section, the political fear of the "fatherless world" was clearly recognizable in the texts of Malthus, who assumed the political task of saving the constitution from "unceasing change and carnage," hoping to end Condorcet's endless calculations, Paine's revolutionary optimism, or Godwin's anarchical use of individual judgment. If it is true that "we still live, at the outset of the twenty-first century, in a world which is defined, in important respect, by [these] events," as Rothschild has contended, this entwinement of political fears and reasoning with economic reasoning is part of our history of the present.[83]

Knowing the Economy and Political Reason

Malthus's essay on population presented itself to be about the body, mate-riality, and economic laws. But, above all, it set out to determine the very line that distinguishes the "real and . . . [the] imaginary state of things."[84] Malthus's self-assigned task was to rectify a dangerous intermeshing of the domain of mere dreams and reality that he finds on the political scene. He promised that his book amounts to piercing through "a phantom of the imagination" and to "awaken[ing] to real life, and [to] contemplat[ing] the genuine situation of man on earth."[85] According to Malthus, the faults of Condorcet, Paine, or Godwin had been to dwell in "gorgeous palaces of happiness and immortality" that would "dissolve like a baseless fabric of a vision": "This beautiful fabric of the imagination vanishes at the severe touch of truth."[86] Hence, ascertaining the question of rights, which Paine and Condorcet prominently posed, demands first know which rights are possible on the basis of economic facts:

> The circulation of Paine's Rights of Man, it is supposed, has done great mischief among the lower and middling classes of people in this coun-try. This is probably true, but not because man is without rights, or that these rights ought not to be known, but because Mr. Paine has shown himself totally unacquainted with the structure of society. . . . Nothing would so effectually counteract the mischief occasioned by Mr. Paine's Rights of Man as a general knowledge of the real rights of man.[87]

The opposition between the sphere of imagination, vision, or dreams, on the one hand, and the sphere of economic facts and necessities, on the other, installed a polemical opposition. But one has to be careful not to follow these lines of opposition without scrutinizing them first. As Foucault suggested, if one is attending to the period of the eighteenth century, the genealogy of knowledge "must first—before it does any-thing else—outwit the problematic of the Enlightenment" that stages a battle "between knowledge and ignorance, of reason against chimeras . . . we have to see . . . something very different: an immense and multiple battle, but one between knowledge and ignorances, but an immense and multiple battle between knowledges in the plural."[88] Thus, instead of sid-ing between imagination and reality in this battle, the task lies in under-standing the stakes of epistemology in this context.

Malthus's writings are significant in the history of economic fact because they ground a novel "epistemological authority" over and against the skepticism of the eighteenth century.[89] The turn toward the "real state of things" was more than the sober awakening from the "imaginary state of things" that Malthus' rhetoric desires to make us believe.[90] It was a step into to a different epistemology—that is, a different account of how to address the objectivity and ultimate reality of social order. In his own accord, Malthus followed the ideal of scientific objectivity that Newton had established. The *Essay on Population* aspired to belong to the "the most just and sublime theories, founded on careful and reiterated experiments," just like the "grand and consistent theory of Newton." According to Mal-thus, his adversary Condorcet made "facts bend to systems, instead of establishing systems upon facts" and put the theory of Newton "upon the same footing as the wild and eccentric hypothesis of Descartes."[91] But already Condorcet had taken Newton's experimental science has his model for his "social mathematics" and took "post-Cartesian science" to be his blueprint because it had displaced the faith in systems with a more probing accumulation of general facts from experiment.[92] But "facts" and "systems" related differently for them. Hence, oppositions are not what they seem. Within these debates, the making of "economic facts" itself was at stake.

Malthus's search for a new way of relating facts to systems was governed by a particular fear of the indeterminacy that existed between them. The danger that Malthus detected in this indeterminacy stems from how experience could be used by "mischievous theorists" to draw unjust inferences. He was at pains to distinguish what kind of observation would count as "general experience" that could give rise to the "general principles" that the science of political economy was about. It is worth quoting at length how this translation of observations into facts and systems is wrought with danger:

> But when from this confined experience, from the management of his own little farm, or the details of the workhouse in his neighbourhood, he draws a general inference, as is frequently the case, he then at once erects himself into a theorist; and is the more dangerous, because, experience being the only just foundation for theory, people are often caught merely by the sound of the word, and do not stop to make the distinction between that partial experience which, on such subjects, is no foundation whatever for a just theory, and that general experience, on which alone a just theory can be founded . . . but these advocates of practice do not seem to be aware that a great part of them may be classed among the most mischievous theorists of their time.[93]

Especially in regard to issues of political import, this indeterminacy appeared as a dangerous opening to all sorts of misapprehensions of the "general good," "which we may not distinctly comprehend, or the effect of which may be weakened by distance and diffusion."[94] Siding with Hume, he found that, in the domain of politics, "first appearances are more deceitful" than in any other domain.[95] The knowledge of political economy was taken to provide a beneficial epistemological authority against this susceptibility to misapprehension of the general good: "Political economy is perhaps the only science of which it may be said that the ignorance of it is not merely a deprivation of good, but produces great positive evil."[96]

As one can gather from many passages in Malthus's text, this "great evil" of not knowing how to assess "general principles" was seen to bring about a particular condition of limitlessness in the domain of political judgment and reasoning. A rhetorical tirade against the dangerous domain of unrestrained speculation and excess colored Malthus's account of the exercise of political reason regarding the subject of economy: Men have become "elate and giddy," they have substituted "wild flights and unsupported assertions" for patient investigation.[97] The poor have been inculcated with "false expectations" and "extravagant demands," and "everything that could tend to deceive them to aggravate and encourage their discontents, and to raise unreasonable and extravagant expectations . . . has been as sedulously brought forward."[98] A "late rage for wide and unrestrained speculation seems to have been a kind of mental intoxication, arising perhaps from the great and unexpected discoveries, which has been made in various branches of science." The excesses of reason and political demands brought about excessive measures of repression in turn: "They [the demands] are naturally calculated to excite some alarm . . . but alarm, when once excited, seldom knows where to stop, and the causes of it are particularly liable to be exaggerated . . . it has been under the influence of exaggerated statements, and of inferences drawn by exaggerated fears . . . furnished by the extravagant expectations of the people."[99]

In this account, exaggeration bred exaggeration. The figure of the mob, excited by a reason that did not know its bounds, initiated this chain of excess under which the possibility of liberal order faltered: "It fosters a prevailing tyranny, and engenders one where it was not; and thought, in its dreadful fits of resentment, it appears occasionally to devour its unsightly offspring; yet no sooner is the horrid deed committed, that, however unwilling it may be to propagate such a breed, it immediately groans with a new birth."[100] It is peculiar that biological metaphors of breeding and dying that will become central to the figure of population were ubiquitous in this account of the fate of the political constitution: "The English constitution will be seen hastening with rapid strides to the euthanasia."[101] The death of the liberal constitution was fundamentally linked to a lack of a proper objectivity in matters of "economic facts." It was because the firm foundation in ascertaining what belongs properly to the "real" rights of man was missing that unrestrained reason engendered unrestrained politics, which in turn drowned the liberal constitution.

Viewed in this context, the new boundary established between the domain of economy and the domain of politics became legible as a measure against the dangers of a political reason out of bounds. The question of economy became wholly embroiled in this *problematique*; it had to offer the firm basis, the epistemological authority and novel objectivity that could control how the common order is to be understood and negotiated. The laws were to be simple and need to be "intelligible to the humblest capacity."[102] They also needed to be uniform and universal:

> "We have reason to think," he says, "that it is more conducive to the formation and improvement of the human mind that the law should be uniform": If the laws of nature be thus fickle and inconstant . . . the human mind will no longer have any incitements to inquire, but must remain sunk in inactive torpor, or amuse itself only in bewildering dreams and extravagant fancies. The constancy of the laws of nature, and of effects and causes, is the foundation of all human knowledge.[103]

Economy was an economy of knowledge: it saved on the means necessary to render the economic world visible. It had to offer a closed conception of causal chains that were limited in number. This commitment to general laws that offered simplicity and uniformity to the mind is in a certain sense curious since Malthus was also adamant of the fact that "general principles should not be pushed too far." In fact, Malthus admitted that, in a different context, these general principles and the causal relations they posit were often to be taken with a grain of salt.[104] Yet, in spite of the hesitancy in regard to such "general rules" that promised undue simplification and generalization, economy was still taken to be a reality that was governed by unequivocal laws:

> We know from experience, that these operations of what we call nature have been conducted almost invariably according to fixed laws. And since the world began, the causes of population and depopulation have been probably as constant as any of the laws of nature with which we are acquainted. . . . There is no subject to which general principles have been so seldom applied; and yet, in the whole compass of human knowledge, I doubt if there be one in which it is so dangerous to lose sight of them.[105]

The simultaneous assertion of impervious laws of necessity and their qualification in the making of economic facts is less curious if placed in the context of the epistemological-political contestation at the time. Only against the assumed dangers of excessive political reason, it seemed to be important to assert without qualification that "necessity, that impervious, all-pervading law of nature, restrains [natural life] within the prescribed bounds . . . and man cannot by any effort of reason escape from it."[106]

Malthus did not announce the immutable laws of economic necessity because he sought to mute the sphere of politics. Much to the contrary, it was because Malthus understood public debate as an important part of a liberal constitution that he hoped to furnish the proper foundations for such debate. As Donald Winch has pointed out, Malthus stood between those who enshrine the sanctity of judgment and those who feared it.[107] Malthus did not assume, as Burke did, that people are "destined to obscurity" or that the "good laws" could equally be framed under despotism. Censorship was to him not a desired policy, and he was a supporter of general education. Malthus insisted on the need for general education for the benefit of a democratic public.[108] But he feared, like Burke, that the exercise of political reason had "no fundamental law, no strict convention, no respected usage to restrain it."[109] Malthus did not set out to condemn "all political speculations in the gross," but he sought to bring the "speculative philosopher" back to the grounds of truth and experiment.[110] Accordingly, the understanding of economic laws was supposed to prevent that "we will be thrown upon a wide sea of experiment."[111]

The metaphor of the "wide sea" is conspicuous in this context.[112] At the end of the eighteenth and the beginning of the nineteenth century, the image of a dangerous "sea" belonged to the debate on the dangers of unrestrained reason. Kant's critique of reason famously used this metaphor of the "shoreless ocean" that "after alluring us with ever-deceptive prospects, compels us in the end to abandon as hopeless all the cessations and tedious endeavor" and to "return to the coastline of experience."[113] To Kant, the deception that an unlimited reason held out required a critique that articulated the proper limits of what can be known and hoped for. In an analogous fashion, Malthus presented the science of political economy as such critique of the limits and foundations of political reason.

Malthus's fears about the exercise of political reason belong to the long tradition of liberal skepticism, which is unsure about the merits of individual judgment. It can be traced back to John Locke's apprehension that the great majority would not arrive at an understanding of natural law. Since "natural law," which provided the foundation for legitimate power and spaces of freedom, was, as Locke admitted, "unwritten, and so nowhere to be found but in the minds of Men," the judgment about its content was precarious.[114] The question of which "knowledge and [which] criteria of judgment" is appropriate to the political realm has "both guided and disquieted" the intellectual efforts of liberal thinkers to date.[115] As Rothschild has put it, "the great difficulty for the political theorist of the enlightened disposition was how to describe a universe, or a society, in which everybody has opinions and theories and conflicting, changing desires."[116] Condorcet and Paine even more than Hume and Smith link liberal economy to an ongoing political reasoning. It is considered an unruly world of uncertain judgment. The invention of economic necessity counters this unruly world of judgment. The announcement of such laws is a theoretical act that aspires to end all theories—it is full of "disdain for the speculative or explanatory views people have formed about collectives."[117]

Twentieth-century neoliberalism still capitalizes on this moment. Friedrich von Hayek explains the merits of liberal economic theory today by referring to its epistemological modesty: market economies do not need anybody to reflect about socioeconomic relations; they arrange our bits and pieces of knowledge in the best possible and most productive ways. "The most significant fact about this system is the economy of knowledge with which it operates, or how little the individual participants need to know."[118] These rules of conduct are simple; the required knowledge is limited. The critique of "hubristic reason" turns into a prohibition for critical vision.[119] The understanding of liberal economy as being governed by a simple set of laws and principles is not to the least an effect of the fear that the economic world is an issue too hybrid and too open to the "wide sea of experiments," and hence too dangerous for debate.

Political Theory and Liberal Economy—Malthusian Moments

The preceding sections argue that the invention of economic laws of necessity can be understood as a political argument that is preoccupied with the fear that economic issues are too contentious, too indeterminate, and too complex for the judgment of the many. Malthus's essay on population, scarcity, and necessity has been deciphered as an answer to a situation of dissensus. This interpretation shifts emphasis away from the question of naturalism associated with the question of population. The question of life appears in this context first and foremost in terms of an illicit or wrong politicization. Those who do not know how to debate these issues in reasonable ways have entered the political stage. The naturalism of life is submerged in a question about how to properly negotiate "what is given, of what is visible, and therefore of what can be said about it and done with respect to it."[120] It concerns the modes of configuring the object and the subject of politics, which is "biologically and anthropologically unlocatable."[121]

Some passages in Malthus's text show how the political question of economic life is governed by the fear of an impossible politicization of life. As cited earlier, Malthus fears a mob that articulates its "cries for hunger" on the political stage: "A mob, which is generally the growth of a redundant population goaded by resentment for real sufferings, but totally ignorant of the quarter from which they originate, is of all monsters the most fatal to freedom."[122] In this passage, the monster that undoes the political order is redundant species-life. The metaphor of a monstrous animal that only growls and groans in a single sentiment signals the appearance of the excluded on the political stage.[123] It affirms, dramatizes, and enshrines the impossibility of a differentiated, conflicting, piecemeal, and experimental politicization of economic life in a situation of dissensus.

It is remarkable how closely Malthus's account of this misapprehension of the question of life on the political stage resembles Arendt's critique of the course of the French Revolution presented at the beginning. Reading these thinkers alongside each other is illuminating for both of them: one the one hand, it buttresses a reading of Malthus in terms of the implicit political theory that his economics contain. It emphasizes the political stakes in his argument on economic laws. On the other hand, it sheds a new light on Arendt's critique of the politicization of life. As this concluding discussion shows, Arendt, just like Malthus, feared the politicization of life due to a lack of faith in the ability of political reason to deal with issues that are not wholly political but concern the malleable economic.

In her reading of the French Revolution, Arendt argues—very much in accordance with Malthus—that the articulation of suffering and needs on the political stage is by its own nature limitless and undifferentiated:

> Rousseau's image of a 'multitude . . . united in one body' and driven by one will was an exact description of what they actually were, for what urged them on was the quest for bread, and the cry for bread will always be uttered with one voice. Insofar as we all need bread, we are indeed

all the same, and may as well unite into one body. It is by no means merely a matter of misguided theory that the French conception of the people has carried, from its beginning, the connotation of a multi-headed monster. . . . Robespierre once compared the nation to the ocean; it was indeed the ocean of misery and the ocean-like sentiments it aroused that combined to drown the foundations of freedom.[124]

Again, the image of the boundless ocean appears in this problematization of a political reasoning that has been corrupted by a lack of differentiation and fails to distinguish between what can and what cannot be achieved by politics. She contends, no "revolution has ever solved 'the social question' and liberated man from the predicament of want."[125]

Just like Malthus, Arendt fears the dangerous intermingling of politics and economics. Even though Arendt writes in a different historical situation and is certainly no defender of the liberal understanding of politics, she shares with Malthus this fear. According to her reading, modern politics suffers from what she calls the most "pernicious belief of the modern age," which means to take life and economy to be the center of the human endeavor and the prime object of politics.[126] The goals of national welfare have given rise to a particular mingling of politics and economics that she links with conformity, totalitarian extension of state power, and administrative rule. The genuine dimension of the political as a sphere of plurality, action, and freedom dissolved therein. The nation becomes one gigantic household in this reading, transforming politics into the managerial rule and administration.[127] The stark divisions that Arendt maintains between what she calls the social and the political have often been critically commented upon. The purification of the political has been declared to be a nostalgic call for what would become an empty political game, conservative in its sensibilities and ignorant of what is at stake in negotiating the technical and economic complexity of modern society.[128] But this division has rarely been discussed as expressing a particular fear on the side of the theorist: that the precarious domain of political judgment will not be exercised properly when matters of economy are allowed into its domain. A remarkable passage in her book *On Revolutions* is revealing in this respect.

In this passage, Hannah Arendt discusses Karl Marx's take on the liberal divide between economy and politics. She utters respect for the attempt of the young Marx to link the political concerns for freedom with the economic issue of poverty by framing it as an outcome of violation: "By reducing property relations to the old relationships which violence, rather than necessity, establishes between men, he summoned up a spirit of rebelliousness that can spring only from being violated, not from being under the sway of necessity." Marx, she continues, persuaded the poor that "poverty itself is a political, not a natural phenomenon, the result of violence and violation rather than of scarcity." Doing so might fulfill revolutionary aspirations but runs up against the demands of analytical sincerity: the domain of life and economy, of body and needs—we might add, of things and money—"can never be simply reduced to and completely absorbed by violence and violation."[129] The entanglement of conceptual categories for societal order cannot be brought to a simple conclusion that reduces it to the political forces of power and violence in toto. It remains an equivocal entanglement.

According to Arendt, this entanglement appeared unsatisfying to Marx because it defied scientific rigor. Being committed to this scientific explanation, the later Marx hence exchanged this political reading of economic poverty—incomplete as it had to remain—for the sake of an economic reading of politics. Arendt is not known for her knowledge or careful interpretations of Marx, and this reading she gives should not be mistaken for one.[130] But her interpretation of the entangling of politics and economics in Marx is still interesting. It points out that the attempt to read economy in political terms defies the reduction of one into the other. It opens a *problematique*. To Arendt, the very interpretation of the economy of life as a political phenomenon always comes up against the problem that it can never be *completely* traced to a political origin.[131] The intermingling of the economy of life with the political domain is thus full of pitfalls and wrong-headed excesses. It is a dangerous frontier, so to speak.

Interestingly, Arendt does not keep this unsettling frontier open in her own accounts. While she criticizes Marx for having succumbed politics to the irresistible laws of economic necessity, she adopts a more naturalized version of economic necessity into her political theory that Marx had long left behind. Her account of economy remains by definition hostile to any intermingling with political reason. The strict boundaries between economy and politics are enshrined in the depiction of these realms: there is no meddling with necessity. But the account of the economy in terms of unrelenting necessity already contains the limits of politicization. It closes off the very indeterminacy that is a site for the exercise of political judgment. To distinguish a "wrong," as Rancière calls it, from an event to be endured as a given fact forms the very matter of politics and political subjectivation: "Where exactly do we draw the line between the unpleasant feeling of having received a blow and the feeling of having suffered an 'injury' through this same blow? We could say that the difference is marked precisely in the logos that separates the discursive articulation of a grievance from the phonic articulation of a groan."[132]

Both Malthus and Arendt seem to find this task to be too complicated for political reason. Their accounts of the economy in terms of laws of necessity shield politics from having to deal with a realm that is not reducible to it. But as this chapter has shown, liberal economy did not always appear too dangerous to negotiate. At the end of the eighteenth century, liberal economy had been linked to an experimental cast of political reason. A more open and porous relation between the socioeconomic realm—understood as a corporeal, affective, mutually dependent collectivity—and political reason had emerged at that time. The deepening and absolutizing of the conceptual boundary of liberal economy was a reaction to this experimental openness and to the fears that it engendered. To adapt a phrase by Rancière, one might say that it was political philosophy in the guise of economic thought that invented economy—if one takes political philosophy to mean a "philosophical project of achieving politics by doing away with it."[133] As the next chapter demonstrates, this displacement of the political has a parallel displacement of the economic as its corollary.

CHAPTER 2

Savage Life, Scarcity, and the Economic

T he notion of population designates an aggregate of living beings who reproduce, eat, live, and die. It raises issues of subsistence, resources, space of living, peaceful coexistence, and reproduction at once. Like the political figure of the people, the population addresses a mode of collectivity. But very much unlike the people, population is not about the subjects of rights, democratic constitution, and political sovereignty. The notion of population concerns human beings in their "biological rootedness."[1] The doubling of the body politic into the people, on the one hand, and an excitable, desiring, needy, and reproducing population, on the other hand, encapsulates and rearticulates a long-standing division in Western political thought—that between man and citizen, between private and public, between economic needs and political freedom.[2] But while the notion of population enshrines this division, it confounds it at the same time: debates and politics about population cross over the domains of economics, biology, politics, health, and sexual reproduction.[3]

Michel Foucault ingeniously suggests that the notion of population is central for understanding modern liberalism. In his *Security, Territory, Population* lectures, Foucault argues that the population emerged as an "absolutely novel" object in the eighteenth century and transformed the meaning of liberal politics: "The relation between the individual and the collective, between the totality of the social body and its elementary fragments, is made to function in a completely different way."[4] Hence, telling the history of liberalism through the notion of population changes our understanding of it. According to Foucault, the problematization of how the population "exists, is preserved, subsists, and subsists at an optimal level" belongs to a historically new type of liberal governmental apparatus that he calls security dispositif, and to a new type of power that he calls biopolitical.[5]

Although Foucault claims the centrality of the problem of population for the historiography of liberalism, he does not elaborate in any detail on the most peculiar economic aspect of the problematization of population in the history of liberalism: the overriding concern with the scarcity of resources.[6] Since the beginning of the nineteenth century, the question of economy became deeply linked to the fear that a population will eat away the resources it needs to subsist. This fear changed the face of economic liberalism. A population out of bounds was assumed to generate poverty, a loss of standards of living, and scarcity. Accordingly, the "absolutely novel" object of population did not only transform the political side of liberalism, it also changed its economic side: Reproach of reproducing masses, questions of survival, and the economic facts of scarcity mingled in the question of population ever since the "threshold" of biopolitical modernity has been crossed.

Speaking of a "threshold" that has been crossed at the beginning of the nineteenth century might appear as an exaggeration, which would lead to an undue unification of liberal thought in the long nineteenth and twentieth century that were to come. Yet, without assuming that the question of economy, the problem of population, and the invocation of scarcity have always been tied together the same way, one can find a perplexing continuity of linking these issues to each other in the history of economic liberalism. The question of population has been used and reused in order to render the question of scarcity palpable and to explain what economic necessity is about. It seems as if the question of population consistently serves to demonstrate how a liberal economic order answers best to the demands of the human condition, to life, and to reality itself—regardless how "denaturalized" or "knowledge-based" liberal economics has otherwise become.

At the beginning of the nineteenth century, the use of population discourse for defining the economic problem in terms of scarcity was most visible. The science of political economy became preoccupied with the limits that land and the reproduction of the species imposed on the accumulation of wealth. The link between population, land, and scarcity provided the new science of political economy with a unifying and systematizing core that it would have otherwise lacked: the nexus between population and scarcity organized the causal relations between rent, capital, labor, and wealth.[7] Malthus's *An Essay on the Principle of Population* was the most famous, decisive, and influential text that enshrined this tenacious link between population and scarcity in the history of liberalism. None of his predecessors in the sciences of wealth "was greatly troubled with the prospect of over-population" and none turned scarcity into an ontology of human life.[8] It was Malthus who turned the positive view of population growth that the Scottish Enlightenment had entertained into a scenario of catastrophic scarcity. "Malthus's main contribution to this intellectual tradition [of thinking about the population problem] was to posit the problem of scarcity as something that no human community could escape."[9] The notion of scarcity changed its meaning accordingly: it became a quasi-ontological condition of mankind founded in the biological nature of the human.[10] The historians of economic thought leave no doubt about the crucial role of this novel understanding of population for shifting the notion of liberal economy: "The introduction of the principle of population into British political economy in the late 1790s marked the most significant transformation that occurred in the subject as it moved into the nineteenth century. It could not have been more influential."[11] Even though Malthus's economic doctrines as a whole did not last, the tie between population and scarcity that his work stands for has remained virulent. With him, scarcity became a central presupposition of political economy.

Population and scarcity turned out to be perennial themes in liberal economic thought, but the way they were linked did not remain the same. Toward the end of the nineteenth century, questions of bodies, reproduction, and land moved to the background in economic arguments about scarcity. Economic discourse is said to have "denaturalized" over the course of the century. The historian Margaret Schabas coined this term in order to show that liberalism increasingly eschews any reference to biological limits or corporeal necessities for defining the economic problem.[12] Notwithstanding these changes, scarcity remained central to economics, with the issue of population constantly lingering in the background. For example, the economist Stanley Jevons, who is known for his psychological account of utility, preferences, and scarcity, wrote a book about the coal question. Not land but energy appeared as a limiting factor for economic wealth. This book is commonly taken to be one of the landmarks in economic thinking on resource depletion. Again, population growth has a central role in this argument as the prospect of further population growth together with higher rates of consumption make these limits of energy tangible.[13] The issue of population comes to the fore when arguments about scarcity are linked to material limits.

Even through the "denaturalization" of liberalism seems to have continued in the twentieth century, the question of population does not disappear—but it changes its role for defining the economic problem. For example, Friedrich von Hayek is known for his criticism of the ecological limits imposed by natural conditions. He does not fear "too much life" on earth, and he questions the notion of "overpopulation." But these criticisms should not be taken as a sign that population has become less important to demonstrate that unavoidable necessity reigns in a liberal market order. Precisely because there are so many lives to sustain, the market order becomes vital as it deals most aptly with limited resources and capacities. To Hayek, population life and market order are inextricably wedded together as the latter protects and makes possible the former. This vital market order is not without its own "calculation of lives," as Hayek puts it: evolutionary demands might impose the need to sacrifice the current lives for the unknown future lives. Again, life-threatening choices, vital necessity, and liberal economy are tied with the issue of population.[14]

The importance of population discourse for liberal economics continues unabated after the Second World War. It moved to the forefront of the agenda in policies of economic development roughly at the same time that the question of ecological limits moved to the foreground of public debates. In the 1960s the World Bank announced that "population has become a major obstacle to social and economic development."[15] It produces scarcity where there should be growth and plenty. Not much later, the Meadows report on the limits to growth presented population as an endogenous cause in a single global system that connected demographics, economics, and ecology. Population control turned into a matter of survival since the world population as a whole was exhausting the "carrying capacity of the earth" and threatening the ecological system from within while ruining economic prospects at the same time.[16] The "population bomb," as the famous title of Paul Ehrlich's international bestseller warned, will exhaust the resources of the earth.[17] Economics of scarcity and ecological limits conjoin in these images of a population out of bounds.

This cursory account of various instances of liberal arguments about population and scarcity since the beginning of the nineteenth century does not offer an historical argument—it merely signals that debates about population have been again and again about life and its economic (and ecological) limits. What does this perennial presence of the theme of population tell us about the crucial tenet of scarcity and the attendant notion of economic necessity for defining liberal economy? How does it shape the notion of liberal economy and the economic imagination?

This chapter takes up this question. It goes back to the historical moment when this nexus between population and scarcity was first established in order to reconstruct this event from the perspective of the genealogy of the economic. I take Malthus's *Essay on the Principle of Population* as a scene of emergence for the definition of liberal economy in terms of scarcity and necessity; I further assume that analyzing the link between population and scarcity provides the opportunity to uncover the malleable economic behind the notion of scarcity. Rereading Malthus's texts from this vantage point allows me to unpack scarcity as a black box that covers the more complicated question of how to engender economic futurity. Scarcity appears as a type of "objectivity" in the sense that Lorraine Daston and Peter Galison have given this term: as a historically contingent articulation of a virtuous relation between subject and object.[18] This argument avoids the polemics that questions of scarcity often induce between those who claim to recognize the hard facts of scarcity and those who mistrust the political implications of this assertion and seek for this reason to show that scarcity is "merely" constructed. The gist of this chapter is a different one: I target one of the most taken-for-granted notions of what makes things economic in order to unfold the malleability of the economic behind it.

As this chapter demonstrates, the tight link between population and scarcity that Malthus establishes rests on a particular notion of species-life, which is inextricably tied to a cultural-racial hierarchy. "Savage life," as Malthus coins it, stands at the heart of the principle of population.[19] It designates a form of life that is always ruining the prospects of material progress by the acts of immediate consumption. "Savage life" is defined by its lack of foresight and appears as a form of "abject," monstrous life, which undoes economic futurity because it is not able to wait until future benefits are secured.[20] While the more civilized life undoes this catastrophism of the population principle, savage life produces scarcity and misery for all. Not species-life itself, but a cultural and colonial differentiation between brute life and civilized life makes the connection between population and scarcity. Detecting this racial-cultural hinge between species-life and scarcity allows extricating the question of futurity and temporality from the notion of scarcity.

The argument pursued here does not consist in the claim that liberal economics necessarily encapsulates such colonial and racial hierarchies linked to a biopolitics of population. The aim is much the contrary: I use a particular historical-conceptual constellation at the beginning of the nineteenth century to uncover the malleable economic from putative laws of necessity that are based on an assumption an all-pervasive and quasi-ontological condition of scarcity. In this specific historical case, the question of species-life and the colonial-racial hierarchies it entailed prove to be the major transmission bolt for turning an open plane of the economic into such understanding of necessity. There are many reasons to assume that the historical constellation unpacked here shaped the liberal economic imagination in lasting ways—as the rough sketch of the debates on population presented above indicates.[21] But laying bare the moment at which these issues became linked is meant as a critical operation that establishes historical difference rather than continuity: it hopes to raise the ability to discern the multiplicity of what liberal economy might mean and how it is open to political debate and experiment.

Given the prominence of the issue of species-life and its racial-cultural differentiation for the analysis presented in the following, this chapter contributes to two prominent theoretical debates in political and social theory. One the one hand, it speaks directly to the debate on biopolitics. Stated in the most general terms, this debate concerns the political consequences of what is termed the "biopolitical fracture" between people and population, between citizen and man. The very division that parcels out the proper political life from its private, natural, or material substrate is taken to be a highly contingent and political act. Modern politics is said to be characterized by the way it relates to what it excludes and yet takes as its most important object: life itself. Michel Foucault and Giorgio Agamben are the two main protagonists of this debate. Both have developed their respective notions of biopolitics with reference to political questions of sovereignty, rationalities of governing, and law. The question of economic liberalism has a deceptive presence in these debates: these thinkers tend to subsume the discussion of economy under the heading of biopolitics. But the link between biopolitics and liberal economy remains tenuous, overstated, or unexplored in these writings. Foucault explicitly acknowledged at the end of his lectures on biopolitics that he has not properly sufficiently answered the question of how liberal economic governmentality and the biopolitics of population are tied. The historical analysis presented below allows clarifying and specifying what the debate so far leaves indeterminate. It offers a new reading on how to link the biopolitics of population with the articulation of liberal economy that revolves around the question of economic norms.

Above and beyond this contribution to this theoretical debate, this chapter belongs to the growing exploration of a postcolonial perspective on liberal economic thought. In many ways, it should not come as a surprise that the discourse on liberal economy cannot be "chartered in Europe alone." Just as any other European discourse in the eighteenth and nineteenth century, the notion liberal economy is wound up with thinking about empire.[22] While the constitutive relations between liberalism and British Empire have been thoroughly analyzed in political and social theory, the issue of economy has received comparatively little attention. "With scarcely any exceptions, every British political thinker of note wrote on the empire."[23] The same could be said of economic thinkers of note, and yet political economists do not figure in Edward Said's canonical critique of orientalism, to take one prominent example.[24] In recent years, liberal economics has become a more prominent subject on the scholarly agenda of postcolonial studies.[25] This chapter contributes to this salient discussion by demonstrating how the colonial image of a savage, reproducing, and naked life is constitutive for a historically specific but enduring notion of liberal economy.

The remainder of this chapter is structured as follows: The first section unfolds how the principle of population is constitutively linked to a notion of "savage life." The second section reframes the notion scarcity in liberal economic discourse on the basis of this discussion. The third section explicates how this newly interpreted nexus between population and scarcity changes our understanding of the conceptual relation between biopolitics and liberal economy.

Savage Reproduction and Catastrophic Abundance

The novelty of the principle of population as explored by Malthus would be ill understood when taken to be a simple statement about the confrontation between too many bodies with too little food. As Malthus puts it, asserting that "population must be always kept down to the level of the means of subsistence" is to state an "incontrovertible" and "abstract truth" that has been pronounced many times before since Plato.[26] Malthus offers a more complicated argument with high stakes: he seeks to investigate the foundation of a liberal economic order. Malthus's essay on population sets out to reconstruct the essential principles for a viable "body economic." He does so by presenting what appears as an economic state of nature equivalent to the state of nature in modern political theory.[27] The *Essay on the Principles of Population* commences with lengthy descriptions of how the laws of population have been playing themselves out across the globe. Malthus's account juxtaposes different geographic areas to the civilized order at home. These areas are not only spatially but also temporally distant to the European societies: they appear as a past that Europe has left behind. Akin to the canonical political treatises of modernity, the state of nature is not just a thought experiment but has a concrete historical-empirical referent in the colonies and at the shores of European expansion.[28]

What Malthus finds described in the travel diaries of James Cook, Alexander von Humboldt and by colonial administrators of India serves him as witnesses' reports of the degrees of civilization found in different spots on the earth.[29] It is less Rousseau's benign vision of "savage life" than Hobbes's descriptions of the hardships in the state of nature, which stands as a model for Malthus account: "I am inclined to think that our imaginations have been carried beyond the truth by the exuberant descriptions which have sometimes been given of these delightful spots."[30] His narrative about the savage state commences with "the wretched inhabitants of Tierra del Fuego [that] have been placed by the general consent of voyagers, at the bottom of the scale of human beings."[31] Malthus depicts a bodily and social state of utter despair and dissolution. The description of the "race of savages," which are "half starved . . . shivering with cold, and covered with filth and vermin" embellishes the Hobbesian account a life that is "brutish, nasty and short" with further details. The misery is written all over the individual body: "Their stature seldom exceeds five feet;

their bellies are protuberant, with high shoulders, large heads, and limbs disproportionally slender . . . in general, [they] are neither tall nor well made."[32] The children are "deformed, dwarfish, mutilated, blind and deaf."[33] In extended descriptions, Malthus pictures a savage body that is marked by "perpetual diseases," by "pleuritic, asthmatic, and paralytic disorders," and that suffers from "inconsiderate gluttony in one case, and their severe abstinence in the other."[34] It is a disgusting body that is presented in these lengthy portrayals: Savages are "swarming with vermin," live in cabins that "have a nastiness and stench to which the den of no known animal in the world can be compared."[35] These "naked and despicable" beings are depicted as ugly and deformed members of the human species. They are "at twenty two . . . more wrinkled and deformed by age than an European women at sixty."[36] Their whole being arouses disgust in the gaze of the European observer: "Nothing could be so disgusting as their mode of living."[37]

It is not only the deformation of the individual body that is described in these scenes. Both the individual and the collective body merge in an image of mutilation. The individual body appears as literally torn apart by the laws of population, so that "skulls, limbs, ribs and backbones, or some other vestiges of the human body, were scattered promiscuously in great numbers."[38] But inasmuch as the individual body has lost its living cohesion, so are the socioeconomic bonds in utter disarray. The natural bond between parents and children is severed as "children desert their parents and parents consider their children as strangers. The ties of nature are no longer binding. A father will sell his son for a knife or a hatchet."[39] The epitome of such undoing of familial ties is the cannibalism of those "reduced to the dreadful extremity of supporting themselves on the flesh of two of their children."[40]

As scholars have pointed out, the colonial imagination has a "lengthy and timeless fascination with colonial nakedness." The depiction of the native's nakedness signifies a lack of shame, a state of unconsciousness and a "monstrously and overly sexual" being.[41] Racism and sexuality are inextricably linked in modern discourses on the proper civil order. Corporeal vulnerability, savagery, and sexuality are conjoined in the image of the naked native, who is in all respects the opposite of what counts as social and economic refinement in the eighteenth century.[42] But how far and in which ways are these lengthy references to the colonial body constitutive for the articulation of liberal economy? How has the "disciplinary development of economics been implicated in the West's strategy of alterity"?[43]

The context of Malthus' writings suggests a relation between the development of liberal economics and colonialism. The administrative changes in colonial government and the revolutionary upheavals abroad formed the backdrop of Malthus's writings on population.[44] The East India College, later renamed Haileybury College, where Malthus obtained the first chair for political economy, had been founded by the British East India Company. Its purpose was to train company servants for administrative purposes. At the beginning of the nineteenth century, the British East India Company was in the course of becoming a governing body instead of being merely a trading body; the British Empire commenced to understand itself less and less as a purely commercial undertaking.[45] But this contextual backdrop does not yet allow the pinpointing of a profound link between the invocation of the abject colonial body and the reframing of liberal economy. It signals a conjuncture but no systematic connection. For exploring such systematic connection, it is instructive to compare the role that the "savage state" has played for Adam Smith's account of liberal economy to the role it played for Malthus.

For Smith, just as it has been the case for John Locke before, the savage state is characterized by a lack of differentiation in the division of labor, of property, and of trade.[46] At the same time, it is depicted a state of deprivation that makes progress the inevitable consequence of a life that is too precarious for humanity.[47] The movement from this savage state toward civilization occurs through growth of population, intensification of invention, and the slow emergence of the division of labor. For Smith—as for the eighteenth century in general—population is one element of an evolving order that hinges on exchange, specialization of needs, and property rights: bodies, exchange, and the division of labor are assumed to grow in tandem, one element pushing the others forward. But the very "spatiotemporal" narrative of a progressing economic order, which dominates Smith's understanding of population, changes with Malthus.[48] The savage state is no longer characterized by a mere absence of the division of labor. It is no longer the unproblematic vantage point of a progressing order. The principle of population introduces a moment of rupture within this narrative of progression: it becomes a dominant and threatening element— the needy and reproducing body appears as undoing the progressive mechanism.

As Catherine Gallagher argues, Malthus's "bioeconomics" valorizes and problematizes the body to a novel extent: "Malthus, thus, turns the body into an absolute social problem."[49] Hence, in order to understand how the colonial image of the savage and naked body is tied to the conceptualization of liberal economy, one needs to ask two questions: What turns the body into an "absolute social problem"? How is this problematic body tied to the re-articulation of the economic problem? In other words, how is economy at stake in these scenes populated by vulnerable, suffering, but also disgusting and "monstrously sexual" bodies?

As one can gather from Malthus's explanations, it is not the economic interest of self-preservation that is missing in the savage state. On the contrary, Malthus imputes the alleged cannibalism and the modes of warfare in the "savage state" to the laws of self-preservation that unite the human species: "It seems to be a worse compliment to human nature and to the savage state, to attribute this horrid repast [of cannibalism] to malignant passions, without the goad of necessity, rather than to the great law of self-preservation, which has at times overcome every other feeling, even among the most humane and civilized people."[50] Unexpectedly, it is neither economy in the sense of scarcity that conditions this destruction of the state of nature. Quite the contrary, the condition of man in the state of nature is usually defined by a "gift of nature to man," as Malthus explains. "If the earth had been so niggardly of her produce as to oblige all her inhabitants to labour for it, no manufactures or ideal persons could ever have existed. But her first intercourse with man was a voluntary present."[51]

Not scarcity but abundance or even "extreme fertility" of the soil is the original situation of man in the state of nature.[52] It is the very precondition for the history of progression to commence, allowing "a greater number of people to subsist together [and therefore] . . . give the fairest chance to the inventive powers of the human mind."[53] But this "gift of nature" is perpetually transformed into a state of misery, as we learn from Malthus's tireless descriptions of how the principle of population works its course in all quarters of the world. "In whatever abundance the productions of these islands may be found at certain periods . . . the average population . . . presses hard against the limits of the average food." Thus, "savage life" vibrates "between two extremes, and consequently the oscillations between want and plenty are strongly marked, as we should naturally expect among the less civilized nation."[54]

This account of the state of nature ties the lack of economy to a lack of history. History appears as frozen in this oscillation between want and plenty. It is immobilized, but not because it has reached its end, as Foucault describes it in his analysis of economic discourse in the nineteenth century, but because the temporal sequence of material progress has not even commenced.[55] The principle of population is a principle that locks the human species into its savage slot because it fails to unlock historical and material progression from the initial gift of nature. The temporal dimension of development becomes thus an "ultimate parameter of judgment."[56] But what is the cause for this failure to unlock the temporal passage into civilization. What produces the endless circle of abundance and destruction?

The *Essay on Population* reveals that the catastrophic principle of population is nothing but the "law" of savage life. The unchecked growth of population results from the immediacy by which these reproducing bodies react to any increase in the means of subsistence. Humans, animals, and plants are equally governed by the laws of life itself, which react like a "spring," "making a start forwards at every temporary and occasional increase of food by which means it is continually going beyond the average increase and is repressed by periodical returns of severe want."[57] But the apparent unity of the concept of life that ties the human and the animal species is marked by a fundamental caesura: It is only among "animals and the uncivilized states of man" that abundance calls a "large proportion of the procreative power into action, the redundancy from which was checked by violent causes." Hence it is only among the savages that population is much below what the soil could support.[58]

The principle of population, cast as the procreative force of life itself, is understood here in terms of a savagery defined by the immediacy with which it reacts to resources. The Irishman, the improvident savages, and the laboring poor at home embody this savagery of species-life. "The ignorance and indolence of the improvident savage would frequently prevent him from extending the benefits of these supplies much beyond the time when they were actually obtained."[59] Hence, Malthus concludes that resources that are "not distributed to the lower classes consequently would give no stimulus to population."[60] Ireland, with its cheap potato, is a much-preferred example for this immediate multiplication of food into more bodies.[61] The improvident savages and ignorant Irishmen are just like the "labouring poor" at home, who "live from hand to mouth," and "enjoy themselves while they can," never thinking about tomorrow: "The providence foresight and postponement of present gratification for future benefit and profit, which are necessary for this purpose, have always been considered as rare qualities in the savage."[62]

To present the "savages" as "presentist animals" without any sense of history is a common colonial trope.[63] Banerjee has explored in depth how the status of being primitive has been linked to the lack of temporal distance: "For the 'primitive,' the 'object' of desire (and knowledge) existed as merely a thing of immediate satisfaction, while money represented a civilised temporal distance—an awaiting between desire and its satisfaction, between subject and object. The 'primitive,' therefore, had no idea of means and mediation, no idea of money, no temporal sense of deferral."[64]

The principle of population is in this sense a narrative about savage life: it is because savage life reacts immediately with its procreative consumption to any resource offered to it that the population will exceed the resources available to it in the future. "The improvident barbarian who thinks only of his present wants," is just like the "labouring poor," whose "present wants employ their whole attention; and they seldom think of the future," or the miserable savage, who only ever learns in a belated and deathly fashion about its real resources that would be available not only today but also tomorrow: they all bring about a "stream of mortality" that will only "run with greater force through some channels" if "we stop up any other channel."[65]

The principle of population and its attending scarcity are thus not about a simple confrontation between too many bodies and too little resources to sustain them. It is rather about a missing temporal orientation toward the future that is ascribed to the savage condition. The alleged presentism of the "primitive" life is diagnosed as a destructive blindness toward the future. The mathematical expression of the law of population—famously depicted by the divergence of a geometric and arithmetic rate of growth in population and in foodstuff—needs to be related to this discursive articulation of savage life, its blindness and lack of futurity regarding the use of present resources for being adequately understood.[66] As the following section explores, the experience of scarcity is presented in this context as a regulatory and epistemological device that teaches savage life how to use resources for the future and, more radically, how to produce futurity and history itself.

The Economic: Scarcity as the Epistemology of the Future

Scarcity seems to be a self-evident and simple presupposition of liberal economic thought that anyone can relate to: there are simply not enough goods for the many desires that people have. As a contemporary textbook of macroeconomics puts it: "You can't always get what you want."[67] Economics tells us how to deal with this essential limitation. The definition of economy and economics given by Lionel Robbins at the beginning of the twentieth still captures this economic common sense quite nicely: "We have been turned out of Paradise. We have neither eternal life nor unlimited means of gratification. Everywhere we turn, if we choose one thing we must relinquish others—scarcity of means to satisfy given ends is an almost ubiquitous condition of human behavior. Here, then, is the unity of the subject for Economic Sciences, the forms assumed by human behavior in disposing of scarce means."[68]

Some liberal economists explicitly define the boundary between economy and non-economy as the boundary between abundance and scarcity. Goods that are abundant are "non-economic" while scarce goods require the subject to order his choices and to act economically.[69] Non-economy rarely applies since even "the need for aesthetic beauty or religious inspiration is no less potentially subject to scarcity of means than bread and butter . . . the domain of economics is principally unlimited."[70] This translation of every situation into a situation of scarcity is a sine qua non for liberal economics, for otherwise there are "no prices, no budget constraints, and no basis for choice"—it is only for the economic problem in terms of scarcity that "the intellectual machinery" of liberal economics has "come to be so well designed."[71] Assuming scarcity appears as a tenable vantage point for economics, even though "many great problems of our era are problems of excess," as the sociologist Andrew Abbott notes. But we are accustomed to pose these problems in terms of scarcity. It simply seems to be more realistic to do so and rather "immature at best, if not altogether pathological . . . to reject scarcity, to pretend it does not exist, to wish it away."[72] From the vantage point of a genealogy of the economic, one does not have not to choose between being realistic or immature: it becomes possible to investigate the link between scarcity and realism in economic matters and to uncover the malleable economic behind the facts of scarcity.

From Malthus's texts, one learns that scarcity is not merely a given state of reality. As recounted above, the immediate experience in the state of nature is not characterized by scarcity but by abundance. In this context, abundance is tied to a deceptive allure: it tends to signal a situation of plenty in the present that is not viable. Coupled with the presentism of savage life, abundance induces a misapprehension of the given and the possible. Indeed, scarcity and realism are linked. But not because scarcity is the reality to be acknowledged but rather because it answers to an epistemological problem of how to properly discern what is given in the light of what will become.

Accordingly, status of scarcity as an ultimate reality is paradoxical. On the one hand, Malthus asserts that there can be no doubt about the existence of the absolute boundaries to human and animal existence. The absolute limits of scarcity are demonstrated by referring to the image of an island. The island is a very typical "schematic fiction" that is assumed to contain the "essentials of reality."[73] As the historian of the question of population, Alison Bashford, notes: "Malthus liked writing about islands":[74]

> And the whole earth is in this respect like an island. . . . The bounds to the number of people on islands, particularly when they are of small extent, are so narrow, and so distinctly marked, that every person must see and acknowledge them. . . . The difficulty here is reduced to so narrow a compass, is so clear, precise and forcible that we cannot escape of it. It cannot be answered in the usual vague and inconsiderate manner, by talking of emigration, and further cultivation.[75]

But paradoxically, these absolute limits are declared to be inconsequential and irrelevant for the very question of population. While on the one hand there is no doubt about the objective limits, on the other hand these limits do not matter: "Allowing produce of the earth to be absolutely unlimited, scarcely removes the weight of a hair from the argument."[76] In fact, the limits that scarcity presents are defined as independent from the absolute limits of the earth: "In this supposition no limits whatever are placed to the produce of the earth. It may increase for ever and be greater than any assignable quantity; yet still the power of population being in every period so much superior, the increase of the human species can only be kept down to the level of the means of subsistence by the constant operation of the strong law of necessity."[77]

It is indeed the very question of *how* scarcity is to be conceptualized that differentiates Malthus from his adversaries. Marquis de Condorcet and William Godwin assume—in the words of Malthus—that "no difficulty would arise from this cause, till the whole earth had been cultivated like a garden." If indeed the question of limits waited only at the end of history, the "contemplation of so remote a difficulty" would be futile, as Malthus concedes.[78] Yet, a "man who is locked up in a room maybe fairly said to be confined by walls of it, though he may never touch them."[79] The absolute limits of resources, which are objectively there, apparently do not matter, except for the fact that they need to be present within experience constantly. It is precisely because "savage life" always misapprehends the situation of abundance that it only belatedly learns about its unwise use of resources. "Savage life" translates abundance into a permanent and imminent threat of death at each moment of history since it lacks the experience of scarcity.[80] Scarcity has to be made present, since it is not present at the moment. The unfailing presence of scarcity is paradoxical: it is there and not at the same time.

Curiously, the question of scarcity ultimately tilts over into a political argument about war and peace. Whereas the absolute limits of the earth are presented to be of little importance for understanding the economic scarcity of resources, the acknowledgment of the absolute limit of the earth is central for the political prospects of peace: "It is not easy to conceive a more disastrous present, one more likely to plunge the human race in revocable misery, than *an unlimited facility of producing food in a limited space* . . . a limitation in the power of producing food is obviously necessary to man confined to a limited space."[81] The "perpetual struggle for food and room" is the result of such unlimited expansion within a limited space. Space figures as the "barrier that cannot be passed."[82] One moves from an economic argument about resources to a political argument about territoriality. Rhetorical excesses accompany the warning of the ultimate limits of space in Malthus's text. He fears that "all the planets of our solar system" will be filled in the same way, "and not only them, but all the planet revolving around the stars which are visible to the naked eye."[83]

The figure of the "barbarian" embodies the political prospects of an unlimited reproduction in limited space. "Barbarians," as Malthus explains, always solve the problem of a redundant population by "plunder and emigration."[84] If Malthus were to have written the "Perpetual Peace," it would have included the threat of "savage life" that eats away the future and will ultimately result in hostile expansion. The "peaceful spirit of commerce" that "sooner or later takes hold of every people" that Immanuel Kant invoked belongs more to the world of Smith than to the world of Malthus.[85] The lack of a proper orientation toward futurity that defines to Malthus how "savage life" deals with a given redundancy of resources results in political instability more than in economic misery. While scarcity appears on first sight as the most economic category of liberal thought, it turns out to have as much political valence.

In sum, scarcity—understood as an experience of limitation and as a condition of finitude—has an uncertain status. It vacillates between what is given and what is not yet; between what is and what should be apprehended and averted; between economy and politics. This wavering status of scarcity results, as I want to argue, from its role as a regulatory and epistemological device. It is cast as an "epistemic virtue" that teaches us to view the given abundance in terms of the future. Rather than being a present condition, it amounts to an epistemology of the "as if," which ensures that resources are used in order to produce a viable future. The notion of "as if" has been coined by the philosopher Hans Vaihinger. He asserts that the "as if" lacks an "objective correlate, but functions as an "instrument for finding our way about more easily in this world."[86] To act in the present "as if" scarcity prevails is to disrupt the presentism of immediate consumption that Malthus associates with "savage life." Instead it produces economic futurity. Scarcity is about a particular composure regarding the given: it views resources in light of their finitude. In these texts, the objectivity of the notion of scarcity does not consist in pointing out an ever-present, ubiquitous, and universal reality—the objectivity of scarcity should rather be understood in the sense that Daston and Galison have given this term. As indicated earlier, they understand objectivity as a historically contingent articulation of a virtuous relation between subject and object. Objectivity is about historically shifting "epistemic virtues" that delineate moral ideals as to how the knowledge-seeking subject *should* comport itself vis-à-vis the given.[87] As the foregoing showed, the virtues of scarcity control and civilize the abject figure of "savage life" that ruins the possible of a material civilization since it fails to relate "objectively" to its surroundings.

If one adopts this perspective on scarcity as belonging to the "virtuous" definition of economic objectivity, one can detect the cultural and moral valorization of the notion of capital that goes along with it. Malthus ascribes the role of objectivity that "savage life" lacks to capital itself. In the *Principle of Political Economy*, capital—and, with it, private property—is introduced as the very agent that enacts the regulatory limit and its attendant epistemology of the future. The employment of capital requires "providence, foresight, and postponement of present gratification for the sake of future benefit and profits, which . . . have always been considered as rare qualities in the savage."[88] Different than savage life, which only halts in its reproduction if it is checked by death and exhaustion, capital halts much earlier, that is, when those "employed on the soil [do] not produce more than the value of [their] wages."[89] Without this "practical limit" to employment and subsistence, "the whole people of a country might thus be employed during their whole time in the production of mere necessaries, and no leisure be left for other pursuits of any kind. But this state of things could only be effected by the forced direction of the national industry into one channel by public authority. Upon the principle of private property, it could never happen."[90] Capital, which Malthus defines as that "particular part of these possessions or of accumulated wealth, which is destined to be employed with a view to profit in the production and distribution of future wealth," ensures that something beyond life's necessities will be left.[91]

Capital thus imposes a limit to population that is conducive to material civilization. Not only will the "check from want of employment . . . be much more steady in its operation and much more favourable to the lower classes of the people, than the check from the immediate want of food," capital also renders finitude operative in a way that always ensures some abundance, leisure, luxury, and, hence, civilization.[92] It is the very task of capital to form a body economic that civilizes savage life, organizes futurity and material progression, and preserves the very abundance necessary for civilized life.[93] Capital enacts a proper amount of scarcity that will result in preserving abundance for the sake of civilization. Its "objectivity" is inextricably linked to the fear that "savage life" would otherwise undo the possibility of a civilized life beyond the reign of necessity. Malthus contrasts the civilization brought about by capital with the case of China. Within the hierarchical order of civilizations that Malthus discusses, China is singled out as the exemplary case of a population that has developed all resources without any abundance left. Malthus cites the accounts of European observers to illustrate such a situation: "The labours and efforts of these poor people are beyond conception. A Chinese will pass whole days in digging the earth, sometimes up to his knees in water, and in the evening is happy to eat a little spoonful of rice, and to drink the insipid water in which it was boiled."[94] The outlook of a life at its limits, without abundance left, reduced to the mere survival, is what frightens Malthus most. Population, as the negative example of China clarifies, needs an epistemology of limits that halts the deployment and use of a resource before the absolute limit for population is reached—that is to say, before there would indeed be a general and ever-present scarcity that would reduce living to surviving at the lowest common denominator.[95]

Malthus thus offers a cultural-political definition of capital: it is said to unite all epistemological and regulatory virtues on its side. On the one hand, it interrupts the recurrent catastrophe of the state of nature and mobilizes historical development; on the other hand, it shields the population from reaching the absolute limit of the earth at the end of history. While "savage life" consumes abundance away, capital makes sure that there is abundance in the midst of scarcity without which there would be no "enjoyment and leisure" and without which a republic could not be maintained. Using the notions of objectivity and the "as if," as introduced earlier, one could say that capital is to Malthus more "objective" insofar as it is conceived of as a more suitable "instrument for finding our way . . . in this world."[96]

In sum, Malthus's text articulates a richly layered meaning of liberal economy. The analytical unfolding of this layering makes it now possible to dissect "the economic" from this "economy." First, scarcity becomes legible, as belonging to a regulatory epistemology of how to ascertain the given. It is not simply a reality to be acknowledged but appears as an "epistemic virtue" and regulatory device that should organize the use of resources. Second, this epistemological rendering of the notion of scarcity is deeply wedded to a question of futurity. Understood from the vantage point of the genealogy of the economic, scarcity is a shortcut for the malleable and multiple devices that organize economic futurity that are open for design and debate.[97] Third, this issue of futurity becomes black-boxed due to the biopolitical and colonial rendering of the population in terms of "savage life." To the extent that economic discourse has been mired to a cultural hierarchy of civilization, the malleable economic disappears and is turned into an argument about economic necessity. Putting it differently, without this fear of "savage life," the question of economic futurity would be opened up, offering itself to political negotiation and a broadened liberal economic imagination. Likewise, without being defined as the opposite to "savage life," the notion of capital would lose its a priori cultural valorization as a virtuous and "objective" device of creating economic futurity. Detecting the question of futurity, of culture and epistemic virtues behind the apparently simple but ultimately complicated and paradoxical reality of scarcity opens up economic necessity to the malleable economic. None of these elements would help to create a closure on the question of what kind of economic order liberalism could and should give rise to; all of these elements open up a critical space for debating and discerning economic difference.

Biopolitics and Liberal Economy

The foregoing analysis has demonstrated that a fundamental civilizational hierarchy is at work in establishing the nexus between population, economy, and scarcity in liberalism. This argument has important consequences for the current debate about the relation between biopolitics and liberal economy. In this concluding section, I explicate these theoretical ramifications. The term "biopolitics," however differently employed and defined, suggests that the question of life is of particular valence for understanding modern politics, its lines of exclusion, and its logics of power. The works of Foucault and Agamben stand for the main positions in this debate: whereas the former emphasizes how liberal modernity is shaped by the way it includes life into the orbit of governmental care, the latter focuses on how the fundamental division between life and politics characterizes the Western political tradition. Both assume that liberal economy is part of this biopolitical predicament, but as I show in the following, both remain ultimately indecisive or unclear on how one should conceptualize the entanglements among economy, biopolitics, and life in liberalism. Hence, within the debate on biopolitics, the role of economy is a central but relatively unchartered dimension that still awaits conceptual clarification.[98]

Based on the foregoing historical argument, I suggest that the linkage between population and scarcity belongs not to economic liberalism per se but has become part of it at the beginning of the nineteenth century. In its wake, a particular and historically contingent convergence between liberal economy and biopolitics takes place on the level of norms: Biopolitical norms become tied to the question of economy in such a way that an economic "calculation of lives" turns out to be homologous to a biopolitical decision over the worth and value of life. Based on this argument, I contend that, pace Foucault, the structures of biopolitical valuation within liberal economic governmentality are different from the statistical type of normalization that Foucault has focused on. Pace Agamben, I argue that the biopolitics of modernity does not only rest on a biopolitical fracture of "mere life" and "political life" but also on the way that the nexus of population and life has come to shape liberal economic discourse. The latter determine as much as the former how the issue of life is taken up political terms within liberalism. I will shortly present how the question of economy appeared to Foucault and Agamben, respectively, before I outline the conceptual difference that the historical argument presented above makes.

At the end of *Birth of Biopolitics*, Foucault himself suggested that he has not even properly begun to answer the question of how liberal, economic governmentality and the biopolitics of population are related: "What should now be studied, therefore, is the way in which specific problems of life and population have been posed within a technology of government which, although far from always having been liberal, since the end of the eighteenth century has been constantly haunted by the question of liberalism."[99] These closing remarks in *Birth of Biopolitics* seem to indicate that Foucault does not assume a necessary link between these poles. Their relation appears as a puzzle, as something to be "studied now."

The assertion of a nonidentity between biopolitics and liberal governmentality is surprising, given that it very much differs from how Foucault had set out at the beginning of the lecture course *Security, Territoriality, Population*. Initially, he had been sure that liberal governmentality is two things at once: economic and biopolitical. To understand the divergence between his closing comment and his starting point, it is helpful to recall how Foucault has established the interrelation between the biopolitics of population and the genealogy of liberal economy in the first place. Between his initial certainty and the later circumspection lies an unchartered conceptual space. The analysis presented earlier helps to probe this conceptual space in order to determine more precisely the points of convergence between biopolitics and economy.

Foucault's starting point for assessing the identity between biopolitics and liberal governmentality is the naturality of the population. The emergence of the population as a novel object of politics signals the advent of biopolitics: Liberal politics becomes preoccupied with governing "the life of the species."[100] The "naturality" of the population, its milieu, and its conditions of subsistence and existence are primary objects of politics. According to Foucault, governing this "naturality" of the population is especially amenable to an economic rationality. Political economy looks at individuals not primarily in terms of legal subjects capable of voluntary actions but as a "multiplicity of organisms, of bodies capable of performance."[101] Economic rationalities of governing eschew a "regulatory system of injunctions, imperatives, and interdictions on these principles [of circulation]."[102] Foucault defines economic rationalities of governing as indirect modes of governing that seek to entice, channel, and modulate the interests and conduct of the subject.[103] He claims that sovereign power that works through juridical decree and claims the power to take life is limited by a governmental political rationality that takes population as "the final end of government." Such government uses instruments that are "immanent to the field of population" and focuses for this reason on needs, aspirations, and interests of the living that it seeks to govern.[104]

As Foucault maintained, one central link between the economic and biopolitical governing of the population consists in the type of normalization that the latter impels. Foucault has argued that "a normalizing society is the historical outcome of a technology of power centered on life."[105] Liberal governmentality gives rise to a specific type of normalization. According to Foucault, the norms associated with the figure of population shun any transcendent foundation or idealization. These norms are not imposed from without but are derived from the given: they stem from statistical regularities such as death rates, distributions of disease, migration, and accidents.[106] Statistical regularities are based on events that are "aleatory and unpredictable when taken by themselves or individually" but display constants "at the collective level."[107] Distinct from juridical or disciplinary norms, these statistical normalities do not posit any normative demand vis-à-vis the given but are used to influence events and choices through calculations of probabilities and changes in risk exposure.[108]

This understanding of biopolitical-cum-economic norms that Foucault furnishes in his lecture course stands in marked contrast to his earlier remarks on biopolitical norms. A power interested in life, Foucault says, aims at "distributing the living in domain of value and utility"; it has to "qualify, measure, appraise, and hierarchize." Foucault elaborates on such biopolitical hierarchization in the context of a discussion on sovereign politics. Sovereign biopolitics differentiates between inferiority and superiority in a decision about whose life is to be fostered and whose is disallowed "to the point of death."[109] A specific type of biopolitical racism occurs when the well-being of the whole is understood to depend on the eradication of some parts of the group. But Foucault is adamant in pointing out that these lines of fragmentation and inner hierarchization, which cut through the collective body of the population, do not have any ties to the constitution of the modern understanding of economy. Foucault explicitly states the non-economic nature of these biopolitical caesuras: the act of an economic divestment of privileges and the purely economic questions of management and planning do not rest on such biopolitical logic of fragmentation and exclusion.[110] Hence, Foucault presents two accounts of biopolitical norms: an economic rendering of biopolitical norms that is tied to statistical normalities and a sovereign-political rendering of norms that emphasizes racial exclusions and hierarchizations of value and worth.

As the analysis here demonstrates, the differentiation of species-life into catastrophic forms of savage and animal life, on the one hand, and civilized and more human life, on the other, imparts its own norms that differ from both of these biopolitical norms Foucault has presented: they are neither tied to a sovereign and political decision about who is disallowed to live nor are they merely statistical regularities. These ranks of civilization do not necessarily impose a strict division between the inside and the outside of an economic-cum-political collectivity. These scales articulate an evolutionary ladder of difference.[111] They order a continuum of humanity that reaches down to the most animal, on the one hand, and the most human, on the other, touching on the "imaginary boundaries of the human 'species.'"[112] These political and cultural codes of difference linked to the notion of population import an implicit hierarchy of civilized life into the liberal understanding of economy. When it comes to deciding who is to be saved and for whom resources are to be spent, these registers of valuation come to the fore.[113] They link the notion of liberal economy to a historically specific "calculation of lives," borrowing here an expression by Hayek.[114] This "calculation of lives," understood as an act of valuing life in economic terms, is often presented as a tragic choice that has to be made in the context of scarcity. Scarcity appears as external to the necessity of making a choice about the more or less valuable life. But as demonstrated above, the way scarcity is called upon in economic discourse is not independent from these biopolitical norms of the population. It already befits an implicit fear about the lesser civilized who will use the resources in the wrong way.

One can detect within Malthus's text such convergence of biopolitical and economic norms in the discussion of the Poor Laws. Malthus establishes a "calculation of lives" in which the support of the "unworthy" harms the "worthy members" of the collective:[115] "The quantity of provisions consumed in workhouses, upon a part of the society that cannot in general be considered as the most valuable part, diminishes the shares that would otherwise belong to more industrious and more worthy members, and thus, in the same manner, forces more to become dependent."[116] The consumption on the side of some members of the community will render the whole worse than before, while withholding the means of life from the "unworthy" becomes equivalent to strengthening the economic life of the community. Foucault has described this logic as a form of biopolitical racism that distinguishes between what "must live and what must die," "fragmenting the field of the biological that power control."[117] Malthus leaves no doubt that the "calculation of lives" undoes political liberalism if it were to be transposed onto a political plane. One reason for his opposition to the Poor Laws—a system of social provisioning that has been part of English politics since the seventeenth century and was mostly administered by local authorities, which I discuss in the following chapter—derived from the prospect that such political decisions about worth and value would constitute an illiberal regime par excellence:[118] "If an inquisition were to be established to examine the claims of each individual, and to determine whether he had or had not exerted himself to the utmost, and to grant or refuse assistance accordingly, this would be little else than a repetition upon a larger scale of the English poor laws, and would be completely destructive of the true principles of liberty and equality."[119]

The political power and authority that distributes living on a scale of worth and value in this way—what Foucault would call biopolitics—is exposed as "tyranny."[120] Yet, what is deemed to be a political impossibility is at the same time firmly tied to the articulation of the economic side of liberalism. The way in which liberal economy has been tied to the nexus between population, "savage life" and scarcity carries these scales implicitly as an unwanted shadow. To Malthus, the only way to solve this political impossibility was to leave it to "nature" to make these decisions, which no one could possibly make within any liberal regime—it would "draw upon ourselves the odium of executioner."[121] As a political liberal, he was certain that these decisions of worth and value ought never to be taken in the political realm, but as an economist and theorist of population, he had already placed the hierarchies of worth and value at the heart of his understanding of scarcity and population.

Based on this reading of Malthus, one can say that his specific understanding of the notion of population in terms of "savage life" embodies the biopolitical norms that "qualify, measure, appraise, and hierarchize" life and imports them into the understanding of liberal economy. As long as such transmission of biopolitical norms into notions of liberal economy remains undetected, economic necessity appears to be unrelated to a political valuation of worthy and unworthy lives. It is the very combination of a division between politics and economy, on the one hand, and the constitutive link between economy and population, on the other, that creates a peculiar biopolitical horizon for liberalism. Foucault was right to suspect that the link between liberalism and biopolitics is more complicated and historically contingent than he initially thought it to be. It hinges not only on turning population into the "final end of government" but is also based on how the life of the population has been linked to a civilizational hierarchy, on the one hand, and how this imparts the notion of liberal economy, on the other. Moreover, this articulation of life, population, and economy does not only bespeak an inclusion of life into the orbit of politics but enshrines a particular division between politics and economy in liberalism at the same time.

In contrast to Foucault, Agamben has always accentuated the formative role of the division between life and politics. Agamben commences his account of biopolitics with the problematization of the division between the political sphere vis-à-vis the sphere of life, the household, and the economy. The Western political tradition, so Agamben, has divided *zoe*, a stratum of natural and apolitical life, from *bios* that designates its proper political form. Whereas *zoe* or natural life belongs to the economic commands of the household, only *bios* allows enacting the practices of freedom and equality.[122] But casting out a form of life as utterly nonpolitical is itself a political act, as Agamben argues. What has been excluded from the political sphere is indelibly marked by this exclusion. For Agamben, apolitical life preserves the "memory of the originary exclusion." This means that it is exposed to politics while distinguished from it. Life and politics are not external to each other even though they are divided from each other. Mere life becomes "bare life," which is exposed to the possibility of being killed.[123]

The discussion of how the division between the biological life of the population and the political notion of the people informs and shapes liberal modernity appears to be of immediate relevance to a discussion on the economic, population, and scarcity in liberalism. And, indeed, Agamben does suspect that the "biopolitical fracture" between man and citizen, between population and the people, has an economic valence. He insinuates that the images of utmost poverty—such as embodied in the "imploring eyes" of the Rwandan child displayed for obtaining money for humanitarian help or in the "fragmentary multiplicity of needy and excluded bodies"—are somehow related to this "biopolitical fracture."[124] Agamben argues that, at bottom, the economic and social concepts—or the "economism" and "socialism" that seem to dominate modern politics— actually have a political or, rather, a biopolitical meaning.[125] Yet the political meaning of this economism is not developed in its specificity.[126] Agamben does not clarify how the question of economy is tied to a "biopolitical fracture" between politics and life.

This comparative silence is because Agamben relates this "originary exclusion" to the politics of sovereignty. His discussion of biopolitics essentially revolves around the political foundation of law, sovereignty, and territory without any consideration of how economy is constituted in this divide. In other words, one cannot address the question of liberal economy from the vantage point of this theory—except by assuming that the question of economy is part of the founding of political sovereignty.[127] Trying to think of the link between population and economy with Agamben would thus imply subsuming the question of economy in the founding of political sovereignty—which is tantamount to ignoring the specificity of this form. Accordingly, Agamben's work on biopolitics can serve only as an inspiration to inquire about the formative role of the divisions and relations between economy, life, and politics respectively.

This chapter demonstrates that the (economic) notion of population is indeed constituted by a (biopolitical) fracture. But the type of fracture that constitutes the figure of population and relates it to the political and economic horizon of liberalism is more complicated than Agamben's theoretical perspective suggests. On must note the division between life and politics as much as one must understand how a particular notion of life has informed central tenets of liberal economy. Only by addressing the hierarchies ingrained in the notion of life and by tracing how the definition of the economic problem is linked to it can one understand how the division between economy and politics in liberalism is part of a biopolitical horizon. There is no direct and necessary relation between biopolitics and liberal economy but a contingent one that is open for renegotiation.

Nevertheless, as long as the fear that a putative "savage life" will always use resources to the detriment of all, the basic assumption of scarcity will appear as an indispensable regulatory shortcut and the account of the laws of necessity turn into safe-guards against a political reason that is feared to be unfounded. It is only consistent that Malthus assumes there can be no "right to live," as the next chapter explores in further detail. The way such a boundary between politics and economy is drawn, the way that economic reality is defined and the elaboration of particular governmental rationalities befitting such economic reality are all falling into place in one stroke—behind this does not stand self-same "biopolitical fracture" but a desire to provide foundations and delimitation for a "fatherless world" of political reason and the malleable economic.

CHAPTER 3

The Right to Live

Economic Man, His Wife, and His Fears

There is no right to live—this declaration made Malthus infamous. The passage, in which Malthus maintained that "a man who is born into a world already possessed . . . has no claim of right to the smallest portion of food, and, in fact, has no business to be where he is," was removed in later editions due to the uproar it caused. But Malthus remained sure about the matter in principle: "There is one right which man has generally be thought to possess, which I am confident he neither does nor can possess—a right to subsistence when his labour will not fairly purchase it." He observed that the politics of rights is neither effective nor viable in respect to the question of economy. But, above all, Malthus believed that such right would remove the fear of want and would thus only produce more poverty and despair: "The plenty that before reigned" would be changed "into scarcity."[1]

The declaration about the rights that man does *not* have followed the declaration of such rights during the French Revolution. Against this background, Malthus expressed his skepticism and caution against the high running hopes of revolutionaries and radicals to ameliorate the social question by political means. As detailed before, at the beginning of the nineteenth century, the social question presented itself to liberalism as a conundrum. It appeared as a political problem in need of redress. But according to Malthus, no "proper calculation," "no application of knowledge and ingenuity," and "no effort" could help against the laws of necessity that stood against the right to live.[2] With this announcement Malthus sets a limit to politics on the basis of the laws of economic reality that he established. His contention of the non-rights of man is not based on the mere recognition that economic relations have their own specificity and density that are different from political ones. Malthus's statement of the impossibility to grant a "right to live" is not just motivated by a critique of rights as a tool of policy—although it is that as well: Malthus poignantly asserts that no one can "command the wheat to grow." But such an acknowledgment of difference between the economic and the political would not offer a sufficient foundation for his strict and categorical assertion regarding the right to live. Something more is required to turn difference and specificity into such a categorical boundary.

Malthus enacts a boundary between politics and economy. But what does it mean to speak about a boundary between politics and economy? It certainly does not mean a relation of externality or nonintervention. As Karl Polanyi has painstakingly demonstrated a long time ago, emergence of the "self-regulated market" during the nineteenth century amounted to an political act of institutionalization: "Laissez-faire was not a method to achieve a thing, it was the thing to be achieved . . . The road to the free market was opened and kept open by an enormous increase in continuous, centrally organized and controlled interventionism."[3] Even a most ardent believer in the spontaneity of market processes would concede the importance of a regime of rights for a commercial society. And Malthus, for that matter, does not shun away from commending political intervention into economic processes other than granting the "right to live."

While the boundary, hence, does not imply nonintervention, it neither circumscribes neatly bounded spheres. The notion of different spheres is deeply ingrained in the modern "social imaginary." It lends itself to a depiction of the economy in territorial terms, assuming it to be a more or less extended area governed by a quasi-sovereign law. Viewed from the genealogy of the economic, the portrayal of the economy and politics in terms of such spheres is a misleading image. It does not adequately address the impure processes by which the malleable quality of the economic and the political are turned into determined sets of practices and institutions, conventions and authorities that delineate what counts as economic objectivity and what counts as proper politics. Understanding the economy in terms of a bounded sphere with its own logic or laws lends foundation and fixation to such process but is not a useful guide for understanding it. Associating the notion of boundary with the image of distinct spheres gives rise to the much-used notions of de- and reregulation regarding the economy: these notions represent the economy as something to be put on a leash, or something in danger of being suffocated because it needs to be free to reign. Instead, I suggest that drawing a boundary between economy and politics is about deciding which policies are beneficial or harmful, practical or effective, desirable or detestable. Talking about a boundary akin to establishing a sieve that forms and sifts out what comes to pass as proper politics or what is rejected as improper.

Seen in this light, Malthus's indictment of a "right to live" is not just an announcement of a limit of politics but is a negotiation of proper "interventionist" politics vis-à-vis "the economy." The concrete regulatory and political question, to which Malthus's declaration of the limits of politics belonged, concerned the reform of the Poor Laws. These laws were an old English institution dating from the end of the sixteenth century. It was a tax-based system that granted support to the locally "settled" poor. This relief policy became the subject of discussion in 1770 in papers and pamphlets that swelled to a "sizeable stream" by the 1830s as the "social question" moved toward the center of public debate. The debate drew to a close with the reform bill in 1834.[4] "After Malthus developed his case for the adverse demographic and economic effects of legal relief . . . no political economist could avoid the issue"—and no policy maker either. The author of the 1817 Report from the Select Committee on the Poor Laws "wrote the science of population into his findings," challenging the old forms of governance of the poor. Malthus's doctrines were crucial "to the delineation of the objectives, if not the means of the official strategy of 1834, the legislative centerpiece of liberal poor policy."[5]

The "right to live" had been subject to a string of reform efforts during this protracted debate. Karl Polanyi chronicled how the first reform effort in 1795 had turned the "right to live" effectively into "death trap." The so-called Speenhamland Law introduced an allowance that would subsidize wages that were too low to live from. It became a widespread practice to grant the poor money doles, work, child allowances, or supplements for insufficient wages from the rates. The effect of this allowance system was a downward spiraling of wages: it undermined the market value of labor.[6] Malthus's intervention took place against this background. The final reform of the Poor Laws in 1834 did not completely repeal the right to relief as Malthus had asked for in principle, even though he also admitted a gradual change. The reform did abolish the eligibility for able-bodied men to receive support. After the reform, it was only the aged, the infirm, the insane, and the widowed women who were eligible for outdoor support. No "able-bodied" man could hope to find supplementary assistance anymore unless willing to enter the workhouse.[7] Most importantly, for the first time, assistance was withheld from unwed women with children. Single women were made legally and economically responsible for their illegitimate children. The policy change toward single mothers followed Malthus's reasoning to its full extent.[8]

This chapter looks at Malthus's arguments about the "right to live" and the Poor Laws as an instantiation of a novel boundary between politics and economy, which entails a specific type of political intervention—the making of economic man. I show that the re-articulation of the boundary between economy and politics, based as it was on a new "ontology" of scarcity, gives rise to a type of political intervention that focuses on turning "savage" life into economic-cum-civilized life. As this chapter demonstrates, Malthus's proposals for the reform of the Poor Laws constitute an important episode in the political genealogy of economic man. Malthus does not take the proper calculation of economic self-interest and the desires of economic man as given—as Adam Smith has done—but assumes that they need to be calibrated and created. The comments on the reform of the Poor Laws, on conjugal relation, on subsistence or the love of luxury can all be deciphered as elaborating the political and cultural devices that help to produce what was no longer naturally there: the economic-cum-civilized subject, which was supposed to function as the main hinge for creating a prosperous liberal economic order.

As I want to argue, a politics of affect plays a constitutive role for this genealogy of economic man. Fear is its main lever. But although fear is presented as central and indispensable, it is not sufficient for making economic man. The hope to acquire objects, including the precious ones from the colonies, has to accompany this fear. Most importantly, the politics of affect includes a differential treatment for those deemed to be more or less civilized. Whereas the more civilized are to be governed by hope, the lesser civilized require fear to become economic subjects. Furthermore, I argue that the politics of making economic man does not target an isolated figure but takes economic man as a subject nested in social relations. In this historical conjuncture, the conjugal relations of economic man become part of his sentimental education. Tying economic man to a wife and withholding support for single mothers is for Malthus a crucial element in ensuring the triumph of economic rationality over "savage life."

This reading of fear and hope as economic sentiments takes Albert Hirschman's seminal work *The Passions and the Interest* as its historical vantage point. Hirschman has long ago offered an argument on how a political discourse on the passions is part of the history of economic interest. In this perspective, rationality and irrationality, interest and passions are not opposites but ingredients for delineating what counts as "rational" or as economic" within a specific set of circumstances.[9] This chapter takes up the thread at the moment that Hirschman's historical and theoretical narrative ends. Whereas Hirschman assumes that the political arguments about economic interests recede with the triumph of economics at the beginning of the nineteenth century, the story told here continues his analysis of the political arguments implicit in the debate about economic interests.

Foucault's analysis of liberal governmentality offers the conceptual vantage point for this chapter. As discussed in the introduction, seen from the perspective of the genealogy of the economic, Foucault has presented an insufficient account of liberal governmentality. His account of liberalism does not attend to the struggles surrounding the meaning of liberal economy, its inner multiplicity and openness, which the genealogy of the economic can seize upon. In general, the genealogy of the economic traces the acts of delimitation that were foregone by such governmental elaboration. But eventually the two genealogies align at the point at which such openness is replaced with the elaboration of a set of governmental practices that befit a particular understanding of liberal economy.

Foucault summarizes his "interpretation" of liberalism as pointing out those "types of rationality that are implemented in the methods by which human conduct is directed through a state administration."[10] He identifies the notion of interest as the single key to understand the economic form of liberal governmental power: "Government is only interested in interests. . . . It no longer deals with these things in themselves. It deals with the phenomena of politics, that is to say, interests, which precisely constitute politics and its stakes."[11] Foucault briefly discusses how the economic subject is also cast in terms of sensibility and sentiment, but he quickly subsumes the question of sentiment and the notion of desire to the key concept of interest.[12] A rich literature on liberal governmentality has hitherto analyzed the manifold ways that shape the interest of the economic subject through techniques of responsibilization, evaluation, accreditation, and motivation. "Advanced liberal rule," as Nikolas Rose concisely defines it, "governs through the regulated choices of individual citizens."[13] Notably, Mitchell Dean has shown how the reform of the Poor Laws belongs to a form of liberal governmentality that aims at the responsibilization of the subject.[14]

This chapter adds important qualifications to this burgeoning literature. Not only does it deepen the understanding of how important hope and fear were for the making of economic man and his rationality; it also draws attention to how liberal governmentality enlists the gendered, sentimental bonds of the subject, and it demonstrates the importance of civilizational hierarchies for differentiating different policies for different classes of subjects. Overall, the chapter shows that the "constructive" nature of liberalism is much older than it is often portrayed to be.[15] Neoliberalism is usually distinguished from liberalism by its acknowledgment that markets and economic subjects are not naturally there—instead, they have to be fashioned. But as will become clear throughout this chapter, this "insight" is much older than the twentieth century—liberalism has been beset in the past by insecurities about the rationality of the subjects that it relies on.

The remainder of this chapter commences with a general introduction to the history of economic man and the notion of the politics of affect. It is followed by a historical section that explains how the account of economic rationality changed after the Scottish Enlightenment as it gave place to a radical doubt about the subject's capacity to pursue his or her interest properly. The third section shows how fear and hope became important levers in the governmental making of economic man. The forth section unfolds how Malthus's position on conjugal relations is a constitutive element of this politics of affect.

The History of Economic Man and the Politics of Affect

The figure of economic man is undoubtedly central to the liberal understanding of the market. The rationality of this figure as he weighs, calculates, and decides about options of conduct is crucial for framing the market as an emergent, flexible, natural, and rational order. Modern economics can even be defined by the central role it grants to this figure: It is the "attempt to explain human behavior by employing the assumption that individuals behave 'rationally.' "[16] This simple definition tends to hide the historically shifting definition of what counts as rational conduct and self-interest. This history ranges from Adam Smith's portrait of economic man as someone who is governed by the "desire to better his condition" to the late-nineteenth-century depiction of a "pleasure machine" that can be modeled within mathematical terms, and it includes the early-twentieth-century account of it as a "slot machine" that neither "competes nor higgles."[17] In the midst of the twentieth century, the depiction of economic man is closer to a "caricature" than anything else, as the historian of economics Mary Morgan argues. Economics assumes that economic man has complete information and calculates the best possible option instantaneously.[18] Since these heydays, rationality has become a more bounded affair and economic man a less "heroic" abstraction: economic man might have limited information and all sorts of motivations; his rationality consists only in a consistent form of choosing.[19]

Critiques of orthodox liberal economics have for a long time targeted the claims of economics about this "model man." Economic man is derided as an unrealistic overstatement of a purely maximizing and isolated individual. This model man is accused of generating inappropriate models of economic life. As the most recent accounts of the "animal spirits" in economic life suggest, the notion of economic rationality is too limited: it cannot account for the irrationality of economic conduct and thus for the irrationality of the market itself. Affects, beliefs, narratives, passions, gut feelings, and contagious behavior are said to govern economic man, more than any concept of bounded rationality would admit.[20] As a consequence, economic man becomes a more "well-rounded and more interesting character—a man who can learn, bargain, act strategically, has memory, and may even be happy."[21]

But however much these assumptions about economic man have been adapted, one constant can be found: economic man remains a "model man," "thin enough in characterization for us to reason with."[22] His rationality—however defined—remains the key to understand what economics and the market is all about.[23] Whereas the political subject is deemed to get lost in the maze of ideology and is criticized for entertaining unrealistic beliefs about the possibility of a good life for all, the economic subject is regarded as less burdened with cognitive demands, moral hopes, and erroneous beliefs. In comparison to the political subject, economic man appears to be modeled according to more realistic assumptions and hence is supposed to be the more realistic figure. Economic model man does not need to imagine or to realize the common good as a conscious undertaking. In contradistinction to the political subject, the economic subject is allowed to follow only what he knows best: his own interests. Even if economic man acts without perfect knowledge, he at least acts systematically according to his own preferences. Within a world that is impossible to grasp as a whole, economic man is for liberalism—despite or even because of his limited cognitive and moral devices—the "island of rationality," as Foucault has put it.[24]

Social theory has always emphasized that economic rationality is not an innate trait, but it part of our cultural and political history. As Max Weber has famously argued, the rationality of economic man is a culturally defined and religiously sanctioned form of rationality.[25] Hirschman has taken up this general argument but has replaced the religious genealogy with a political one. Not so much interested in understanding the religious addendum necessary to spur economic conduct, Hirschman concentrates on how the creation of the economic subject belonged to a political vision of order. As is well known, Hirschman argues that the notion of economic interest was initially endorsed as part and parcel of a political tradition that had taken the passions as the key for understanding human beings and human order. He alerts us to the fact that striving to find an anthropological model man that depicts man as he "really is" is not at all specific or unique to economic thought. On the contrary, the turn toward how man "really is" is the hallmark of modern *political* thought: Niccolò Machiavelli announces to replace the "imaginary republics" with the "effective truth of things." Thomas Hobbes and Baruch Spinoza follow this gesture. Instead of taking one's vantage point in a reflection on the kind of political or ethical virtues necessary for a proper political order, modern political theory aspires to ground itself in an "anthropological empiricism."[26] The passions of man are regarded as anthropological reality that political theory has to reckon with. As Hirschman puts it, "controlling passions by playing one off against the other" promises to provide "at least a realistic conception of human beings."[27]

According to Hirschman, it is only with Adam Smith that this political genealogy of economic interest disappeared. "The main impact of the Wealth of Nations was to establish a powerful economic justification for the untrammeled pursuit of individual self-interest, whereas in the earlier literature that has been surveyed here the stress was on the political effects of this pursuit."[28] Hence, Smith gives the economic "coupe de grace" for economic man. Accordingly, the political story that Hirschman writes about economic man comes to a halt the moment at which the economic horizon appears as self-sufficient. The beginning of the nineteenth century is often characterized as a turn toward a more purely economic discourse. Political economy starts to argue on the basis of the systemic laws of the economy.

But looking at the genealogy of economic man, this break becomes "chimerical," as Mitchell Dean has argued.[29] The emergence of neat bounds around the disciplines of economics and around the realm of liberal economy does not end the concrete policies that aim at intervening into economic matters. One crucial site of intervention is the economic subject: his interests, fears, relations, and desires. Accordingly, this chapter suggests that it is fruitful to continue the inquiry about economic man as a figure that is linked to a political elaboration of the ordering of the passions. The term "politics of affect" is loosely employed here to signal how the passions are addressed with the intention of molding (economic) subjectivity and rationality.[30] The notion of the politics of affect points out that the economic subject is made and that this making occurs in the abode of the heart and the feelings—even if something as supposedly "cold" as economic self-interest is at stake.

The beginning of the nineteenth century is a particularly instructive period for an analysis of the politics of affect, which aims at inculcating the rationality of economic man. On the one hand, the rationality of economic man becomes, for the first time, a key for modeling the dynamics of the economy. While Smith's character, as Morgan argues, is already a "fictional character," he is still too "thickly" described and "too complicated to reason with": "Smith's economic man character does not function as a model in his economics." One cannot derive any scientific laws from this figure of economic man. Among the early classical economists, Malthus's work is an exception, as he indeed does use economic "model man" to derive such laws: "Malthus's man is a character with whom we can think. He is a model man in the sense that he is thin enough in characterization for us to reason with. He has simple motivations, from which we can derive population and economic outcomes."[31] Malthus's writings thus present a more "modern" account of economic man than did Smith— he is much more adamant in defining economic man as part and parcel of a self-governing economic system. Malthus's *Essay on the Principle of Population* signals the widening reach of the "rhetoric of self-interest" vis-à-vis the "timid egoism" of the British and Scottish Enlightenment.[32] There is, so to speak, an additional "coup de grace" after Smith.

But this strengthening of economic rationality is, on the other hand, paradoxically tied to a pervasive uncertainty about the manifestation of this rationality in each subject. The "reasoning powers" ascribed to the *homo oeconomicus* become central but are also thought to be more easily overwhelmed by other motives and stronger passions. The understanding of the passions as naturally inclining men toward sociality and improvement does not appeal to the postrevolutionary context, in which Malthus is writing. Malthus assumes the prevalence of passions that are neither calm nor steady. In his somber outlook on the destructiveness of the passions, Malthus resembles Thomas Hobbes much more than Adam Smith or David Hume, who are his immediate predecessors in the history of economic and political thought.[33] This difference is worth exploring.

From Social Sentiments to Savage Affects

Adam Smith's *The Wealth of Nations* has for a long time been taken to articulate the canonical version of liberal economic man. As the famous phrase puts it, "it is not from the benevolence of the butcher, the brewer, or the baker, that we expect our dinner, but from their regard to their own interest."[34] Economic man is characterized by the single-mindedness of the purpose to serve himself. But what does his self-interest consist of? For Smith, it is defined by a very general aspiration for improvement that the *Wealth of Nations* consistently aligns with "ease," "plenty," "opulence," "preservation," and the "conveniences and elegancies of life."[35] "The desire of bettering our condition comes with us from the womb, and never leaves us till we go into the grave. In the whole interval which separates these two moments, there is scarce perhaps a single instant in which any man is so perfectly and completely satisfied with his situation, as to be without any wish of alteration or improvement, of any kind."[36] Regarding the "great mob of mankind," Smith assumes that the desire for improvement manifests itself in the desire for the "augmentation of fortune." Ordinary man still wants to better his condition but does so in the most "vulgar and obvious" way.[37]

Smith is wrongly made out as the culprit for defining economic man as an isolated and single-minded figure that aspires to nothing but more goods and more money. On the contrary, economic man is a thoroughly social figure for Smith; his conduct is shaped by "sentiments" that draw him into sociality.[38] His desire for goods is spurred by a concern for how he appears to others and thus motivated by "regard to the sentiments of mankind." The many luxuries or conveniences ultimately serve a social aspiration to be "observed, taken notice of," and "recognized." As Smith puts it, "it is the vanity, not the ease or the pleasure, which interests us."[39] Unlike for Hobbes, vanity for Smith is not a passion that engenders hostility but constitutes an inclination for being approved of. It turns economic man into a social being.[40] Even economic exchange is depicted as being engaged in a social intercourse of communication or, rather, persuasion: "The offering of a shilling, which to us appears to have so plain and simple a meaning, is in reality offering an argument to persuade one to do so and so."[41]

According to Smith, the desire for material improvement leaves economic man as much or sometimes more exposed than before to anxiety, fear, and sorrow. But it also engenders a steady and calm conduct. Parsimony, industry, and the disposition to save result in capital accumulation and therewith opulence. They are the virtues that are generated by this steady and incessant drive to "better one's condition."[42] Most importantly, for Smith, this desire is constant and prevalent. He contrasts the "passion for present enjoyment" with the "desire of bettering our condition" and finds the former "though sometimes violent and very difficult to be restrained . . . only momentary and occasional." In contrast, the latter is "calm and dispassionate"; it "never leaves us till we go into the grave."[43] Economic man thus becomes frugal, prudent, and industrious, and economic conduct turns out to be a form of virtuous conduct.[44] Luckily, according to Smith, the "principle of frugality" predominates "very greatly" among the greater part of man.[45]

For Adam Smith, the desire to improve one's condition is a universal aspiration akin to a "naturalized motivating principle" internal to the subject.[46] The progress from the savage to the civilized stage acquires a certain "naturalness and universality": "Little else is requisite to carry a state to the degree of opulence from the lowest barbarism, but peace, easy taxes and a tolerable administration of justice; all the rest being brought by the natural course of things."[47] Smith's four-stage history is certainly wedded to the hierarchical distinction between the savage and the civilized.[48]

But Smith does not suggest that differences in development are due to the inferior character of an "ignoble savage" in respect to economic man. He concedes that too many "less obvious factors" contribute, if people "live primitively on good soil."[49] There is no "ignoble savage" that held back that course of progress.[50] Accordingly, the civilized economic man and his savage counterpart are not distinguished in principle. They both engage in the same "social calculations," both "judge their own action by comparing his view of himself with the view he thinks others will take; actors in societies at all stages are concerned to avoid the contempt of those around them and, it would seem, to be both praised and praiseworthy."[51] The difference between the savage and the civilized state consists in the relative coarseness of these judgments due to fewer experiences and less interaction and differentiation. The increase of complex interactions, interdependencies, and divisions of labor are assumed to result in such bourgeois virtues as moderation, generosity, humility, and frugality.[52] Such universalizing and naturalizing accounts of the aspiration to better one's condition assumes economic man to be, in nuce, always already present.[53]

This account of the gradual, social, and historical making of economic man is no longer taken for granted after the revolutionary upheavals at the end of the eighteenth century. While endorsing the same "bourgeois virtues" as Smith, Malthus cannot find in everyone the ubiquitous desire to better one's condition. This most material and vulgar desire for improvement, as Smith has called it, is to Malthus's eyes alarmingly absent. The natural state of man is not characterized by "restlessness and activity," as Smith would have it, but by state of "sloth." The more barbarous and savage a being is, the more it prefers "indolence" to a "new coat":[54]

> If the labourer can obtain the full support of himself and family by two or three days labour; and if, to furnish himself with conveniences and comforts, he must work three or four days more, he will generally think the sacrifice too great compared with the objects to be obtained, which are not strictly necessary to him, and will therefore often prefer the luxury of idleness to the luxury of improved lodging and clothing. This is said by Humboldt to be particularly the case in some parts of South America, and to a certain extent prevails in Ireland, India, and all countries where food is plentiful compared with capital and manufactured commodities.[55]

Whereas the eighteenth century has debated the perilous effects of consumption of luxury goods, Malthus fears that the great mass of people would not even desire such goods but would multiply themselves instead. The following sentence from David Ricardo, whose economic thought had fully adopted the dynamic of population as presented by Malthus, exemplifies these doubts regarding economic desires: "The friends of humans cannot but wish that in all countries the labouring classes should have a taste for comforts and enjoyments, and that they should be stimulated by all legal means in their exertions to procure them. There cannot be a better security against a superabundant population."[56] There is always a temptation not to want commodities. A "stalled desire for commodities," early breeding and loss of productive inclination was all too probable.[57] Malthus observes: "Temptations to indolence will generally be too powerful for human weakness when the question is merely about a work which may be deferred or neglected, with no other effect than that of being obliged to wear old clothes a little longer."[58] The cause for this lack of taste for goods lies in the immediacy of desires and cravings that govern those at the "bottom of the human scale," as the last chapter detailed.

Immediacy needs to be understood here as an unmediated material attachment. Immediate consumption means to react in an automatic, bodily way to the resources present. Appetite for other bodies, out of sexual desire, or for food governs the forms of immediate consumption that Malthus describes. They are "bodily cravings," such as "hunger, love of liquor, and the desire of possessing a beautiful woman that urge men to actions."[59] These "natural passions" thus lead to the "wildest and most fatal extravagancies." "As animals," Malthus conceded, "our only business is to follow these dictates of nature, but as reasonable beings, we are under the strongest obligation to attend to their consequences."[60]

It is interesting that these scenes of savage consumption are without of any of the social sentiments that govern consumption for Smith. It is always the object at hand and at sight that is wished for—but it is not the symbolically or socially charged object held out as the fruit of one's exertions.[61] The immediate reaction between an individual body and the objects of his appetite is thus not mediated by the games of social recognition or social intercourse. The scene of consumption stages only bodies, attracted to bodies or goods, in an automatic and immediate way. There is no interval, no future, and no calculation. There is only the present and a subject lost among and enthralled by objects. Economic man and his rationality are dangerously absent.

Fear and the Making of Economic Order

Malthus poses a problem of order akin to the Hobbesian problem of order: how does the catastrophic state of nature, in which the reign of human passions displays its destructive consequences, end? What kind of passion leads the subject to subscribe to a different order? Like Hobbes, Malthus takes the passions as the most fundamental basis of any social, political, or economic theory. Regarded itself as neither good nor bad, "passions are the material of all our pleasures, all our pains all our happiness, all our misery." They are beyond moral reproach when considered in isolation and can only be judged by the consequences their gratification entails.[62] Malthus searches, just as Thomas Hobbes does, for a way to arrange, enlist, and mold the passions that are conducive for the constitution of order. Even though Malthus and Hobbes are concerned with radically different orders—one aspires to found a sovereign body politic and the other, an orderly and progressing body economic—they both single out two passions particularly relevant for producing social order: fear of the future and hope for goods.

As Hobbes declares, and Malthus was to follow, "Feare of death, Desire of such things as are necessary to commodious living; and a Hope by their Industry to obtain them" are passions that incline men to leave the state of nature.[63] Among these two, fear appears to be much more important for leaving the state of nature. As the political theorist Corey Robin points out, Hobbes is the first to grant fear special pride of place. Fear is to him not a "primitive passion" but a "rational, moral emotion."[64] If the pursuit of self-preservation is to political order, a proper understanding of this pursuit is necessary. Hobbes assumes that the appetites focus the individual on the present while the "real good of a person" is to be found in the long term. Fear, defined as a "certain foresight of future evil"—in its purest form, the fear of death—produces the beneficial orientation toward the long term: "The fear of death had an elective affinity with reason. . . . It offered a perfect coincidence of thought and feeling."[65] Strong enough to counter the passions for glory and vanity, fear teaches the individual to understand his self-preservation with an eye toward the future. It produces the coherent self that could form the basis for a pursuit of self-interest:[66] "Fearful men were to be thought of not as cowards, but as purposive and reflective, focused upon their own ends. . . . Frightened of death, he could construct a purposeful life. He would be capable of rationality. The fearful, in other words, do not simply freeze or flee. They move forward, maximizing whatever means they have at their disposal in order to obtain their future ends."[67]

The Hobbesian man fears nothing more than the state of nature and the sovereign. He becomes a political subject submissive to the power of the sovereign and busy in mending his own life. Malthus's "model man" has a different task: he is to found not the body politic but the body economic. But the same passion will lead the way. Malthus follows Hobbes's "distinctly modern conception" of fear as a constituent of a proper form of subjective reasoning, thus bespeaking the continuity between political and economic thought.

Malthus accredits fear—"misery, and the fear of misery"—a necessary role and he declares that fear can "never be removed."[68] "If the rising generation were free from the fear of poverty, population must increase with unusual rapidity." In sum, "men cannot live in the midst of plenty."[69] This praise of "misery, and the fear of misery" implies a reversal of the Enlightenment's attitude toward fear. To the political theorist at the close of the eighteenth century, the "slow vanquishing of fear" is the most cherished achievement of civilized societies. Both political and economic fears appear as being most hostile to further progress—in commercial, political, or moral terms. Linked to the "terrors of religion," the arbitrariness of feudal institutions, political despotism but also to an "agitated fear of scarcity," fear belongs to the dark orders of the past. As the Marquis de Condorcet puts it, "fear is the origin of almost all human stupidities, and above all of political stupidities," and Smith writes "fear is in almost all cases a wretched instrument of government."[70]

To Malthus, fear becomes necessary because hope was not sufficient to lead the savages out of their state of nature. There is no natural love of the "elegancies and conveniences of life" that would propel any subject forward in a desire to better his or her condition. Instead Malthus finds a pervasive indifference to the objects of commercial life: "Few indeed and scanty would be the portion of conveniences and luxuries found in society, if those who are the main instruments of their production had no stronger motives for their exertion than the desire of enjoying them. It is the want of *necessaries* which mainly stimulates the labouring class."[71] Want rather than desire is necessary to produce a subject that is eager to exert himself. More precisely, as Malthus qualifies, it is not want itself, but the fear of want that truly makes economic man: "It is the hope of bettering our condition, and the fear of want, rather than want itself, that is the best stimulus to industry; and its most constant and best directed efforts will almost invariably be found among a class of people above the class of the wretchedly poor."[72]

Malthus maintains that poverty itself, "which appears to be the great spur to industry, when it has once passed certain limits, almost ceases to operate."[73] Fear, aside from hope, is much more conducive for economic calculation than the experience of poverty itself. Whereas for Smith the liberal reward of labor would engender the comfortable hope of bettering his condition and thus "motivate him to exert that strength to the utmost," for Malthus, the mechanisms of hope needed a more powerful companion: the fear of misery. Hence, he added to the Smithian "desire of bettering our condition" "the fear of making it worse." Both together form the "*vis medicatrix republicae*."[74] If men lived within "plenty" alone and without the fear of the provisions in the future, the next catastrophe would be pending:

> Alas! What becomes of the picture, where men lived in the midst of plenty, where no man was obliged to provide with anxiety and pain for his restless wants; . . . where the mind was delivered from the perpetual anxiety about corporal support, and free to expatiate in the field of thought which is congenial to her? This beautiful fabric of the imagination vanishes at the severe touch of truth. . . . The rosy flush of health gives place to the pallid cheek and hollow eye of misery.[75]

This dire outlook of a world in which there is no "perpetual anxiety" is governed by a particular understanding of savage immediacy, which Malthus has described in so many words in his account of the colonial world. Condorcet observes "one is more sure of subjugating people's minds by frightening them, than by speaking to them of reason, for fear is an imperious passion."[76] But it is exactly the imperious nature of this passion that made it most susceptible to counter the dangerous presentism of the savage mind.

Malthus takes fear or anxiety to be a crucial and constitutive passion for making economic man. But he does not assume that such fearful gaze at the future is sufficient. It had to be accompanied by a hopeful outlook as well. "Hopeless indolence," no less than fearlessness, is thus a condition that undermines economic man.[77] In this sense, Malthus's account of the passions that make economic man does not reject what Smith has written about this subject. He retains an equally crucial role for hope in the politics of passions. But the constellation of hope and fear proved to be different. Especially with respect to the savage subject, the effects of hope were less certain. Hence, making economic man requires a particular constellation of these passions dependent on the state of civilization the subject is deemed to be in. Only slowly does the "goad of necessity" give place to the more refined fears and hopes of civilized life. The fear of misery pushes the less civilized man, and the lure of the "elegancies and conveniences of life," as Smith puts it, pulls civilized man into "bettering his condition." Hence, Malthus finds, "the civilized man hopes to enjoy, the savage expects only to suffer."[78]

The relevance of hope for constituting and modulating the economic subject has recently caught the attention of social theorists. Different scholars have commenced addressing the role of hope for economy and the economic subject. Hope's role seems to lie in how it enfolds a cognitive understanding of future possibility or expectation with a desire. "Hopes lies in the reorientation of knowledge."[79] These authors emphasize that there is no necessary connection between hope and the activity to make events come true. One might say that Malthus was equally uncertain about the extent to which hope would necessarily awaken both an orientation toward the future and the activity to make it true. Not any commodity could capture the mind of the subject with a promise of deferred gratification: Malthus assumes that the "clumsy manufactures" produced in Glasgow would barely incite the hopes of the subject.[80] But he speculates that the "peasant, who might be induced to labour an additional number of hours for tea or tobacco, might prefer indolence to a new coat."[81] Colonial goods are objects of passionate attachment and enjoyment—powerful enough to render the economic subject more forward-looking in his desires and exertions. Thus, the diffusion of luxury among the mass of the people seems to be advantageous since it is the tastes for these comforts and conveniences that "prevent people from marrying, under the certainty be being deprived of these advantages."[82]

To his critiques, Malthus wholeheartedly endorses the untrammeled pursuit of economic self-interest. He asserts that to the "apparently narrow principle of self-love, which prompts each individual to exert himself in bettering his condition, we are indebted . . . for everything that distinguishes the civilized from the savage state."[83] But this announcement should not be understood as praise for economic self-interest as a universal motivation innate to the human subject. Rather, it is a praise of those civilized enough to desire to better their condition. Underneath this praise lies the fear of the savage and an-economic subject that follows his inclination toward immediate consumption. The figure of economic man has a shadow: the pauper or the savage at home, who is "antisocial" and an-economic at once, "stubbornly indifferent to the lures of well-being." As the historian Giovanna Procacci puts it, this figure is the "internal limit" of economy.[84] Inculcating fear and creating hope were thus the levers to turn this an-economic subject into both a civilized and properly calculating subject, which is willing to "reason from the past to the future."[85] The degree of civilization determines if the subject is to be frightened or lured.

Economic Man and His Wife

The reformed Poor Laws from 1834 include a "notorious bastardy clause" that changed the existing arrangements for the provision of mothers. The former regulation allowed women to name the father to the local parish, who would collect, if possible, the means for provision from the father or else supplement the missing funds. Under the new legislation "single mothers would no longer be able to expect the parish to extract money from the father or to receive any cash payment from the parish." Women would be given the choice of supporting themselves or entering the workhouse. "It was only during the 1830s that many commentators started to blame women rather than men for sexual immorality."[86] The Poor Laws actually strengthened the patriarchal relations of authority.[87]

Malthus agreed with this regulation. According to him, women were to carry the burden of any illegitimate offspring, either through moral indignation or through financial reprobation. Even if it constituted a "breach of natural justice" that a "woman should at present be almost driven from society for an offence, which men commit nearly with impunity," Malthus was sure that blame has to fall on her shoulders and the children: "The sins of the fathers should be visited upon the children."[88] The rationale behind this responsibilization of women was not to turn them into "free agents economically responsible for themselves."[89] Malthus held that, "by laws of nature, a child is confided directly and exclusively to the protection of its parents. By the laws of nature, the mother of a child is confided almost as strongly and exclusively to the man who is the father of it."[90]

In this section, I show how these policies of sexual regulation are constitutively wedded to the cultural and political project of fashioning economic man. One can detect how the changed eligibility for able-bodied men and the new reproach of single mothers are conjoined in a politics of affect that seeks to produce the proper understanding of economic self-interest in economic *man*.[91] This politics of affect targets the familial and conjugal relations of economic man in order to inculcate the orientation to the economic future into his "heart" and "body."[92]

As the arguments for the bastardy clause of the Poor Laws from 1834 show, the libidinal and emotional ties of economic man are part and parcel of fashioning his rationality. Economic man becomes a being that calculates present and future gain *because* the passionate attachment to his offspring and his wife lead him to do so: it is the "heart-rending sensation of seeing his children starve" that impels the subject to exercise economic virtues:[93]

> Many who are in such a state of mind, as to disregard the consequence of their habitual course of life, as far as relates to themselves, are yet greatly anxious that their children should not suffer from their vices and follies. In the moral government of the world, it seems evidently necessary, that the sins of the fathers should be visited upon the children; and if in our overweening vanity we imagine, that we can govern a private society better by endeavouring systematically to counteract this law, I am inclined to believe, that we shall find ourselves very greatly mistaken.[94]

Withholding any provision for single mothers thus aims at the sentiments of economic man. Malthus admits that "it may appear to be hard that a mother and her children, who have been guilty of no particular crime themselves, should suffer for the ill conduct of the father; but his is one of the invariable laws of nature" since only if the man was "convinced that the women and the child depended solely upon him for support" he would abstain from deserting them.[95] The woman becomes, in this reasoning, an object in the calculations of economic man—more precisely, the passionate attachment to a wife induces him to reckon with the future in the first place. The patriarchal family, the utter reprobation of single mothers, the denial of the right of subsistence or any piece of land—all these elements are tied in this discourse by a single objective: to inculcate futurity to the mind of economic man. Even the desire for objects are thought to be amplified by these conjugal relations: "The evening meal, the warm house and the comfortable fireside would lose half their interest, if we were to exclude the idea of some object of affection, with whom they were to be shared."[96]

In this discourse, heterosexual familial arrangements and the virtues of economic man are two sides of the same coin. The affective conjugal relations and the forms of conduct and calculation appropriate for economic man are bound in a mutual reinforcement. According to Malthus, both conjugal relations and economic calculations are furthered by a practice that he called "moral restraint"—meaning delayed marriage and sexual abstinence until the resources could be garnered for supporting the children. The demand for the control of the sexual passions by moral restraint is part of a thoroughly secular argument. Malthus makes the case for moral restraint and against contraception but not because he subscribes to any religious dogma or because of moral indignation of the passion. On the contrary, Malthus takes these passions to be pleasurable and essential.[97] He opposes "illicit" sexual intercourse because it presents a form of immediate gratification of a passion without consequences for the future; it unburdens the subject from becoming a moral and economic agent that calculates distant consequences. Giving in to the immediacy of (sexual) appetites thus leaves one of the most powerful passions of the subject within the state of savage immediacy instead of molding and modulating it by linking it to a temporal delay. Malthus opposes all types of sexual conduct that weaken this roundabout fulfillment of desires: he shuns "promiscuous intercourse" as well as a "state of celibacy": both are likely to weaken this delayed gratification, either by extinguishing the passions or by gratifying them indiscriminately.[98]

In some of the southern countries, where every impulse may be almost immediately indulged, the passion sinks into mere animal desire, is soon weakened and almost extinguished by excess, and its influence on the character is extremely confined. But in European countries, where, though the women are not secluded, yet manners have imposed considerable restrains on this gratification, the passion not only rises in force, but in the universality and beneficial tendency of its effects; and has often the greatest influence in the formation and improvement of the character, where it is the least gratified.[99]

Delayed gratification has multiple roles to play in this account of economic civilization. The necessity to wait and to defer the gratification of passion is conducive to the economic act of saving. It replaces consumption with deferred consumption. At the same time, the ability to wait links with the willingness to work for the object desired. Furthermore, it also civilizes these passions, sends them into detours, makes them "gentler," but only "where obstacles are thrown in the way of very early and universal gratification." They are kept alive and "burn with a brighter, purer, and steadier flame" after they had been "repressed for a time."[100] Economic man and civilized man are created in a single stroke. By attending to the questions of celibacy, sexual desire, and early marriages, one seems to have strayed far from the questions of economy. But they are integral to this politics of affects that hopes to create the attributes of key character: the rationality of economic man.

This chapter demonstrates the continuity between economic and political liberalism regarding the role of fear (and hope) for the constitution of order. More than hope, fear appears to be the key lever for this liberal politics of affect since fear promises to be the most imperious and most activating passion: Jeremy Bentham is sure that "'the real question,' concerning all living beings" is not "can they reason? Nor, can they talk, but, can they suffer?"[101] But it looks as if the question "will they fear to suffer" is the most important of all, followed by the question "are they worthy to be governed by hope." As demonstrated here, an alleged state of civilization functions as a crucial variable for differentiating how hope and fear are used in the making of economic interests. This liberal politics of affect targets different groups of people differently: some are allowed to hope and others must fear.

Undoubtedly, economic man turns out to be a deeply cultural figure, linked to the hierarchies of modernity. But the genealogy of this figure is not only interesting because it reveals that economic man is never a "thin" figure that has no history, no politics, or no culture. This genealogy is also able to show why the making of the rationality of the economic subject turns into a key focus of liberal politics. Foucault has merely observed that liberal governmentality is "only interested in interests"; but it is equally important to ask why economic man is such central figure for any liberal governmentality. It is because the liberal economic has been constitutively linked to a notion of "savage life" that the governing the economy hinges on the virtuously rational subject, which defers and anxiously expects. Behind the politics of fear (and hope) stands the broader question: to whom or to what can one entrust the resources that are to be employed for the sake of the future? The crisis of liberalism a hundred years later will put the question of economic futurity on the agenda again but will find the virtuous economic subject of the nineteenth century failing in this respect.

Part II. Money

CHAPTER 4

The Return of the Political and the Cultural Critique of Economy

T
he attempt to identify historical periods is a contentious undertaking. The edges of such periods are always fuzzy, and the putative terms of identification betray the disunity and multiplicity of historical time. But with this caveat in mind, the period between the 1880s and 1930s is still aptly circumscribed as a time of growing crisis and contestation. As the historian Robert Colls puts it, "between 1890 and 1920, Liberalism represented the English to themselves and to others in ways that were increasingly regarded as inadequate for a nation facing serious social 'issues' within, and carrying a large and growing empire without."[1] Multiple challenges to the established understanding of liberal politics and liberal economy permeated the social fabric. The liberal hope of taming political passions under the auspices of the alleged neutrality of law, reason, and trade unraveled. Whatever was deemed to be neutral, reliable, or natural turned out not to be so. Concrete sites of social and political contention were tied to a general undoing of established hierarchies and conventions. In 1936 Virginia Woolf wrote: "Things—empires, hierarchies, moralities—will never be the same again."[2]

The reasons for this increasing sense of fundamental change were manifold. The background for the growing uncertainty was set by a long-standing economic instability since the 1873 that had shattered the confidence that the liberal economy could be looked upon as "a fixed entity, sanctified by free trade and expressive of the genius of the greatest industrial nation in the world."[3] It undid the expectation of increased prosperity and the hopes for reconciling competing interests, which had governed the two previous decades. Economic depression appeared to "drag on interminably" and the "economic system appeared to be running down."[4] Meanwhile, on the international scene, the Russian Revolution and the First World War were the galvanizing events that indelibly colored the perceptions of a profound break with the past. At the same time, pessimism and uncertainty accompanied the imperial expansion. While the period marks, on the one hand, the heyday of British imperialism, it is also a time of doubt. Chamberlain's phrase that "the wary Titan staggers under the too vast orb of its fate" captures this sense of pessimism about a "baggy and boundless empire."[5] The unprecedented territorial expansion during the last decades of the nineteenth century had created a "too large body" that contemporaries feared would not last.[6] The South African War (1899–1902) was taken to be the "death-blow to the optimistic idea that the Englishman was the born ruler of the world."[7]

The sense of crisis abroad went hand in hand with a rising tide of politicization and a growing attention to what was called the social question at home.[8] Toward the end of the nineteenth century, the application and publication of sociological statistics had made visible the "depth and extent of a great mass of ingrained and obstinate poverty" in tables, reports, and interviews. The official report by the Royal Commission on the Poor Laws in 1909 announced that "something in our social organization is seriously wrong." The Poor Law Commission on the Poor Laws surveyed the history of poverty since the 1834. While the report from 1909 emphasized again the Victorian view that poverty is linked to "bad moral character," it also grew out of a new sense of poverty as more than a question of individual fate. It had a majority report and a minority report. The latter, drafted by Beatrice and Sidney Webb, demanded a comprehensive set of public services that would target the "disorganization" of society. In reaction to this report, the controversial "People's Budget of 1909" was passed, which "declared, for the first time in British history, a government's willingness to use taxation as a means of redistributing wealth."[9] Liberalism was confronted with an account of a social body that had its own laws of growth and decay insufficiently grasped within the liberal purview. "The notion of society as an organism— living, reproducing, degenerating, dying" started to inform "social criticism of the late-Victorian period powerfully informing the critique of classical liberalism."[10] Liberalism, as the historian George Dangerfield famously wrote, died a "strange death" at that time.[11]

The rise of the social question and the questioning of liberalism coalesced again, like a hundred years before, with a widening of the political sphere: the bounds that had defined who and what belonged to politics were undone. The franchise had already been a vividly debated issue in Britain during the 1860s, "crucial to the redefinition of what the political nation was and might become."[12] The extension of the electoral constituency became again an open and pressing concern in the first decades of the twentieth century, especially due to the militant struggles of the suffragettes.[13] In between these years, an organized labor movement made its appearance, achieving political representation in 1906, when Labour gained for the first time the status of an independent parliamentary party. Finally, in 1918 the Representation of the People Act granted general suffrage to men and allowed restricted rights to vote for women. It institutionalized the shift toward mass democracy. Hence, during first decades of the twentieth century, the inherited regimes that delimit the status political subjectivity and determine the issues of proper political debate were in question. The women's vote challenged the symbolic organization of society and called upon fears that indicate the fundamental nature of change implied. Symptomatic is a conservative in 1908 who predicted nothing less but a national calamity "worse than a German invasion" if female suffrage were to take hold.[14] Skepticism regarding the ability of ordinary man to think independently about the important issue of the day accompanied this undoing of the former bounds of political participation.

One might justly speak of a "return of the political" to characterize this historical situation. This phrase indicates that the very modes of defining and accounting for the social reality and the political sphere were newly at stake. Befitting Rancière's definition of politics, at this historical moment, political contention mingled with epistemological uncertainty regarding the "system of self-evident facts."[15] The question "what is reality?" was not just a concern of a specialized branch of philosophical inquiry but was probed in political struggles, in debates about social question, and in the renegotiations of relations of race and gender. Undoing the former orthodoxy regarding the belief in deterministic laws and ultimate necessity was a "modernist" preoccupation that could be found in the visual arts, psychology, literature, and science, among others.[16] The question of economy was caught up in the midst of this fundamental probing: it returns as a contentious and disorderly subject, which it had been a hundred years before.

As this chapter details, the political language that allowed negotiating the crisis of liberalism, the uncertainty regarding the status of empire, the franchise, the rise of the social question, and the challenge to inherited notions of universality, objectivity, and truth revolved prominently around the notion of culture. Cultural critique was used to particularize, to render conventional and parochial what had been deemed to be general and objective during the nineteenth century. The question of economy was as much the object of cultural critique as was the status of civilization or democracy. Culture linked these debates and contentions; it undermined beliefs in determinism, and it organized the critique of liberal economy. At the same time that the term "culture" was used to undo established hierarchies, the ascendancy of "culture" as a term of debate also belonged to the renegotiation of the boundaries and hierarchies of the body politic at home and abroad. Notions of particularism, primitivism, and degeneration allowed questioning but also reaffirmed exclusions and hierarchies. Cultural critique cut in different ways: it decentered former authorities and informed the desires for new boundaries.

The aim of this chapter is to elucidate how this specific language of cultural critique served to destabilize the established boundary between economy and politics. I explore in this chapter what cultural critique meant at this particular time, and what its stakes, arguments, and limits were regarding the question of economy. As I will show, this destabilization of the boundary between economy and politics through the language of culture consists in an undoing of the epistemological privilege that nineteenth-century liberalism has accorded to the economic subject vis-à-vis the political subject. The dethroning of the economic subject takes place through the deployment of tropes of degeneration and primitivism. But this type of critique is not exhausted by these tropes of degeneration; neither does it center on the irrationality of economic man and his "animal spirits."[17] One can find a much richer type of cultural critique that reconfigures economic rationality as a question of judgment vis-à-vis a world of economic conventions and temporal flux. As a consequence, political judgment and economic judgment, political subjectivity and economic subjectivity are depicted as sharing a common basis: both are faced with the task of navigating uncertain grounds, conventional artifice, and futurity; both are threatened by conformity and the inability of independent judgment. As a consequence, the boundary between the economy and politics becomes porous, and one side cannot function anymore as a foundation for the other.

This chapter detects this richer type of cultural critique in Keynes's writings. As Jed Esty has observed, Keynesian macroeconomics very much partakes in this "anthropological turn" and "metropolitan autoethnography" that "projected England qua nation as newly representable in the holistic terms of anthropology."[18] He elucidates how Keynesian discourse belongs to this wider intellectual current on culture. But his argument emphasizes the recuperative, nationalizing, and holistic aspect of this cultural discourse. Before returning later to this aspect, the critical valence of this cultural critique needs to be explored first. I will show that Keynesian critique of economics bears a family resemblance with a philosophical critique of universalism and reason that is prominently associated with the work of Friedrich Nietzsche. Nietzsche placed the analysis of culture as the foremost task of philosophy and social theory alike.[19] In this context, he stands as a model for a particular type of cultural critique. The parallelization between Nietzsche and Keynes helps excavate the *problematique* of judgment and convention that is at work in this particular undoing of established notions of liberal economy.

The remainder of the chapter begins with a historical overview of the specificity of the discourses on culture and cultural critique at the beginning of the twentieth century. "Culture" is a notoriously vague and complicated term whose meaning historically shifts.[20] A cultural critique of economy cannot be defined out of the discursive nexus in which it functions. This insight is especially pertinent today since "cultural economy" has become again a watchword for an innovative perspective on economy that eschews the naturalizations of economic discourse.[21] Following this call for historicization, I trace the tropes of cultural degeneration, parochialism, and civilization that were prevalent at that time. On this basis, I demonstrate in the second section how notions of primitivism and degeneration were employed in a critique of the economic subject. The third section unfolds how these tropes of degeneration need to be understood against a background of a broader Nietzschean critique of culture, convention, and subjectivity. The fourth section reveals how this type of critique destabilizes the boundary between liberal economy and politics. The chapter concludes with a reflection of the limits of this type of contestation that revolves around the subject as its main concern.

The Rise of Cultural Critique

According to the political theorist Sheldon Wolin, twentieth-century political and social thought is characterized by the ascendancy of culture as a main locus of critique and reflection. This ascendancy has as its corollary, he maintains, a descent of economy as an object of concern. Nietzsche's writings, due to their salience and paradigmatic status, receive the credit or blame for encapsulating this historical shift "from economy to culture": "When a challenge emerged to the primacy of economy, it brought not only a new focus but a different locus . . . this new site can broadly be described as 'culture.'"[22] But this image of a seesaw between economy and culture needs qualification. Economy was not replaced as a locus of concern, but the type of cultural critique that emerged around the turn of the twentieth century furnished new grounds for the conceptualization of economic reality and its bounds. Cultural critique in this case did not mean the "romantic criticism of commercial society" that has a long tradition since romanticism. It is not a purely "sentimentalist" attitude that has "no alternative system to offer," as Bernard Shaw complained in a letter to Keynes.[23] The rise of culture as a term and target of critique was part of the "anthropological turn" during the first decades of the twentieth century.[24] Against the universal claims of the concept of civilization, culture emphasized the particularity, historicity, and geographical specificity of collective forms of living.[25]

Culture, in this sense, refers to a set of customs and skills, patterns of thought and actions that defined a particular mode of existence. "Cultural critique" meant that the anthropological gaze turned toward its own society. As anthropologist Bronislaw Malinowski reasoned, the "average member" of European society is equally governed by the "inertia of custom" as the "present-day savage," although by a different set of rules.[26] This anthropological turn and its attendant notion of culture provided the conceptual means for rearticulating "English universalism" into "English particularism."[27] A fascination with primitivism became widespread in literature, art, and philosophy. Both Freud and Nietzsche framed their analysis of civilization in terms of an always-present "primitive" or "savage" element. The "primitive mind is, in the fullest meaning of the word," said Freud, "imperishable."[28] The claim that European societies embodied the pinnacle of civilization tout court lost its ground—instead, these societies became itself more and more particularized, threatened from within as much as from without. As a consequence, civilization was a title that could be withheld from one's own society and the meaning of civilization was up for redefinition. It turned into a historical task not yet completed. The crisis of Victorian order was greeted as the possible "beginning of the Age of Reason," as Lytton Strachey, a member of the Bloomsbury Group, put it. Leonard Woolf recalled that "in the decade before the 1914 war, there was a political and social movement in the world, which seemed at the time wonderfully hopeful and exciting. It seemed as though human beings might really be on the brink of becoming civilized." English society, as it were, could aspire to her critics, at best to the title of semicivilization: its acts of imperialism and war had only used civilization as mantle for exploitation and destruction; likewise, Virginia Woolf titled Victorian society as being "half-civilized barbarism" due to the hierarchies of gender that it upheld.[29]

The reimportation of colonial tropes to Europe indicates that this anthropological questioning of one's own culture did not take place on an isolated domestic scene. They were spurred, haunted, and inflected by the inedible context of British Empire. As postcolonial scholarship has convincingly argued, the inner bounds of the political nation and its outer bounds are simultaneously negotiated. These negotiations are processes full of tension depending on continuous "boundary work." The period between the 1880s and 1930s brings this simultaneity of concomitant "boundary work" exemplarily to the fore. "The shift in imperial thinking that we can identify in the early twentieth century focuses not only on the Otherness of the colonized, but on the Otherness of colonials themselves."[30] The period sees an intensifying critique of "insane and irrational" imperial policies and rivalry that had characterized the preceding decade. These critiques did not necessarily imply that Empire should be abandoned in factor of "Little Englandism." The Liberal Party and the Labour Party favored a form of "sane imperialism."[31] But in its very uncertainty, Empire became a "sharply contested category" that spurred the interlocking of domestic and colonial issues: politics of "national efficiency," the Boy Scout movement, eugenics, conscription, "imperial motherhood," social reform, and liberalism all gained "irresistible moment within the context of the need to re-engine the Empire."[32]

Robert Young has described the double role of the notion of culture for questioning and affirming hierarchies and exclusions in this context: "What emerges from this history is the startling fact that the notion of culture developed so that it was both synonymous with the mainstream of Western civilization and antithetical to it."[33] In this period, tropes of degeneration assumed a dominant role in the double movement of questioning and reaffirming cultural hierarchies. The diagnosis of degeneration typically refers at once to "moral depravation," "cultural debasement," and "biological deterioration."[34] It calls for an image of a retrograde movement *within* a civilizing body and predicts a pending reversal of cultural development. A discourse on degeneration expresses a loss of certainty in respect to the mechanisms of progress. Accordingly, civilization loses all automatism and becomes a project of willful intervention, selection, breeding, and decision: "There is no certain progress, not evolution, without the threat of 'involution,'" José Ortega y Gasset wrote in the 1930s.[35] Against the desired state of civilization, tropes of degeneration portrayed the primitive, the savage, and the lower race as a danger to the whole, which was present in the very midst of civilization and brought about its reversal.

Notions of degeneration, civilization, and culture pervaded the debates about the social, economic, and political order. The rise of the social question is a case in point. Both conservative and progressive reformers depicted the social realm as governed by interdependent processes of civilization and degeneration. The Majority Report on the Poor Laws and the dissenting Minority Report are exemplary here. While they differed in where they located the ultimate causes of this decay—in the poor themselves or in their unfortunate circumstances—they both employed a language of "national efficiency" and the health of the social body, whereby health and efficiency were both taken to be threatened by cultural and physical degeneration. The reports assumed that a "decayed and predatory underclass was battening upon and dragging down the rest of the social system." These savages resided not abroad but were to be found at the heart of the metropolis itself: "Down there in the abyss, south of Waterloo and east of Liverpool Street, a new and frightening race was evolving." The poor in London's East End were accordingly cast in biological and anthropological terms as a "backward people" and a "race apart"—to the extent that a spokesperson of the London Working Men's Association protested "against the fashion for talking of the working classes as though they were some new found race or extinct animals."[36] The arguments for social welfare were tied to the project of breeding an "imperial race" at home at the same time that critiques of imperialism bemoaned the moral and aesthetic degeneration through Empire.[37] "New" or "Progressive" liberalism became permeated by eugenicist argument about how to improve the "stock of race." A prominent example for this intersection is the Committee on Physical Deterioration that was established in 1904 to investigate the causes of the poor physical condition of the British soldiers after the Boer War. It found that overcrowding of the "lowest type," steeped in every kind of degeneration, to be the culprit of this situation, and it demanded to "take charge of the lives of those who, from whatever cause, are incapable of independent existence up the standards of decency."[38]

Significantly and importantly, these discourses on cultural degeneration also navigated liberalism's relation to "the political." As Daniel Pick puts it in his book *Faces of Degeneration*: "The notion of degeneration was used at once to signify the urgency of intervention and, still more alarmingly, the potential impossibility of constituting the nation from society in its entirety. . . . It was not a question of rejecting the whole urban working class as a 'rabble' nor of accepting it wholesale" but of constructing categories to mediate among them.[39] The poor and the "rabble" were therefore subjects of both intervention and the fear that "social mass" would transmute into a "political mass" unfit to constitute an informed electorate. Images of a savage crowd made up by degenerated poor banding together or depictions of an effeminate mass that was governed by flickering sentiments— all these figures dramatized the lack of proper political judgment.

The new subject of mass psychology portrayed a liberal public sphere that was enthralled by "instinct, prejudice and habit." It would hence cease to function as a "neutral ground wherein individual impulses and emotions might be checked and harmonized": Mass psychology and political critique conjoined in fearing that "public opinion" is the chief source of the irrational, synonymous with prejudice and stereotype throughout this period. As Michael North explains, "in fact, the idea that crowds are ruled by their least intelligent members, who betray the whole to its social unconscious, is a common place of crowd psychology." Walter Lippmann's influential book *Public Opinion* warned against the fickle insubstantiality of public opinion, and to Gustave le Bon the masses presented the more primitive, uncivilized part of human nature that could always gain the upper hand.[40] Bernard Shaw, one of the prominent members of the Fabian Society, announced: "We must either breed political capacity or be ruined by Democracy." He envisioned a "State Department of Evolution" with the task of producing healthy citizens: "King Demos must be bred like all other kings, and with Must there is no arguing." Otherwise, civilization would rush "downward and backwards with a suddenness that enables an observer to see with consternation the upwards steps of many centuries retraced in a single life time."[41]

As the concerns over breeding and cultural quality indicate, cultural critique and tropes of degeneration focused on the question of modern subjectivity. The modern individual appeared not any longer as the most prized achievement of civilization but turned into an object of analysis and concern: its degree of civilization, its genealogy, its strength and weaknesses became nodal points of the debate. Even socialists, as the historian of intellectual history Stefan Collini points out, "preferred economic arrangements on the grounds that they would produce 'a higher type of character.' . . . As one Socialist commentator put it in the 1890s: 'Today the key word . . . in economics is "character." ' "[42] The Fabian Society, whose critique of liberalism and championing of socialism was very influential, makes this link between breeding cultural quality and socialism prominent.[43] The subject was dethroned from its sovereign position as the founder of order, but it was also in a way enthroned as a "practical achievement" and the most prominent task of creation that society could set itself. The question of what type of individuality has been "bred" has preoccupied sociologists, philosophers, imperialists, reformers, and democrats alike.[44] Roger Fry, a member of the Bloomsbury Group, puts this focus on the question of the individual paradigmatically:

> I am gradually getting hold of a new idea about the real meaning of civilization, or what it ought to mean. It's apropos of the question of the existence of individuals. It seems to me that nearly the whole Anglo-Saxon race especially of course in America have lost the power to be individuals. They have become social insects like bees and ants. They just are lost to humanity, and the great question of the future is whether that will spread or will be repulsed.[45]

The modern individual appeared as a task for further improvement, cultivation, and intervention. The figure of economic man was not unscathed by this cultural critique of modern individuality—with destabilizing consequences for the inherited notions of liberal economy.

The Primitivism of Modern Economic Man

Around 1900 economic man appeared to neoclassical liberal economics as a threatened achievement. Especially the virtue of foresight seemed in danger of extinction. Tropes of degeneration expressed this danger and helped to reaffirm the nexus between civilizational hierarchies, the notion of economic rationality and the question of economic futurity that the foregoing chapters have traced back to the beginning of the nineteenth century. It might come as a surprise that such cultural tropes of degeneration can be found in this branch of economic reasoning that had become prevalent at the end of the nineteenth century. Neoclassical economics is mostly known for its pristine schemes of equilibrium in which utility functions of economic agents intersect. If anything, it has been charged for its rampant and abstract individualism that is devoid of social context: "A particle in Mechanics corresponds to an individual in Economics. . . . Energy in Mechanics corresponds to utility in Economics"—these mechanical analogies, as declared by the economist Irving Fisher in 1892, are exemplary for this type of economic discourse that has become predominant in the second half of the nineteenth century.[46] But also within this pristine setting of mechanical forces, the question of culture, character, and degeneration is present.

Irving Fisher proclaimed that the capacity of considering the future in due proportion is a particular advantage that the white economic man has in contradistinction to the "communities of peoples from India, Java, the negro communities of both North and South, the peasant communities of Russia, and the North and South American Indians, both before and after they had been subjugated by the white man." In almost similar words to those Malthus used about a hundred years before, he explained, "In the case of primitive races, children, and other uninstructed groups in society, the future is seldom considered in its true proportion."[47] Regarding this cultural advantage, he is worried about the cultural degeneration of the economic subject: "One of the first symptoms of racial degeneracy is decay of foresight." After 1906 he records with increasing eugenicist temper how much economic foresight might decay through the "multiplication of the unfit" within civilized societies.[48]

These fears of a cultural "debasement" were not merely cultural but pertained to the core of economics proper. In the eyes of Alfred Marshall—the most authoritative exponent of classical liberalism at that time—English character had reached the highest point of development insofar as it exhibited "more self-reliant habits, more forethought, more deliberateness and free choice" than the rest of mankind. He confirmed that economics is in its essence a "study of man" dealing with the "strongest of the forces that shape man's character."[49] Marshall explained to his readers how cultural "degenerations" would challenge the workings of the economy at its heart: "Everyone is aware that the accumulation of wealth is held in check, and the rate of interest so far sustained by the preferences which the great mass of humanity have for present over deferred gratifications, or in other words, by their unwillingness to 'wait.'"[50]

Like these prominent classical and neoclassical economists, Keynes, in his cultural critique, employed the tropes of degeneration—but with different intention and effect. He used them for a "revaluation of all values," borrowing here the Nietzschean phrase. This revaluation concerned the relation of economic man to futurity. Just as the question of temporality and futurity had defined for the nineteenth century the rationality and civility of economic conduct, so was the question of temporality the cause for the dethroning of economic man. Keynes recast the preference to wait and the willingness to postpone gratification endlessly into the future as a pathological, religious, and primitive trait of modern economic man that endangered further civilization and future wealth. *Homo oeconomicus* became a figure that no has longer the most productive and most refined relation to the future—instead, this relation is depicted as sterile and weak, and as inviting retrograde movements in the process of economic civilization.

For modern economic man, the future never arrives but always recedes. Economic man appeared as a figure that postpones the arrival of the future. The future retreated endlessly.

> The "purposive" man is always trying to secure a spurious and delusive immortality for his acts by pushing his interest in them forward into time. He does not love his cat, but his cat's kittens; nor, in truth, the kittens, but only the kittens' kittens, and so on forward forever to the end of catdom. For him jam is not jam unless it is a case of jam tomorrow and never jam today. Thus by pushing his jam always forward into the future, he strives to secure for his act of boiling it an immortality.[51]

For nineteenth-century economics, this postponed fulfillment of gratification had been the very key for proper economic conduct. Futurity itself and the possibility of material progress appeared to depend on this act of postponing consumption. In fact, futurity was produced through acts of saving. But according to Keynes this deferral had pathological features. Postponement and deferral impeded material progress because they favored abstaining from transforming potentiality into an actual course of consumption or investment. They undid futurity by not making it happen and keeping it away from the world. Business men, Keynes derided, "fall back on the grant substitute motive, the perfect *ersatz*, the anodyne for those who, in fact, want nothing at all—money. . . . [They] flutter about the world seeking for something to which they can attach their abundant libido. But they have not found it."[52] While classical liberal political economy had found that the proper use of present means for future ends is corrupted by a lack of foresight, it is now the lack of action that corrupted the relation to the future.

Money allowed this withdrawal from action since it provided the possibility of storing value for later use. A "fetish of liquidity," Keynes assumed, has taken hold of economic man.[53] The "love of money as possession" becomes a "superstitious belief."[54] Money was not cherished for the things it can procure but for its capacity to be "re-embodied if desired in quite a different form."[55] In Georg Simmel's *Philosophy of Money* one finds a very similar emphasis on money as a potentiality: "Since money is not related to any specific purpose at all, it acquires a relation to the totality of purposes"; money represents "mere possibility of unlimited uses."[56] Such love of money's potentiality changed the workings of economy, since modern economic man demanded a "premium" and a "reward" for holding wealth "in some form other than hoarded money." The interest gained on money "has been usually regarded as the reward of not-spending, whereas in fact it is the reward of not-hoarding."[57] The very narrative about the course of material accumulation focused not any longer on the savage's lack of foresight, but the fetishization of liquidity: "That the world after several millennia of steady individual saving, is so poor as it is in accumulated capital-assets, is to be explained, in my opinion, neither by the improvident propensities of mankind, nor even by the destruction of war, but by the high liquidity-premiums . . . now attaching to money."[58]

It is revealing how the metaphors of savagery and primitivism shifted in this account of economic man. Primitivism consisted not any longer in immediate gratification but in the superstitious love of money as an object in itself. Accordingly, the colonial "other" was charged with this newly detected savagery: India's "love of the precious metals" and the wish to "hug her sterile favourite" becomes the preeminent example for the misguided and savage passions of natural man. "Vague stirrings of the original sin of mercantilism [is] always inherent in the mind of the natural man urging him to regard gold as beyond everything essential wealth."[59] Keynes announced, "Solon represents the genius of Europe, as permanently as Midas depicts the bullionist propensities of Asia."[60] To remind the reader, it had been the fault of the ancient King Midas to mistake gold as the ultimate end and not understand its character as a mere means—he had wished for everything turning gold upon his touch. In contrast, Solon, the king of Babylon, had in Keynes's view the wisdom of lowering the value of metal coins for the sake of economic well-being, thus challenging the status of money as an end in itself. The two figures of Midas and Solon thus stood for the savage fetishisms regarding money, on the one hand, and the civilized ability to pierce through them, on the other.

The reimportation of tropes of fetishism as present in Keynesian thought was a common discursive device for detecting the internal Otherness of European societies.[61] These tropes were typically overlaid and accompanied by sexualized and gendered stereotypes. Hence, it is not surprising that metaphors of sterility, impotence, and death were employed in this discourse to render the effects of the economic "fetish of liquidity" vivid. Economic man was depicted as a "frigid creature" that "flap[s] away from our shores with their golden eggs inside them."[62] The "character of liquidity" represented, according to the cultural historian Piero Mini, a "vicious circle of timidity, frigidity, and impotence."[63]

The prevalence of notions of sexualized desire in depicting a new psychology of economic man has led some scholars to make a case for a strong connection between Keynes's psychological account of economic facts and Freudian figures of thought.[64] Keynes's own writings contain several remarks that present psychology as an important part of economics. He maintains that "it is evident, then, that the rate of interest is a highly psychological phenomenon."[65] Furthermore, the very prominent role of the Bloomsbury circle in discussing, disseminating, and publishing the word of Freud in England makes this connection tenable.[66] Yet, a very immediate detour of economy through the psychology of the subject misses a more encompassing horizon of this critique. Keynes himself suggests that "[it] might be more accurate, perhaps, to say that the rate of interest is a highly conventional, rather than a highly psychological, phenomenon.

For its actual values is largely governed by the prevailing view as to what its values is expected to be."[67] Taking up this lead, I argue that paralleling Keynes with Nietzsche rather than with Freud helps us to understand much better the nexus between subjectivity, temporality, and convention that underlie this novel account of economic man and his relation to the world.

Nietzschean Economics: The Economy as Convention

The name of Nietzsche is not usually associated with issues of economy. But it is not for his remarks on economy that Nietzsche is referred to in this context. Rather, the way in which Nietzsche frames and problematizes the question of culture illuminates the Keynesian cultural critique of economic rationality. The argument presented below draws attention to the implicit proximity between some familiar Nietzschean figures of thought and Keynesian cultural economy. This very general reference to Nietzsche does not intend to prove any direct influence or total congruence of perspectives—even though an argument could be made (and has been made) in favor of partial influence.[68]

For unfolding the similarity in framing the question of culture, some cursory remarks on Nietzsche as a philosopher of culture need to be made. Nietzsche provides an account of culture that emphasizes its historical and artificial character. Cultural conventions are artifacts that provide stability against a world that is fundamentally characterized by flux, complexity, and incertitude. "Cultural interpretations sustain and are inscribed in practices by lending familiarity, stability, and continuity to the world. . . . It is the intrinsically human way of transforming the phenomenal realm of experience into a universe within which agency is possible."[69] But, while lending necessary stability, cultural forms are always threatened by ossification. While the task is "to carve out a horizon, making possible a mode of acting and providing an interpretative space" for the experience of agency, culture might outlive itself in ways that impede the "basic exigencies of life and action." Humans tend to "mistake their own interpretive constructs for natural ones, their own conditioned perspectives for universal ones."[70] Hence, a critical genealogy of their emergence is necessary in order to "reevaluate the value of these values"—just as Keynes reevaluates the virtues of saving and hoarding.[71] In this sense, cultural conventions are the artificial grounds in a world without certain grounds. They are necessary yet prone to become "mere conventions," which is to say that they become unrecognizable as cultural artifice and are followed out of conformity.

For Nietzsche, culture thus needs a historical sense that ascertains its aptitude in the light of the present and the future. Hence, temporality and futurity are a significant preoccupation of Nietzsche. For example, Nietzsche judges Christian morality, *inter alia*, for its failure in "ensuring the future of humanity."[72] The follower of Christian morality "lived at the expense of the future."[73] Culture, in this historical sense, requires creative construction and destruction in order to be a guide to the future. The role of the subject is to "revaluate," to define ranks, and to summon the conviction necessary in a world without certainty. The subject has to simultaneously nourish the constructive impulses for building conventions and has to have the ability to discard outworn ones. The subject who is capable of this task is taken to be the "ripest fruit" that culture has to offer.[74]

This Nietzschean perspective sheds a revealing light on the critique of the economic man that Keynes furnishes. It brings to view the intersection between subjectivity, cultural conventions, and temporality that governs this critique. Instead of positing valuations and conventions against the flux of time, Keynes depicts economic man as being unable to deal with temporality. Economic man is said to desire liquidity because he shuns the very decision that would entangle him with the fortune and fate of a specific choice. In other words, he fails to summon the conviction for a leap into the future, to which he could commit. At the stock market, he behaves as "a farmer, having tapped his barometer after breakfast, could decide to remove his capital from the farming business between 10 and 11 in the morning and reconsider whether he should return to it later in the week." Economic man is a nervous and wavering subject. There is a "delicate balance" of the moods, Keynes finds, and one has to yield "to the nerves and hysteria and even the digestions and reactions to the weather" that influence the temperament of those upon whose spontaneous activity investment depends.[75]

This wavering and nervous subject stands in a stark contrast to how Keynes depicts the businessmen of former times, who were "individuals of sanguine temperament and constructive impulses who embarked on business as a way of life. . . . The affair was partly a lottery. . . . If human nature felt no temptation to take a chance, no satisfaction (profit apart) in constructing a factory, a railway, a mine or a farm, there might not be much investment merely as a result of cold calculation."[76] The heroic businessman of the past was "the master-individualist, who serves us in serving himself, just as any other artist does." He is portrayed as a creature with a strong imagination "disciplined by a stronger will"; he had a "strong nervous force."[77] The sanguine temperament of the businessman of the past is an example of the famous "animal spirits" that Keynes finds indispensable for economic action and, one should add, for any agency in general. Animal spirits are defined as a "spontaneous urge to action rather than inaction"; this urge toward action is not animated by "the outcome of a weighted average of quantitative benefits multiplied by quantitative probabilities."[78] Rather, it connotes a pleasure in construction, in doing and in acting, which is linked to health and life force itself.

The "animal spirits" are conspicuously close to that definition of the will proposed by Nietzsche: a physiological and psychological *compositum* that signals vitality.[79] It is the necessary condition for entering into a productive relation with the future. "We are," as Keynes explains, "merely reminding ourselves that human decisions affecting the future, whether personal or political or economic, cannot depend on strict mathematical expectation, since the basis for making such calculations does not exist."[80] Within the realm of economy, the need for such "animal spirits" that can substitute for the lack of certainty is amplified for the simple reason that the future is an especially prominent concern for economy: "The whole object for the accumulation of wealth is to produce results, or potential results, at a comparatively distant, and sometimes at an indefinitely distant date."[81] The "dark night of uncertainty" as one commentator puts it, afflicts economic man in constitutive ways.[82] Thus, the uncertainty about a pending total loss needs to be "put aside as a healthy man puts aside the expectation of death."[83] Such "strong roots of conviction" and "spontaneous optimism" are said to elude the modern economic man. Thus, he behaves like a farmer who pulls out the seeds he has planted.[84]

The very prevalent historical discourse on "nervous excitability," neurasthenia, and the "weakness of the will" is recognizable in this critique of economic man.[85] It unites both Keynes and Nietzsche's critique of modernity. Nietzsche finds the "irritability" and "incapacity to withstand a momentary impression" a flaw of modern subjectivity.[86] "Nothing is as contemporary as weakness of will," Nietzsche writes and Keynes unconsciously echoes: "We are suffering today from the worst of all diseases, the paralysis of will. Nothing can be more dangerous than that. We have become incapable of constructive policy or decisive action. We are without conviction, without foresight, without a resolute will to protect what we care for."[87]

The famous passages on "animal instincts" have often been discussed as an account of the irrationality of the economic subject. Uncertainty and irrationality are taken to define the ultimate contention of the neoclassical tradition. George Shackle takes this novel account of the economic subject to be the core of the Keynesian revolution: "The message of the General Theory is that investment is an irrational activity."[88] Other scholars have pointed out that it is not irrationality or affect per se that are portrayed here.[89] Instead, one should understand it as a form of reasonableness. In this sense, the rationality of Keynesian economic man participates in the "extended family of rational expectation." Conventions function thus as a "companion to reason."[90] "Keynes was neither a (strong) rationalist or an irrationalist. He stood in a middle-way position as far as his epistemology is concerned."[91] When a contemporary of Keynes suggested to him that the arbitrariness in judgments of probability "implies a criticism or at least calls for further analysis, of the basic concept of economic man," Keynes accorded in response, "It may well be . . . [that] we have to abate somewhat from the traditional picture of economic man."[92] Investment is rather a medley of knowledge and affects; its rationality is more a question of degree than of principle.

From within the discipline of economics, dominated as it is by the question of rationality, means/ends calculations, and complete information, the concentration of the debate on issues of rationality is plausible. Engaged within a tug-of-war with the neoclassical theory, the question of the rationality of economic man is automatically taken to be the decisive issue. But sometimes merely attending to oppositions of a field means to stay within the old order of thought. It is easy to miss the changes that pertain to the more fundamental level of discursive formation, as I argue below. The very lack of passions in Keynes's answer points to the possibility that the rationality of economic man is not the core issue.

Thus, viewed from a genealogy of the economic, the most remarkable aspect of these pages might not even be that economic man is now harboring irrational propensities or affects and has only a vague knowledge of things. The striking shift lies in the fact that the purity of rationality is no longer important to define economic actions at its core.

Reasonableness of degree, gambling, animal spirits, and conventions are allowed to converge as rationality ceases to function as a *differentia specifica* of economic man and economy. Instead economy is problematized as a field of necessary conventions that need to be carried through time but that nevertheless lack objective grounds. How to relate to the conventions to the past, how to open up the future, and how to judge these issues—these questions define the *problematique* of economy, just as any other realm of conduct.

This claim that convention becomes a key category for this cultural critique of economy requires elucidation, and even more so since "convention" is a term that is used by Keynes himself in different ways. But they all fit the Nietzschean term of "culture." First, conventions are defined as the artificial substitutes for the absolute certainty. The subject in a world without foundations falls back "on what is, in truth, a *convention*."[93] Radical uncertainty and the irreducibility of conventions are two sides of the same coin. "We are assuming, in effect, that the existing market valuation, however arrived at, is uniquely correct in relation to our existing knowledge . . . though philosophically speaking, it cannot be uniquely correct, since our existing knowledge does not provide a sufficient basis."[94] Conventions provide quasi-objective grounds where there are none "in an absolute view of things."[95]

The second characteristic of this world of convention is also present in these passages: the preeminence of valuation. Conventions entail specific modes of "valuations" that contains all "sorts of considerations."[96] Valuation on the market place is a process much more mediated than the model of a straight reckoning of scarcity would suggest—it is full of estimation, opinion, and convention. A third aspect of convention is intimately linked to the foregoing: it addresses the role of social conformity in adhering to "conventional valuations." The meaning of "convention" is here a merely conventional—that is, conformist—way of acting and thinking. "Knowing that our own individual judgment is worthless we endeavour to fall back on the judgment of the rest of the world which is perhaps better informed. That is, we endeavour to conform with the behavior of the majority or the average endeavoring to cope the others leads to what we may strictly term a conventional judgment."[97] Only a particularly strong and independent individual can avoid this conformity and summon the "wit" and individual strength that is needed to go against this average opinion. In respect to a "long-term investor" who is most socially useful,

Keynes finds that "it is in the essence of his behaviour that he should be eccentric, unconventional and rash in the eyes of average opinion."[98]

Thus, the world of economy is one of artificial foundations, "conventional" valuations, and accustomed conformity—these elements provide the main terms of problematization of economy. Those who merely follow the established conventions compromise the achievements of individuality *and* of economy in the sense of general welfare. But at the same time, the very adherence to conventions is also necessary as it offers a direly needed stability. It functions as a minimal guarantee for behavior: In "conventional morality" there is "a great deal of it rather tiresome and absurd once you begin to look into it, yet nevertheless it is an essential bulwark against overwhelming wickedness."[99] Keynes understands financial politics in terms of such conventional morality and describes the Treasury in identical terms to morality per se: "In some ways I think Treasury control might be compared to conventional morality."[100] Conventions are not lightly to be discarded: Even though "metaphysically we can give no rules," "there are rules, which though not immutable have nevertheless so wide and general a validity that they ought to be obeyed as universally as if they were universal."[101] Yet they also need to be opened to genealogical criticism at times, for they mistakenly represent themselves in the garb of universal objectivity. Keynes finds this problem paramount regarding the interest rate, which rests too high for the mere fact "that the level established by convention is thought to be rooted in objective grounds much stronger than convention."[102] Genealogical critique of conventions as well as the ability to uphold them and to posit them, if necessary, against the pressures of conformity—these new virtues of economic man appear mostly ex negative, but they outline the very different grounds on which economic man and economy are conceptualized.

Without objective grounds and certain foundations, the realm of decision, guesswork, and experiment grows larger. Individual judgment has a crucial role to play. "To such fanatics of the individual judgment as many of us are born to be," Keynes asserted, the "right of the individual to judge its own case" is paramount.[103] Ethical, economic, and political conducts coalesce around the importance of individual judgment. "With rules and duties bereft of ultimate philosophical guarantee, they [moral rules] became practices 'to be used or disused according to the circumstances and the nature of each individual case,'" summarizes R. M. O'Donnell of the resultant role of judgment that has to decide the merits of each case.[104] It has been precisely the question of individual judgment that had spurred Keynes's interest in probability before turning to economics. He explicitly claims that the general question of conduct was an "important contributory cause to my spending all leisure hours of many years on the study of that subject."[105] The radical uncertainty announced in his *General Theory* did not, it is important to note in this context, "put a bar towards individual judgment, on the contrary, but [was] a way of neutralizing the unknown" so that individual judgment would be possible.[106] Granting such an exalted role of the virtues of judgment is not peculiar to Keynes alone. As Lorraine Daston and Peter Galison have shown, the very conception of scientific objectivity at the turn of the century started to revolve around the virtues of "trained judgment": "The real emerged from the exercise of trained judgment"[107]—the economic real, no less.

It is interesting to note that Friedrich von Hayek and Keynes share this critique of rationality, and they both emphasize the role of conventions but take different positions regarding the role of individual judgment. Both Keynes and Hayek "asserted that the nineteenth-century positivist attempt to treat economics as analogous to the physical sciences was doomed to failure." Both proclaimed the habitual and customary basis for thought and action.[108] But they differ in respect to the amount of individual judgment regarding the established rules governing the institutionalization of the market and the conventions of monetary policy. Hayek demands the utter obedience to rules "because of the 'sea of ignorance,' in which they move, they are not in a position to form a genuine and reasonable judgment of concrete situations that involve expectations about the future. They have to resort to the unique wisdom they possess against ignorance: the wisdom of tradition."[109] In a world that lacks grounds, the unconditional adherence to well-tried tradition seems to promise the best available mode of conduct for Hayek. Keynes had a more critical and experimental position, and in the historical moment the critical valence reigns more supreme: Nietzschean genealogical critique takes precedence as it allowed claiming the "immoralism" that repudiates the "duty to obey general rules."[110] The difference in economic doctrines is not in the least a difference in how the duties of obeying and the capacities of judgment are conceived of. At the same time, Keynes differentiated and hierachized between those apt to be immoralist and those in need of morality: "We," he announced to his friends, "are not part of the machine, but we consume its products; we have hardly any duties, as I understand the word. We can see enough to perceive that many of the old moralities may be unfounded." But within the "Kingdom of moralities and duties" the "need for an adequate and relevant morality" remains paramount.[111]

Indeterminate Frontiers—Politics and Economics

For classical liberalism, the economic subject is an "island of rationality" because he or she calculates the sensations of pain and pleasure, follows only his or her own interests, exercises a consistent form of choosing, or calculates all information available. But seen from the perspective of culture, the economic subject is situated in a world of convention and is uncertain about it and enthralled by it. As I reconstruct below, both economy and politics are diagnosed to suffer from the incapacity of its subjects to deal with such a world of convention, which requires nonconformity, strength of individual judgment, and conviction simultaneously. Hence, it is their common failure that makes the spheres of economy and politics alike. These failures of subjective judgment do not only pertain to the political and economic masses but also to the institutional or political authorities: political leaders, the treasury and bankers are as much part of the problem as average economic man and the political masses. All of them would either lack firm principles of conduct, be lost in conventions, or miss out on the constructive impulse for institution building. The next paragraphs offer a montage of depictions of the stock market and of democracy. They show the striking extent to which the problematization of these spheres relies on homological and sometimes even identical terms.

As described before, the institutionalization of mass democracy in the first decades of the twentieth century was accompanied with anxieties regarding the value and effect to mass enfranchisement. Resonating with the antidemocratic skepticism of his time, Keynes holds that "there is not very general a priori probability of arriving at desirable results by submitting of the decision of a vast body of persons, who are individually wholly incompetent to deliver a rational judgment on the affair at issue."[112] The democratic party has "to depend on this mass of ill-understanding voters, and no party will attain power unless it can win the confidence of these voters by persuading them in a general way either that it intends to promise their interests or that it intends to gratify their passions." In the Labour

Party, which is presented as the most democratic party, "too much will always be decided by those who do not know *at all* what they are talking about."[113]

Turning toward the account of the stock market, we find an analogous diagnosis about how ignorance and incompetence undermine judgments in economic matters: The vast majority "knows almost nothing whatever about what they are doing. They do not possess even the rudiments of what is required for a valid judgment, and are the prey of hopes of fears easily aroused by transient events and as easily dispelled. This is one of the odd characteristics of the Capitalist System."[114] In any case, the "conventional valuation, which is established as the outcome of the mass psychology of a large number of ignorant individuals is liable to change . . . opinion due to factors which do not really make much difference to the respective yield." Not knowing what they base their judgments on, the masses also lose their conviction quickly, as there are "no strong roots of conviction to hold it steady."[115] The triad of judgment, conviction, and healthy animal spirit is replaced by conformity, lack of conviction, and fear. "Speculative markets are governed by doubt rather than by conviction, by fear more than by forecast."[116] Proper judgment is lacking all around.

The political as well as the economic masses do not only lack the capacity for exercising proper judgment; they also corrupt the last vestiges of skilled judgment. Due to the influence of the masses the "expert professional and speculator" are mainly concerned "not with making superior long-term forecasts of the probable yield of an investment over its whole life, but with foreseeing changes in the conventional basis of valuation a short time ahead of the general public. . . . For it is not sensible to pay 25 for an investment of which you believe the prospective yield to justify a value of 30 if you also believe that the market will value it at 20 three month hence." Hence, it is not even rewarded "that anyone should keep his simple faith in the conventional basis of valuation having any genuine long-term validity."[117] Within such flickering mass, the "skilled individual" finds no support. To the same extent that the skilled investor is torpedoed by the stupidity of the economic masses, the political leader is undermined by the political masses. The leader of the Labour Party will not be rewarded for following his own judgment; instead it is "necessary for a successful Labour leader to be, or at least to appear, a little savage." Only a less democratized party guarantees that an "intellectual element will . . . exercise control."[118]

In this perspective, democracy and wrong-headed speculation exemplify the same dangers of corrupted judgment. America comes to stand as a stereotyped signifier for both: "In one of the greatest investment markets in the world, namely, New York, the influence of speculation [understood by Keynes as forecasting the psychology of the market] is enormous. Even outside the field of finance, Americans are apt to be unduly interested in discovering what average opinion believes average opinion to be; and this national weakness finds its nemesis in the stock market." One unlikely but nevertheless sensible measure would be thus to exclude the masses: "It is usually agreed that casinos should, in the public interest, be inaccessible and expensive. And perhaps the same is true of stock exchanges. That the sins of the London Stock Exchange are less than those of Wall Street may be due, not so much to differences in national character, as to the fact that to the average Englishman Throgmorton Street is, compared with Wall Street to the average American inaccessible and very expensive."[119]

These quotations exemplarily show how the political and economic sites of judgment are constructed in similar ways. Parliament and parties, on the one hand, and the stock market, on the other, exhibit a fundamental homology as both are discussed in terms of conventions, conformity, and the virtues of independent judgment. It is worthwhile to note that this homology does not only appear on the level of the critique of mass psychology but also pertains to political and economic authorities.[120]

The leaders of the city and the treasury are presented as paramount examples of the institutional elites of the economy and their ill of judgment. "Bankers," Keynes asserts "are the most romantic and least realistic of all persons": "It is part of their business to maintain appearances and to profess a conventional respectability." A banker, he continues, "is not one who foresees danger and avoids it, but one who, when he is ruined, is in a conventional and orthodox way along with his fellows, so that no one can really blame him." It is conformity and conventionality that holds sway in their economic judgment. The rhetoric used by Keynes to question the policy of the bank is unanimously that of blindness and "ignorance" due to "absence of thought" and "belief in old customs." Discussing with them thus is "like discussing the *Origins of Species* with a bishop sixty years ago. The first reaction is not intellectual, but moral." Not cognizant of the circumstance, the treasury remains enthralled by a moral bond: The "financial fashion plates" display "marriage with the gold standard as the most desired, the most urgent, the most honorable, the most virtuous, the most prosperous, and the most blessed of all possible states."[121]

It seems, Keynes speculates, that the recognition of their "vast responsibility" surpasses the banks, and, being so huge, "there is a great temptation to them to cling to maxims, conventions and routine." "Those who sit at the top tier of the machine" fail to perceive the conventional nature of their beliefs; even less are they capable of judging their appropriateness or developing conscious strategies to secure their own position of power. It is thus absurd to assume a bankers' conspiracy, concludes Keynes, as they share with other citizens the utter incomprehension of the dangers ahead: "A bankers' conspiracy! The idea is absurd! I only wish there were one!"[122] Among the economic authorities it is hence the very lack of recognition that they are dealing with a world of convention that unhinges their judgment. They mark the opposite pole to the flickering mass, whose fault it was to form any convention with some conviction that could hold it steady.

Within the realm of politics, one finds both faults of judgment prevalent. There is an inability either to pierce through old conventions or to posit timely ones for the present; there is either a mechanical chant about outworn moralities or the lack of conviction to hold those that fit the order of the day steady. An account of these ills of political reason can be found in the *Economic Consequences of Peace*, which Keynes published in 1919 after attending the peace conferences at Versailles as a part of the British delegation.[123] The three statesmen—Woodrow Wilson, Georges Clemenceau, and David Lloyd George—embody these ills of political reason: Clemenceau stood for clinging without any doubt to the old game of the "balance of power." He represented the inability to engage in a critical review of outworn conventions that no longer fit circumstance.[124] Wilson stood at the other end of the spectrum, in all respects the opposite of Clemenceau: "He had no plan, no scheme, no constructive ideas whatever for clothing with the flesh of life the commandments which he had thundered from the White House." He lacks the constructive impulse that can tie values of heaven with the demands of the world. Lloyd George, the last of them, was cast in the role of the "femme fatale." He was "rooted in nothing," showed "final purposelessness, inner irresponsibility." Hence, "an old man of the word, a femme fatale, and a non-conformist clergyman—these are the characters of our drama."[125] The flaws of the political and economic world bear much resemblance: either there is an excess of allegiance to conventions, blinding one toward the change of circumstance, or there is a lack of principled conduct altogether as conventions are not carried through time. It is either the clergyman or the femme fatale.

In between the ignorant democratic masses and the incapable elites, proper political and economic judgment finds no secure ground. Economic reason and political reason suffer from the same pathologies, and neither can give foundation for the other. Hence, the realm of economic objectivity appears to be as much the effect of the domains of opinion and judgment as the human artifice of political reality. The stock market, banks, and parliament appear as homologous institutions, functioning as central authorities for exercising the judgment from which the "real" emerges. These kinds of objectivities have no ground "in the absolute view of things," neither do they answer to a law of necessity. Speaking of an indeterminate frontier between economy and politics intends to emphasize this homology of both spheres. It refers to the fact that the old grounds for ascertaining these frontiers are undone by this homology. This indeterminacy resides at the level that defines the very conditions for demarcating these spheres. It is no longer the economy of scarcity, the system of forces, and the mechanics of laws that turns economic reality more "real" or more "necessary" than politics. Where and how these conventions of economy emerge and are put into practice, whence and by whom a genealogical criticism of these conventions is effective—these are questions that can now be posed, as they are not foreclosed by a necessity deeper than convention.

The Limits of Cultural Critique

A panoply of characters populates these Keynesian accounts of economy: frigid businessmen, bankers that behave like bishops, jam savers, clergymen, nervous subjects that cannot commit, who outrun those with sanguine temperament and skills. These figures dramatize and render vivid the claim that economic facts and cultural facts have more in common than is usually accorded. They undo the image of the economy as the pristine set of mechanical forces that neoclassical economics had portrayed. These "character masks" exemplify the kind of cultural critique at work in this discourse. This cultural critique has two main and overlapping determinants, as I have shown. First, economic man revealed itself as a limited cultural convention with degenerative traits. Keynesian revolution in economics might be taken as a reversed cultural tale about economic man. But, second, it is not only the "revaluation of values" that is significant of this cultural critique of economic man. To unfold more comprehensively what this turn to culture implied theoretically, this chapter has strategically used references to Nietzsche's writings. Some very general Nietzschean figures of thought have been employed as a means to shed new light on the account of economic objectivity present here. Economic objectivity emerges from the malleable relations between temporality, convention, and subjectivity. The vagaries and virtues of individual judgment and conduct assume an outstanding role within this triad—not as a foundation but as a key concern of this cultural critique. Hence, the role of these subjective characters, their flaws, and anxieties are part of a cultural critique that revolves around a question of judgment.

This cultural critique of economy shifts the field of economic objectivity from truth, scarcity, and law into a domain that cannot marshal such grounds. But it also remains—so far—a drama of subjectivity. The deciding, investing, scheming subject remains the kernel around which this critique revolves. The diagnosis of a "weakness of the will," the pitfalls of "nervous excitability," and the account of the average man who has "lost his power to be an individual"—as Roger Fry has put it—belong this kind of problematization of economy. It plays on a scale of subjectivities and still tells a moral story of their virtues. In this sense, one might even say that such cultural critique also affirms the tradition of liberal economic thought as it remains a tale about economic man and his conduct, however twisted this tale has become. As vivid as these character masks are and as much as they dramatize the deeper *problematique* of temporality and convention, they cannot be taken as the endpoint of the theoretical inquiry. They dramatize a novel account of the ontology of economy, but they do not expose to full extent what makes it possible to depict the economy as a domain of convention and judgment. What is the ontology in which this kind of moral drama finds its conditions of possibility? What is economy, when it no longer about scarcity and the laws of necessity but tilts over into the contingency of cultural conventions? The next chapter provides the answers to these questions as it excavates the malleable economic from these cultural tales about money, economy, and the subject.

CHAPTER 5

The Economic Unbound

Material Temporalities of Money

The beginning of the twentieth century witnesses a curious multiplication of meanings pertaining to the notion of economy. In 1925 the *Palgrave's Dictionary of Political Economy* defined economy unequivocally as the "principle of seeking to attain, or the method of attaining, a desired end with the least possible expenditure of means."[1] Hence, the best use of scarce resources circumscribed the notion of economy for the individual and for the social totality alike. In diametrical and polemical opposition to this understanding, Keynes found that there is a harmful and "exclusive concentration on the idea of 'economy,' national, municipal, and personal meaning by this the negative act of withholding expenditure." He defined inversely that "economy can have no other purpose or meaning except to release resources," and warned his contemporaries "if we carry 'economy' of every kind to its logical conclusion, we shall find that we have balanced the budget at naught on both sides, with all of us flat on our backs starving to death from a refusal, for reasons of economy, to buy one another's services."[2] A breach appeared between the logic of economy revolving around the individual strategies of saving, on the one hand, and the proper ways of thinking about the economy as a domain of systematic interrelations, on the other hand. According to Keynes, one had to stop reasoning "by false analogy from what is prudent for an individual" to what benefits the economy as a whole or govern the "conduct of the State [by] maxims which are best calculated to 'enrich' an individual."[3]

It is of course possible to see in this polemical opposition to the individual economy of saving nothing more than the seeds of the managed macroeconomy and the call to deficit spending that Keynes has become, not quite rightly, infamous for.[4] But reading this injunction against the "economy of means" solely in the context of economic policy would mean to miss a much broader conceptual shift that is taking place. Keynes's rethinking of liberal economy was only one voice in a larger choir of social theorists and philosophers who partook in the inquiry into the "ontology" of the economy and its relation to culture and politics. In this historical period, the fundamental terms of liberal economy, such as "exchange," "rationality," and "scarcity," were subjected to novel forms of historical and philosophical questioning. Max Weber's exploration of the meaning of rationality and its genealogy in religious striving for salvation comes to mind, as does the ethnologist and sociologist Marcel Mauss's work on the social relation of gift giving as a moral foundation of an exchange economy. Georg Simmel's *Philosophy of Money*, which retraces the cultural meaning of value, subjectivity, and sociality, needs to be added to this list as well as Joseph Schumpeter's rewriting of capitalist economies as relations of debts and creative destruction. Not to the least, Georges Bataille's elaboration of a "general economy" of expenditure that is ontologically superior over the restrictions of means belongs to this group.[5] But unlike the philosophical, sociological, or ethnological queries about liberal economy and the economic, Keynesian discourse was not condemned to "march round the citadel of orthodoxy blowing the trumpets and waiting for the walls to crumble":[6] no disciplinary boundaries shielded economics proper from this challenge from within.

To conceptually isolate what the pluralization of the meaning of economy is about, it is necessary to turn toward "the economic." This conceptual coinage has been introduced to highlight a mode of analysis that seeks to isolate the specificity of a relation that is not yet tied to a definite model of the economy as an ordered and firmly bounded totality. It aims at addressing what distinguishes economic relations from political or religious ones while it simultaneously recognizes the impure constitution of things economic. The economic is thus a notion that highlights what is malleable, yet specific, about economy. As I want to show in this chapter, the multiplication of the definition of economy at that time is a symptom of the resurfacing of "the economic" in liberalism. A space was opened up that allowed a debate about the fundamental reality principles of liberal economy. In sum, the beginning of the twentieth century not only sparked new debates about "the political"—as widely discussed and most prominently linked to the work of Hannah Arendt and Carl Schmitt—but was equally preoccupied with a novel account of reflection on the economic.[7]

As will be further elucidated below, the elaboration of the economic at that time revolves around a novel understanding of money and temporality. Money became a central theme for the rethinking of liberal economy. Historical circumstances favored such focus on money as a vehicle for a critique of the inherited orthodoxy of classical liberalism. The last decades of the nineteenth century and the first decades of the twentieth century had seen abrupt changes in price levels and monetary value that "made us lose all sense of numbers and magnitude," as Keynes remarked.[8] An "unbroken sequence of currency crises" after the Great War swept through Europe. Whole populations became "currency-conscious," meaning that they calculated the effect of inflation on real income and regarded stable money as "the supreme need of human society."[9] As Thomas Mann explained to his American audience, "a market woman who demanded in a dry tone 'one hundred million' mark for a single egg, had lost during inflation the capacity to be amazed at anything anymore."[10]

The political and economic response to the currency instabilities after the First World War consisted of attempting to restore the gold standard, which had defined the wisdom of monetary policies for several decades before the war but had been impossible to maintain due to the large amount of debts accrued during the war.[11] Throughout the 1920s the return to gold was seen as synonymous with a return to stability, free trade, and prosperity after war and crisis. A large concerted and coordinated effort was made to reinstall the standard. This effort took place between "1923, when the German mark was pulverized within a few months," and the beginning of the 1930s, when "all important currencies of the world were on gold."[12] The effect of this attempt was deflationary policies of prices, wages, and rents that resulted in economic and political instabilities of unexpected proportions. The endeavor to restore the gold standard failed spectacularly, and in September 1931 Britain went off gold; the United States followed in 1933.

In this historical context, the neutrality axiom of money championed by classical liberalism became increasingly hard to maintain. For classical liberalism, money is an insignificant layer upon economic forces more substantial and real than money. Keynes rejected the axiom of the neutrality of money and with it the sanctity of the gold standard. He regarded monetary relations as a force in its own rights and turned money into object of analysis in itself.[13] But money turned out to be more than a newly added, important topic of economic thought—even though it was that as well. Money becomes the vehicle for reorganizing economic thought. As the Keynesian scholar Paul Davidson passionately asked, "Can there be anything more revolutionary? Keynes rejects the neutral money axiom."[14] Many years after Keynesianism's rise and decline, the issue of money still functions as a rallying point for reclaiming the question of economy from some designated orthodoxy in economics.

From the vantage point of a genealogy of the economic, Keynes's writings on money are important to the extent that they entail a reconfiguration of the "ontology" of liberal economy. Keynes's positions on money, debt, the gold standard, and the interest rate are discussed in this chapter not for the sake of these issues per se but in regard to a different aim: to explore the economic that is at stake in them.[15] Keynesian recipes of monetary policy are not the subject of this chapter; rather, the critical space of the economic that opened up between the old orthodoxy of classical liberalism and the new orthodoxy of Keynesianism that was to follow are the focus here.

The question of temporality is crucial for the following discussion of the economic, as it has been for the analysis of the economic in the previous chapters. It is by no means uncommon to focus on the question temporality for a discussion of Keynes. Especially heterodox types of Keynesianism share this focus.[16] The analysis of the economic provided here differs from these interpretations with respect to how the importance of temporality is understood and framed. Within the debates on Keynesianism, the importance of temporality is seen to consist in the role of expectation and uncertainty that time introduces to economics. In this perspective, taking temporality seriously means to acknowledge the uncertainty that the economic actor is confronted with. The limit that uncertainty poses to the rationality of the economic actor is understood to question the assumptions about market equilibrium. One prominent example for this interpretation is the work of George Shackle, who argues "that the Keynesian revolution concerned time. The essence of time is that it is irreversible and that we can know nothing about the future." Giving the uncertainty of the future "the Keynesian revolution [is] overthrowing precisely the type of rational-choice theory on which the neoclassical synthesis was based."[17]

The analysis of the economic offers a different take on the question of temporality: the notion of uncertainty is not ignored but loses its centrality if seen from the genealogy of the economic. In this chapter, I argue that the economic that surfaces in Keynes through his writings on money is based on an "ontology" of divergent and intersecting material temporalities that are understood to be governed by conventions of measurement. The attribute of the economic becomes a question of degree: there are shades of being more or less economic due to the conventions that end up "giving measure" to these material temporalities. The difference between the perspective offered here and the discussions on uncertainty is best characterized by the different role it grants to the economic subject. While the emphasis on uncertainty implies a focus on the deciding and calculating economic subject, the genealogy of the economic accentuates the analysis of a relational "ontology." As I argue, behind the diagnosis of uncertainty and "expectational time" stands the more general role of conventions of temporality for redefining "economic objectivity."[18] Hence, instead of tying the question of temporality to the subject's decision, this chapter explores further how temporality and conventions of measurement are turned into a heuristic for thinking *economic relations* that have their own specificity without forming a purified system or law.

The remainder of this chapter unfolds this account of the economic step by step. The first section concentrates on how the classical account of the neutrality of money is challenged by the constitutive relation that Keynes establishes between money and temporality. This section provides the background for the following discussion, which excavates the link between Keynes's notion of money and the elaboration of the economic. I emphasize how the novel understanding of money belongs to an elaboration of the economic in terms of material temporality and measurement that undermines the divide between the monetary and the "real" economy. The third section concentrates on how this configuration of the economic allows for an analysis of monetary regimes in terms of the conventions of measurement that they entail. I discuss specifically the type of critique that Keynes mounted against the gold standard. The fourth section discusses the fate of this notion of the economic, foreshadowing the next chapter on the closure of this critical space in the form of the birth of the managed macroeconomy.

From Money as Representation to Money as Temporality

For elucidating how money became the entry point for a new account of the economic, it is helpful to juxtapose this notion of money with the one that classical political economy had maintained throughout the nineteenth century. As indicated earlier, the economic doctrines of classical liberalism have largely subscribed to the axiom of the neutrality of money, assuming that money in itself is only a layer upon economic forces.[19] In mid-nineteenth century, John Stuart Mill encapsulates this understanding of money by declaring that there cannot be a more "intrinsically insignificant thing in the economy of society."[20] This delegation of money into an object of secondary importance rests on two main pillars: first, it is based on an understanding of money as a medium of exchange. Second, it assumes that money represents the values in exchange without distortion.[21] As a neutral medium of exchange "money enters the picture only in the modest role of a technical device that has been adopted in order to facilitate transactions."[22] As the neoclassical economist Carl Menger explains, money's role and function is tied to relations of exchange, which engender this "technical device": "As each economizing individual becomes increasingly more aware of his economic interest, he is led by this interest, without any agreement, without legislative compulsion, and even without regard to the public interest to give his commodities in exchange for other, more saleable, commodities"—this more saleable object is money in its nascent form.[23] Hence, money makes the commercial wheel run smoother and faster, but it does not define what the logic of economy is about: "Even in the most advanced industrial economies, if we strip exchange down to its barest essentials and peel off the obscuring layer of money, we find that trade between individuals or nations largely boils down to barter," Paul Samuelson assures the students in his famous standard textbook on economics.[24]

From this vantage point, the gold standard appeared in the nineteenth century as the most natural choice for a monetary system: gold, regarded as a scarce and valuable commodity itself, would ensure that the monetary sign would not stray from the values and utilities defined in relations of exchange. It makes sure that money remains connected to the realities of value defined elsewhere. As a mere placeholder for the exchanging of goods, money becomes the universal symbol and numéraire for the value of goods. Many scholars have pointed out that the philosophical presupposition of this notion of money is a representational logic. As a layer upon the real, money is akin to a token or a sign whose role is to represent the values of the commodities in an accurate way. "As a symbol, it can *directly* represent real commodities."[25] Money is regarded as a sign that exemplifies how the commodities come to stand in definite and measurable relations to each other. Inasmuch money is assumed to be a neutral medium of exchange, it is expected to function as a neutral medium of representation for the exchanging values.[26] Historically, the debates about paper money during the nineteenth century bring this function of representation to the fore as they are concerned with "the relation between the substantial thing and its sign."[27] The following phrase, uttered by a witness to the monetary controversies in post–Civil War America, captures this representational understanding and might thus be taken as a motto for this monetary discourse of the nineteenth century: "If we shall once get the thought fairly and fully into our minds of the difference between a thing and the representative of a thing, we will be . . . safe."[28]

The fundamental shift in thinking about money that occurred at the beginning of the twentieth century displaces this representational logic with a temporal one. Keynes's critique of the neutrality axiom of money at the beginning of the twentieth century targets both of the pillars on which this representationalism rests. He neither assumes that the question of exchange most aptly circumscribes the genealogy and function of money nor subscribes to a representationalist account of money as an "honest" mirror of real values.[29] Instead, Keynes favors a temporal problematization of money.[30] Money turns from a medium that is "honest" or "dishonest" to a medium that measures and formats temporality. What this means is elaborated below. For the moment, it is important to note that such shift from a representational frame to a temporal does not mean that money's capacity to adequate values does not emerge as a problem anymore. Quite the contrary, the problem of keeping a "sense of magnitude and numbers"—to use Keynes's phrase—retains its commonsense importance. The representational attributes of money will surface again but within a different conceptual space and, hence, with different implications.

Like many heterodox theories on money, Keynesian thought about money finds its starting point in the relations of credit and debt.[31] Instead of imagining the multiple but instantaneously happening exchanges of goods as the foundational scene for understanding money, relations of credit and debt are seen to provide a window to the essence of money. In this way Keynes counters what Mauss has called a misleading "unconscious sociology." This "unconscious sociology" in thinking about money mistakenly assumes that credit is a phenomenon of developed societies alone. Mauss's work on gift exchange paradigmatically encapsulates this shift from exchange to credit as the more salient and more fundamental social relation. As Mauss puts it: "The evolution in economic law has not been from barter to sale, and from cash sale to credit sale. . . . Barter has arisen through a system of presents given and reciprocated according to a time limit."[32] Credit was first. Keynes reasons along similar lines.

Having occupied himself with the study of the origin of money in Near Eastern ancient societies, Keynes finds that it is only with relations of contract that a monetary economy comes into existence. Not exchange itself but the expression of customary or contractual obligations through time captures money's impact in society: "The introduction of a money, in terms of which loans and contracts with a time element can be expressed, is what really changes the economic status of a primitive society; and money in this sense already existed in Babylonia in a highly developed form as any years before the time of Solon."[33] Measuring and expressing this obligation in terms of value is a monetary phenomenon par excellence: "An article may be deemed to have some at least of the peculiar characteristics of money (1) if it is regularly used to express certain conventional estimates of value such as religious dues, penalties or prizes, or (2) if it is used as the term in which loans and contracts are expressed."[34] This quote links the emergence of money not to the exchange of goods but to expressing an obligation through time. Against this expression of obligation through time, Keynes finds coinage and the invention of "sealed money" of rather "trifling significance." It does not constitute the "veritable introduction of money" but should rather be seen as "bold vanity, patriotism, or advertisement with no far-reaching importance."[35]

Economists have widely commented on the difference between the understanding of money as a representative commodity and of money as a standard for expressing relations of obligation or debt. As Schumpeter puts it, the difference lies within a "credit theory of money" as distinct from a "monetary theory of credit."[36] The first one is essentially a "claim theory." It conceptualizes money as a promise to pay or as a promise to satisfy a debt, and it emphasizes the making of a standard that measures if the promise of payment has been fulfilled. Whereas the second one looks at credit from the vantage point of a particular understanding of money, the first one uses the relation of credit to understand the essence of money. Within monetary theory and the sociology of money, such making of standards is often tied to the question of political authority and the sovereign state.[37] But here the focus lies on a different aspect of the "credit theory of money." Most important for elaboration of the economic is the primordial importance that such theory of money grants to temporality. Relations of credit, debt, or customary obligation contain, as Keynes points out, an "element of time." They demarcate a temporal durability. It is this link through time that turns for Keynes into a characteristic of money par excellence. As Keynes puts it in the *General Theory*: "Money in its significant attributes is above all, a subtle device for linking the present to the future. . . . We cannot get rid of money even by abolishing gold and silver and legal tender instruments. So long as there exists any durable asset, it is capable of possessing monetary attributes and, therefore of giving rise to the characteristic problems of a monetary economy."[38]

This is indeed a remarkable statement, in which the usual discussion of money in terms of its own value or lack thereof is replaced by a discussion of money in terms of time. It could not be stated clearer that "moneyness" is foremost tied to temporality. *"For the importance of money essentially flows from its being a link between the present and the future."*[39] In this perspective, neither the metal basis of money nor legal tender defines money as much as temporality does. Only when money comes linked to time through the relation of credit does it "make . . . its entry into human institutions."[40] The importance of the temporal dimension is closely related to a question of measurement. Money is not only about time but also about the measurement of time. A credit relation or a debt specifies both a temporal bracket and an obligation that is due at a marked point in time.[41] Credit is granted on the expectation of a return; therefore, the temporal horizon is enmeshed with a measure of what is due at a future point in time. Measuring and expressing this obligation in terms of value becomes the monetary phenomenon par excellence. Keynes argues that the origins of money are not to be found in relations of exchange but in the measurement of duties linked to religious and political relations. Money was introduced to measure whether these "non-economic" obligations had been sufficiently discharged. Within this context, the "conventional orders of value" could be vague but were still "perfectly satisfactory"—a cow could function as a measure as it expressed a "handsomer prize, a severer penalty, a richer sacrifice than a sheep, a copper pot or a measure of barley."[42] But these measures of value would not allow to be "generalized and expressed without reference to the particular. . . . No-one would ever price goods or advance a loan in terms of cows in general without reference to the particular. . . . Even a particular cow does not have a steady value throughout the year but fluctuates in accordance with the seasons or difficulty of finding fodder and the expected date of its calving."[43]

The purity of a monetary standard that emerges from these religious and political relations results from a process of abstraction. In other words, what creates a truly *monetary* standard for expressing obligations through time is the abstraction from the particularities of duties and obligations, and from time and space. The cow that is used to discharge a political obligation will therefore never be a monetary standard to a full extent, since it is tied to a body that is exposed to change and decay. Money emerges when it sheds such exposure—when a different time-space is created for a monetary standard to remain stable. Paradoxically, money will therefore be a link through time by abstracting from the particularities of time: it should not be subjected to waste or decay. It is this abstraction or generalization that creates money's main characteristic: its liquidity—that is, its character of being exchangeable for other goods, its ability to be "re-embodied if desired in quite a different form."[44]

Interestingly, "moneyness" becomes a gradual attribute in this perspective, which depends on the degree of abstraction from the vagaries of time and space, which always imply danger of deterioration or expense: "It may be worth emphasizing . . . that 'liquidity' and 'carrying-costs' are both a matter of degree, and that it is only in having the former high relatively to the latter that the peculiarity of 'money' consists."[45] A nonmonetary economy is for Keynes not just an economy without legal tender, given that any durable asset is capable of possessing monetary attributes. What makes a durable asset "nonmonetary" is the following: "There exists nothing, that is to say, but particular consumables and particular capital equipments more or less differentiated according to the character of the consumables which they can yield up . . . all of which, unlike cash, deteriorate or involve expense, if they are kept in stock, to a value in excess of any liquidity-premium which may attach to them."[46] In other words, moneyness entails a particular organization of materiality, which is low in costs and high in liquidity. One could say, the more abstracted money is from the vagaries of time-bound and material existence, the more liquid it is. But abstraction is here not to be understood as a form of dematerialization; instead, it rests on a specific organization of materiality, temporality, and space that furnishes protection from the dangers of embodiment. The notion of "relative carrying costs" indicates these inedible links to materiality, which have to be organized in a specific way to minimize exposure and maximize liquidity in order to create high degrees of "moneyness."

It is important to note that such elaboration of money, temporality, and measurement does not ignore money's role as a token that stands in for the value of other commodities. Money keeps its role as a measure of value in respect to other values: The question what a certain monetary numéraire can command in terms of its "purchasing power" remains a paramount monetary issue. But this question is now posed within a conceptual frame that foregrounds the patterns of time and the obligations that are due over the course of time. Therefore, the question of the "purchasing power" of money becomes a question of choosing what standard of measurement will apply to which kind of goods within a context of temporal durations. As Keynes emphasizes, there is no "unique centre, to be called the general price level. . . . There are various prices indexes, appropriate of various purposes. There is nothing else."[47] Keynes puts the *problematique* of money regarding temporality and measurement in the following metaphors: "A contract to pay ten years hence a weight of gold equal to the weight of the king of England is not the same thing as a contract to pay a weight of gold equal to the weight of the individual who is now King George."[48] If the individual who is now King George weighs half that of the king of England ten years hence, the money due to satisfy the contract would be doubled. What matters is thus not only if a piece of coin or paper represents the value of a thing (or a king) but what standard of value is defined for expressing relations through time. The question of "purchasing power" and value is inextricably tied to measuring temporal sequences. Money as debt thus does not mean that money is in itself a contractual relation of debt that can be enforced by legal means or social sanctions. Rather, it means that the organization of temporality and the conventions of measurement become paramount for understanding what is at stake in monetary arrangements.[49]

Money and the Economic I—Material Time Machines

This genealogy of money in credit and debt draws time, abstraction, representation, and measure into an inextricable relation to each other. The result of this multiple intersection is an understanding of the specificity of money's temporal qualities. Money turns out to be quite a specific link through time because it is a measure of obligations through time that is shielded from the effects of time. Reversing the famous saying of Benjamin Franklin that "time is money," one might say that "money is time."[50] Instead of implying that time gives the opportunity to earn money, the reversed statement points out that money produces and formats (economic) time. Approaching money in terms of a specific time machine opens up the Keynesian monetary theory to a broader ontology of the economic. The following paragraphs unfold the ways in which money appears in this discourse as a medium that organizes and formats a pattern of time in a quite peculiar way. This functions as a bridge to the broader issue of the ontology of the economic contained in this account of money. The first question to be answered is what time is money? The second question to be attended to is what does this tell us about the economic?

What time is money? Following Keynes' exploration of temporality and money, one can single out three temporal specificities of money. First, money produces the *future as a potential*. Because money can be exchanged for (almost) anything, it harbors possibility in itself. Since it ideally neither suffers from waste nor decay, it stores this possibility into the future. In a sense, it creates futurity because it opens a space for a decision yet to be made. The sociologist of money, Geoffrey Ingham, puts this quality of money in following words: "With money, decisions can be deferred, revised, reactivated, cancelled"[51] Money fashions a link from the present to the future by creating and maintaining the future as potential. This form of futurity is quite paradoxical because money links the present to the future precisely by avoiding the vagaries and possibilities that emerge within the unfolding of events. The pure storage of money for the sake of retaining the future as an unspecified potentiality commits itself to a barrenness: "For it is a recognized characteristic of money as a store of wealth that it is barren; whereas practically every other form of storing wealth yields some interest or profit."[52] The miser, as Karl Marx has put it, is "merely capitalist gone mad."[53]

Insofar as the classical political economy did not consider the question of temporality, this quality of money appears as madness or as pure folly: "Why should anyone outside a lunatic asylum wish to use money as a store of wealth?" Keynes asks, and he finds that the only reason is that this potentiality or liquidity of money has its own qualities in terms of time: it opens and stores a futurity that does not yet have to commence and does not suffer from the mishaps of time. For the very reason that this type of futurity matters, money's futurity is prized itself. The price of money expresses thus the "preference . . . for holding cash in hand over cash for deferred delivery"[54]—that is, potentiality over an investment entangled with the fate and fortune of a particular investment, life, or thing.

Second, and intimately connected to the first, money works "back from the future." This enigmatic expression points toward the warped temporal structure inherent in using money. Because any use of money for a present transaction always implies that money's value in the future holds good, the future value of money has to be assumed for its present use. Using money therefore means that one uses the future validity of money for a present payment. Hyperinflation, for example, is the very situation in which this form of using the future for the present has ceased to work: since one cannot even assume the future validity of money for the next day, the purchasing power in the present is severely minimized or nil.

The temporal structure of money, which resides in the most mundane monetary transaction, is therefore not one of a linear succession of events. Neither can it derive its force from its past usage. On the contrary, each payment only works "back from the future" since it rests on the assumption that money is also a valid token for tomorrow.[55] French Journalist Marcel Labordère, who stood in close correspondence to Keynes on questions of money, has put this use of the future for the present in the following words: "If we look at it closely, we invest our savings before we have made them. . . . We work on fantasy."[56] Money, in this way, injects the future into the present moment because using money and accepting money is governed by its futurity, not by its sources. There exists something because it will exist in the future: savings will be called into being once the action starts.

Some people find it a paradox that, up to the point of full employment, no amount of actual investment, however great, can exhaust and exceed the supply of savings, which will always exactly keep pace. . . . If the banking system chooses to make the finance available and the investment projected by the new issues actually takes place, the appropriate level of incomes will be generated out of which there will necessarily remain over an amount of saving exactly sufficient to take care of the new investment.[57]

Given this warped temporal structure that proceeds from the future rather than from the past, it is no wonder that Keynes finds it a "fascinating task to rewrite economic history." Keynes's historical narrative about the British nation commences not with any material accumulation of things but like a fairy tale with a found or stolen treasure. The "privateering" of Spanish treasure ships in 1573 becomes the "fountain and origin of British foreign investment." In a historical and calculative sequence fashioned by money, Keynes links the stolen treasure in 1580 with the aggregate foreign investment in 1930.[58] In this historical narrative, the material progress of the British nation begins with an accidental influx of money that is, with the magical properties of money, to commence a course of events by relying on the future. Put differently, only because money has a capacity for letting a process begin, the writing of history can begin with money itself, leaving the whereabouts of this treasure up to historical accident or to political history. This recalls, of course, Marx's famous account of the violent means of expropriation that allowed "primitive accumulation" to set off the history of capital, but the different emphasis on the futurity inherent in money itself is noteworthy: money adds a type of temporality that is irreducible.[59]

Money is, last but not least, a medium that measures a particular circular temporality. In this respect, the temporality of money is most closely tied to the relation of credit or debt proper. Money is, as the above discussion has shown, the standard that articulates the obligations over the course of time. It belongs to the peculiarity of a credit relation that it demands a return with an increment added at a certain point in time. "Credit money 'brackets' time since a period of the future is reserved or 'colonized' as a stream of obligations."[60] Within a monetary economy, it is the interest rate that defines the increment that is "obtainable on current cash over deferred cash."[61] The bracket of time is thereby subjected to a measure: it costs a premium to obtain money for a particular amount of time. As part of a relation of credit or obligation, money itself is linked to a return due at a defined point in time. Adapting Benjamin Franklin's saying that time is money, one might say that interest defines to what degree and for whom time has to be money—for the given time has to be used to procure the increment, which can be paid in addition to the repayment of the original sum. In this sense, credit money not only fashions a circular temporality by organizing a return of money to the point of origination. Through the interest rate, it also measures this temporality because it defines not only when but also under which conditions the circular movement needs to be completed.

The closed circuit as an essential moment of order can be found in numberless accounts of economy.[62] Schumpeter contends that the "circuit flow that in each period returns upon itself" belongs to the very essence of economic science proper.[63] Several thinkers have dwelled on this circular structure, fitting it to their own respective theoretical frameworks. For example, Fernand Braudel describes the economic logic of long-distance trade during the early modern period under the heading "no closure, no deal": "Trade circuits are like electrical circuits: they only work when the connection is unbroken." Likewise, Marx took pains to distinguish the circular movement of capital, governed by the limitless drive to make "money beget money," from more limited engagements for the sake of consumption. In contrast with the final dissipation of funds through consumption, the logic of capital lives by the closure of the circle so that the funds travel back to their site of emanation. Seemingly most distant from more narrowly defined economic thinkers, Jacques Derrida has pursued the same line of reasoning when he says in *Given Time* that one needs to attend to the odysseic structure of economy.[64] At the beginning of the twentieth century, this general figure of circularity is taken up in terms of the variable and conventional measure of temporality that it entails. Here Keynes follows the same trajectories of thought that one can find in Mauss's analysis of gift giving. Both understand the element of time and the measure of return as social, conventional, or moral facts. The genealogy of credit links money's beginning to religious or political obligations, thus emphasizing the "total social fact" that this measure encapsulates.

The question of interest, the measurement of circular time, the importance of the future validity of money—these elements all belong to a monetary theory that foregrounds the question of temporality. In what way does this monetary theory expose a different configuration of the economic? What does money tell us about the economic? Explicating the ontology of the economic entailed by this monetary theory requires attending more closely to the role of materiality in this account of money and temporality. Looking at money in terms of temporality and materiality reveals that "moneyness" is a variable attribute that consists in a specific configuration of materiality. As elaborated earlier, Keynes argued that a cow, due to the variability of its body over its life course, could assume the attribute of "moneyness" in principle, yet it could do so only to a little degree. But any materiality that is less variable and equally durable would potentially assume this quality to a larger extent. According to Keynes, land—different from cows—is, just as money, a durable asset that links the present to the future while offering protection against the gnawing of time.[65] Land could assume the same liquidity-function as money and thus accrue sufficient degrees of moneyness. This analogy between money and land strains the inherited notion of money as a token or a sign of representation that is disconnected from the reality that it must represent. Seen within a representationalist framework, money and land seem not to have much in common—one is deemed to be an immaterial sign, the other stands for the most material and earthly condition of production. But the account of money in terms of temporality, materiality, and measure suddenly draws both money and land into a single frame of analysis. As quoted earlier, Keynes assumes that "so long as there exists any durable asset, it is capable of possessing monetary attributes and, therefore, of giving rise to the characteristic problems of a monetary economy." Land and legal tender share this durability. Seen through the lenses of temporality, money appears as just one "durable equipment" among others. Interestingly, discussing capital in terms of the facilities of production, Keynes uses the very same words: "It is by reason of the existence of durable equipment that the economic future is linked to the present." The "real" and the "monetary" economy meet on this plane of organizing time: they are all "subtle devices" for linking and formatting time: in other words, they are material time machines.[66]

Money and matter have thus become homologous in an analytical perspective that foregrounds the making and measuring of temporalities. Adopting this perspective allows linking the material and the monetary in novel ways, countering the ontological divide between money and the real: "We have all of us become used to finding ourselves sometimes on the one side of the moon and sometimes on the other, without know-ing what route or journey connects them, related apparently, after the fashion of our waking and our dreaming lives." The aim is to "escape from this double life," and the *General Theory* should therefore not be misunderstood as a "separate 'theory of money.' "[67] Money and its link to the "real economy" is modeled in terms of the homologies between these formerly distinct spheres in terms of materialized and multiple measures of temporality.

The temporal patterns and measures that define these economic tem-poralities are bound by the materiality to which they belong. This crucial role of materiality can be taken from a very technical discussion of interest rates in Keynes. Interest rates or temporal measures, Keynes argues, exist for all objects that are articulated in economic ways: "For every durable commodity we have a rate of interest in terms of itself—a wheat rate of interest, a copper-rate of interest, a house-rate of interest, even a steel-plant rate of interest." There "is no reason why their rates of interest should be the same . . . why the wheat-rate of interest should be equal to the copper-rate of interest."[68] The measure of temporality varies depending on the specificity of the context and materiality at hand: They differ, as the probability of yield, the affordance of the material substance at hand, the danger of loss, and the costs of storing them differs from one to the next.

The technical term of interest rate should not mislead about what is implied in this rendering of economic temporality: that there are as many time machines as there are things or bodies used in processes of procuring services or commodities. In other words, there is not a single clock for measuring economic temporality and the obligations tied to it—instead, different measures are implied depending on the specificities involved. "Every reference body has its own particular time"—this sentence encapsulates what this list of copper, houses, wheat, or steel is about. Curiously, it is a sentence that stems from Albert Einstein, not from Keynes. Nevertheless, it explicates the discursive frame in which these economic things appear at the beginning of the twentieth century. Keynes has indeed been called the "Einstein of Economic Theory" more than once.[69] The link between them is to be found in this multiplication of the "clocks" that tie temporality and measure. The cultural historian Stephen Kern has put this shift in the understanding of temporality implied here as follows: "He contrasted the older mechanics, which used only one clock, with his theory which requires that we imagine 'as many clocks as we like.' The general theory of relativity had the effect, figuratively, of placing a clock in every gravitational field in the universe . . . each telling a different correct time."[70]

Keynes echoes in an early piece on time. "There is no absolute measurement of time that is intrinsically more correct than any other measurement," insisting "on the essential relativity of all time measurement."[71] If there was such absolute time, "it would of necessity be out of all relation and connection with all other reality; it could neither act on it, nor be acted on by it, nor be in any way in relation to it. And I cannot conceive a portion of reality thus completely separated off from the sum of all other reality."[72] It is only for the reason of the "interaction of time and matter" that the perspective on temporality offers to cut across the monetary and the real, unfolding each time how the peculiarity of a material medium implies a specific format and measure of temporality.

Keynes maintains that one can only arrive at a "purely conventional measure of time."[73] This understanding undermines the notion that the economy is governed by a uniform and universal set of laws due to some principles of self-interest, calculation, and scarcity on which it is seen to rest. Instead, we have now a plurality of temporalities and measures. What kind of futurity, what kind of return, and what kind of circularity are fashioned—these questions are not answerable by assuming a set of given variables in an economic system. These questions point toward the intersecting temporalities, measures, and conventions that mold and modulate the economic. There is not yet "the economy" as a hydraulic system, governed by a single lever. From the genealogy of money in credit—and the questions of obligation and time that it raises—one has arrived at a simple figure of thought: the economic as a multiplicity of intersecting material "time machines" that tie materiality, measurement, and convention to each other.

In this perspective, temporality, materiality, and its measurements become the specific heuristic for delineating the economic attribute of relations or undertakings. The economic is defined by the triad of time, measure, and circularity. The task of the cook is, Keynes exemplifies, not to cook "the absolutely best dinner" at "an hour that would suit him best if time counted for nothing" but to "provide the best dinner he can for service at that hour." Discounting time would import "a large element of unreality" into economic thought. The paramount role of the "link between to-day and to-morrow" is not to be misunderstood as consisting of the linear sequence of hours or days.[74] The making of temporality is at stake—that is, the constitution of patterns and measures of time. These are inextricable from the materiality to which this temporality belongs.

Money and the Economic II—Monetary Temporalities

After having traced how this specific account of money and temporality belongs to a novel understanding of the economic, it is important to note that Keynes, as an author, does not explore all implications of this frame of thinking the economic. Whereas one could use this heuristic of the economic for an analysis of the various sites and mechanisms that determine these measures and patterns of material temporality—ranging from the temporality of the soil, the body to the technologies of controlling the work space or the management of resources—Keynes himself does not. Money and the monetary rate of interest are Keynes's main theoretical concern: "So far, therefore, the money-rate of interest has no uniqueness compared with other rates of interest, but is on precisely the same footing. Wherein, then, lies the peculiarity of the money-rate of interest?"[75] While Keynes approaches the question of money from a broader ontology of the economic, he leaves this broader ontology unexplored and focused on the question of money instead. But it is worth unfolding in further depth how money and monetary policies appear when looked at from this perspective of the economic. A different language of understanding the politics of money comes to the fore.

According to Keynes, this focus on money is warranted by the fact that money is peculiar among other economic temporalities. It is "ruling the roost," as Keynes puts it, which means that it produces a measure and a temporality that governs the rest, simply by being the "greatest of the own-rates of interest (as we may call them)."[76] Keynes poses himself the task to understand and to analyze this peculiarity of the money rate of interest.[77] Whereas classical liberalism assumes that the monetary interest is a variable determined by equilibrating market forces, Keynes aims to show that this variable is determined by forces that do not belong to any equilibrating market mechanism.[78] The Keynesian theory detects two main determinants of the monetary measure of time. One determinant is to be found in the fears of economic man and his fetish of liquidity, which

I discuss in the previous chapter. The second resides in the conventions of monetary policy, notably the gold standard.

From the vantage point of the genealogy of the economic, it is instructive to look at how Keynes's critique of the gold standard is articulated. Following Keynes's critique renders visible how the different understanding of the economic shifts the problematization of gold away from a question of representation to a discussion of economic measures, demonstrating them to be "logically indeterminate" and impure, thus fragmenting the understanding of a self-bound economic system.[79] Hence, the following sections recall the argument in favor of the gold standard in order to demonstrate subsequently what it means to approach this issue from the vantage point of the economic understood in terms of material temporality and the conventions of measurement.

Gold had provided "the framework for domestic and international monetary relations" for many decades during the nineteenth century. Currencies "were convertible into gold on demand and linked internationally at fixed rates of exchange."[80] It is an interesting detail in the history of economic thought that not only the representatives of classical liberalism assumed that gold is the best choice of a monetary standard—Marx also subscribed to this axiom to a considerable extent.[81] The real side of economy was defined either by the calculations of utility or by the amounts of abstract labor. Both are juxtaposed to money, understood as a layer upon this reality. Karl Polanyi has recorded the curious unanimity of the positions in respect to gold across politically and philosophically diverse schools of thought:

> Belief in the gold standard was the faith of the age. With some it was a naïve, with some a critical, with others a satanistic creed implying acceptance in the flesh and rejection in the spirit. Yet the belief itself was the same, namely, that bank notes have value because they represent gold. Whether the gold itself has value for the reason that it embodies labor, as the socialists held, or for the reason that it is useful and scarce, as the orthodox doctrine ran, made for once no difference. The war between heaven and hell ignored the money issue, leaving capitalists and socialists miraculously united. Where Ricardo and Marx were at one, the nineteenth century knew not doubt. Bismarck and Lassalle, John Stuart Mill and Henry George, Philip Snowden and Calvin Coolidge, Mises and Trotzky equally accepted the faith.[82]

Viewed from an account of money in terms of exchange within a representational logic, gold appeared as the most natural choice: it promised to tie the workings of money to the workings of the real economy in the most transparent way. Instead of handing the management of money to the "rule of man," the gold standard was cherished as the neutral "rule of law."[83] Whenever any country had an imbalance in its payments, the relative position of its own currency toward gold would weaken: its gold reserves would deplete in order to balance its international bills. Reversing this tide would require a country to take measures that would restore the position of its currency and correct the imbalances of its trade. Prices had to fall so that exports would be comparatively cheaper for other countries and imports would become dearer. The interest rate for money had to rise so that the value of currency would rise. The gold standard effected these adjustments or led to them. For example, the very commitment to gold would motivate the inflow of foreign currencies on the expectation that soon this currency would again become more valuable. Budget discipline, a flexible interest rate, and free flows of capital are corollaries of the gold standard. Hence, within the model, a quasi "automatic" adjustment would emerge.[84]

Within a discourse that was governed by a representational account of money as a neutral medium of exchange, this self-equilibrating mechanism of the gold standard appeared both as the most theoretically consistent and elegant resolution to the complexities of international trade and the conundrums of money. Adherence to the gold standard could claim both a foundation in an objective standard and the adherence to a universal rule. It was not only theoretically guaranteeing "honest money" but also promising the actual rule of "honest money" through its regulative powers.

But this assessment of the elegant and theoretically consistent workings of the gold standard changes if gold is considered from a vantage point of the economic in terms of temporality and measurement. Within this perspective, the gold standard assumes a new quality. It is not simply a regulative medium that ensures money's representational qualities; insofar as it governs the monetary interest rate, it is also inevitably a measure of economic temporality. According to Keynes, the key to a prospering economy is the transformation of the accumulated resources into novel investments. But investments that are planned always have to match or, rather, exceed the monetary interest rate; otherwise they will fail to materialize. The gold standard will most likely hamper this transformation because it induces a measure of economic returns that is comparatively high and inconsiderate of the domestic situation.[85] Instead of being the most "natural," "automatic," or elegant way of regulating money, the gold standard comes into view as a measure of the economic that is disruptive and prone to produce unemployment and unnecessary restrictions on the used resources. "For example, in a country linked to an international gold standard . . . a domestic rate of interest dragged up to parity with the highest rate . . . may be much higher than is consistent with domestic employment."[86]

To put it with the metaphors used before, the "clocks" and measures of temporalities and returns are governed by a monetary measure of return much tighter and dearer than they can deliver. Gold is a measure of economic temporality that imposes too much economy—in the old sense of the restrictions of resources—on economy, understood now as a field of interconnecting and continuing services, goods, productions, and consumptions—even more so since the more plentiful a material provision already is, the less return is to be expected on a further piece of the same.[87] This is why "two railways from London to York" are not as good as only one: its scarcity value would diminish, and, hence, the returns to be fetched would be lower. But in material terms, it might be valuable to have two railways instead of one.[88] One might say that the gold standard tends to impose a particular and ultimate conventional standard for the "economic" that undermines the useful release of resources.

In this perspective, the gold standard becomes visible as a convention of economic objectivity instead of being "rooted in objective grounds much stronger than convention," as Keynes puts it.[89] Instead of emanating from the necessities and coherence of the system itself, the gold standard produces an interest rate understood to be unnecessarily high and disruptive.[90] If one mistakes conventions for objectivity, any other interest rate that is not linked to the gold standard has the disadvantage of being "viewed with a justifiable lack of confidence."[91] But from the temporal perspective, it is rather the old financial orthodoxy that should inculcate doubt because it is due to "forces of old custom and general ignorance" or due to "golden fetters of the Bank of England."[92] In this perspective, the gold standard has turned from being the most elegant regulatory mechanism that ensures that the economic system is well balanced and in accordance with reality, into an "emblem and idol."[93] Metaphors of religion and belief, but also of political provenience, proliferate in these accounts of the gold standard. A monetary institution that has been considered in terms of an economic mechanism of supply and demand is rearticulated as a contingent and conventional measure of economic temporality governed by religious reverence and morality.

The Fate of the Economic

The previous chapter already recorded that the economic subject and the gold standard have been objects of a cultural critique in Keynes's writings. Only now one can properly appreciate how and why such cultural critique could affect the question of economy in fundamental ways. This chapter has laid bare the conditions of possibility opening up the question of economy to a cultural critique. By recasting money as a time machine, among other things, the economic becomes visible as a contingent patterning of material temporalities—open to such cultural and political determinations without being "merely" cultural or political. On this basis, it is possible to understand how economy intersects with culture as, for example, in the conventions of the gold standard; one can now comprehend to full extent how the domain of economic reason could possibly become as indeterminate and contingent as the domain of political reason.

The age of the gold standard waned long ago, and the current monetary regime, with its flexible exchange rates and busy capital markets, seems to suffer from quite different problems than this critique of gold targets. But this account of the gold standard as a particular convention, which constitutes economic temporality, demonstrates how the novel account of the economic gives rise to a "rethinking" of economic institutions that is still fertile today: the making of economic futurity in novel financial instruments, the intermingling of political and economic obligations in the debt crisis, and the question of economic measure are themes that resonate with the current discussions on the role of rating agencies, the temporalities and measures imposed by financial markets, and the "total social fact" of debt. But today's debates often give the impression that there is only something technical and functional involved that is too complex to negotiate. It capitalizes on the assumption that economy is a pure matter of "so-called hard facts," as Keynes has put it.[94] Approaching these debates from the side of the malleable economic allows us to ask instead how and in which way the economy of material temporalities is molded and modulated by politics and culture.

Discursive formations exceed the specific theoretical positions of an author. They are fields that determine what can become "visible and articulable" as Gilles Deleuze once put it.[95] They provide the grounds for new questions and different answers that are not exhausted by a particular theoretical position. Being historically bound and limited themselves, they are also used in limited ways. Keynesian theory is an exemplary case for such limited articulation of a discursive horizon. While Keynesian thought explicates how the monetary institutions and monetary measures, like the interest rate, are modes of fashioning economic temporality, it never ventured to explore the conventions of economy outside of money. To Keynes, the "ordinary forces of the market" accounted for the rest, accepting, in his own words, "a large part of the established body of economic doctrine."[96] But as the history of measurement and disciplinary technologies of power amply demonstrate, the conventions of economic temporality are not only described in monetary terms. The history of Taylorism is only one example, albeit a fitting one from the same period, showing how economic measure of corporeal temporalities is fashioned. But the exploration and analysis of the formatting of the economic is not confined to relations of work—it is a perspective that allows connecting the analysis of materialized, organized, measured, intersecting, and hierarchized temporalities of finance, bodies, plants, soils, or climate. The economic as articulated here should thus by no means be confounded with the economic theory of Keynes. Rather, the economic exceeds the author's intentions—it forms the very condition of possibility for his argumentation. It made it possible to open economic issues to questions of conventions and contingency, but it does not preempt how this openness is employed.

CHAPTER 6

The Archipolitics of Macroeconomics

At the beginning of the twentieth century, the national economy emerged as a novel object of "representing and intervening."[1] While the economy had been conceptualized before as a distinct sphere of social relations, the new macroeconomic models were markedly different. They framed the economy as a totality of interdependent *and* manageable statistical variables that were amenable to national administrative steering in a new way. The rate of unemployment, output, and growth became "an object of politics that could be scientifically predicted and manipulated by the politically neutral techniques of the state's economic engineers."[2] There emerged a new separation between the economy and politics that juxtaposed a clearly bounded and controllable economic system to managerial politics. Liberalism turned into what has been called "embedded liberalism." It became tied to a conception of a macroeconomic entity that belonged to the territorial unit of the nation-state.

The macroeconomics that articulates the national economy as a manageable entity has been baptized "hydraulic Keynesianism" because it suggests an analogy between governing the national economy and engineering a system of flows. The actual construction of a three-dimensional hydraulic model of the economy that was sloshing around differently colored liquids conveys the spirit of this time.[3] Keynesian economics was not the sole element that brought this hydraulic conception of the national economy about, but it played a decisive role for its articulation.[4] Keynesian economic thought was translated, clarified, and rendered persuasive in and through such mathematical and mechanical models—both with and without the approval of Keynes as an author.[5] The molding of Keynesianism into a "neoclassical synthesis" after the war completed this translation of "the Keynesian Revolution" into postwar economic and political orthodoxy. The "mathematical and econometric conversion of Keynesianism created an unbeatable coalition" that determined macroeconomic thought in lasting ways.[6] *Time* magazine commented in 1965, "we are all Keynesians now," pointing out that even his severest detractors use his macroeconomic terms and framework.[7] In terms of policy, Keynesianism became a "magical tool-kit, which would not only patch up the engine but, with fine tuning, keep it running at maximum horse-power."[8]

Usually, the emergence of the managed national economy and its accompanying welfare programs are regarded as the most politicized model of the economy in liberalism. It is seen as having granted the administrative apparatus of the state the highest leverage of influence and political choice. In this perspective, the "fundamental shift in the scale, scope, and ambitions of government in relation to the economy" is understood as having led to a political model of economy.[9] But as I argue in this chapter, this account omits the fact that the national economy was not just a politicized model of the economy. It was at the same time and rather paradoxically an "antipolitical economy" as well.[10] It narrowed the ways, in which the economy could become an object of negotiation; it transformed politics into a version of economic management. The macroeconomic model allowed transforming "political controversies into technical objectives that might be pursued by relatively de-dramatized means within the space called 'the economy.'"[11] Keynesian macroeconomics invested as much in purifying the fuzzy bounds of the economic and narrowing politics as it did in "politicizing" economic matters.

This chapter demonstrates that the emergence of macroeconomic management should be understood in terms of a simultaneous displacement of the economic and the political. What is meant by this? As the previous chapter has elucidated, a critical space for rethinking the economic had opened up. The economic problem did not appear any longer as being about individual choices in a context of scarcity. Instead, it was framed in terms of an "ontology" of intersecting planes of material temporalities, conventions of measurement, and precarious acts of judgment. This understanding of the economic had a permeable and uncertain boundary toward political reason and could potentially give rise to multiple types of politico-economic order. As shown, the critical space of the economic belonged to a political scene of contestation in which neither the system of facts nor the types of politics appropriate for it had been agreed upon. The transformation of this open plane of the economic and the political into a "hydraulic" model of the economy that could be governed by neutral expertise appears in this perspective not as an act of politicization but as an act of closing off the "essential ambiguities" of the economic.[12] It displaces the "symmetrical space" in which the economic becomes visible as malleable "ontology" of liberal economy open to political artifice.

In the following, I explore the "archipolitics" that constitutes the macroeconomics of the national economy. By "archipolitics" I mean—following Rancière—the paradoxical operation of "achieving politics by doing away with it."[13] As I show, the transposition of the economic to "the economy" rests on two "archipolitical" acts. First, Keynesian macroeconomics resorts to the notion of the population as a figure of economic, cultural, and political collectivity for articulating the bounds of "the economy."[14] This part of the argument draws attention to the continuing importance of the notion of population for defining liberal economy.[15] Second, Keynesian macroeconomics defines politics as an "act of giving measure" and delegates the authority to define this measure to an economic expert. As I show in detail, this act of "giving measure" is specifically linked to the tools of monetary policies in the hand of the economic expert. By granting the authority of "giving measure" to such experts and by assuming that such unified measure can be found, Keynesianism ends up with a narrow and problematic version of politics.

The story about the paradoxical politics of Keynesianism told in this chapter understands itself as an important supplement to the current scholarly research on the governmental and technical "invention" of the national economy. In the last decade, a range of interdisciplinary works have started to examine the politico-epistemological genealogy of the national economy.[16] It has been shown that macroeconomics constitutively depends on the innovations in the statistical representation of the economy. The "accounting effect of extraction and abstraction [helps] to separate the economic from what is political, social, and natural, among other facts."[17] The statistical rendering of the macroeconomy is understood in terms of the "persistently close ties" between "economic measurement" and "administration and reform."[18] The emphasis in these debates is on the technical aspects of calculating "the economy," on rendering it visible and manageable.

The current argument does not so much question the importance of such emphasis on the technical and mundane aspect of rendering an economy governable. Rather, I suggest that one needs to contextualize this approach with an understanding of the constitution of the horizon in which the technologies of "governing the economy" appear as viable. It is not sufficient to recount the types of political rationalities and techniques that are invented for making an economy governable. It is also important to account for delimitation and concretization of the horizon, to which these technologies belong. Accordingly, this chapter does both: it discusses the "magical tool-kit" of Keynesian macroeconomics as a liberal technology of governing the economy through money and it explains the narrowing of the political-economic horizon within which these technologies are applied.

The reminder of this chapter starts with a short historical discussion of the multiple sites of emergence of the "national economy," with a specific emphasis on the role of the two world wars for the framing of "the economy" as a national entity. This section elucidates that even though the organization of national resources in view of a war effort played an important role for the emergence of the "national economy" in this period, it cannot wholly account for the specific type of Keynesian macroeconomics that became prevalent after 1945. This section functions as a historical and contextual backdrop for opening up the question that is discussed in this chapter: What are the "archipolitical" acts that turn the economic into a new macroeconomics? How does governmentalization of the question of money that is typical of Keynesianism belong to this "archipolitical" framing?

Multiple Emergences of the National Economy

In the decades after the Second World War, the macroeconomic conceptions of the national economy achieved a widespread naturalization. "The idea that society was spatially bounded within particular state structures assumed a self-evident status in late-nineteenth-century sociological and philosophical paradigms as well as in emergent nationalist discourse."[19]

The project of "national developmentalism" was increasingly taken for granted as a political and economic framework for conceiving postwar national and international politics. The emergence of the national economy was part and parcel of the "re-imagination of the nation-state" against the disintegration of Empire and the experience of social and political crisis at the beginning of the twentieth century.[20] Keynesianism thus belonged to the "new languages for collective experience designed to supersede the forms and languages of the laissez-faire 1920s."[21] The welfare arrangements of Western states and the development discourse about the Third World as well as the struggles for political and economic independence of postcolonial states took recourse to the model of a national economic system.[22]

Especially the colonial context has been an important source for the proliferation of a nationalized account of "the economy." Both the British colonial administration of India and Egypt and the struggles against it were crucial nodes in the making of a national economy.[23] While the context of colonialism and "recuperative nationalism" will be part of the story told here, the management of the war economy in Britain and the United States will not. Even though the management of resources for the sake of the war effort played a significant role in the genealogy of the "national economy" in general, the specific Keynesian articulation of it did not follow the model of a nation at war.[24] Some clarifications are therefore helpful in order to understand both the importance of the question of "how to pay for the war" and the negligible role the war plays for understanding Keynesianism as a "new language for collective experience."[25]

At the beginning of the twentieth century, managerialism and military planning were instrumental for conceptualizing a manageable economy. The First World War had spurred the overall professionalization of social scientific expertise in political and economic planning, which functioned as important ingredient to the conception of a managed economy.[26] At that time, the accumulation of statistical knowledge seemed to promise that unemployment and the instability of the business cycle could be alleviated simply by knowing the exact position one occupied within the course of a business cycle. Daniel Breslau summarizes this understanding, which was prominently held by Wesley Mitchell, the founder and first director of the National Bureau of Economic Research: "If entrepreneurs, managers, and bankers . . . were including the entire picture of the business economy in their calculation, and not simply the price signals they were getting from suppliers, customers, and competitors, they would avoid overinvestment and overextension of credit that breeds crisis." He cites Mitchell with the statement: "If we could foresee the business cycle, there would be none."[27] But this production of statistical economic knowledge gained new purpose and urgency during the next war, which showed how modern economic analysis is useful in the realization of national objectives.

The Second World War functioned as "proverbial hothouse" for the "application of the new macroeconomic accounting methods to the needs of the state. Indeed, it is hard to imagine, in the absence of the forced stimulant of militarization, a more rapid elaboration of what is, to this day, the national accounts system."[28] The "problems of financing the war" and the efforts of "establishing a structure of interlocking national accounts" coincided.[29] Faced with the problem of minimizing the use of resources and maximizing outputs, the state appeared as an economic body that reckons its costs and incomes like a single firm.[30] Theoretical and accounting innovations merged in the undertaking of "how to pay for the war" in the case of Britain.[31] Keynes, then at the Treasury, collaborated in devising the interlocking accounts of the national economy that were modeled as "manual constructs of [his] theory":[32] "While others, most notably the eminent British economist John R. Hicks, would devise the specific accounting identities ultimately and universally used in national product estimates, Keynes . . . supplied the conceptual map necessary to the completion of their task."[33]

But while the war and its national accounts suggested conceiving of "the nation as an economic unit," one should not be too rash in taking these elements as key for understanding the framing of the kind of manageable economic system that Keynesianism is about. On the contrary, the managerial governing of the war economy suggested a conceptualization of a national economic unit that was rather different from the Keynesian model.[34] Roosevelt's "war on depression" and the New Deal did not speak the same language as the "magical tool-kit" of Keynesianism. Whereas the former conceived the common national effort against the depression in terms of administering and mobilizing the resources of an organizational unit, the latter eschews such kind of intervention: "The Keynesian system, in its exclusive reliance on aggregated variables and its apparent deference to the allocational functions of the price mechanism, separated the idea of economic management in the public interest from the detailed specification of prices and outputs that had always been associated with it."[35] Keynesianism explicitly denied the viability of understanding the national economy as a household writ large, whereas Franklin Roosevelt's New Deal remained in essence bound by a particular household conception of economy more closely tied to a "nation at war." Roosevelt and Keynes therefore remained skeptical toward each other's policies even though they shared a belief in managerial expertise and national efficiency. Richard Adelstein concludes that "Roosevelt's macroeconomics of war" and "Keynes's macroeconomics of peace" are, hence, not identical.[36]

In view of the current argument, one can thus maintain that the context of a "nation at war" did not predetermine the kind of conceptualization of a manageable economic unity that Keynesianism presented. A story therefore remains to be told about the "archipolitics" at work in the emergence of macroeconomics. As I argue in the following, Keynesian macroeconomics was part of a wider intellectual current during the 1930s and 1940s that sought to reimagine the foundations of a cultural body politic that would "recover a usable core of English national culture from the derelict body of British imperialism."[37] To Keynes, the experience of the First World War held the lesson of employing caution with respect to political frontiers created "between greedy, jealous, immature and economically incomplete, nationalist states."[38] Hence, the Keynesian national economy was imagined as being part of a cooperation in larger economic units and multilateral exchanges.[39] With exception of a short flirtation with "national self-sufficiency" in 1933, the vision of national development nested within international relations of trade determined the understanding of Keynesian economic government, which assumed supposedly homogenous "cultural and political units" as the basic building blocks for such international order:[40] "One view of the post-war world which I find sympathetic and attractive and fruitful of good consequences is that we should encourage small political and cultural units. . . . It would be a fine thing to have thirty or forty capital cities in Europe, each the centre of a self-governing country entirely free from national minorities (who would be dealt with by migrations where necessary) . . . each with their own pride and glory and their own characteristics and excellent gifts."[41]

As I want to show in the following, this envisioning of cultural and political units and the "invention" of macroeconomics were related. In order to understand this relation one has to revisit a perennial theme of liberal political and economic thought: the question of population.

Population, Biopolitics, and the Economy

A manuscript of Keynes titled "Prolegomena to a New Socialism" lists the "chief preoccupations of the State." The first point on this list is "Population, Eugenics," followed by "Money" and then by issues of savings, investments, utilities, industrial dispute, wages, insurance, natural resources, defense and peace.[42] He asserted that "there is no more important object of deliberate state policy than to secure a balanced budget of population."[43] "Size and quality" must become "in future the subject of deliberate state policy and centralized state control."[44] Besides the need to determine the size of the population, Keynes projected that the time will arrive "when the community as a whole must pay attention to the innate quality as well as to the mere numbers of its future members."[45] "I believe that for the future the problem of population will merge in the much greater problem of Heredity and Eugenics."[46] In a speech to the Eugenic Society, Keynes praised Francis Galton "as founder of the most important, significant and, I would add, genuine branch of sociology, which exists, namely eugenics."[47] Not only politics but also economics were defined in important respects in reference to population. A good economist, he suggested in 1923, "remains a sound Malthusian."[48] In 1937 he reaffirmed Malthus as an important reference point for economic thought. The fact that Keynes "from the earliest years of his academic life . . . repeatedly discussed population issues . . . throughout his career" suggests that population remains, as it was to Malthus, a key for understanding the economy and its relation to politics.[49]

But the above-mentioned quotes do not only signal continuity in how population remained a pivotal object of liberal political reason, intimately tying political and economic questions. For understanding the importance of population for the invention of macroeconomics at that time, it is crucial to understand the changed historical context in which the question of population became a hotly debated issue. In general, one can say that population functioned in the first decades of the twentieth century as an important "boundary concept," transgressing and uniting several

distinct fields of debate.[50] The question of population was simultaneously part of the articulation of national unity, the debate about imperial
demise, internationalism, geopolitics, degeneration, immigration, reproduction, gender relations, statistics, and social reform.[51] During the interwar
years, numerous conferences, organizations, and committees on population
appeared that generated transdisciplinary arenas.[52] The first International
Conference on World Population in Geneva in 1927 (which Keynes
attended), the annual conferences on Malthusianism since 1900, the
founding of a committee to study "demographic problems in their international aspects" at the Economic Section of the *League of Nations* in
1939—these were only the most prominent instances of new international
and national arenas of an intensifying debate.[53]

It is important to notice that the question of population not only targeted issues of reproduction, gender, and economy but also had been
equally prominent in the renegotiation of national space, expansion, and
geopolitics. The economist Alfred Marshall made this geopolitical and
national frame of population visible in exemplary ways when he
announced, "There can be no doubt that this extension of the English
race has been a benefit to the world," fearing that it would "harm the
more intelligent race if Englishmen multiply less rapidly than the Chinese."[54] Prescott F. Hall, veteran leader of the U.S. Immigration Restriction League, argued that "superior races, more self-limiting than the
other, with the benefits of more space and nourishment will tend to still
higher levels."[55] The innovator of statistics, Karl Pearson, feared that "we
are ceasing as a nation to breed intelligence."[56] These statements indicate
how much population simultaneously became tied to issues of degeneration and "quality," to questions of reproduction and statehood, to science
and politics. Keynes was thus one among many when he stated in his early
lecture on population in 1914—a lecture that has curiously not been
included in the edition of his collected writings:[57] "The advantage of a fall
in the birthrate in any country is shared by the whole world, while there
maybe a racial or military disadvantage to the country where it occurs.
What is the use for weakening internationally the stock which we think is
the best[?]"[58] And he concludes:

> While large parts of the world fit for a white population were waiting
> to be filled up by European emigration, racial arguments rightly carried
> considerable weight. This temporary state of affairs is rapidly coming to

an end. In the future we can act without our attention chiefly directed towards the economic wellbeing of the population of our own country, with but secondary regard to the numerical position of our race in the world as a whole. . . . Almost any measure seems to me to be justified in order to protect our standard of life from injury at the hands of more prolific races.[59]

Although Keynes also maintained a skeptical distance regarding the assumed "ultimate verities" of "frontiers, races and patriotism," he obviously shared the kind of racial hierarchies and antagonisms inscribed in the discourse on population.[60]

The prominent role granted to eugenics and race in his writings brings up the question of how far Keynes's remarks on population, eugenics, and race are connected to forms of state racism prevalent at the beginning of the twentieth century. The recent debate on biopolitics suggests that the question of population, with its attendant politics of eugenics and racial purity, is inherently tied to the murderous and exclusionary politics at that time, of which Nazism is the most extreme manifestation.[61] But, as the philosopher Roberto Esposito has carefully discussed, the biopolitical paradigm of modernity has many facets. The links between biopolitics and thanatopolitics are "more limited and more complex" than is often suggested.[62] The fact that Keynes declared quality and size of population, including eugenics, as belonging to the priorities of the states puts him into the biopolitical orbit. But this is still different from the forms of thanatopolitics that characterizes the extreme forms of state-racisms at the beginning of the twentieth century.[63] Hence, it is important to delineate carefully how population, economy, and politics are articulated in this national body economic.

To understand the biopolitical role of population for articulating the national economy, one has to recognize that the relation between economy and population underwent a profound change in Keynesian macroeconomics compared to how these issues were related according to Malthus and the liberal tradition of economics in the nineteenth century that was to follow. First clues on how the relationship between economy and population changed with the birth of macroeconomics can be gathered from the radical shift in Keynes's economic and political writings about economy and population before and after he had "worked himself out of a tunnel of economic orthodoxy."[64] Previously, Keynes had cherished Malthus for his "simple, clear, and irrefutable" thesis on population.[65] "That men are not better off than they are, is because there are too many of them, because their quality is inferior, because they and the earth together do not produce more and also because they have destroyed in war and still waste in preparation for it, too much of the fruits of their toil."[66]

In contradistinction, the *General Theory* held that "the world after several millennia of steady individual saving, is so poor as it is in accumulated capital-assets, is to be explained, in my opinion, neither by the improvident propensities of mankind, nor even by the destruction of war, but by the high liquidity-premiums formerly attached to the ownership of land and now attaching to money."[67]

This quote signals that the culprit had changed. It was no longer an overabundant population that ruined the prospects of material well-being. Rather, it was the convention of putting an exorbitant price—the liquidity premium—on land or money. Population seemed to have disappeared as a sole key for understanding economy.[68] The reason to commemorate Malthus as an important economist changed accordingly—Keynes complained in 1935 that "Malthus's name has been immortalized by his *Principle of Population*, and the brilliant intuitions of his more far reaching *Principle of Effect Demand* have been forgotten."[69] Not the fear of redundant bodies but the recognition of the possibility of redundant capital became Malthus's treasure, and Malthus became a member of "a long line of heretics" who survived only as isolated groups.[70] "The great puzzle of effective demand with which Malthus had wrestled vanished from economic literature. . . . It could only live on furtively, below the surface, in the underworlds of Karl Marx, Silvio Gesell or Major [C. H.] Douglas."[71]

The crucial question, then, is how exactly does the question of population retain its importance for defining liberal economy while changing its role for doing so? For tracing this novel relationship, it is helpful to recall how Malthus had tied the figure of population and the notion of economy. Against this background it becomes possible to pinpoint how the relation between population and economy changed with Keynes.

As the first part of the book has shown, for Malthus the "savage life" of the population and its impending catastrophe had functioned as "quasi-ontology" for defining what economy is about. The relentlessness of this "savage life" regarding the consummation of food and the reproduction of itself was only to be matched by an "eternal pressure" of scarcity that had a cultural-political task to fulfill: to instill futurity and civilization by teaching postponement and deferral. As a vehicle for producing futurity, scarcity was to mediate between the resources of today and tomorrow. In this discourse, scarcity was needed as a permanent remainder and eternal governor for producing orderly subjects, civilization, cohesion, and wealth at once. Malthus announced consequently: "A strict inquiry into the principle of population obliges us to conclude *that we shall never be able to throw down the ladder,* by which we have risen to this eminence" (emphasis added).[72] Since "savage life" embodied an eternal threat of beastly immediacy, the economy of scarcity needed to be eternal as well, up to the point at which the resources of the earth are fully developed to their limit. At that point, man would face its condition of finitude, and history would "quiver for an instant upon its axis, and immobilize itself forever," as Foucault has put it in *The Order of Things*: Liberal economics formulates an "uninterrupted history of scarcity" until history itself comes to a standstill.[73]

Unlike Malthus, Keynes assumed that the English population had already achieved a higher degree of civilization as a whole. It could be controlled by the means of education and the distribution of contraceptive devices.[74] As the chairman of the Malthusian League, Keynes stated: "In my opinion that battle is now practically won—at least in this country. . . . Man has won the right to use the powerful weapon of the preventive check [contraception]. . . . We are now faced with a greater problem which it will take centuries to solve. . . . I believe that for the future the problem of population will merge in the much greater problem of Heredity and Eugenics. . . . Mankind . . . has taken into his own hands out of the hands of Nature the task and the duty of molding [body and mind] to a pattern."[75]

It is exactly this "right" to use a measure other than scarcity that signaled the privileges of "civilized" life. Since the threat of savage reproduction receded, the tenet of scarcity could be dethroned as an internal governor. Population changed its status as an economic and political object—it was no longer circumscribed by the ontology of "savage life" but became a political-cultural community that proceeded on the path of material civilization by means other than purely economic ones. The more civilized and wealthy this community was, the "more gifted and more spending" it could be. Its economic measure lay between restriction and waste.

> Pyramid-building, earthquakes, even wars may serve to increase
> wealth, if the education of our statesmen on the principles of the

classical economics stands in the way of anything better. It is curious how common sense, wriggling for an escape from absurd conclusions, has been part to reach a preference of *wholly* "wasteful" forms of loan expenditure rather than for *partly* wasteful form, which because they are not wholly wasteful, tend to be judged on strict "business" principles. . . . It would, indeed be more sensible to build houses and the like; but if there are political and practical difficulties in the way of this, the above would be better than nothing.[76]

The economy could be harmed by too much and too little consumption, too much or too little immediacy—somewhere in between immediacy and deferral, dissipation or accumulation, enjoyment and work, abundance and scarcity lies what qualifies as "economically sound" and conducive to material civilization. In a speech given to the Society for Socialist Enquiry in 1931, Keynes defines socialism as "obtaining political power with a view to doing what is economically sound in order that the community may become rich enough to afford what is economically unsound."[77] Hence, economy became a question of degree and historical specificity—sometimes more postponement, at other times more immediate consumption is needed. Far from championing purely consumerist policies, Keynes sought to balance the increase of capital stock and the dispersion funds through more equal distribution.[78]

It is decisive that Keynes tied this understanding of the variable and malleable measure of economy to a figure of a population as a political-cultural community that had various degrees of civilization and proceeded on a temporal axis of development. Outside the orbit of the "developed" or even already "degenerating" civilization, the presumed "backwardness" and uninhibited forms of reproduction of the "underdeveloped world" required different economic measures. In 1914 Keynes argued, "If we look to the East, I believe that the Malthusian doctrine has never ceased to be applicable there to its fullest extent." The reduction of numbers through what Keynes called the "beneficent visitation" of the plague, which reduced the population of India by 10 percent, is thus recorded as a means of economic development. Hence, he concludes that

cosmopolitan humanitarianism must be indulged in but very moderately if evil consequences are to be avoided. Almost any measure seems to me to be justified in order to protect our standard of life from injury at the hands of more prolific races. Some definite parceling out of the world may well become necessary. . . . Countries . . . are entirely justified in protecting themselves from the fecundicity of the East by very vigorous immigration laws and other restrictive measures. I can imagine a time when it may be the right policy even to regulate the international trade in food supplies, though these are economic reasons, which I cannot go into now.[79]

The image of "rapidly multiplying millions of inhabitants" continued to underlie the postwar accounts of the national economy of less-developed countries.[80] Development economics, largely influenced by the new orthodoxy of Keynesianism, focused on topics such as the relationship between population, resources, and output, and between cultural factors and birth control. The definition of three-quarters of the world as underdeveloped and as being enthralled in the combined catastrophes of savage population growth and insufficient capital furnished the precept for development policies that included illiberal measures of population control abroad and promised to fix "underdevelopment" by improving the ratios of saving and capital.[81]

In contrast, the most-developed populations assume the gestalt of a cultural-political community of higher civilization. It was a political and economic task to actualize the experience of its cohesion and its further development by governing the quality of the population as well as by financing public works and supporting public arts. In a piece called *Art and the State* Keynes suggests that "architecture is the most public of the arts, the least private in its manifestations and the best suited to give form and body to civic pride and the sense of social unit."[82]

Even more important than the permanent monuments of dignity and beauty in which each generation should express its spirit to stand for it in the procession of time, are the ephemeral ceremonies, shows and entertainments in which the common man can take his delight and recreation after his work is done, and which can make him feel, as nothing else can, that he is one with, and part of a community, finer, more gifted, more spending, more care-free than he can be by himself.[83]

The unity of this community is as much cultural as it is political, "each with their own pride and glory and their own characteristics and excellent gifts."[84] Economic measure, national unity, and cultural homogeneity coalesced in this community that perfected the "art of life." Each "cultural and political unit" was on its way to a promised land in which economy eventually ceases to apply: "I draw the conclusion that, assuming no important wars and no important increase in population, the economic problem may be solved . . . within a hundred years. This means that the economic problem is not . . . the permanent problem of the human race."[85] This envisioned end of economy was still to come—there is still a "tunnel of economic necessity" that lies between the present and the future end of economy.[86] The crucial aspect of such eschatology is the space in between the now and the envisioned end. This temporal interval circumscribes and confirms the governmental powers that are necessary until the "end of history" and the "end of economy" is reached.[87]

It is telling that the development toward the end of economy was depicted as the "euthanasia of the rentier." The "rentier" was for Keynes a figure that derives his returns and profits from a monetary realm kept artificially scarce. Being kept scarce, it offered profits that are no longer possible otherwise, given the material abundance that exists. Rents proscribed a measure of economy to the economy that was out of step with its material civilization. The "euthanasia of the rentier" accordingly described "a gradual disappearance of a rate of return on accumulated wealth."[88] It signaled an economy that worked with little returns in a world that is already filled by machines and goods. The metaphor of the "slow death of the rentier" envisioned this development as a constant purification of a historically vital but ultimately obnoxious element of the community. One can see very clearly at this point the consequences of tying a notion of a contingent measure of economy to a particular cultural-political understanding of the population in terms of a community. Tied to an underlying biopolitical frame of population and eugenics, the change of the economic order becomes a "benign death" that gradually frees the community from its "foul" elements.[89]

Given this image of a national economic body that had hosted the "rentier" in its midst until no longer necessary, it is not surprising that the writings of Keynes mobilized the long-standing link between anti-Semitism and the critique of unproductive money.[90] In his biographical sketch of Einstein, written in 1926, Keynes compares:

He is that kind of Jew—the kind which rarely has its head above water, the sweet, tender imps who have not sublimated immortality into compound interest [different from . . .] the other kind of Jews, the ones who are not imps but serving devils, with small horns, pitch forks, and oily tails. It is not agreeable to see civilization so under the ugly thumbs of its impure Jews who have all the money and the power and the brains. I vote rather for the plump hausfraus and thick-fingered Wandering Birds. The result of which is that *Left* and *Right* in German politics do not quite mean what we think they mean. The Right is Nationalist, anti-Semite, anti-Dawes Scheme. The Left is for twisting and turning and lying, and accommodations with International Finance and Red Russians and everything.[91]

This juxtaposition between an image of a destructive, homeless, baseless, and de-territorial Jewish finance and the economic fate of a nationally bounded population demonstrates how the question of population retained its cultural hierarchies and racial distinctions that it had before. At the same time, these racial divisions were no longer entwined with a notion of scarcity that served to civilize "savage life." In the case of Keynesianism, the biopolitics of population and the question of economy intersected differently: as a question of the proper measure of economy for this culturally and politically distinct unit of development. But how is this measure of what is "economically sound" determined? There seems to be much truth to Hayek's remark to Keynes that "it is reassuring to know that we agree so completely on the economics of scarcity, even if we differ on when it applies."[92] In other words, scarcity no longer applies unconditionally. But when and how does it apply? What is the right measure?

The Economic Expert and the *Nomos* of the Economy

Political economy appeared in this context not as purely economic discipline but as part of the art of "statecraft" as far as it was concerned with "the system as a whole."[93] A truly economic problem was, in this perspective, neither an engineering problem nor a business problem but blended with the "art of statesmanship," as Keynes suggested.[94] This "art" could not be displaced with an economics of scarcity, of which Keynes had declared it is "positively wicked for the state to spend a halfpenny on

non-economic purposes . . . so low have we fallen today in our conception of the duty and purpose, the honour and glory of the state."[95] Instead,
the question of what is "affordable" and what is "economic" had to be
answered in respect to the national population and its stage of civilization.
The role of "sound economy" for this community consisted of finding the
right and proper measure: politics turned into an act of "giving measure."
This coinage is adapted from the etymology of the word economy. As
Jacques Derrida has unfolded, the notion of economy comprises the meaning of "law (*nomos*) and of home (*oikos*, home, property, family, the hearth,
the fire indoors)." In this context, nomos "does not only signify the law in
general, but also the law of distribution (*nemein*), the law of sharing or
partition [*partage*] the law as partition (*moira*), the given or assigned part,
participation."[96] The notion of *nomos* refers to an inextricable link between
a normative and material act that seeks to "enclose, contain, take care of
and preserve."[97] One might say, then, that in Keynesian macroeconomics
the *nomos* of the *oikos* was not given by the equilibrium of market forces
per se but included a political-economic act of "giving measure."

The economist assumed in this discourse a paramount role. It was the
subject position that united the political virtues necessary for the "art of
statecraft" and the economic expertise to exercise this art through the
means of economy: "The economist's essential gifts were to be a dealer
in the general and the particular, the temporal and the eternal at the
same time."[98] This weaving together of the perennial oppositions of political thought claimed to solve the conundrums of political order in the
domain of a managed economy. Managing this collective body was linked
to a claim of neutrality of the republican state.[99] The horizon of economic
management delineated a domain of scientific objectivity that circum-
navigates the domain of politics as a realm of democratic contention: "I
believe that in the future, more than ever, questions about the economic
framework of society will be far and away the most important of political
issues. I believe that the right solution will involve intellectual and scientific elements which must be above the heads of the vast mass of more or
less illiterate voters."[100]

Lateralizing the "art of statecraft" into this domain, which is modeled
upon a biopolitical notion of community, thus turned the question of the
economic and the political into the parable of pastoral care:[101] "If we have
the welfare of the giraffes at heart, we must not overlook the sufferings of

the shorter necks who are starved out, or the sweet leaves which fall to the ground and are trampled underfoot in the struggle, or the overfeeding of the long-necked ones, or the evil look of anxiety or struggling greediness which overcasts the mild faces of the herd."[102]

Hence, the governing of economy is framed as an "auxiliary arts of politics" along the lines of Plato's *Statesman* and the *Republic*. The political dreamer "of the school of Plato," as Keynes asserted, required the economist "to give a platform from which his imagination can leap."[103] The economist provided the material foundations for reaching what he termed the "ideal social republic of the future."[104] It does not seem accidental that the name of Plato is referenced to in Keynes writings.[105] Plato's ideal vision of a republic entailed a conception of the socio-material division of labor that accorded to each the proper place and function. Plato's republic is in this sense "a masterpiece of economy," as the philosopher Jacques Rancière puts it.[106] It seems as if Keynes hoped to develop a new "masterpiece of economy" befitting liberal modernity.

The economist had a curious role for establishing this "masterpiece of economy." This role encapsulated the whole gamut of contingency that politico-economic judgment contained but hid it at the same time. The expert knowledge that the economist could claim was supposed to be merely technical and scientific; at the same time, this knowledge was described as uncertain, full of judgment and pragmatism. On the one hand, the economist was portrayed as an electrician or a dentist. A "sounder economic theory, which is as obviously applicable to our problems as electrical theory is to the practical problems of the electrician, will make a vaster difference to our outlook than Shaw and Stalin yet foresee."[107] In this account, both Stalin and Shaw erred in assuming that the old accounts of the economic system hold true and that the old lines of conflict are accurately drawn.[108] According to Keynes, a new expertise was needed that could claim scientific rigor on its side: "Our pressing task is the elaboration of a new standard system which will justify economists in taking their seat beside other scientists."[109] The economic problem, he maintained, "should be a matter for specialists," like dentistry: "If economists could manage to get themselves thought of as humble, competent people, on a level with dentists that would be splendid."[110] These metaphors fit the understanding of "hydraulic Keynesianism" and implied a mechanical application of codified knowledge.

But, on the other hand, the kind of objectivity that economic knowledge could claim was not consistently modeled as a "mechanical objectivity."[111] One can detect a quite different ideal of objectivity in these writings as well—one that is much more inclusive of "trained judgment" and lacks the certainty that the economist as an electrician hopes to claim:[112] Economics should not be misunderstood, Keynes warned, as a "way of applying our formal principles of thought" and "blindly manipulating" a given set of variables. "The object of our analysis is, not to provide a machine, or method or blind manipulation, which will furnish an infallible answer, but to provide ourselves with an organised and orderly method of thinking out particular problems."[113] The classification of variables and determinants was taken to be "quite arbitrary from any absolute standpoint"; variables needed be attuned to the questions and complexities at hand.[114] Keynes describes "economics as a science of thinking in terms of models linked to the art of choosing models which are relevant to the contemporary world. It is compelled to be this, because, unlike the typical natural science, the material to which it is applied is, in too many respects, not homogeneous through time."[115] Hence, an epistemological indeterminacy of economic knowledge appeared in these statements that matched the indeterminacy of its scientific object, which differentiates from the physicist's study of gravity: "It is as though the fall of the apple to the ground depended on the apple's motives, on whether it is worthwhile falling to the ground, and whether the ground wanted the apple to fall, on the mistaken calculations on the part of the apple as to how far it was from the centre of the earth."[116]

The "discreteness and discontinuity" of the economy as a whole and its "lack of a uniform and homogeneous continuity" required therefore a flexible "toolbox" for thinking particular problems.[117] Hence, in this second model of objectivity, economic knowledge was much more attuned to a creative act of problematization and analysis. This second ideal of objectivity incorporated the contingency of judgment that the first model sought to subdue. But both moments of contingency *and* closure remained virulent in this figure of the economist, who was all at once an electrician, a founding statesman, and a bearer of contingent judgments.

The political model for this role of the economist as a statesman can be gauged from Keynes's discussion of the political philosophy of Edmund Burke. Keynes did not engage very deeply with the tradition of political thought.[118] An unpublished manuscript on Burke represents "his most extensive foray into political theory."[119] This piece on the conservative critic of the French Revolution foregrounded the contingency of judgment and the displacement or containment of the political that are crucial for how Keynes's envisions political-cum-economic expertise of the economist.

Keynes introduced Burke as "perhaps the only political writer, the direct bearing of whose works is wholly topical and contemporary."[120] The reasons for this praise of Burke were manifold: Keynes referred to the wisdom of Burke, which led him to prefer a circumspect, slow, and pragmatic stance in ethics and politics in opposition to general principles of truth, right, and the call for revolutionary or violent forms of change. Two aspects stand out in Keynes's discussion of Burke: first, Burke's recognition of the fundamental lack of foundation of judgments and principles, and, second, his disdain for the sphere of politics as a realm of principles and virtues of its own. Both illuminate why Burke was presented as "the source of a consistent and coherent body of political theory" that is apt for the twentieth century.[121] Ironically, it is his abnegation of political ends and virtues as a good of its own that turned Burke into such a "topical" political thinker for Keynes: "It is his antagonism to those who maintain that there are certain ends of a political nature, universally and intrinsically desirable" that Keynes picked as the decisive matter: "Burke's arguments fall to the ground if we admit that one of the best possible things in the world is the possession by the bulk of the people of the power of immediately carrying into effect whatever they will, and of directly supervising their own affairs, regardless of the nature of their desires or of their performances."[122]

In contrast to this elevation of the political and its democratic manifestation, Burke took politics to be a utilitarian device that helped to achieve the happiness of the governed. The science of politics was a doctrine of means for him.[123] In serving the "happiness of the governed," government had to reckon with the "temper of feelings of the governed," the possible and the feasible. Clemency, moderation, and mercy therefore belonged to the virtues of a successful administration.[124] Keynes was only critical of Burke in two respects. He found the "timidity" of Burke regarding the scope of political experimentation an unnecessary obstacle for achieving the aim of happiness. Even more, he regarded Burke's unfailing commitment to the principles of laissez-faire as entirely untenable: "All this is a matter of great complexity and difficulty and it is not likely that the problem is capable of any very simple solution, but Burke's treatment is wholly inadequate and he seems to convince himself in passages which certainly ought to convince nobody else."[125]

Hence, for Keynes, government is about experimenting with means in the administration of "happiness." Government might require bold but circumspect experimentation that does not follow dogmatic precepts— but this experimentation should be a matter of competent and impartial judgment that could neither be found among the masses nor among those that adhered to general principles in matters of politics. It is telling how Keynes commented in a different context on the development in Russia as a venerable experiment in the wrong hands: Thus, while he is disgusted with "the dictatorship of the proletariat . . . [that] keeps control in the hands of the most incompetent and ignorant members of the population" he lauded the "Russian innovators" that have moved beyond the "revolutionary and doctrinaire stage":[126]

> They are engaged in the vast administrative task of making a completely new set of social and economic institutions work smoothly and successfully over a territory so extensive that it covers one sixth of the land surface of the world. Methods are still changing rapidly in response to experience. The largest scale empiricism and experimentalism which has ever been attempted by disinterested administrators is in operation. . . . It leaves me with a strong desire and hope that we in this country may discover how to combine an unlimited readiness to experiment with changes in political and economic methods and institutions, whilst preserving traditionalism and a sort of careful conservatism.[127]

The virtues necessary for this "readiness to experiment" and "careful conservatism" were located in a single figure: the economist. The ideal expert dared to decide, was knowledgeable about economic principles without adhering to them blindly, was oriented toward the greater good of the whole, and embodied the virtues of courage, boldness, and pragmatism. It was, in other words, a most superb and civilized individual who was supposed to make possible an ideal politics beyond politics.

Governing (Through) Money—Silently and Unobserved

The preceding sections outline how a biopolitics of population and a notion of politics as "giving measure" partook in framing "the economy" as a governable entity. But Keynesianism was not only an "archipolitics" that newly settled the division between liberal economy and politics. It also articulated the political and economic technologies for governing that befitted this division. In the words of Peter Miller and Nikolas Rose, " 'technologies of government' seek to translate thought into the domain of reality": They "establish 'in the world of persons and things' spaces and devices for acting upon those entities of which they dream and scheme."[128] Liberal technologies seek to govern indirectly: they hope to modulate, incite, and govern the choices of the subject instead of ordering or prohibiting a particular conduct from above.[129] Keynesianism followed this precept—it was not about a central plan about how to use resources. It aimed at "the powers to spend, not the powers to plan."[130]

As I show below, two aspects make Keynesianism a particularly interesting case for the study of liberal governmentalities. On the one hand, Keynesian technologies foreground the role of the passions. Just as the preceding chapters emphasize, the passions that make up economic interests remained a key concern for liberalism. Albert Hirschman's insights about the constitutive link between the passions and the interest held true for the nineteenth and twentieth century, pace Hirschman's own historiography that drew to a close at end of the eighteenth century. On the other hand, Keynesian technologies of governing added to the toolbox of liberal technologies a specific lever that very much helped to widen and innovate the ways of governing indirectly. This specific lever was money. "Now there is no part of our economic system which works so badly as our monetary and credit arrangements; none where the results of bad working are so disastrous socially; and none where it is easier to provide a scientific solution."[131]

Money became central for this technology of governing for two reasons. First, it was considered as the very point at which the "economic sentiments" and governmental technology met. As the preceding chapters explain, money was linked to the fears and hopes of the subject. "Our desire to hold money as a store of wealth is a barometer of the degree of our distrust of our own calculations and conventions concerning the future. . . . The possession of actual money lulls our disquietude."[132] Second, money's significance as a governmental tool also rested on its nature as a "general cause," as Keynes once put it: it traversed the whole socioeconomic body, affecting several relations at once. Money appeared as an ideal governmental medium because it interlinked economic passions with economic relations. "And since the public always understands particular causes better than general causes, the depression will be attributed to the industrial disputes which will accompany it, to the Dawes Scheme, to China, to the inevitable consequences of the Great War, to tariffs, to high taxation, to anything in the world except the general monetary policy which has set the whole thing going."[133] Money promised to act on everyone and everything; it was presented as a paramount liberal tool for governing. It not only addressed the economic-political totality as a whole but also the individual. Even if many did not understand this "general cause," in the hand of the economist it became a proper tool for this very reason.

Keynesianism differed from classical liberalism in how it took the medium of money more seriously as a tool for governing. It also differed from this tradition in how Keynes set up the problem of the passions. Keynesian liberalism targeted savage passions—but, as discussed in the previous chapters, Keynesian economics revolved around a set of "savage" passions quite distinct from those that classical liberalism had feared: it was no longer solely the presentism of "savage life" but the fears and wavering of the civilized subject that stood at the center of this problematization. Not the savage body but the "degenerate" mind was the focus of attention. "In fact, our predicament . . . comes from some failure in the immaterial devices of the mind, in the working of the motives which should lead to the decisions and acts of will."[134] According to Keynes, the entrepreneurial subject wavered constantly between undue optimism and undue pessimism; it was prey to collective emotion and erred in general on the side of indecision, fear, and the love of money's potentiality: "Investment is being made in conditions which are unstable and cannot endure because it is prompted by expectations which are destined to disappointment. . . . When disillusion falls upon an overoptimistic and over bought market, it should fall with sudden and even catastrophic forces."[135] Instead of investing, the individual retreated into the perceived safety of hoarding. While this might be a viable strategy for an individual, it did not apply to the economy as a whole: "We cannot, as a community, provide for future consumption by financial expedients but only by current physical output. In so far as our social and business organization separates financial provision[s] for the future from physical provision for the future . . . efforts to secure the former do not necessarily carry the latter with them."[136]

It is the variability of these expectations, which tended to a fearful retreat after a disappointed of undue optimism, that became the very object of this governmentality. Given that Keynes located the key problem in fear, lack of conviction, and unwillingness on the side of the economic subject, the main governmental strategies were geared to mitigate the excessive wavering of the passions and to counter the reign of fear. Monetary politics aimed at instilling a steady and moderate hope for the future. The governmental task was to "abolish slumps thus keeping us permanently in a quasi-boom."[137] It had to address "the weakness of the inducement to invest [which] has been at all times the key to the economic problem."[138]

The targets of this monetary governmentality were the interest rate and the variability of the exchange rate. The aim was to make these rates less variable and to give it a ceiling beyond which the interest rate would not rise. For it is "the uncertainty as to its future course" and the "degree of divergence from what is considered a fairly safe level" that hampered the weak powers of commitment of the weak subject—and consequently the level of investment that resulted from its choices.[139] While under the international regime of the gold standard, the interest rate, as well as the price for money, would vary according to the imbalances of trade, Keynesian monetary policies aimed at steadying these rates by subjecting them to public authority. A measure was to be set that "appeals to public opinion as being reasonable and practicable and in the public interest, rooted in strong convection and promoted by an authority unlikely to be superseded."[140] This measure had to be comparatively lower than that offered by the domains of material undertakings. In other words, the returns expected from retreating into the monetary potentiality should be lower than those to be expected from any material course of action. Money was to be made available on more stable and less expensive terms, diminishing its attractiveness in comparison to other forms of material investment. The wisdom of the heretic Gesell, Keynes announced, lay precisely in recognizing that the economic subject needs to be lured away from the potentiality of money: "Those reformers, who look for a remedy by creating artificial carrying-costs for money . . . have been on the right track."[141]

Such monetary measure, given by a public authority, aimed at tempting capital into the circumscribed material world of *homo faber* and his community. It did so by controlling the "reward for parting with liquidity" and its variability.[142] But it also hoped to achieve this effect by creating a more hopeful and steady perspective on the future. According to Keynes, when prices rose a little due to the cheapness of money while the steadied interest rate did not offer much ground for speculation, such hopeful outlooks flourished. Even more so, he reasoned, since the price of labor would not be part of such monetary rise of prices: contracts were fixed and the increasing costs of living were rarely turned into an object of conflict among the social groups that negotiated the labor contract. In this sense, "workers, though unconsciously, are instinctively more reasonable economists."[143] In other words, they unconsciously sacrificed part of their returns for the greater good of increasing material investments, which in turn created more employment and more abundance, making good the initial sacrifice.

Ceiling the level and reducing the variability of the interest rate were supposed to diminish the gains derived from potentiality of money alone. The "slow death of the rentier" found here its concrete application. Hence, without juridical decree and even without deliberation or revolution, the relation between debtor and creditor, between labor and capital were to be transformed little by little. Cheap money would ease the "dead hand of the past"—that is, it would dampen the claims of debt, whose value falls with cheaper money. The claims to income from money alone would fade, while the investor would be lured with higher prices while a veil of plenty would be cast over the reward of labor. Money is supposed to work as a "general cause"; silently and unobserved, it would usher toward the "end of economy."

Such governing through money had a condition and effect: it depended on and resulted in a financially bounded economy. Capital had to stay within the bounds of a national economy, at least to a large degree. In an open system, the increase of investment might occur elsewhere. But according to Keynes, even then "our own country may recover a portion of this leakage through favourable repercussions."[144] Still, the financially bound community, in which capital controls territorialized money's circulations, was necessary in order to achieve further material development.[145] Restricting capital mobility was supposed to create a more stable exchange rate that would reduce uncertainty about the value of money and minimize the irreducible uncertainty that any economic undertaking is beset with. The controlled mobility of capital would also induce material investments for lack of any other venue. Furthermore, only within such geographic bounds would debt and credit appear as "a link in the transformation of the community's surplus resources."[146] Keynes explained how money and community intertwine: "For 'finance' is essentially a revolving fund. It employs no savings. It is for the community as a whole, only a book-keeping transaction. As soon as it is 'used' in the sense of being expended, the lack of liquidity is automatically made good."[147] The *oikos* of the nation is secured in the *nomos* of such circulation folding back upon itself.

In an alluring mixture of lightheartedness and hubris Keynes wrote, "The economic problem is not too difficult to solve. If you will leave that to me, I will look after it."[148] Yet this optimism tied to monetary policies was not consistent. Money appeared as an omnipotent tool of governing but was also potentially weak for the same reason: it might work so indirectly as to lose its aim: "If, however, we are tempted to assert that money is the drink which stimulates the system to activity, we must remind ourselves that there may be several slips between the cup and the lip."[149] Governing through money faced a potentially insurmountable difficulty: overbearing fear together with the lack of confidence could be "insusceptible to control" when they are the effects of recent disappointments.[150] Accordingly, Keynes envisioned the point at which the state had to supplement what monetary policy did not achieve on its own: to settle the general level of activity through schemes of investment undertaken by public bodies.[151] Hence, the weakness of monetary tools had to be supplemented with "semi-public bodies" that would invest where the fears of the private investor turned out to be beyond the politics of hope. The fiscal policies of spending were only the wisdom of last resort. But at the moment at which the roundabout and indirect means of monetary policy ceased to work, this increased direct lever was needed to keep up the volumes of investment.

Keynesianism offers a particular toolkit for how to govern the economy. This toolkit is firmly based in the liberal tradition. It is historically specific insofar as it answers to a particular diagnosis of the "savage passions" to be countered and rests on a particular notion of collectivity and politics. Keynesianism has as its condition of possibility the rethinking of the economic in terms of material temporalities, conventions of measurement, and contingent judgments. But it submerges this critical space of the economic to a biopolitics of population, a Burkean notion of expert judgment, and an understanding of politics in terms of an act of "giving measure" to a community as a whole.

Political Languages and the Economic

Opening up a space between the particular historical articulation of "the economic" and its attendant articulation of "the economy" induces a sense of historical possibility. It invites us to inquire about different forms of translating the more open plane of the economic into a concrete institutionalization of economic order. It makes one wonder how else one could have negotiated and debated this "critical space" of the economic. Instilling such sense of historical possibility has been one aim of this book. As a historical argument, the book must stay within the bounds of history and remain tied to the limited and particular ways that liberal economy had been opened up for debate. In this vein, it is noteworthy that the political languages that Keynes used to think about the governing of economy and money were not uniform in his writings—not all problematizations of money and economy revolved around the "savage passions" of the subject; not all tools of monetary policy were linked to the biopolitics of the community.

Specifically, the political language that was used to debate and negotiate the international dimension of money differed from the biopolitical language of community and the cultural critique leveled at the degenerate passions of the modern economic subject. Keynes's explorations of an international monetary regime are complementary to the envisioning of the national economy as a unit. But even though they are hence not truly different, they still provide telling instances of how political languages allow for different ways in which "the economic" is taken up. By way of conclusion, I give some examples of this diversity of the political idioms for debating the economic. This provides me with a perspective for my epilogue that focuses on the conceptual implications of my historical argument on the double movement between opening up "the economic" and closing it into "the economy."

In the first decades of the twentieth century, international monetary politics revolved around three issues: outstanding debts accrued during the wars, the gold standard, and the monetary arrangements that followed the demise of the gold standard. Keynes frames these issues in a openly political language that revolves around the terms "constitutionalism," "enmity," "war," "authority," and "compromise." The examples given below are culled mainly from debates about war debt and the international monetary system after the war. What follows is not a systematic discussion or a deep elaboration but a collage of the different forms of articulating the malleability of the economic in political terms.

After the First World War the question of debt loomed large on the political agenda. Keynes's best-selling book *The Economic Consequences of Peace* addressed the question of war debt. He did so in a distinct political vocabulary as he framed the issue of debt in terms of dependency, sacrifice, solidarity, and sovereign autonomy. He described debts between nations as "paper shackles" that undid the political and economic prospects of development and peace:

> The war has ended with everyone owing everyone else immense sums of money. . . . The whole position is in the highest degree artificial, misleading, and vexatious. We shall never be able to move again, unless we can free our limbs from these paper shackles. . . . Will the discontented peoples of Europe be willing for a generation to come so to order their lives that an appreciable part of their daily produce may be available to meet foreign payment, the reason of which . . . does not spring compellingly from their sense of justice or duty?[152]

This understanding of debt was markedly different from how Keynes understands debt within the bounds of the national economy. What appeared in the one case as a "revolving fund" turned into "vexatious" and "artificial" bond in the other case. The external relations of debt were reflected in terms of the obligations and dependencies they entailed. Keynes compared the "entanglements of cash owing" to the entanglements of a political alliance, finding the former much more binding, untransparent, and full of hostilities counteracting the spirit of latter.[153]

Keynes's suggestions for an international postwar order after 1945 took up these themes of hostility, enmity, and war that such economic bonds would further. In arguing for the postwar monetary order—first pondered as a "Clearing Union" and later known under the term "Bretton Woods"—Keynes described the proposed arrangements as a "measure of *financial disarmament*. They are very mild in comparison with the measures of military disarmament which, it is to be hoped, the world will be asked to accept" (emphasis added).[154] The underlying rationale for the international system of Bretton Woods was to control these relations of obligation and to keep these entanglements under "neutral rules" that would mitigate and reduce the dependency and political-cum-economic distress tied to debt.[155] Again, the debate about the international monetary system was couched in political terms: shared responsibility, the balance of power, dependence, autonomy, and neighborliness determined how to think about debt. Hence, the questions in how far and to what extent the debtor bears the whole responsibility for the debt, or if the creditor also stands in a relation of obligation toward the debtor became possible. Imbalances were to be avoided in order to turn dependence into mutual dependence. Bretton Woods was supposed to engender a symmetrical process of readjustment from both creditors and debtors.[156] It was to discipline both creditor and debtor in order to allow "favorite experiments" toward an "ideal social republic" of the future on both sides.[157]

The envisioning of a bounded national economy that stands in horizontal, carefully guarded relations of independence and exchange to other national economies form two sides of the same coin. Still, this difference in the political idiom is instructive; it demonstrates how deeply our political languages inform the way "the economic" turns into the economy or multiple economies. Without providing an in-depth analysis and without wanting to suggest that the political language of constitutionalism, war, and compromise are more apt or desirable, this short foray into the debates on international finance strengthens the sense of the historical malleability of the economic and the diverse possibilities of negotiating it politically. Unfolding the opening of the critical space of the economic and recording the multiple ways of how it is closed, translated, and institutionalized into a political and economic order holds a lesson for the contemporary situation: it is a remainder of the internal openness of liberalism. The very horizon of what liberal economy is, what can be said and done about it, might be wider than we assume.

Epilogue

Critical Effects

This book focuses on specific crises in the history of liberalism that rendered the meaning of liberal economy and its boundary to politics uncertain. Rereading these crises in light of how they opened and closed a critical space for rethinking liberal economy has unlocked the notion of liberal economy from within. The meanings of scarcity, economic necessity, money, and rationality turn out to be not as unequivocal as they are often assumed to be. The historical material presented in these pages exposes the impure frontiers of economy and its variable historical ontologies. But it does not do so in a straightforward way. The conceptual history of liberal economy must be forced open by studying it through the lenses of a genealogy of *the economic*.

Turning the question of economy into a question of the economic drives a wedge between two terms that are usually tightly aligned. Yet there is an "immense slippage of meaning" between the economy and the economic.[1] Interrupting this slippage has an unsettling effect. It challenges the topographical metaphors linked to the modern imaginary of economy. As I define it, the notion of the economic is a malleable attribute of relations that is negotiable by political and cultural factors. As a consequence, the critique and debate about liberal economy need not revolve around the question of how much terrain and how many practices are subjected to the economic code. It is not just about fencing in the laws of the market or about letting them reign freely for the sake of productivity.

Instead, the notion of the economic allows for focusing on the composite and gradual modulation of the economic inside and outside markets. Studying the economic invites contemplation about the conventions, authorities, and sites that play a role in shaping the degrees of economy.

As I argue in this book, in the history of liberalism the malleability of the economic has been more or less displaced—and with it the concrete sites of experimentation and contestation regarding what liberal economy is about. Liberal economic thought has assumed the role of providing a foundation and delimitation of politics. Displacing the economic makes it possible to define in unequivocal terms what "the economy" demands in terms of the optimal working of its laws or in terms of underlying and fundamental necessities. This is tantamount to speaking in the name of the common good without exposure to a proper debate about the political nature of the argument. In this book, I demonstrate how a political notion of "the economy" is linked to a displacement of the economic. Adopting a notion by the philosopher Jacques Rancière, I call this process of displacement "archipolitics."

By offering the genealogy of the economic and by studying the "archipolitics" of economic foundation, this book argues on two different, albeit deeply related, levels. On the one hand, it furthers an argument about imbrication of the political and economic categories in the history of liberalism. It furnishes an analytical framework for understanding both the impurity and specificity of the economic and political in liberalism. On the other hand, it opens up an analytical perspective for thinking about economic phenomena in a novel way. The contributions of this book to these two fields of interest can be presented independently from each other, even though they have only become visible in a single stroke and are always interlaced.

The Economic: Material Temporality, Conventions, and Capitalism

At the beginning of this book, I introduce the notion of the economic as a "quasi-ontological" notion that addresses our most fundamental assumptions about what turns a reality, a relation, or a situation into an economic one. Referring to the economic as "*quasi*-ontological" is meant to signal historical contingency. The notion of the economic does not rely on a grand philosophical argument about some ontological essence of economy, but refers to the internal malleability that a specific historical articulation of liberal economy harbors. In this book, I use the notion of the economic to write a conceptual history, but this notion is more versatile than that: it can be used and adapted as an analytical tool for studying the contemporary formations of liberal economy. Even though there is no general definition of the economic that could be furnished at the end of this historical narrative, it is possible to adopt the historical findings for an analytical purpose, exploring where it leads us. In this epilogue I outline how the genealogical analysis of the economic can turn into a source of inspiration for rethinking the analysis and critique of liberal economy.

One of the main findings of this genealogy of the economic concerns the role of temporality for understanding what turns matters into economic ones. Emphasizing the analytical value of time is not new: As Marx already put it, all economy comes down to an economy of time. Max Weber assumed to have found the spirit of capitalism in Benjamin Franklin's maxims of time management. The typically modern acceleration of life has been tied to an economic regime that strives for efficiency.[2] Approaching the notion of time from the vantage point of an analysis of the economic furnishes a novel perspective on what it means to say that all economy comes down to an economy of time. Three aspects come to the fore: the cultural and political making of economic futurity, the constitutive relation between materiality and economic temporality, and the conventions and politics of measure that shape these temporalities.

As the historical analysis demonstrated, the question of futurity proved to be central for specifying the economic. In both Malthus's and Keynes's texts the definition of what counts as proper economic rationality hinges on how it organized the relation to the future. Searching for the economic in Malthus's texts reveals that behind the "facts" of scarcity stands an argument about futurity. Malthus depicts the lack of an outlook on the future as a catastrophic absence of an economic comportment toward the resources given. To him, the specificity of an economic relation to the future consists in the ability to defer, to wait, and to postpone consumption. He ties the absence of such ability to save and to wait to a colonial and cultural hierarchy between "savage" and "civilized" life. For Keynes, the question of futurity is equally important for specifying economic rationality. But to him, the ability to decide in a world of temporal flux and uncertainty, not waiting and deferral, defines the proper form of economic conduct. He considers the desire to retreat into the potentiality of money as a sterile and unproductive relation to the future that undoes economic progress. Keynes links this sterility to a weakness of modern individuality that needs to be countered by monetary policies. The definition of economic futurity enlists a notion of virtuous conduct, cultural notions of worth, and monetary conventions.

The analysis of Keynes's texts has brought to the fore how the question of futurity is tied to a relational ontology of layered, intersecting, and hierarchized material temporalities. As I have shown, Keynes's writings on money rested on an ontology that posits that each matter, body, or medium has its own temporality, meaning its own rhythm, rate of growth and decay, duration, and dissipation. Temporality and materiality were co-constituted. Money appeared as one material temporality among others. For Keynes, "moneyness" becomes a question of degree depending on whether a specific medium is durable enough to last into the future while being shielded from processes of decay. The liquidity typical of money hinges on this type of material temporality. In this context, materiality should not be understood in a narrow sense, as "thingness" or raw matter. It can comprise the materialized monetary regimes, legal conventions, and financial instruments that allow money's futurity to be stabilized in a world of flux.[3]

Following this "historical ontology" excavated from the writing of Keynes, one can say that the thoroughly temporal nature of material existence turns into an economic affair insofar and to the extent that it links the duration into the future to a measure and a yield. Without the reference to a future point in time at which exertions are to be made good, payments are received, rent is demanded, credit is to be paid, resources are to be replenished, the body is to be nurtured, and profit is demanded, the attribute of the economic cannot be specified. Decisive for the notion of the economic is therefore a rhythm tied to a measure, meaning here the process of defining units of time and horizons of futurity, calculating the values of what is due, and employing cultural conventions for claiming appropriateness.[4] The specificity of this perspective of the economic consists in the fact that it takes note of the multiplicity of material durations without assuming that some are more foundational than others. Matters have their own durations and temporalities that exceed economic rhythm and measure. Transforming a material temporality into an economic one means taking up their material specificity and aligning them with economic horizons of futurity and yield. This is a question of resonance, institutional framing, and power.

Showing the conceptual implications of this historical analysis would require a book of its own. In this epilogue, I can only indicate, using very broad strokes, the contemporary relevance of such a perspective on liberal economy. The experience of the financial crisis and the ensuing debt crisis can serve as an exemplary case for demonstrating the importance of studying the making of economic futurity. The crisis can be described as a crisis of a specific form of financial futurity: new financial instruments, such as derivatives and securitization, have changed the meaning of economic futurity. Created and managed by large institutional actors, underwritten by legal conventions and political guarantees, and continuously hedged on markets, financial futurity has become a world of its own. The emergency measures in the wake of the crisis were justified in terms of the "systemic importance" of this type of financial futurity. This systemic perspective needs to be pried open in order to study the making of financial futurity and the politics of obligation tied to it. What types of futurity are we securing? How do financial and other futurities intersect? In which ways do financial futurities measure, enlist, transpose, or ignore other forms of material temporality? Whose debt obligations are to be honored, whose were canceled, and whose were paid by the public?

One advantage of the notion of the economic in terms of an ontology of material temporalities consists in how it allows us to trace different forms of economic temporality and futurity. If bodies, plants, soil, infrastructures, and technologies all have different durations that are taken up, molded, and mobilized in the making of economic rhythms and measures, it is of paramount interest to study the relations between them. The determination of patterns of economic temporality is an impure matter. Materials, processes of production or reproduction, human bodies, or ecosystems have their own—although malleable—range of what is possible, desirable, and livable. The question is always: How do relations of power ensure hierarchies of material temporalities and how are different degrees of economy defined for different material temporalities? How do different material temporalities intersect or superimpose each other? How are economic measures defined and tightened and for whom? Whose time is it?

This analytical perspective circumvents the unifying, totalizing accounts on the market and capitalism without losing sight of the critical concerns animating these accounts. In recent decades, the analytical value and political effects of unifying notions such as "the market" and "capitalism" have been increasingly questioned. Imagining the market as a machine of equilibrating forces and as a self-regulating system has been deemed to hamper the understanding of the piecemeal, embedded, limited, and networked nature of concrete sites and acts of exchange that depend on locality, culture, and shared epistemologies.[5] Likewise, understanding capitalism as a historical system that works its way through history that cannot be stopped unless a global revolution takes place has been found to be political immobilizing as it has made it "so difficult for people to imagine its supersession" and has analytically excluded the recognition of "economic difference."[6]

In its place we have been asked to put capitalism on the ground, as Bruno Latour has suggested. Instead of assuming that capitalism is an "intractable entity endowed with a 'spirit,'" one should study the "tiny but expeditious conduits" that connect, for example, Wall Street to the rest of the world, which make or break the economic centrality and power of this iconic place.[7] Social scientists, historians, and political theorists have started to study the practices that create markets. They have disassembled the market or capitalism into the various acts of standardization, valuation, calculation, and accounting that economic actors and institutions undertake. Following, recording, and describing how these actors know and perform "the economy" has been taken as a royal road to understanding what it means to "economize."[8] But this empirically rich and versatile research strategy has created a blank when it comes to determining the "economic difference" that different ways of calculating, comparing, and quantifying make.[9] We need not only to know how different calculations are stabilized, performed, and rendered pervasive in the circumscribed worlds, as these studies allow us to do; we also need to address what this means in terms of relating, modulating, hierarchizing, or intensifying modes of economy and for whom. Studying the economic in terms of material temporalities and their economic measures allows us to ask how acts of calculating, standardizing, and comparing result in the making of economic measures. It enables one to look at such practices, instruments, and institutions in terms of the hierarchies that they enact between different material temporalities. It allows studying the layering, nesting, intersection, and resonance established between different material temporalities and the degrees to which they are economized. In other words, it enables one to determine "economic difference."

Such perspective allows returning to the notion of capital and capitalism without such totalizing gaze. Just as Fernand Braudel has quipped, that even if one "shoots [the word capitalism] out of the door," it almost immediately "climbs in through the window."[10] Seen through the lenses of the economic, capital could be, on the one hand, nothing but a lump sum of money or a capital good that is a "more or less durable human construction" used for procuring for the future, inventing a new one, and reproducing what exists.[11] But it could also be used and governed as to produce the highest returns, using existing hierarchies and producing new ones. This is how Braudel distinguished the market from capitalism by finding only the latter to constitute the upper limit of the economy. His account of capitalism refers to practices and arrangements of power and exchange that serve to mobilize and hierarchize material life. In this sense, capitalism is not a totalizing system encompassing the whole economy but a variable engagement with material life that produces its own "world theater," mobilizing and engaging with material life when it is profitable to do so.

It is not my intention to discuss in detail or to adopt tout court Braudel's conceptual distinctions. But referring to Braudel helps pinpoint what it might mean to study "economic difference" as a question of degree and intensity. Even though the notion of the economic employed here emphasizes gradual distinctions and thus goes against the binaries that Braudel established between the market as a sphere of transparent exchange and capitalism as the "antimarket," Braudel's notion of capitalism broadly fits the study of economic difference. This conceptualization is proximate to what the elaboration of a perspective on the economic might result in.

Making time such a central category for thinking about the economic is an outcome of the historical work that went before. It is due to the scenes, themes, and figures that I have chosen for this history. It is interesting to ask how different histories would yield different inspirations for understanding the economic, and it remains to be studied how this focus on time relates to a theoretical tradition in the social sciences that focuses on exchange as the *differentia specifica* of economy.[12] The scope of this epilogue is too limited to allow for spelling out these lines of questioning and resonances in further detail. At this point, it might be sufficient to name family resemblances, to indicate synergies, and to allude to the questions and connections that become possible. As the philosopher Hans Blumenberg once said, the quality of philosophy is to be measured by the types of empirical descriptions that it engenders.[13] I have tried to lay out in a very cursory manner what the quality of the philosophical coinage of "the economic" might be.

Hybridity, Neoliberalism, and Economic Archipolitics

This book is not only about "the economic." It is to equal extent a story about how the critical space of thinking about "the economic" was closed. It is unavoidable and necessary that the malleability of the economic becomes fixed, institutionalized, and hardened into a version of economy. But such an act of institutionalization and fixation does not need to be an act of foundation and naturalization by which "the economy" is turned into a self-standing system of laws with stark boundaries to politics and linked to a set of necessities that can be announced by experts without having to explicate the political nature of such act. Such notion of "the economy" makes it increasingly difficult to discern and debate the internal openness and political/cultural nature of defining economic order.

In this book I have used a notion from the philosopher Jacques Rancière to describe such an act of foundation or displacement that occurs in the domain of economic thought. He called this act "archipolitics," referring to the Greek notion of the "*arkhe,*" which means ground. Rancière has defined "archipolitics" as a way of instituting politics by doing away with it.[14] This image of order preempts dissensus and it identifies the "*phusis*" (what is natural and corporeal) completely with the "*nomos*" (a notion of order and law) without remainder. I have used this notion to trace how the concept of "the economy" grants the authority to define what is possible, what is given, and what is viable. The premodern definition of economy very openly exposes this political element. *Oikonomia* was considered to be "the science and technique of order and the subordination of the parts to a whole. It refers to the principle of life . . . and the principle of order. . . ." Both vitalist and functionalist, it gives each its proper place and the most perfectly adapted form for its function. *Oikonomia* implied arrangement, use, and practical organization; it is a "concept of the management and administration of temporal realities."[15] This notion of economy contained "the law of distribution, the law of apportionment, the law as apportionment, the given and allotted part, the share."[16]

Modernity appears to have dispensed with such notion of economy as an ordered totality. It breached this link between the meaning of economy and the household. Liberal economy is no longer about a household and cannot be reduced to an organization or corporation. It projects a milieu of circulation and exchange, a complex interlacing, and a pattern of coordination that is no longer the domain of political philosophy. In fact, liberal economy has been understood to undo the confines of any established political order and authority, melting "all that is solid into air." But, as argued in this book, the archipolitical envisioning of economy did not disappear from the liberal account of economy just because the model of "the economy" as a household has been discarded.

Reading Malthus, I have shown how the notion of the economy as a realm governed by laws of necessity emerged. I have traced how the invention of economic necessity constitutively hinged on importing cultural ranks of worth and narratives of civilization into the meaning of liberal economy. Without the colonial order that "coupled sexuality, class, and racial essence in defining what it meant to be productive—and therefore successfully reproductive," Malthus's explorations of futurity would not have resulted in such conception of economic laws. It would not have generated the prohibition to grant a "right to live," and it would have not been linked to a politics of fear and a turn toward scarcity as the single determining essence of things economic.[17] The second part of the book chronicles the undoing of this notion of economic necessity in the writings of Keynes. As I have shown, the centrality of scarcity, the cultural hierarchies of worth, and the definition of economic rationality were all challenged at once. But Keynes not only reopened the question of "the economic" but also closed it. A novel understanding of "the economy" emerged. This time the biopolitical notion of a national community, a Burkean understanding of politics, and a belief in the expert as a superior individual transformed an open plane for thinking the economic into "the economy."

Today this Keynesian version of the managed national economy and its attendant conception of the welfare state belong to the past. The models of the national economy as a "hydraulic machine" that could be governed through monetary techniques are considered to have already failed during the 1970s. Since Keynesianism had been tied to this technical vision of economy, it has been challenged by such "technical failure." The welfare state has been critiqued, rearranged, adapted, and hollowed out to fit the so-called new realities of globalization. "The global market" is juxtaposed to the political sphere in the name of which policies are demanded and repealed while new arrangements of "territory, authority, and rights" are produced. On the surface it looks as if the neoliberal turn to the market has undone the archipolitics of founding politics through economy. But the lack of explicit political terms, such as the nation or the welfare state, does not signal a lack of archipolitics—quite to the contrary. Whenever there is a vision of "the economy" or "the global market" as a unified entity whose laws one can only avoid if one is willing to invite calamities of a higher order, one can suspect that we are dealing with a masterpiece of archipolitics in the clothes of economic thought that has displaced the malleable economic.

How are we to study the current forms of "archipolitics" and retrieve "the economic" from within? This book provides an analytical template for studying the entanglements between political and economic categories without dissolving the conceptual distinctions. Coming to grips with the simultaneity of division and entanglement of the economic and political side of liberalism is no easy task. This book has offered one version of doing so. I have looked at the division between the spheres of "the economy" and politics within liberalism in terms of a conceptual claim to purity and foundation. Such division cannot be taken to describe complete independence or separation. Instead, it enfolds a political dimension in two ways. First, it smuggles a political standpoint of the common into the accounts of "the economy," on behalf of which one can announce the common good. Second, this division is instrumental for devising and conceptualizing what kinds of political interventions are desirable, feasible or not. It guides politics instead of shielding "the economy" from political intervention and institutionalization. It allows for certain imbrications of political power and economic life and prohibiting others.

This work as a whole maintains that an argument about hybridity between politics and economy need not be a call to dissolve the conceptual distinctions and differences between economy and politics. I have suggested retaining the conceptual specificity of "the economic," however defined, on the level of a malleable attribute, which is not yet fixed and given definite shape. Instead of purity, I looked for specificity. I suggest studying the hybrid entanglements of liberalism in light of the malleable attribute of the economic that they define. It is not a virtue to lack conceptual specificity, and it is not politically desirable to opt for hybridity as a good in itself. Hybridity seems to be a reality, but different types of entanglements are possible, and they need to be distinguished and rendered negotiable. Disentangling this hybridity and opening it up for debate lends historical concreteness to what remains otherwise an empty claim: that all orders are contingent, including the economic one. Knowing that the history of liberalism also contains an experimental and open plane counters the poverty of the political imagination and helps to unlock the economic imagination.

Notes

Foreword

1. Tellmann refers frequently to Karl Polanyi's *The Great Transformation* in this regard. Liberalism is not a "natural" state of human society; it is the result of political choice which is, as Tellmann puts it, "displaced."

2. In a footnote to chapter 4, Tellmann thanks a "very helpful archivist at the King's College Archive in Cambridge," which lists the works of Nietzsche in Keynes's personal library (255, n. 68). All the major works are there, and all are in the German original! It should be said that this is not Tellmann's only venture into the archives in her well-documented study.

3. Two of many examples illustrate the quality of the author's research. In 1924, Keynes began to work on what he called a "Prolegomena to a New Socialism," which he left only in outline. The first two points to be considered were "population" and "eugenics," after which came a series of other topics of which the next was "money." Tellmann also notes that Keynes served as president of the Malthusian League for whose fiftieth anniversary he delivered a toast in 1927 called "Malthus in Piam Memoriam."

4. The concept is first introduced conceptually in Tellmann's introduction (29); later it becomes the title of chapter 6 ("The Archipolitics of Macroeconomics"). The importance of the concept for the author is clear in the above citation, which is taken from her brief epilogue (204).

5. Cf., Dick Howard, *The Primacy of the Political: A History of Political Thought from the Greeks to the French and American Revolutions* (2010) and also *Between Politics and Antipolitics: Thinking about Politics after 9/11* (2016).

Introduction

1. Financial Crisis Inquiry Commission, *Financial Crisis Inquiry Report: Final Report of the National Commission on the Causes of the Financial and Economic Crisis in the United States* (Washington, D.C.: Government Printing Office, 2011), xi, xvi, xx.

2. On the self-description of Wall Street in terms of a guardian of efficiency and productivity, see Karen Ho, *Liquidated: An Ethnography of Wall Street* (Durham, N.C.: Duke University Press, 2009), 130. On the failure of the markets to exert the discipline of scarce capital resources, see Greta Krippner, *Capitalizing on Crisis: The Political Origins of the Rise of Finance* (Cambridge, Mass., Harvard University Press, 2011). For a discussion of the "return to realism," see Arturo Escobar, *Encountering Development: The Making and Unmaking of the Third World* (Princeton, N.J.: Princeton University Press, 1995), 89–94.

3. William Davies, *The Limits of Neoliberalism: Authority, Sovereignty and the Logic of Competition* (London: Sage, 2014), 149 and 155.

4. For the argument about the role of interpreting an event as crisis in closing rather than opening such critical space, see Janet Roitman, *Anti-Crisis* (Durham, N.C.: Duke University Press, 2014), 43.

5. For an account of how the initiative of "new economic thinking" in the aftermath of the crisis lacked the element of the new and consisted instead in a return to old masters, see Philip Mirowski, *Never Let a Serious Crisis Go to Waste: How Neoliberalism Survived the Financial Meltdown* (London: Verso 2013), ch. 1. For a lucid and insightful account of how the crisis was governed, see Paul Langley, *Liquidity Lost: The Governance of the Global Financial Crisis* (Oxford: Oxford University Press, 2015).

6. Charles Taylor, *Modern Social Imaginaries* (Durham, N.C.: Duke University Press, 2004).

7. The notion of the political has been defined in more specific ways from a range of authors. But there is no common denominator in how this notion is used. As Oliver Marchart argues, a minimal coherence can be found in how the political always addresses the moment of indeterminate foundation. But many more qualifications are usually added, as, for example, the notion of antagonism, most prominently in Carl Schmitt and later in Chantal Mouffe's and Ernesto Laclau's work. See, for an overview and discussion, Oliver Marchart, *Post-Foundational Political Thought: Political Difference in Nancy, Lefort, Badiou and Laclau* (Edinburgh: Edinburgh University Press, 2007). For the current project, none of these specifications are implied in using the notion of the political. It suffices to understand the "vision of the common" and the contested scene of its foundation as part of the political dimension. I discuss these conceptual issues in further detail below. The works of Jacques Rancière, Sheldon Wolin, and Bonnie Honig have therefore been helpful for this project. For the discussion of how the notion of the common is a specifically political attribute, see Sheldon Wolin, *Politics and Vision: Continuity and Innovation in Western Political Thought*, exp. ed. (Princeton, N.J.: Princeton University Press, 2004), 10.

8. Notions such as the political or the economic implicitly use a distinction that Martin Heidegger has introduced: that between the ontic and the ontological.

Whereas the first denotes the given forms and institutional set ups of a particular being, the latter points toward the specific but not yet articulated type of existence proper to it. Employing such notions does not necessitate adhering to this philosophical lineage in any strict sense. For a discussion of the use of the ontic and the ontological in this sense, see Chantal Mouffe, *On the Political* (London: Routledge, 2005), 8–9. Here the notion of ontology is radically historicized. It designates a level within discourses and dispositifs that articulate what is specific but still malleable about economy.

9. So far the notion of the economic is only scantily appearing in some discussions within economic sociology and cultural economy. Michel Callon, Yuval Millo, and Fabian Muniesa have argued that we need to analyze how the economic is produced: "The meaning of what it is to be 'economic' is precisely the outcome of a process of 'economization,' a process that is historical, contingent and disputable." See Michel Callon, Yuval Millo, and Fabian Muniesa, eds., *Market Devices* (Oxford: Blackwell, 2007), 3. Putting it this way, the definition becomes tautological. But the gist of this analytical perspective points toward the kind of historical analysis pursued here.

10. R. B. J. Walker, "Conclusion: Cultural, Political, Economy," in *Cultural Political Economy*, ed. Jacqueline Best and Matthew Patterson (New York: Routledge, 2010), 228–30.

11. Wolin, *Politics and Vision*, 371, 373, 271.

12. Bruno Latour, *We Have Never Been Modern* (Cambridge, Mass.: Harvard University Press, 1993), 13.

13. Comparing the strict conceptual divisions in modern society to a "double constitution suggests that a political act of founding is involved in dividing society into clearly separated logics and dominions. "Drafting a constitution" is about setting up different orders of justification, representation, subjectivity, and authority. Viewed in this perspective, the conceptual divisions entail a political subtext: "From now on every one should 'see double' and make no direct connection . . . between the artificiality of the facts and the artificiality of the Body Politic." Bruno Latour, "Postmodern? No, Simply Amodern! Steps Towards an Anthropology of Science," *Studies in History and Philosophy of Science* 21, no. 1 (1990): 155.

14. Karl Polanyi, *The Great Transformation: The Political and Economic Origins of Our Time* (Boston: Beacon, 1957), 127.

15. Catherine Gallagher, *The Body Economic: Life, Death, and Sensation in Political Economy and the Victorian Novel* (Princeton, N.J.: Princeton University Press, 2006), 40.

16. Michel Foucault, *The History of Sexuality: An Introduction*, vol. 1 (New York: Vintage Books, 1990), 143. Also see Michel Foucault, *Security, Territory, Population: Lectures at the Collège De France, 1977–78*, ed. Michel Sennellart (Basingstoke: Palgrave Macmillan, 2007), 21 and 43. For the assertion that biopolitics has a continuing but uncertain relation to liberalism, see Foucault's closing comment on his lecture on biopolitics: "What should now be studied, therefore, is the way in which the specific problems of life and population have been posed within a technology

of government which . . . has been haunted by the question of liberalism." Michel Foucault, *The Birth of Biopolitics: Lectures at the Collège des France, 1978–79*, ed. Michel Sennellart (Basingstoke: Palgrave Macmillan, 2008), 323.

17. For a discussion of the notion of scarcity in liberalism, see Nicholas Xenos, "Liberalism and the Postulate of Scarcity," *Political Theory* 15 (1987). For a more in-depth account of these changes in the notion of scarcity, see chapter 1.

18. Vivienne Brown, *Adam Smith's Discourse: Canonicity, Commerce, and Conscience* (London: Routledge, 1994), 151–52.

19. Michel Foucault, *The Order of Things: An Archaeology of the Human Sciences* (New York: Vintage Books, 1994), 257.

20. Karl Polanyi, *Trade and Market in the Early Empires: Economies in History and Theory* (Glencoe, Ill.: Free Press, 1957), 243.

21. R. J. G. Claassen, "Scarcity," in *Handbook of Economics and Ethics*, ed. Jan Peil and Irene van Staveren (Cheltenham, UK: Edward Elgar, 2009), 470.

22. For the argument of a "denaturalization" of economic thought during the nineteenth century, see Margaret Schabas, *The Natural Origins of Economics* (Chicago: University of Chicago Press, 2005). Timothy Mitchell argues that the denaturalization of economics occurred at a different point in time: the first decades of the twentieth century, in which the political-technical arrangements of large oil supplies made it possible to ignore natural limitations and to conceptualize economics as a field of dematerialized flows. Timothy Mitchell, *Carbon Democracy: Political Power in the Age of Oil* (London: Verso Books, 2011). These two diagnoses of naturalization and denaturalization refer to different processes: the first addresses the explicit theoretical foundation of economics; the second relates economic theories to the silenced material conditions of possibility that they must assume. These two perspectives on denaturalization are to be distinguished from the study of "natural images" of economic thought as furthered by Philip Mirowski, *inter alia*. If one looks at the metaphors and the conceptual transfer from nature to economics, economics never denaturalized. Philip Mirowski, ed., *Natural Images in Economic Thought: "Markets Read in Tooth & Claw"* (Cambridge: Cambridge University Press, 1994).

23. Mitchell Dean, *The Constitution of Poverty: Toward a Genealogy of Liberal Governance* (London: Routledge, 1991), 120 and 149. Dean has drawn attention to the fact that Foucault did not use this insight from the *Order of Things* to address the history of liberal governmentality. For a more elaborate discussion, see ibid., 223n2.

24. The exact relation between this naturalism of economic thought and the turn toward political economy as an "innocuous" and "apolitical" science is subject of debate. Donald Winch made an argument that naturalism and demoralization or depoliticization did not go hand in hand with Malthus. In this book, I take the question of life and biological existence as a theme that structured the elaboration of the liberal economic and the boundary to politics. No assumption is made about a logical sequence between naturalism and depoliticization, even though my take on Malthus differs from that of Winch. All depends on the notion of

nature employed and the vision of politics and economics befitted to it. The current debates on "new materialism" show how claims about nature and ecology belong to an elaboration of a new politics and ethics. See William E. Connolly, *The Fragility of Things: Self-Organizing Processes, Neoliberal Fantasies, and Democratic Activism* (Durham, N.C.: Duke University Press, 2013). For the historical moment in question, I concur with Winch's observation that "explaining the shift of focus in political economy" that occurred between Smith and Malthus requires "some attention to circumstance." This attention takes here the form of writing a genealogy of the economic through specific scenes. Donald Winch, "Robert Malthus: Christian Moral Scientist, Arch-Demoralizer or Implicit Secular Utilitarian?," *Utilitas* 5, no. 2 (1993): 251.

25. For a discussion of Adam Smith, see Murray Milgate and Shannon Stimson, *After Adam Smith: A Century of Transformation in Politics and Political Economy* (Princeton, N.J.: Princeton University Press, 2009), 27 and 32.

26. For the notion of society in Smith, see J. G. A. Pocock, "Cambridge Paradigms and Scotch Philosophers: A Study of the Relations between the Civic Humanist and the Civil Jurisprudential Interpretation of Eighteenth-Century Social Thought," in *Wealth and Virtue: The Shaping of Political Economy in the Scottish Enlightenment*, ed. Ivstan Hont and Michael Ignatieff (Cambridge: Cambridge University Press, 1983), 244. The notion of civil society, which not only Smith but the liberal political tradition in general took as the foundation for reasoning about social order, was posited as independent from the administrative apparatus and sovereign politics. For a discussion of the notion of civil society within economic discourse, see Milgate and Stimson, *After Adam Smith*, 46. Also Donald Winch, *Riches and Poverty: An Intellectual History of Political Economy in Britain, 1750–1834* (Cambridge: Cambridge University Press, 1996), 31. See also Ivstan Hont and Michael Ignatieff, eds., *Wealth and Virtue: The Shaping of Political Economy in the Scottish Enlightenment* (Cambridge: Cambridge University Press, 1983), 11.

27. Emma Rothschild, *Economic Sentiments: Adam Smith, Condorcet, and the Enlightenment* (Cambridge, Mass.: Harvard University Press, 2001), 55, 30.

28. Robert Castel, *From Manual Workers to Wage Laborers: Transformation of the Social Question* (New Brunswick, N.J.: Transaction Publishers, 2003), 170.

29. Rothschild, *Economic Sentiments*, 50, 218, 2, 247.

30. Ibid., 6.

31. Pocock, "Cambridge Paradigms," 251.

32. "In fact, for perhaps twenty-five years—during the first quarter of the nineteenth century when classical political economy assumed the form of an orthodoxy—Malthus' essay ranked second only to Smith as a cornerstone text of classical economics . . . [and] he was regarded as the country's foremost living political economist." David McNally, "Political Economy to the Fore: Burke, Malthus and the Whig Response to Popular Radicalism in the Age of the French Revolution," *History of Political Thought* 21, no. 3 (2000): 438.

33. See Thomas Robert Malthus, *The Works of Thomas Robert Malthus*, vol. 2–3, *An Essay on the Principle of Population. Sixth Edition (1826) with variant Readings from the*

Second Edition (1803), ed. Edward Anthony Wrigley and David Souden (London: William Pickering, 1986), 697.

34. Winch, *Riches and Poverty*, 233 and 247. David McNally comments on this, as follows: "It is an interesting irony of the intellectual history of early nineteenth-century Britain that, although he was out of step with a number of the main doctrines of classical political economy, Malthus becomes a central figure in this tradition." McNally, "Political Economy to the Fore," 238. Being out of step refers to Malthus's opposition against the free trade in corn and to his assumption that not only population but also capital could be superabundant, *inter alia*. For a discussion of the "economics" of Malthus, one must turn to the extended study of Samuel Hollander, *The Economics of Thomas Robert Malthus* (Toronto: University of Toronto Press, 1997).

35. D. L. LeMahieu has furnished an argument about the theological underpinnings of Malthus's economic and political thought. He argues that the secularized arguments on economic conduct are only pragmatic versions of "the economy of evil as just and compensatory as the law of supply and demand." The impurity of economic laws, their implicit political more than theological underpinnings, is very much the subject of the argument presented here. But the current argument takes more seriously that Malthus's argument sought grounds other than theological reasoning. D. L. LeMahieu, "Malthus and the Theology of Scarcity," *Journal of the History of Ideas* 40, no. 3 (1979).

36. Anthony Michael C. Waterman, *Revolution, Economics and Religion: Christian Political Economy, 1798–1833* (Cambridge: Cambridge University Press, 1991).

37. Milgate and Stimson, *After Adam Smith*, 122.

38. For a discussion of this term "historical ontology," see Ian Hacking, *Historical Ontology* (Cambridge, Mass.: Harvard University Press, 2004).

39. David Hume, *David Hume: Writings on Economics*, ed. Eugene Rotwein (London: Thomas Nelson, 1955), 37. As John Stuart Mill put it in the nineteenth century, "there cannot, in short, be intrinsically a more insignificant thing, in the economy of society, than money." John Stuart Mill, *Principles of Political Economy with Some of Their Applications to Social Philosophy*, vol. 3 of *The Collected Works of John Stuart Mill*, ed. John M Robson (Toronto: University of Toronto Press, 1965), 506.

40. Irving Fisher, the patriarch of American monetarism, describes his opus *The Purchasing Power of Money* at the beginning of the twentieth century as "at bottom simply a restatement of the old 'quantity theory of money.'" In Jonathan Kirshner, "The Political Economy of Low Inflation," *Journal of Economic Surveys* 15, no. 1 (2001): 56. Nigel Dodd explains the quantity theory of money in its general sense as follows: "In so far as money serves solely as a medium of exchange, there is little which is contentious or surprising about the theorem itself. If there is a definite quantity of money and a definite quantity of goods to be sold, the prices at which those goods will be sold is an elementary question of arithmetic, at least once values for the velocity of money's circulation and the volume of transactions are known." Nigel Dodd, *The Sociology of Money: Economics, Reason & Contemporary Society* (New York: Continuum, 1994), 10.

41. The classical model refers here to the basic tenets of macroeconomic thought from 1776–1936. See Brian Snowdon, Howard Vane, and Peter Wynarczyk, *A Modern Guide to Macroeconomics* (Cheltenham, U.K.: Edward Elgar Publishing, 1994), 56.

42. See, among other the following discussions of money in terms of politics, discourse, representation and culture, Michael Pryke and Paul du Gay, "Take an Issue: Cultural Economy and Finance," *Economy and Society* 36, no. 3 (2007); Marieke de Goede, *Virtue, Fortune and Faith: A Genealogy of Finance* (Minneapolis: University of Minnesota Press, 2005); and Bill Carruthers and Sarah Babb, "The Colour of Money and the Nature of Value: Greenbacks and Gold in Postbellum America," *American Journal of Sociology* 101, no. 6 (1996).

43. Jonathan Kirshner, "Money Is Politics," *Review of International Political Economy* 10, no. 4 (2003).

44. Polanyi, *The Great Transformation*, 196.

45. John Maynard Keynes, *Essays in Persuasion*, vol. 9 of *The Collected Writings of John Maynard Keynes*, ed. Donald Edward Moggridge (London: Macmillan for the Royal Economic Society, 1972), 59.

46. Richard Shannon, *The Crisis of Imperialism, 1865–1915* (London: Hart-Davis, MacGibbon, 1974), 109. David Landes describes the period from 1873 to 1896: "The years from 1873 to 1896 seemed to many contemporaries a startling departure from historical experience. Prices fell unevenly, sporadically, but inexorably through crisis and boom. . . . It was the most drastic deflation in the memory of man. . . . And profits shrank, while what was now recognized as periodic depressions seemed to drag on interminably. The economic system appeared to be running down." David Landes, *The Unbound Prometheus: Technological Change and Industrial Development in Western Europe from 1750 to the Present* (Cambridge: Cambridge University Press, 1969), 231. This stood in marked contrast to the two decades before, which either confirmed or promised expectations of increased prosperity for the future. Liberalism still believed in the "reconcilability of competing interests." Shannon, *Crisis of Imperialism*, 29.

47. Robert Colls and Philip Dodd, *Englishness: Politics and Culture 1880–1920* (London: Croom Helm, 1986), 54.

48. John Maynard Keynes, *The General Theory and After*, part II: *Defence and Development*, vol. 14 of *The Collected Writings of John Maynard Keynes*, ed. Donald Edward Moggridge (London: Macmillan for the Royal Society, 1973), 115.

49. Joan Robinson, "An Open Letter from a Keynesian to a Marxist," in *Collected Economic Papers* (Oxford: Basil Blackwell, 1973) 4:267–68.

50. Keynes, *Essays in Persuasion*, 306.

51. Ibid., 223–24.

52. Keynes, *The General Theory and After*, part II, 85; and John Maynard Keynes, *Social, Political and Literary Writings*, vol. 28 of *The Collected Writings of John Maynard Keynes*, ed. Donald Moggridge (London: Macmillan for the Royal Society, 1982), 42.

53. As J. E. King points out, J. R. Hicks has received the credit or the blame "for devising the first diagrammatic representation of Keynes's ideas . . . but the general equilibrium interpretation of the General Theory, on which the (in)famous

diagram relies, occurred more or less simultaneously to a number of writers, among them Roy Harrod." King, *A History*, 15. Franco Modigliani formulated the most orthodox account of the Keynesian model that became the cornerstone of the neoclassical synthesis. Ibid., 18. On the debate on how revolutionary Keynes really was, see J. W. King, *A History of Post-Keynesian Economics Since 1936* (Cheltenham, U.K.: Edward Elgar, 2002), 16–24. Keynes's work was regarded to be both a minor refinement and addition to classical theories, on the one hand, or a revolutionary undoing of their premises, on the other (ibid.). To settle the question about the "true" contribution of Keynes's economics to economic theory, there are many differing Keynesians: neo-Keynesians, post-Keynesians, or fundamentalist Keynesians. For how post-Keynesian differentiate themselves, see Philip Arestis, *The Post-Keynesian Approach to Economics* (Aldershot, U.K.: Edward Elgar, 1992), 88–89.

54. The first phrase from Russell is cited in Ann Banfield's work on the epistemology of modernism. See Ann Banfield, *The Phantom Table: Woolf, Fry, Russell and the Epistemology of Modernism* (Cambridge: Cambridge University Press, 2000), xiv. The quote from Woolf is cited in Derek Crabtree and A. P. Thirlwall, eds., *Keynes and the Bloomsbury Group* (London: Macmillan, 1980), 47. Keynes became as an undergraduate in 1903 a member of the Apostles, "a secret society with a tradition of philosophical discussion" founded in 1820. See R. M. O'Donnell, *Keynes: Philosophy, Economics and Politics: The Philosophical Foundations of Keynes's Thought and Their Influence on His Economics and Politics* (New York: St. Martin's Press, 1989), 12. For an account of the Apostles, also see Robert Skidelsky, *Hopes Betrayed 1883–1920*, vol. 1 of *John Maynard Keynes: A Biography* (London: MacMillan, 1983), 116. Bertrand Russell and G. E. Moore were members of the Apostles. "Bloomsbury" is the name of the cultural and social group that comprised also Vanessa Bell, Desmond McCarthy, and Adrian and Karin Stephen. The Apostles and Bloomsbury had overlapping membership. Leonard Woolf, Lytton Strachey, and Roger Fry belonged to both. To mention just two of their very important "public activities," not even going into the writings of Clive Bell or Virginia Woolf, or the art of Vanessa Bell or Duncan Grant: Roger Fry organized the first postimpressionism exhibition in London 1910—showing Cézanne, Gauguin, van Gogh, Matisse, Picasso—that became paradigmatic for the change in tastes and perception. See Piero Mini, *Keynes, Bloomsbury and the General Theory* (New York: St. Martin's Press, 1991), 92. Besides introducing the art of the continent to England, the group is also responsible for effectively disseminating Freudian thinking to the British island. Adrian Stephen, Karin Stephen, and James Strachey had all studied with Freud in Vienna. James Strachey was the general editor of the *Standard Edition* of Freud in English and Leonard and Virginia Woolf's Hogarth Press was its publisher. See E. G. Winslow, "Keynes and Freud: Psychoanalysis in Keynes' Account of the 'Animal Spirits' of Capitalism," *Social Research* 53, no. 4 (1986): 554. Shone describes the fate of the group in following terms: "What had appeared in the 1920s as a way of life that was refreshingly free of convention, liberal and delightfully pliant, seemed to many in the later decade

as spineless, frivolous and uncommitted." The death of Julian Bell in the Spanish civil war appears as the most poignant symbol of that confrontation. See Richard Shone, "A General Account of the Bloomsbury Group," in *Keynes and the Bloomsbury Group*, ed. Derek Crabtree and A. P. Thirlwall (London: MacMillan, 1980), 27. For Virginia Woolf and Bloomsbury, see Christine Froula, *Virginia Woolf and the Bloomsbury Avant-Garde: War, Civilization, Modernity* (New York: Columbia University Press, 2005).

55. See Raymond Williams, "The Significance of 'Bloomsbury' as a Social and Cultural Group," in *Keynes and the Bloomsbury Group*, ed. Derek Crabtree and A. P. Thirlwall (London: Macmillan, 1980), 62.

56. Banfield, *The Phantom Table*, 15, 42. Also see Rossana Bonadei's discussion of modernism and Keynes in "John Maynard Keynes: Contexts and Methods," in *John Maynard Keynes. Language and Method*, ed. Alessandra and Francesco Silva Marzola (London: Edward Elgar, 1994), 47. For helpful general account of the philosophical source and implications of modernism, see Michael Bell, "The Metaphysics of Modernism," in *The Cambridge Companion to Modernism*, ed. Michael Levenson (Cambridge: Cambridge University Press, 1999).

57. Alessandra Marzola, "Rhetoric and Imagination in the Economic and Political Writings of J. M. Keynes," in *John Maynard Keynes. Language and Method*, ed. Alessandra Marzola and Francesco Silva (Aldershot, U.K.: Edward Elgar, 1994), 194.

58. Jennifer Wicke argues that the parallel between modernism and Keynes lies on this level of representation: "Like consciousness, the market has come to defy description, in that it is no longer equitable with realist or entirely rationalist models of representation" See Jennifer Wicke, "Mrs. Dalloway Goes to Market: Woolf, Keynes, and Modern Markets," *NOVEL: A Forum for Fiction* 28, no. 1 (1994): 11.

59. Jed Esty discusses the debate on totality and modernist representation that has been famously initiated by Frederic Jameson's claim that modernism's preoccupation with representation is the result of a political unconscious about British imperialism that precipitated a "lost totality." Jed Esty, *A Shrinking Island. Modernism and National Culture in England* (Princeton, N.J.: Princeton University Press, 2004), 6. Keynesian discourse, in this perspective, reeks with the experiments of modernist representation, trying to "open up new vistas on reality which has been passed over by superficial and conventional observation." Bonadei, "Context and Methods," 50, 47, 58; and Marzola, "Rhetoric and Imagination," 220. Anna Carabelli has consistently stressed the question of "organic independence" of economy, referring to a whole that exceeds the sum of the parts. See Anna Carabelli, "Uncertainty and Measurement in Keynes: Probability and Organicness," in *Keynes, Knowledge and Uncertainty*, ed. Sheila and John Hillard Dow (Aldershot, U.K.: Edward Elgar, 1995); and Anna Carabelli, *On Keynes's Method* (London: Macmillan, 1988).

60. See Keynes, *Essays in Biography*, vol. 10 of *Collected Writings of John Maynard Keynes*, ed. Donald Edward Moggridge (London: Macmillan for the Royal Economic Society, 1972, 262.

61. Keynes, *The General Theory and After*, part II, 114.

62. Joan Robinson, "What Has Become of the Keynesian Revolution?," in *Essays on John Maynard Keynes*, ed. Milo Keynes (Cambridge: Cambridge University Press, 1975), 125. Robert Skidelsky summarizes this scholarship in an accessible and lucid fashion. Robert Skidelsky, *John Maynard Keynes: A Biography*, vol. 2, *The Economist as Saviour 1920–1937* (London: Macmillan, 1992), 83.

63. See Teodore Dario Togati, "Keynes as the Einstein of Economic Theory," *History of Political Economy* 33, no. 1 (2001). Keynes has written two essays on Einstein and was alluding himself to such parallel. See Keynes, *Essays in Biography*, vol. 10; and Keynes, *Social, Political and Literary Writings*. In the introduction to the *General Theory on Employment, Money and Interest*, this association with the scientific revolution in physics sounds as follows: "We are thus led to a more general theory, which includes the classical theory with which we are familiar, as a special case." Keynes, *The General Theory on Employment, Money and Interest*, vol. 7 of *The Collected Writings of John Maynard Keynes*, ed. Donald Moggridge (London: Macmillan for the Royal Economic Society, 1973), xxiii. On the importance of temporality for Keynesian economics see also George L. S. Shackle, *Keynesian Kaleidics: The Evolution of a General Political Economy* (Edinburgh: Edinburgh University Press, 1974). See also the discussion in chapter 5.

64. Skidelsky, *The Economist as Saviour*, 82 and 540.

65. Philip Mirowski, *Machine Dreams: Economics Becomes a Cyborg Science* (Cambridge: Cambridge University Press, 2002), 514–17.

66. Robert Skidelsky, *John Maynard Keynes, 1883–1946: Economist, Philosopher, Statesman* (London: Macmillan, 2003), 846.

67. For exemplary discussions, see Sheila Dow and John Hillard, *Keynes, Knowledge and Uncertainty* (Aldershot, U.K.: Edward Elgar, 1995).

68. "I have found it instructive and illuminating and I really have no criticisms. I think that you have re-orientated the argument beautifully." Keynes, *The General Theory and After*, part II, 84.

69. Keynes explains his understanding of economic knowledge and economic models as follows: "It seems to me that economics is a branch of logic, a way of thinking; . . . it is of the essence of a model that one does not fill in real values for the variable functions. To do so would make it useless as a model. . . . Economics is a science of thinking in terms of models linked to the art of choosing models, which are relevant to the contemporary world. It is compelled to be this, because, unlike the typical natural science, the material to which it is applied is, in too many respects not homogeneous through time." Ibid., 296–97.

70. Escobar, *Encountering Development*, 59 and 61; see also J. K. Gibson-Graham, *The End of Capitalism (as We Knew It): A Feminist Critique of Political Economy* (Cambridge, Mass.: Blackwell, 1996).

71. Escobar, *Encountering Development*; James Ferguson, *The Anti-Politics Machine: "Development," Depoliticization, and Bureaucratic Power in Lesotho* (Cambridge: Cambridge University Press, 1990); Stephen Gudeman, *Economics as Culture: Models and Metaphors of Livelihood* (London: Routledge, 1986); and Timothy Mitchell,

The Rule of Experts: Egypt, Techno-Politics and Modernity (Berkeley: University of California Press, 2002).

72. Philip Mirowski's erudite historical reconstruction of the cultural and political history of economic knowledge demonstrates this point in different instances. His works on the rise of neoclassical thought shows how the attempt to emulate the physical sciences by introducing the concept of energy necessarily failed on account of the very metaphor that was to ensure its similarity to physics. Philip Mirowski, *More Heat Than Light: Economics as a Social Physics, Physics as Nature's Economics* (Cambridge: Cambridge University Press, 1989). The postwar interlacing of neoclassical economics and military research offers a different case how economics is shaped by forgotten genealogies. See Mirowski, *Machine Dreams.* Mary Poovey has provided a "historical epistemology" of what counts as fact in economic discourse, undermining the putative independence of these facts from theoretical generalizations. See Mary Poovey, *A History of the Modern Fact: Problems of Knowledge in the Sciences of Wealth and Society* (Chicago: Chicago University Press, 1998). For an account of the contested "soul" of economics in the interwar years, see Yuval Yonay, *The Struggle Over the Soul of Economics: Institutionalist and Neoclassical Economists in America Between the Wars* (Princeton, N.J.: Princeton University Press, 1998).

73. Koray Caliskan and Michel Callon, "Economization, Part 1: Shifting Attention from the Economy Towards Processes of Economization," *Economy and Society* 38, no. 3 (2009): 370. For an up-to-date discussion of the field, see Jacqueline Best and Matthew Paterson, eds., *Cultural Political Economy* (London: Routledge, 2010), 2–5.

74. Donald A. MacKenzie, Fabian Muniesa, and Lucia Siu, *Do Economists Make Markets? On the Performativity of Economics* (Princeton, N.J.: Princeton University Press, 2007). For programmatic overviews and theoretical discussions, see Michel Callon, "Performativity, Misfires and Politics," *Journal of Cultural Economy* 3, no. 2 (2010); Paul du Gay and Michael Pryke, eds., *Cultural Economy: Cultural Analysis and Commercial Life* (Thousand Oaks, Calif.: Sage, 2002); Marieke de Goede, *International Political Economy and Poststructural Politics* (New York: Palgrave Macmillan, 2006); Roger Lee, Andrew Leyshon, and Adrian Smith, "Rethinking Economies/Economic Geographies," *Geoforum* 39, no. 3 (2008); and William Walters, "Decentring the Economy," *Economy and Society* 28, no. 2 (1999). The journal *Cultural Economy* dedicated a whole issue to the notion of performativity of economics. For a critical comment on how the notion of performativity has come to dominate the field, see Judith Butler's contribution "Performative Agency," *Journal of Cultural Economy* 3, no. 2 (2010), 152 and 154. See also Philip Mirowski and Edward Nik-Khah, "Command Performance: Exploring What STS Thinks It Takes to Build a Market," in *Living in a Material World: Economic Sociology Meets Science and Technology Studies*, ed. Trevor Pinch and Richard Swedberg (Cambridge, Mass.: MIT Press, 2008).

75. Callon, "Performativity, Misfires and Politics," 165.

76. Michel Callon has addressed this co-constitution but without assuming that this requires specific methodologies of analysis. Ibid.

77. Andrew Barry, "The Anti-Political Economy," *Economy and Society* 31, no. 2 (2002): 268. For the discussion of the political in finance, see Marieke de Goede, "Repoliticizing Financial Risk," *Economy and Society* 33, no. 2 (2004). For a critique of contingency as the political element per se, see du Gay and Pryke, *Cultural Economy*, 3–5. They maintain that "to highlight the contingent assemblage of the economic in this way is not to endorse a politics . . . for it seems very difficult, if not impossible, to make contingency a matter of either celebration or suspicion as opposed to a brute fact that has to be dealt with." Du Gay and Pryke, *Cultural Economy*, 3–5.

78. Max Weber, *The Protestant Ethic and the Spirit of Capitalism* (London: Routledge, 2001).

79. Max Weber, *Gesammelte Aufsätze Zur Soziologie und Sozialpolitik* (Tübingen: Mohr, 1988), 416 and 419.

80. Gunnar Myrdal, *The Political Element in the Development of Economic Theory* (Cambridge, Mass.: Harvard University Press, 1954), 17.

81. L. Boltanski and E. Chiapello, *The New Spirit of Capitalism* (London: Verso, 2005), 23–24. For the elaboration of the theoretical model of justification and critique, see Luc Boltanski and Laurent Thévenot, *On Justification: Economies of Worth* (Princeton, N.J.: Princeton University Press, 2006).

82. Eve Chiapello and Luc Boltanski avoid this problem to a certain extent by taking a very scaled down yet plausible definition of capitalism as their starting point. Nevertheless, they have to assume an inherently expansive and pure "logic" of capital, which they juxtapose to a set of normative constraints shaping and delimiting it. This produces a theoretical blind spot since one ceases to ask what kind of normative, political, or cultural forces produce such expansive logic in the first place.

83. Jacques Rancière, *Dissensus: On Politics and Aesthetics* (London: Continuum, 2010), 49, 207, 212. Even though Rancière did not address the role of economics, the prime example he gives of such "archipolitics" refers to an economic-cum-political model of the community: Plato's political republic in which "individuals, needs, and the means to satisfy them" cohere into the just order and form a "a masterpiece of economy." Jacques Rancière, *The Philosopher and His Poor* (Durham, N.C.: Duke University Press, 2003), 3.

84. Bonnie Honig, *Political Theory and the Displacement of Politics* (Ithaca, N.Y.: Cornell University Press, 1993), 108.

85. Instead of using the distinction between politics and the political, Rancière uses the distinction between politics and police. But in this context, these distinctions can be mapped onto each other. In order to avoid unnecessary confusion, I use the notion of "the political" to denote what Rancière calls politics proper.

86. Rancière calls this "system of self-evident facts" the "distribution of the sensible," which he defines as an order of "sense perception that simultaneously discloses the existence of some-thing in common and the delimitations that define the respective parts and positions within it." Jacques Rancière, *The Politics of Aesthetics: The Distribution of the Sensible* (London: Continuum), 12.

87. Ibid., 13.

88. Ulrich Bröckling, Susanne Krasmann, and Thomas Lemke, "From Foucault's Lectures at the College de France to Studies of Governmentality: An Introduction," in *Governmentality: Current Issues and Future Challenges*, ed. Ulrich Bröckling, Susanne Krasmann, and Thomas Lemke (New York: Routledge, 2011), 5.

89. Foucault, *Security, Territory, Population*, 95 and 34.

90. For this point, see Foucault, *The Birth of Biopolitics*, 271. See also Foucault, *Security, Territory, Population*, 106, 352. "Advanced liberal rule," as Nikolas Rose concisely defines it, "governs through the regulated choices of individual citizens." Nikolas Rose, "Government, Authority and Expertise in Advanced Liberalism," *Economy and Society* 22, no. 3 (1993): 285. Under the paradigm of neoliberalism, the entrepreneur with his imperative of self-activation has become a ubiquitous form of subjectivity, which is made to traverse the whole social field. See Ulrich Bröckling, *Das unternehmerische Selbst: Soziologie einer Subjektivierungsform* (Frankfurt am Main: Suhrkamp, 2007). In this sense, governmentality is admirably well equipped to understand the pervasive application of these strategies of conducting conduct: historical reality and analytical strategy intermesh perfectly, in both critical and analytical ways.

91. Barry, "Anti-Political Economy," 270. Mitchell Dean also emphasizes the need to tie this governmental analysis to the "mythologies" at work in politics. See Mitchell Dean, "A Political Mythology of World Order: Carl Schmitt's Nomos," *Theory Culture and Society* 23, no. 5 (2006).

92. Nicolas Berland and Eve Chiapello, "Criticisms of Capitalism, Budgeting and the Double Enrolment: Budgetary Control Rhetoric and Social Reform in France in the 1930s and 1950s," *Accounting, Organizations and Society* 34, no. 1 (2009): 29.

93. Denis Meuret has suggested writing a political genealogy of liberal economy that differs from Foucault's. He argues to understand the emergence of the science of political economy as a type of political constitution. Referring mainly to Claude Lefort, he writes: "We should think of it [science of political economy] as a diplomatic treaty a compromise that each player agrees to because its nature appears such as to protect each of them from the other two." He refers to the state, capitalism, and the public as the players involved. His "political genealogy" is to some extent kindred in spirit, but very differently in practice to what is suggested here. Denis Meuret, "A Political Genealogy of Political Economy," *Economy and Society* 17, no. 2 (1988): 228.

94. For a discussion of how to multiply the genealogies of liberalism by addressing the rearticulation, adaptation, and modulation of technologies of power in response to new problematizations, see Stephen Collier, "Topologies of Power. Foucault's Analysis of Political Government Beyond 'Governmentality,'" *Theory, Culture and Society* 26, no. 6 (2009).

95. Michel Foucault, *Nietzsche, Genealogy, History*, in *Language, Counter-Memory, Practice: Selected Essays and Interviews by Michel Foucault*, ed. Donald F. Bouchard (Ithaca, N.Y.: Cornell University Press, 1977), 144, 142, 146, and 151.

96. Foucault, *Genealogy*, 150, 152.

97. This distinction belongs properly to the performing arts but has been also employed by Claude Lefort in the context of his political theory about the symbolic constitution of society. Here it is yet again adapted to refer to a theoretical artifice for writing the genealogy of the economic. For a discussion of Lefort's use of the term, see James Ingram, "The Politics of Claude Lefort's Political: Between Liberalism and Radical Democracy," *Thesis Eleven* 87, no. 1 (2006): 36.

98. Foucault, *Nietzsche, Genealogy, History,* 140. Genealogy includes an archeological analysis of discourse but emphasizes more than the former the struggles that pertain to the institution of discursive orders. Discourse-analysis targets a level of thought that pertains to the "surface of emergence" of scientific objects, asking what "enables [them] to appear, to juxtapose [themselves] with other objects, to situate itself in relation to them, to define its difference, its irreducibility, and even perhaps its heterogeneity." Michel Foucault, *Archaeology of Knowledge* (London: Routledge, 2002), 50.

99. Foucault, *Archaeology,* 50; and Foucault, *The Birth of Biopolitics,* 35–36.

100. Foucault, *Archaeology of Knowledge,* 66.

101. This strategy of reading entertains a certain family resemblance to Albert Hirschman's analysis of the political arguments that are encapsulated in economic concepts. See chapter 3 for a more extended discussion. Albert O. Hirschman, *The Passions and the Interests: Political Arguments for Capitalism Before Its Triumph* (Princeton, N.J.: Princeton University Press, 1997), 100.

102. Michel Foucault, "Methodologie pour la connaissance du monde: Comment se debarrasser du Marxisme," in *Foucault: Dits et ecrits 1954–1988,* vol. 2, *1976–1988,* ed. Daniel Defert and Francois Ewald (Paris: Gallimard, 2008): 599.

103. Jacques Rancière, *Dissensus,* 2016.

1. The Invention of Economic Necessity

1. For these often-recounted events, see Olwen H. Hufton, *Women and the Limits of Citizenship in the French Revolution* (Toronto: University of Toronto Press, 1992), 7–12. Also see Georg Rudé, *The Crowd in the French Revolution* (London: Oxford University Press, 1972), ch. 5.

2. Edmund Burke, *Revolutionary Writings: Reflections on the Revolution in France and the First Letter on a Regicide Peace,* ed. Iain Hampsher-Monk (Cambridge: Cambridge University Press, 2014); see also Thomas Paine, *Rights of Man, Common Sense, and Other Writings,* ed. Mark Philp (Oxford: Oxford University Press, 1995). For a discussion of the rhetoric of Burke, see Isaac Kramnick, *The Rage of Edmund Burke: Portrait of an Ambivalent Conservative* (New York: Basic Books, 1977).

3. Gregory Claeys, "The Origins of the Rights of Labor: Republicanism, Commerce, and the Construction of Modern Social Theory in Britain, 1796–1805," *Journal of Modern History* 66 (1994): 249. For an account of the French Revolution

Debate, see Gregory Claeys, *French Revolution Debate in Britain: The Origins of Modern Politics* (New York: Palgrave Macmillan, 2007).

4. For a discussion of this short period as a forgotten historical moment in the history of liberalism, see Gareth Stedman Jones, *An End to Poverty? A Historical Debate* (London: Profile Books, 2004).

5. Hannah Arendt quotes the *Declaration of the Rights of the Sansculottes*, proposed by Boisset, who was a friend of Robbespiere; see Hannah Arendt, *On Revolution* (New York: Viking Press, 1963), 55.

6. Ibid., 54.

7. Michel Foucault, *Security, Territory, Population: Lectures at the Collège De France, 1977–78*, ed. Michel Sennellart (Basingstoke: Palgrave Macmillan, 2007), 104, 79.

8. Jacques Rancière, *Dissensus: On Politics and Aesthetics* (London: Continuum, 2010), 38.

9. Emma Rothschild, "Political Economy," in *The Cambridge History of Nineteenth-Century Political Thought*, ed. Gareth Stedman Jones and Gregory Claeys (Cambridge: Cambridge University Press, 2011), 753.

10. Cheryl B. Welch, "Social Science from the French Revolution to Positivism," in *The Cambridge History of Nineteenth-Century Political Thought*, ed. Gareth Stedman Jones and Gregory Claeys (Cambridge: Cambridge University Press, 2011), 177–78.

11. Rothschild, "Political Economy," 756; and Alon Kadish and Keith Tribe, "Introduction: The Supply of and Demand for Economics in Late Victorian Britain," in *The Market for Political Economy: The Advent of Economics in British University Culture, 1850–1905*, ed. Alon Kadish and Keith Tribe (London: Routledge, 1993), 3.

12. For a good overview of the reception, Robert Thomas Malthus's biography, and the content of his books, see Patricia James, *Population Malthus: His Life and Times* (London: Routledge, 1979), 69, 116. About the reception of Malthus's book, see John Avery, *Progress, Poverty, and Population: Re-Reading Condorcet, Godwin, and Malthus* (London: F. Cass, 1997), xv, 56. A helpful source is also Elie Halévy, *L'Evolution de la doctrine utilitaire de 1789 à 1815*, vol. 2 of *La Formation du radicalisme philosophique* (Paris: Presses Universitaires de France, 1995), 2: 104.

13. James Bonar, *Malthus and His Work* (London: Routledge, 2014), 2.

14. Avery, *Progress, Poverty, and Population*, 77. The success of the first version led Malthus to undertake a much more extended research, resulting in a much larger second edition, which appeared in 1803. The empirical basis for the new work included, among other things, his own observations during the travels he had undertaken to Norway, France, and Switzerland and the letters of the missionaries from the colonies. One of the most commented upon differences between the editions lies in the "ever-greater emphasis" Malthus placed on the effectiveness of moral restraint while he had removed "those passages which had caused the widest offense." See Thomas Robert Malthus, *An Essay on the Principle of Population. Sixth Edition (1826) with Variant Readings from the Second Edition (1803)*, vol. 2 and 3 of *The Works of Thomas Robert Malthus*, ed. Edward Anthony Wrigley and David Souden (London: William Pickering, 1986), 7. But there are many changes

throughout the editions. The fifth edition, for example, concentrated on the schemes of Robert Owen instead of those of William Godwin to exemplify the peculiar problem the force of population posed against their ideas of improvement. For a discussion of the editions, see James, *Population Malthus*, 81, 376. The reading given in this work relies on the enlarged editions, using the sixth as the reference point, but being cognizant of the changes that occurred since the first edition. The work is treated as a whole and the quotes travel back and forth between the editions, warranted by the fact that the logical structure of the essay was retained throughout. Malthus himself described the difference between the first and second edition in the following words: "To those who still think that any check to population whatever would be worse than the evils which it would relieve, the conclusions of the former Essay remain in full force." Malthus, *Population*, iii.

15. Cited in Arthur E. Walzer, "Logic and Rhetoric in Malthus's 'Essay on the Principle of Population, 1798,'" *Quarterly Journal of Speech* 73 (1987): 2.

16. Francis Barker, ed., *1789, Reading, Writing Revolution: Proceedings of the Essex Conference on the Sociology of Literature, July 1981* (Colchester: University of Essex 1982), 160. The launching of the *Edinburgh Review* in 1802 furthered debates on political economy as well as the Mechanics' Institutes of the 1820. The best-known popular accounts of political economy were Jane Marcet's *Conversation on Political Economy* (1816) and Harriet Martineau's *Illustrations of Political Economy: Easy Lessons on Money Matters* (1833). The latter was intended for children but reached an estimated two million readers. For a discussion of this popularization in terms of a political history, see David McNally, "Political Economy to the Fore: Burke, Malthus and the Whig Response to Popular Radicalism in the Age of the French Revolution," *History of Political Thought* 21, no. 3 (2000): 427–47. For an account from the history of science, see Margaret Schabas, "British Economic Theory from Locke to Marshall," in *The Cambridge History of Science*, ed. Theodore Porter (Cambridge: Cambridge University Press, 2003); and Deborah A. Redman, *The Rise of Political Economy as a Science: Methodology and the Classical Economists* (Cambridge, Mass.: MIT Press, 1997), 275.

17. This quote stems from the contemporary of Malthus, Edwin Chadwick, who commented on Malthus's text in a foreword to Jeremy Bentham's *Observation on the Poor Bill*. Cited in Clara Tuite "Frankenstein's Monster and Malthus' "Jaundiced Eye": Population, Body Politics, and the Monstrous Sublime," *Eighteenth-Century Life* 22, no. 1 (1998), 150. See chapter 2 for further discussion of the Poor Laws.

18. F. Rosen, "The Principle of Population as Political Theory: Godwin's *Of Population* and the Malthusian Controversy," *Journal of the History of Ideas* 31, no. 1 (1970): 37.

19. The quote continues: "The increasing attention which in the interval has been paid generally to the science of political economy; the lectures which have been given at the projected university in the metropolis, and, above all, the Mechanics' Institution, open the fairest prospect that, within a moderate period of time, the fundamental principles of political economy will, to a very useful extent, be

known to the higher, middle, and a most important portion of the working classes of society in England." Malthus, *Population*, 526.

20. It is significant that this chair was founded at a college that was set up set up by the directors of the East India Company to ensure a formal training of its civil servants. For the colonial genealogy of liberal economy, see the discussion in the following chapter. Patricia James gives a very thorough and interesting account of the founding of the East India College at Hertford. She writes that students "should be imbued with reverence and love for the Religion, the Constitution, and Laws of their own Country," and they studied classical literature for writing skills, arithmetic, "general law, politics, finance and commerce" and "oriental learning." The third subject was later transformed into the title of political economy, for which Malthus took the post. James gives a detailed account of the history of its founding and the connections between the parliament, the board, and the company at play. See James, *Population Malthus*, 168–75.

21. Oxford established the Drummond Chair in 1819, followed by Cambridge and University College, London, in 1812 and King's College in 1831. See Schabas, *British Economic Theory*, 178.

22. Margaret Schabas, *The Natural Origins of Economics* (Chicago: University of Chicago Press, 2005), 5. Also see Emma Rothschild, *Economic Sentiments: Adam Smith, Condorcet, and the Enlightenment* (Cambridge, Mass.: Harvard University Press, 2001), 247.

23. Thomas Robert Malthus, *An Essay on the Principle of Population: The First Edition (1798) with Introduction and Bibliography*, vol. 1 of *The Works of Thomas Robert Malthus*, ed. by Edward Anthony Wrigley and David Souden (London: William Pickering, 1986), 97.

24. Immanuel Kant, "The Contest of Faculties," in *Political Writings*, ed. Hans Reiss (Cambridge: Cambridge University Press, 1991), 182.

25. Malthus, *Population*, 319–20.

26. Jean-Antoine-Nicolas de Caritat, Marquis de Condorcet, *Sketch for a Historical Picture of the Progress of the Human Mind* (New York: Noonday Press, 1955), 150.

27. Roger A. E. Wells, *Insurrection: The British Experience, 1795–1803* (Gloucester: A. Sutton, 1983), 21. But the political demands for constitutional reform—that is, improved representation through annual suffrage—had their precursors even earlier in the eighteenth century, reaching back to the 1720s and the activities of Viscount Bolingbroke and Robert Walpole. A continuous strand, weaving earlier and later traditions of English radicalism together, was established through the history of religious dissent, culminating in the writings of Joseph Priestley, James Burgh, and Richard Price. In the last years of the 1780s the agitation to remove the political exclusion of dissenters was linked to more general constitutional critique. Moments of politicization also came through the abolitionist movement. See Edward Royle and James Walvin, *English Radicals and Reformers, 1760–1848* (Lexington: University Press of Kentucky, 1982), 13–40, 43–45, 113.

28. Harry Thomas Dickinson, *British Radicalism and the French Revolution, 1789–1815* (Oxford: Blackwell, 1985), 1.

29. Mark Philp, *Reforming Ideas in Britain: Politics and Language in the Shadow of the French Revolution, 1789–1815* (Cambridge: Cambridge University Press, 2014), 19.

30. Ibid., 17.

31. Royle and Walvin, *English Radicals*, 42–45. See also Dickinson, *British Radicalism*, 2.

32. Philp, *Reforming Ideas*, 22.

33. Royle and Walvin, *English Radicals*, 17 and 30. The foundation of societies like the Society for Constitutional Reform became instrumental in the widening of the public base for political constitution.

34. Dickinson, *British Radicalism*, 19–20.

35. Olivia Smith, *The Politics of Language 1791–1819* (Oxford: Clarendon Press, 1984), 57.

36. Edward P. Thompson, *The Making of the English Working Class* (New York: Vintage, 1966), 107–11.

37. Ibid., 57, 59, 61. See also Wells, *Insurrection*, 21.

38. Thompson, *The Making of the English Working Class*, 110.

39. Gregory Claeys and Christine Lattekt, "Radicalism, Republicanism and Revolutionism," in *The Cambridge History of Nineteenth-Century Political Thought*, ed. Gareth Stedman Jones and Gregory Claeys (Cambridge: Cambridge University Press, 2011), 205–6.

40. Claeys, "Rights of Labor," 252.

41. Royle and Walvin, *English Radicals*, 49.

42. John Dinwiddy, "Interpretations of Anti-Jacobinism," in *The French Revolution and British Popular Politics*, ed. Mark Philp (Cambridge: Cambridge University Press, 1991), 48; see also Rudé, *The Crowd*, 24–29.

43. Dickinson, *British Radicalism*, 57. Dickinson proposes such middling assessment of this contentious issue, whereas Roger Wells, Edward Royle and James Walvin, and Georg Rudé make a stronger case for the politicization of economic issues. See, for example, Wells, *Insurrection*, 21, 76. Well describes how the political societies, like the London Corresponding Society, sought to address the wider public by taking up the issue of food, and Royle emphasizes that the London Corresponding Society started to speak with a "collective voice for London's distressed artisans and, more generally, for the dispossessed throughout the nation." Royle and Walvin, *English Radicals*, 49. For a more skeptical position, see Jan Christie, "Conservatism and Stability in British Society," in *The French Revolution and British Popular Politics*, ed. Mark Philp (Cambridge: Cambridge University Press, 1991), 171; Dinwiddy, "Interpretations of Anti-Jacobinism," also strikes a middle chord in this debate.

44. Dickinson, *British Radicalism*, 43.

45. Philp, *Reforming Ideas*, 21–22.

46. Smith, *The Politics of Language*, 64.

47. In July of 1795 the suspension of habeas corpus had lapsed but was followed by the so-called Two Acts, which banned all meetings of more than forty people and the licensing of lecture halls. "The British government faced widespread,

organized pressure for parliamentary reform, and a public which had been so encouraged to flirt with republicanism . . . that the social and political elite had felt it necessary to organise to an unprecedented extent in defense of the status quo and the constitution." Philp, *French Revolution and British Popular Politics*, 9. See also Royle and Walvin, *English Radicals*, 77; and Wells, *Insurrection*, 23.

48. For the debate before its demise and the account of this apostasy, see Keven Lee Cope and Rüdiger Ahrens, *Talking Forward, Talking Back: Critical Dialogues with the Enlightenment* (New York: AMS Press, 2002), 43.

49. Claeys, "Rights of Labor," 251.

50. Welch, "Social Science," 171; Johan Heilbron, *The Rise of Social Theory* (Minneapolis: University of Minnesota Press, 1995), 91, 140, 168; I. Bernard Cohen, *The Scientific Revolution and the Social Sciences*, in *The Natural Sciences and the Social Sciences*, ed. I. Bernard Cohen (Dordrecht: Kluwer, 1994); and Peter Gay, *The Enlightenment: An Interpretation: The Science of Freedom* (New York: W. W. Norton, 1969), 322.

51. Sheldon Wolin, *Politics and Vision: Continuity and Innovation in Western Political Thought*, exp. ed. (Princeton, N.J.: Princeton University Press, 2004), 281.

52. Karl Polanyi, *The Great Transformation: The Political and Economic Origins of Our Time* (Boston: Beacon, 1957), 84–85.

53. Michel Foucault, *The Birth of Biopolitics: Lectures at the Collège de France, 1978–79*, ed. Michel Sennellart (Basingstoke: Palgrave Macmillan, 2008), 313.

54. Ibid., 308.

55. Elizabeth A. Williams, *The Physical and the Moral: Anthropology, Physiology, and Philosophical Medicine in France, 1750–1850* (Cambridge: Cambridge University Press, 1994), 104, 155, 187, and 130. See also Heilbron, *The Rise of Social Theory*, 180.

56. Margaret Schabas and Neil De Marchi, *Oeconomies in the Age of Newton* (Durham, N.C.: Duke University Press, 2003), 282–84. Sympathy was a notion derived from the study of the nervous system, "which first began to make its inroads into the Edinburgh medical establishment with the appointment of Robert Whytt" (ibid., 290). For a very instructive account of the relevance of the "study of the nervous system" for the Scottish Enlightenment, and thus for Adam Smith and later Malthus, see Christopher Lawrence, "The Nervous System and Society in the Scottish Enlightenment," in *Natural Order: Historical Studies of Scientific Culture*, ed. Barry Barnes and Steven Shapin (Beverly Hills, Calif.: Sage Publications, 1979).

57. Jonathan M. Hess, *Reconstructing the Body Politic: Enlightenment, Public Culture and the Invention of Aesthetic Autonomy* (Detroit, Mich.: Wayne State University Press, 1999), 31 and 226.

58. Elie Halévy, *The Growth of Philosophic Radicalism* (Boston: Beacon Press, 1966), 126, 127, 90.

59. This quote stems from John Thelwall, one of the main protagonists of British radicalism at that time. It is quoted in Philp, *French Revolution*, 54. For a discussion of the language of right in British radicalism, see Elie Halévy, *The Growth of Philosophic Radicalism*, 139.

60. See Keith Michael Baker, "The Idea of a Declaration of Rights," in *The French Idea of Freedom: The Old Regime and the Declaration of Rights of 1789*, ed. Dale Van Kley (Stanford, Calif.: Stanford University Press, 1994), 159, 167.

61. Regarding its aim and promise, the language of rights proved to be incomplete at best. In respect to the declaration of the "rights to subsistence" and the "public relief as a sacred debt" that the French famously announced in the constitution of 1793 and that were echoed by Paine, this insufficiency became palpable. The declaration of economic rights was bound by the understanding that the abolition of workhouses and regulated labor combined with guarantee of subsistence in case of sickness or disability would by itself end all "man-made" misery. Not only the lack of public finance in a context of war and inflation, but also the "conundrum" that plenty did not spring forward only because archaic structures were dismantled, weakened its purchase. For an extended discussion of social rights at that time, see Robert Castel, *From Manual Workers to Wage Laborers: Transformation of the Social Question* (New Brunswick, N.J.: Transaction Publishers, 2003), 148–65. Castel quotes from the declaration of the National Convention in 1793 and the Constitution passed June 24, 1793, which states that "society owes subsistence to its unhappy citizens." Ibid., 165.

62. Welch, "Social Science," 172.

63. Halévy, *The Growth of Philosophic Radicalism*, 238.

64. Malthus, *Population*, 334.

65. Welch, "Social Science," 173.

66. Condorcet, *Sketch for a Historical Picture*, 175. Condorcet thought that the social sciences are a peculiar achievement of his age. See, for a discussion, K. M. Baker, "The Early History of the Term 'Social Science,'" *Annals of Science* 20, no. 3 (1964): 213. "The social art, he wrote, is a true sciences based, like all the others, on experiments, reasoning, and calculation." Gay, *The Enlightenment*, 344. See also Rothschild, *Economic Sentiments*, 178.

67. Malthus, *Population*, 554.

68. Rothschild, *Economic Sentiments*, 131.

69. Ibid., 219; see also 162.

70. Condorcet introduced the term "social mathematics" in 1793, hoping for an exact social science in the service of political reform. Heilbron, *The Rise of Social Theory*, 168.

71. Lorraine J. Daston, "Mathematics and the Moral Sciences: The Rise and Fall of the Probability of Judgments, 1785–1840," in *Epistemological and Social Problems of the Sciences in the Early Nineteenth Century*, ed. H. N. Jahnke and M. Otte (Dordrecht: Springer Netherlands, 1981).

72. Rothschild, *Economic Sentiments*, 178.

73. Daston, "Mathematics and the Moral Sciences."

74. Lorraine Daston, "Condorcet and the Meaning of Enlightenment," *Proceedings of the British Academy* 151 (2007).

75. Mary Poovey, *A History of the Modern Fact: Problems of Knowledge in the Sciences of Wealth and Society* (Chicago: Chicago University Press, 1998), 264.

76. Rothschild, *Economic Sentiments*, 162.

77. Albert O. Hirschman, *The Passions and the Interests: Political Arguments for Capitalism Before Its Triumph* (Princeton, N.J.: Princeton University Press, 1997), 104. For a discussion of the political skepticism of Smith, see also Elie Halévy, *Le Radicalism philosophique*, vol. 3 of *La Formation du radicalisme philosophique* (Paris: Les Presses Universitaires de France, 1995), 177.

78. Vivienne Brown, *Adam Smith's Discourse: Canonicity, Commerce, and Conscience* (London: Routledge, 1994), 196.

79. Condorcet, for example, specified conditions and exclusions for political subjectivity, the primary "condition of eligibility being that of property ownership," while Paine did subscribe to a radical democratic understanding of political judgment—to him, universal suffrage was a natural right. David Williams, *Condorcet and Modernity* (Cambridge: Cambridge University Press, 2004), 199. Donald Winch has argued for understanding Malthus not simply as an anti-Jacobin opposed to Condorcet but more or less in a potential dialogue with him, differing on some issues such as methodology or social policy. While Winch's argument against those who see in Malthus nothing but a hard-nosed defender of the status quo is well taken, the fundamental difference between Condorcet and Malthus on issues of political subjectivity, the role of fear, and the bounds of liberal economy are too substantial as to reduce them to some minor divergences. For the argument on Condorcet and Malthus, see Donald Winch, "Malthus Versus Condorcet Revisited," *European Journal of the History of Economic Thought* 3 (1996).

80. It pertains to the curiosities of Godwin's form of liberalism and utilitarianism that the calculation of this utility was the exclusive domain of the subject who was not reasoning from his or her hedonistic pleasures or pains alone. William Godwin, *An Enquiry Concerning Political Justice*, vol. 3 of *Political and Philosophical Writings*, ed. Mark Philp and Austin Gee (London: W. Pickering, 1993), 59. Godwin's position in the history of utilitarianism is unequivocal, as Halévy asserts, because the role of individual judgment and the conception of utility beyond pleasure and pain distinguishes him in this tradition. Halévy, *Le Radicalisme philosophique*, 61. For Condorcet's relation to the principle of utility and the quote given in the text, see Rothschild, *Economic Sentiments*, 200.

81. Rothschild, *Economic Sentiments*, 216; see also Rancière, *Dissensus*, 207.

82. Paine's writings are a case in point. On the one hand, his liberalism did imply both political and economic equality. The question of how to engender these equalities pertained to both spheres. But it is also true that a liberal-democratic optimism about social structures could turn into a "trap" and the denial of "sources of coercion" at work in this realm. For example, in Paine's defense of the Bank of Pennsylvania on the basis of the obligation of contract, he eschews the question of power pertaining to such institutions. See Michael Foot and Isaac Kramnick, "Editor's Introduction: The Life, Ideology and Legacy of Thomas Paine," in *Thomas Paine Reader* (New York: Penguin Books, 1987), 26–30.

83. Rothschild, *Economic Sentiments*, 6. The quote "unceasing change and unceasing carnage" stems from Malthus, *Population*, 501.

84. Malthus, *Population*, 320.

85. Ibid., 329.

86. Ibid., 329 and 334.

87. Ibid., 504.

88. Michel Foucault, *Society Must Be Defended: Lectures at the Collège de France, 1975–76*, ed. Mauro Bertani, Alessandro Fontana, François Ewald, and David Macey (New York: Picador, 2003), 179.

89. Poovey, *History of Modern Fact*, 265.

90. Malthus comments on Condorcet: "A few observations will be sufficient to show how completely this theory is contradicted, when it is applied to the real, and not to an imaginary, state of things." Malthus, *Population*, 320.

91. Ibid., 325.

92. Williams, *Condorcet and Modernity*, 97. See also Condorcet, *Sketch for a Historical Picture*, 158.

93. Malthus, *Population*, 558.

94. Ibid., 438.

95. Ibid., 558.

96. Ibid., n526.

97. Ibid., 328.

98. Ibid., 512.

99. Ibid., 513.

100. Ibid., 501.

101. Ibid.

102. Ibid., 524.

103. Ibid., 471 and 324.

104. Ibid., 562. "It may be confidently stated that the frequent combination of complicated causes, the action and reaction of cause and effect on each other, and the necessity of limitations and exceptions in a considerable number of important propositions, form the main difficulties of the science." Malthus, *Political Economy*, 8.

105. Malthus, *Population*, 321 and 559.

106. Ibid., 8.

107. Donald Winch, *Riches and Poverty: An Intellectual History of Political Economy in Britain, 1750–1834* (Cambridge: Cambridge University Press, 1996), 253.

108. See also the discussion by Halévy of Malthus's attitudes on education, especially on the utilitarian foundation of his argument in comparison to the already existing institutions of public education and their foundation in the hands of dissidents and Methodists, who had recourse to a notion of justice: "Entre 1796 et 1807, l'influence de Malthus s'est exercicée sur le parti liberal. Elle a été une influence démocratique. Pour ce qui touche en particulierer a l'éducation des pauvres, la théorie radicale de l'instruction populaire est d'origine malthusienne." Halévy, *L'Evolution de la doctrine utilitaire*, 133 and 116.

109. Edmund Burke, *The Portable Edmund Burke*, ed. Isaak Kramnick (New York: Penguin Books, 1999), 436.

110. Malthus, *Population*, 6.

111. Malthus, *Political Economy*, 303.

112. The metaphor of a "wide sea" for the dangers of politics has a long history in the tradition of political thought that reaches back to Plato's Gorgias, as Rancière reminded us. Rancière contends that "the whole political project of Platonism can be conceived as an antimaritime polemic. The *Gorgias* insists on this: Athens has a disease that comes from its port. . . . The great beast of the populace, the democratic assembly of the imperialist city, can be represented as a trireme of drunken sailors. In order to save politics it must be pulled aground among the shepherds." Jacques Rancière, *On the Shores of Politics* (London: Verso, 1995), 1.

113. Immanuel Kant, *Critique of Pure Reason* (Cambridge: Cambridge University Press, 1998), 439.

114. John Locke, *Two Treatises of Government*, ed. Peter Laslett (Cambridge: Cambridge University Press, 1988), 358.

115. Kirstie Morna McClure, *Judging Rights: Lockean Politics and the Limits of Consent* (Ithaca, N.Y.: Cornell University Press, 1996), 63 and 69.

116. Rothschild, *Economic Sentiments*, 49.

117. Ibid., 149–50.

118. Friedrich A. Hayek, "The Use of Knowledge in Society," *American Economic Review* 35 (1945): 527.

119. For an extended discussion of this aspect in Hayek's work, related to Foucault's argument about visibility and invisibility of the economy, see Ute Tellmann, "Foucault and the Invisible Economy," *Foucault Studies*, no. 6 (2009).

120. Rancière, *Dissensus*, 207.

121. Ibid., 92.

122. Malthus, *Population*, 501.

123. Jacques Rancière, *Disagreement: Politics and Philosophy* (Minneapolis: University of Minnesota Press, 1998), 30, 22, and 26.

124. Arendt, *On Revolution*, 89–90.

125. Ibid., 108.

126. Ibid., 58.

127. Hannah Pitkin has pointed out that Arendt mingles in the category of the social seemingly unrelated things, such as the biological necessity of the natural body, an account of the forces pertaining to the market place, no less than norms that impel conformity or the understanding of the economy as a gigantic household to be managed or planned. Hanna Fenichel Pitkin, *The Attack of the Blob: Hannah Arendt's Concept of the Social* (Chicago: University of Chicago Press, 1998), 12 and 192.

128. For using Arendt's notion of the political against her own divisions, see Bonnie Honig's discussion in *Political Theory and the Displacement of Politics* (Ithaca, N.Y.: Cornell University Press, 1993), 120–25.

129. Arendt, *On Revolution*, 57–59.

130. Arendt asserts that Marx replaced the political understanding of economy with an economic understanding of politics that was much more "theoretically elegant" and scientifically appealing, but unfortunately ended up surrendering the

political to the economic. Ibid., 58. Marx's argument is of course much more complex and mediated. His critique of the liberal politics of rights and the political economy of capitalism—notably the question of labor—were depicted as co-constituted. The reason for still presenting Marx through the lenses of Arendt lies in the fact that the problem of economism still remains a true theoretical problem for Marx's rendering of capitalism. There is indeed one curious similarity between Arendt and Marx: both conceive of the economy as a domain of necessity that is opposed to a domain of freedom.

131. Arendt, *On Revolution*, 59.
132. Rancière, *Disagreement*, 2.
133. Rancière, *Dissensus*, 92.

2. Savage Life, Scarcity, and the Economic

1. Michel Foucault, *Security, Territory, Population: Lectures at the Collège de France, 1977–78*, ed. Michel Sennellart (Basingstoke: Palgrave Macmillan, 2007), 75; see also Catherine Gallagher, *The Body Economic: Life, Death and Sensation in Political Economy and the Victorian Novel* (Princeton, N.J.: Princeton University Press, 2006), 3–4.

2. For the feminist problematization of this division, see Susan Moller Okin, "Gender, the Public, and the Private," in *Political Theory Today*, ed. David Held (Oxford: Blackwell Polity Press, 1991).

3. About the multiple valences of the notion of population and its global history, see Alison Bashford, *Global Population. History, Geopolitics, and Life on Earth* (New York: Columbia University Press, 2014). Also see Matthew Connelly, *Fatal Misconception* (Cambridge: Harvard University Press, 2008); and Edmund Ramsden, "Carving Up Population Science: Eugenics, Demography and the Controversy Over the 'Biological Law' of Population Growth," *Social Studies of Science* 32, no. 5–6 (2002).

4. Foucault, *Security, Territory, Population*, 66.

5. Ibid., 44.

6. Foucault did address the question of limits and finitude in the biological discourse at the turn toward the nineteenth century in his *Order of Things*, but he only makes cursory mention of this in his lectures on governmentality. See Michel Foucault, *The Order of Things: An Archaeology of the Human Sciences* (New York: Vintage Books, 1994), 256. In his lectures, he raises his older findings in order to redefine them in terms of shifting techniques of power but falls short of this task. See Foucault, *Security, Territory, Population*, 78–79. Mitchell Dean has already drawn attention to this curious omission of Foucault, arguing that the emergence of "bioeconomic necessity" therefore largely eluded Foucault. See Mitchell Dean, *The Constitution of Poverty: Toward a Genealogy of Liberal Governance* (London: Routledge, 1991), 69 and 120. Interestingly, Foucault does address the change of the political meaning of scarcity at that time. He points out that the

liberal security dispositif detaches the notion of scarcity from being a common "scourge" of hunger that gives rise to a "kind of immediate solidarity" and becomes instead a factual reality for some who will "die of hunger after all." The relevant quote reads as follows: "Thus, the scarcity event is split. The scarcity-scourge disappears, but scarcity that causes the death of individuals not only does not disappear, it must not disappear." Foucault, *Security, Territory, Population*, 42. Foucault remains silent about the nature of the "must not" that he alludes to in this passage. For an extended discussion, see Ute Tellmann, "Catastrophic Populations and the Fear of the Future: Malthus and the Genealogy of Liberal Economy," *Theory, Culture & Society* 30, no. 2 (2013).

7. See the discussion in Murray Milgate and Shannon Stimson, *After Adam Smith: A Century of Transformation in Politics and Political Economy* (Princeton, N.J.: Princeton University Press, 2009), 127. Elie Halévy makes this point in *L'Evolution de la doctrine utilitaire De 1789 À 1815*, vol. 2 of *La Formation du radicalism philosophique* (Paris: Presses Universitaires de France, 1995) as well: "On voit quel rôle joue, dans la formation de la nouvelle économique politique, le principe de population, complété par la loi de la rente, que en dérive: c'est un principe d'unification. Désormais, les variations de la rente, du salaire, des profits, ne peuvent plus, comme elles le pouvaient du temps d'Adam Smith, être étudiées séparément: elles dérivent d'une seule et unique loi. Et l'économique politique, conformément au rêve de James Mill, va reprendre, quoique en un sens nouveau, le caractère rigoureusement systématique qu'elle avait présenté, en France, au XVIIIe siècle, chez Quesnay et les physiocrates: en 1817 paraissent les *Principes de l'économie politique et de l'impôt*." Ibid., 162.

8. Donald Winch, *Malthus* (Oxford: Oxford University Press, 1987), 234 and 247.

9. Matthew Connelly, "To Inherit the Earth: Imagining World Population: From the Yellow Peril to the Population Bomb," *Journal of Global History* 1, no. 3 (2006): 299–319, 302.

10. As Nicholas Xenos has demonstrated at length, scarcity has already been part of the texts of classical liberalism "before there was any formal postulate of scarcity in the economic theory." He recognizes that scarcity only became the true focus of political economy later but claims that Smith and Hume opened up the "sources and role of social scarcity in their analysis of wealth." He qualifies C. B. MacPherson's assumption that liberalism adopted scarcity as a legitimizing device for the emerging market order since Thomas Hobbes. Instead, he argues, the Scottish Enlightenment—notably, David Hume—should be regarded as a precursor of the economics of scarcity avant la lettre. Nicholas Xenos, "Liberalism and the Postulate of Scarcity," *Political Theory* 15, no. 2 (1987): 233. As he argues, Hume derives from this condition the importance of property rights, the dynamics of emulation and social need, and a conception of justice. It is in the theory of justice that Xenos sees the significance of scarcity for liberal political theory. John Rawls is the paradigmatic case of a liberal theory of justice that adopts the condition of "moderate scarcity" as its very vantage point. Neither Smith nor Hume assumed the notion of scarcity to be that unifying principle of economy as a

totality. In Xenos's reading, the significance of the concept of scarcity lies in the fact that it produces a cultural experience of lack in a world of plenty: According to Xenos, this experience is due to the "fluid, ever changing social world of emulation and conspicuous consumption" that creates a "world of dramatically increased excitation and frustration of desire, and therefore in a world of perpetual scarcity." Nicholas Xenos, *Scarcity and Modernity* (London: Routledge, 1990), 10. Marshall Sahlin's argument about the specific modern experience of scarcity is canonical in this respect. Anthropological evidence suggests that societies of hunters and gatherers must have been seen as "societies of affluence" that organize their livelihood not with reference to scarcity. Marshall David Sahlins, *Stone Age Economics* (Chicago: Aldine-Atherton, 1972), 1–39.

11. Milgate and Stimson, *After Adam Smith*, 121.

12. For the overall argument on "denaturalization," see Margaret Schabas, *The Natural Origins of Economics* (Chicago: University of Chicago Press, 2005). It is important to point out that the term "denaturalization" does not imply that liberal economics eschews naturalizing metaphors for depicting economic laws. See note 22 in the introduction for an elaboration of the different uses of "naturalization" and "denaturalization" regarding economic discourse.

13. Of course, such cursory remark cannot do justice to Jevons's economics of scarcity and the relation to his book on the coal question and to the question of population. Jevons's discussion puts much emphasis on the nonrenewability of coal and the industrial dynamics, but population assumes an important role. His "argument in the *Coal Question* entailed a straightforward application of Malthusian population growth." For an extended discussion of the role of population in the *Coal Question*, see Sandra Peart, *The Economics of W. S. Jevons* (London: Routledge, 1996), 20–34.

14. Friedrich A. von Hayek, *The Fatal Conceit: The Errors of Socialism* (Chicago: University of Chicago Press, 1989), 120–34. For an important argument on how neoliberalism refers to an altogether different notion of life that give rise to a critique of ecological limits, and to limitless expansion of capital while maintaining the notion of scarcity and vital necessity, see Melinda Cooper, *Life as Surplus: Biotechnology and Capitalism in the Neoliberal Era* (Seattle: University of Washington Press, 2008), 15–50.

15. Mohan Rao, *From Population Control to Reproductive Health: Malthusian Arithmetic* (London: Sage, 2004), 112. For an overview, see Barbara Duden, "Population," in *The Development Dictionary: A Guide to Knowledge and Power*, ed. Wolfgang Sachs (London: Zed Books, 1999). Also see Arturo Escobar, *Encountering Development: The Making and Unmaking of the Third World* (Princeton, N.J.: Princeton University Press, 1995); and Timothy Mitchell *The Rule of Experts: Egypt, Techno-Politics and Modernity* (Berkeley: University of California Press, 2002).

16. Donella H. Meadows, *The Limits to Growth: A Report for the Club of Rome's Project on the Predicament of Mankind* (New York: Universe Books, 1972). For a discussion of the concept "carrying capacity," see Bashford, *Global Population*, 93–97.

17. Paul R. Ehrlich, *The Population Bomb* (New York: Ballantine Books, 1968).

18. Lorraine Daston and Peter Galison, *Objectivity* (New York: Zone Books, 2007), 40.

19. This is an expression Malthus introduces. See Thomas Robert Malthus, *An Essay on the Principle of Population. Sixth Edition (1826) with Variant Readings from the Second Edition (1803)*, Vol. 2 and 3 of *The Works of Thomas Robert Malthus*, Edward Anthony Wrigley and David Souden (London: William Pickering, 1986), 59.

20. The notion of the "abject" refers to the effects of exclusion on the excluded. This term highlights that the divisions between subjects leave their mark on how they can be recognized as subjects. See, for a discussion, Judith Butler, *Bodies That Matter: On the Discursive Limits of "Sex"* (New York: Routledge, 1993), 3.

21. For a discussion of Malthusianism old and new, see Rao, *Malthusian Arithmetic*, 75–122. In a reference handbook on world population in 2001, Malthus's text is included and still functions as the landmark for basic theoretical wisdoms on population. Geoffrey Gilbert, *World Population: A Reference Handbook* (Santa Barbara, Calif.: ABC-CLIO, 2001), xi, 58.

22. Ann Laura Stoler, *Race and the Education of Desire: Foucault's History of Sexuality and the Colonial Order of Things* (Durham, N.C.: Duke University Press, 1995), 7.

23. Uday Singh Metha, *Liberalism and Empire: A Study in Nineteenth-Century British Liberal Thought* (Chicago: Chicago University Press, 1999), 4.

24. Robert W. Dimand, "Classical Political Economy and Orientalism: Nassau Senior's Eastern Tours," in *Postcolonialism Meets Economics*, ed. Eiman O. Zein-Elabdin and S. Charusheela (London: Routledge, 2004), 74.

25. See Bhikhu Parekh, "Liberalism and Colonialism," in *The Decolonization of Imagination: Culture, Knowledge and Power*, ed. Jan Nederveen Peiterse and Bhikhu Parekh (London: Zed Books, 1995); Metha, *Liberalism and Empire*; David Armitage, *The Ideological Origins of the British Empire* (Cambridge: Cambridge University Press, 2000); Anthony Pagden, "Human Rights, Natural Rights, and Europe's Imperial Legacy," *Political Theory* 31, (2003); and Bruce Buchan, "The Empire of Political Thought: Civilization, Savagery and Perceptions of Indigenous Government," *History of the Human Sciences* 18, no. 2 (2005). For how colonialism constitutively shaped the framing of historical development and the nation—both intimately tied to nineteenth-century liberalism—see Dipesh Chakrabarty, *Provincializing Europe: Postcolonial Thought and Historical Difference* (Princeton, N.J.: Princeton University Press, 2000); Partha Chatterjee, *The Nation and Its Fragments: Colonial and Postcolonial Histories* (Princeton, N.J.: Princeton University Press, 1993); and Akhil Gupta, "Imagining Nations," in *Companion to the Anthropology of Politics*, ed. David and Joan Vincent Nugent (Malden, Mass.: Blackwell 2004). For the general discussion of the universalisms of liberalism in respect to colonial difference and racism, see Etienne Balibar, *Masses, Classes, Ideas: Studies on Politics and Philosophy Before and After Marx* (New York: Routledge, 1994). The following works prominently discuss the relation between economic thought and colonialism: David L. Blaney and Naeem Inayatullah, *Savage Economics: Wealth, Poverty, and the Temporal Walls of Capitalism* (New York: Routledge, 2010); Eiman O. Zein-Elabdin and S. Charusheela, *Postcolonialism Meets Economics*

(London: Routledge, 2004); Uma Kalpagam, "Colonial Governmentality and the 'Economy'," *Economy and Society* 29, no. 3 (2000); David Colander, Robert E. Prasch, and Falguni A. Sheth, ed. *Race, Liberalism, and Economics* (Ann Arbor: University of Michigan Press, 2004); and Prathama Banerjee, "Debt, Time and Extravagance: Money and the Making of 'Primitives' in Colonial Bengal," *Indian Economic and Social History Review* 37, no. 4 (2000). Dipesh Chakrabarty has discussed Marx's economic philosophy within a postcolonial perspective. See chapter 2 of his book *Provincializing Europe*. The earliest discussion of economics in the context of postcolonialism is of course Gayatri Chakravorty Spivak's discussion of value. See "Scattered Speculations on the Question of Value," *Diacritics*, Winter 1985.

26. Malthus, *Population*, 291, ii–iii.

27. As Shapiro argued, Adam Smith's "spatio-temporal" narrative also employs this juxtaposition between a state of nature and a civilized state for his economic theory. Yet, as we will see, the state of nature changes dramatically with Malthus. Michael Shapiro, "Adam Smith: Desire, History, and Value," in *International Political Economy and Poststructural Politics*, ed. Marieke de Goede (Basingstoke, U.K.: Palgrave Macmillan, 2006), 46.

28. Several scholars have argued that the state of nature is not merely a "hypothetical primordial state" of human existence but is intimately linked to the colonial context. "Locke's state of nature was constructed from a range of colonial sources on Indigenous peoples, depicting a condition without settled private property and legislative authority." Buchan, "Empire," 5. See also Armitage, *Ideological Origins*.

29. Malthus refers to James Cook's *A Voyage Towards the South Pole, and Round the World: Performed in His Majesty's Ships the Resolution and Adventure in the Years 1772, 1773, 1774 and 1775* (1777) to Comte Jean François La Perouse's *A Voyage Around the World: Performed in the Years 1785, 1786, 1787 and 1788* (1789) and to Friedrich Heinrich Alexander von Humboldt's *Essay politique sur le royaume de la Nouvelle Espagne* (1811).

30. Malthus, *Population*, 58.

31. Ibid., 22.

32. Ibid., 22–23.

33. Ibid., 32.

34. Ibid., 33.

35. Ibid., 35.

36. Ibid., 96.

37. Ibid., 102. Matthew Connelly has chronicled the tropes of catastrophism and disgust associated with the problem of population far into the twentieth century. He quotes Claude Lévi-Strauss, who describes after having been in the streets of Calcutta the "herding together of individuals whose only reason for living is to herd together in millions, whatever the conditions of life may be. Filth, chaos, promiscuity, congestion; ruins, huts, mud, dirt; dung, urine, pus, humours, secretions and running sores." Connelly, "Inherit the Earth," 315.

38. Malthus, *Population*, 34.

39. Ibid., 36.

40. Ibid., 41.

41. Philippa Levine, "States of Undress: Nakedness and the Colonial Imagination," *Victorian Studies* 50, no. 2 (2008): 189 and 192–93.

42. Stoler, *Race and the Education of Desire*, 35; Susan Buck-Morss, "Envisioning Capital: Political Economy on Display," *Critical Inquiry* 21 (1995): 450; and Robert C. Young, *Colonial Desires: Hybridity in Theory, Culture, and Race* (London: Routledge, 1995).

43. Antonio Callari, "Economics as the Postcolonial Other," in *Postcolonialism Meets Economics*, ed. Eiman O. and S. Charusheela Zein-Elabni (London: Routledge, 2004), 114. The role that these strategies of alterity play within economic discourse has been so far reconstructed in very different ways. David Blaney and Naeem Inayatullah, for example, discuss how the "savage" is constructed by a "temporal wall" that splits and shields commercial society from ethical critique that emerge from different ways of life. Implicitly, Blaney and Inayatullah thereby employ a Roussean strategy of critique that uses a benign account of the state of nature as a foil against which the pathologies of modern societies can be put into relief. Blaney and Inayatullah, *Savage Economics*. In opposition to this argument, Davis Levy and Sandra Part have shown how economics has been historically tied to a radical claim of equality among the races. It has been the romantic critique of economics that bemoaned this assumption of radical equality that united the antislavery movement and economics baptized by Thomas Carlyle as "negro science." They argue that economics has been succumbing to racial accounts of economic man only since later in the nineteenth century, betraying its original anti-discriminatory outlook. While their historical reconstruction of the discourse of economic critique excavates its imbricated racism, the strategies of alterity employed by classical political economy and by neoclassical economics elude the authors. Davis M. Levy and Sandra Peart, "The Negro Science of Exchange: Classical Economics and Its Chicago Revival," in *Race, Liberalism, and Economics*, ed. David Colander, Robert E. Prasch, and Falguni A. Sheth (Ann Arbor: University of Michigan Press, 2004).

44. For a discussion on how the European debate on the French Revolution and the French Enlightenment was also informed and preoccupied with the revolutionary events in the colonies, notably the Haitian Revolution, see Susan Buck-Morss, "Hegel and Haiti," *Critical Inquiry* 26, no. 4 (2000). As she argues, the very question of slavery, cast by European thinkers as a matter of the private affairs of the household, turned into a public question thereby undoing the neat conceptual boundaries between economy, household, and politics. Also see the extended work on this matter: Susan Buck-Morss, *Hegel, Haiti and Universal History* (Pittsburgh: University of Pittsburgh Press, 2009), 42, 87–104.

45. Jennifer Pitts, *A Turn to Empire: The Rise of Imperial Liberalism in Britain and France* (Princeton, N.J.: Princeton University Press, 2005), 13.

46. Blaney and Inayatullah, *Savage Economics*, 43.

47. Christian Marouby, "Adam Smith and the Anthropology of the Enlightenment: The 'Ethnographic' Sources of Economic Progress," in *The Anthropology of the*

Enlightenment, ed. Larry Wolff and Marco Cipolloni (Stanford, Calif.: University of Stanford Press, 2007), 94.

48. For an account of the narratological logic of Smith history of economic development, see Shapiro, "Adam Smith." Blaney and Inayatullah discuss in their recent book *Savage Economics* how a "temporal wall" of development is constitutive for economic discourse: "The savage operates thereby as a null point against which Smith assessed the progress of his own and other commercial societies." The difference among them is conceived as the absence of division of labor. Blaney and Inayatullah, *Savage Economics*, 43.

49. Gallagher, "The Body Versus the Social Body," 86.

50. Thomas Robert Malthus, *An Essay on the Principle of Population. Sixth Edition (1826) with Variant Readings from the Second Edition (1803)*. Vol. 2 and 3 of *The Works of Thomas Robert Malthus*, ed. Edward Anthony Wrigley and David Souden (London: William Pickering, 1986), 37.

51. Ibid., 393; and Thomas Robert Malthus, *Principles of Political Economy: Second Edition (1836) with Variant Readings from the First Edition (1820)*. Vol. 5 and 6 of *The Works of Thomas Robert Malthus*, ed. Edward Anthony Wrigley and David Souden (London: William Pickering, 1986), 113.

52. "It appears then, that the extreme fertility of these countries, instead of affording an adequate stimulus to a rapid increase of wealth and population, has produced, under the actual circumstances in which they have been placed, a degree of indolence which has kept them poor and thinly peopled after the lapse of ages." Malthus, *Political Economy*, 270–71.

53. Malthus, *Population*, 44.

54. Ibid., 58 and 154.

55. Foucault, *Order of Things*, 257 and 259.

56. Banerjee, "Debt, Time and Extravagance," 4. Prathama Banerjee explores how colonialism has been the critical condition of the modern ontologies of temporality. For the question of time and colonialism in respect to politics and economy, see Chakrabarty, *Provincializing Europe*.

57. Malthus, *Population*, 20 and 171. For the metaphor of the "spring," Malthus refers to James Steuart as a source.

58. Ibid., 153 and 87.

59. Ibid., 28.

60. Ibid., 21.

61. "I shall only observe therefore, that the extended use of potatoes has allowed of a very rapid increase [of population] during the last century. But the cheapness of this nourishing root, and the small piece of ground which, under this kind of cultivation, will in average years produce the food for a family, joined to the ignorance and the depressed state [this expression replaced the original "barbarism"] of the people, which prompted them to follow their inclinations with no other prospect than an immediate bare subsistence, encouraged marriage to such a degree, that the population is pushed much beyond the industry and present resources of the country; and the consequence naturally is, that the lower classes

of people are in the most impoverished and miserable state. The checks to the population are of course chiefly of the positive kind, and arise from the diseases occasioned by squalid poverty, damp and wretched cabins, by bad and insufficient clothing and occasional want." Ibid., 277–78; see also 389 and 545.

62. Malthus, *Political Economy*, 72; see also Malthus, *Population*, 366.

63. David Spurr, *The Rhetoric of Empire: Colonial Discourse in Journalism, Travel Writing and Imperial Administration* (Durham, N.C.: Duke University Press, 1994).

64. Banerjee, "Debt, Time and Extravagance," 429.

65. Malthus, *Population*, 453. 366, 495.

66. The passage unfolds as follows: "Taken the whole earth, instead of this island, emigration would of course be excluded; and, supposing the present population equal to a thousand millions, the human species would increase as the numbers, 1, 2, 4, 8, 16, 32, 64, 128, 256, and subsistence as, 1, 2, 3, 4, 5, 6, 7, 8, 9. In two centuries the population would be to the means of subsistence as 256 to 9; in three centuries as 4096 to 13, and in two thousand years the difference would be almost incalculable." Malthus, *Population*, 12.

67. Paul Krugman and Robin Wells, *Macroeconomics* (New York: Worth, 2009), 6.

68. Lionel Robbins, *The Nature and Significance of Economic Science* (London: Macmillan, 1932), 15.

69. Carl Menger, *Principles of Economics* (New York: New York University Press, 1981), 101.

70. Rutger Claassen, "Scarcity," in *Handbook of Economics and Ethics*, ed. Jan Peil and Irene van Staveren (Cheltenham, U.K.: Edward Elgar, 2009), 470.

71. Andrew Abbott, "The Problem of Excess," *Sociological Theory* 32, no. 1 (2014): 5.

72. Blaney and Inayatullah, *Savage Economics*, 202.

73. Hans Vaihinger, *The Philosophy of as If, a System of the Theoretical, Practical and Religious Fictions of Mankind* (London: Kegan Paul, 1924), 25.

74. Bashford, *Global Population*, 29.

75. Malthus, *Population*, 47 and 50.

76. Ibid., 461.

77. Ibid., 13.

78. Ibid., 319.

79. Ibid., 460.

80. Ibid., 319.

81. Malthus, *Political Economy*, 169.

82. Ibid., 222.

83. Ibid., 169.

84. Malthus, *Population*, 73.

85. Immanuel Kant, "Perpetual Peace: A Philosophical Sketch," in *Political Writings*, ed. Hans Reiss (Cambridge: Cambridge University Press, 1991), 114. In this respect, Malthus is peculiar in the tradition of liberal economic thought: His account of population is as much about a universalizing economic fear of "savage life" as it is about the fear of a potential dissolution of political bounds. Dreading the former as much as the latter, he maintains territorial vision of liberal economy other than

the planetary, cosmopolitan articulation of liberalism. His articulation of economics and politics had a territorial backdrop: he opposed free trade in grain and the policies of emigration and colonization as mechanisms to calibrate territorial bounds and population. For a short but instructive account, see David McNally, "Political Economy to the Fore: Burke, Malthus and the Whig Response to Popular Radicalism in the Age of the French Revolution," *History of Political Thought* 21, no. 3 (2000).

86. Vaihinger, *Philosophy of as If*, 15.
87. Daston and Galison, *Objectivity*, 40.
88. Malthus, *Political Economy*, 72.
89. Malthus, *Population*, 405.
90. Ibid.
91. Malthus, *Political Economy*, 212.
92. Malthus, Population, 451.
93. It belongs to the peculiarity of the Malthusian system of political economy that it modeled capital in identical terms to the figure of population. "The laws which regulate the rate of profits and the progress of capital, bear a very striking and singular resemblance to the laws which regulate the rate of wages and the progress of population." Malthus, *Political Economy*, 262–63. Both can be redundant; that is, they increase beyond the limit of their productive employment or their subsistence. But in conjunction with the laws of population, this redundancy of capital will quickly be dissolved, if the production of the necessities of life has must catch up with the additional bodies produced by the laws of population. Ibid., 263–65. As John Maynard Keynes would later claim, the possibility that capital itself might become redundant marks Malthus as one of the "heretics" of economic thought. See the essay on Malthus in Keynes, *Essays in Biography*, vol. 10 of *The Collected Writings of John Maynard Keynes*, ed. Donald Edward Moggridge (London: Macmillan for the Royal Economic Society, 1972). Most notably, he compares him to David Ricardo and Jean-Baptiste Say. But this peculiarity of this system of political economy is of less interest here than the establishment of the question of limits and scarcity as the core tenets of liberal economy.
94. Malthus, *Population*, 131.
95. Ibid., 405.
96. Vaihinger, *Philosophy of as If*, 15.
97. For a discussion on how to understand economic structures in terms of experimental forms, see Philip Mirowski, *Machine Dreams: Economics Becomes a Cyborg Science* (Cambridge: Cambridge University Press, 2002), 545 and 567.
98. There is a growing debate on how to understand the relation between biopolitics and economy, or bioeconomy. The scholarly works in this field are rather disparate in how they go about defining the links between biopolitics and economy. Most prominently, Michael Hardt and Antonio Negri have rearticulated the Foucauldian account of biopower and biopolitics with a Spinozist-Marxist understanding of capitalism. Michael Hardt and Antonio Negri, *Empire* (Cambridge, Mass.: Harvard University Press, 2000), 421. Michael Dillon and Luis

Lobo-Guerrero have suggested widening the understanding of "species-life" employed by Foucault for exploring the connection between economy and population. They suggest that the biopolitical imaginary of species-life is tied to an ontology of connectivity, circulation, and complexity. Michael Dillon and Luis Lobo-Guerrero, "The Biopolitical Imaginary of Species-Being," *Theory, Culture and Society* 26, no. 1 (2009): 8. A whole different strand of the debate investigates economic logics in biotechnology and biomedicine. They trace the intersection of logics of profit, value, and life. See Cooper, *Life As Surplus*; Kaushik Sunder Rajan, *Biocapital: The Constitution of Postgenomic Life* (Durham, N.C.: Duke University Press, 2006); Nikolas Rose, *Politics of Life Itself: Biomedicine, Power, and Subjectivity in the Twenty-First Century* (Princeton, N.J.: Princeton University Press, 2007); and Cathy Waldby and Robert Mitchell, *Tissue Economies: Blood, Organs, and Cell Lines in Late Capitalism* (Durham, N.C.: Duke University Press, 2006). Jacqueline Best has combined Foucault's understanding of economic governing with Agamben's exploration of modern "thanatopolitics" for a critique of economic policies of international organizations that increase the vulnerability for many citizens of developing countries. Jacqueline Best, "Why Economy Is often the Exception to Politics as Usual," *Theory, Culture & Society* 24, no. 4 (2007). For a discussion of the reception of biopolitics, see Thomas Lemke, *Biopolitics: An Advanced Introduction* (New York: New York University Press, 2011).

99. Michel Foucault, *The Birth of Biopolitics: Lectures at the Collège de France, 1978–79*, ed. Michel Sennellart (Basingstoke, U.K.: Palgrave Macmillan, 2008), 323–24.

100. Foucault, *History of Sexuality: An Introduction*, vol. 1 (New York: Vintage Books, 1990), 143.

101. Foucault, *Security, Territory, Population*, 21, 66 and 73.

102. Ibid., 352.

103. Foucault, *Birth of Biopolitics*, 45.

104. Foucault, *Security, Territory, Population*, 105.

105. Foucault, *History of Sexuality*, 144.

106. Foucault, *Security, Territory, Population*, 63 and 104.

107. Michel Foucault, *Society Must Be Defended: Lectures at the Collège de France, 1975–76*, ed. Mauro Bertani, Alessandro Fontana, François Ewald, and David Macey (New York: Picador, 2003), 246.

108. Foucault, *Security, Territory, Population*, 62–63.

109. Foucault, *History of Sexuality*, 144 and 138.

110. Foucault, *Society Must Be Defended*, 255, 262.

111. Young, *Colonial Desires*, 180.

112. Balibar, *Masses, Classes, Ideas*, 197. As Etienne Balibar has put it, no "definition of the human species, or simply the human . . . has ever been proposed which would not imply a latent hierarchy. This has to do with the impossibility of fixing the boundaries of what he calls 'human.'" Ibid.

113. Ulrich Bröckling has recently discussed how economic calculations become instrumental in the political governance of both individuals and the populace. One conclusion of his discussion has been that one can detect an "expansion of

economic rationality to all realms of life." Every aspect of human life becomes valued in these terms. Bröckling finds a radicalized "political economy" that turns into biopolitical economy—that is, into an economic and political calculation of life worth living. Ulrich Bröckling, "Human Economy, Human Capital: A Critique of Biopolitical Economy," in *Governmentality: Current Issues and Future Challenges*, ed. Ulrich Bröckling, Susanne Krasmann, and Thomas Lemke (New York: Routledge, 2011), 248, 262.

114. Hayek, *Fatal Conceit*, 132.

115. Foucault analyzes the establishment of a causal link between elimination or weakening of one part of the population to the automatic strengthening of the other part as a biopolitical act par excellence. Foucault, *Society Must Be Defended*, 258.

116. Malthus, *Principle of Population*, 365.

117. Foucault, *Society Must Be Defended*, 255.

118. The Poor Laws will be discussed in the next chapter in more detail. For a discussion of illiberal forms of government as inherent to liberalism, see Mitchell Dean, "Liberal Government and Authoritarianism," *Economy and Society* 31, no. 1 (2002); Sven Opitz, "Government Unlimited: The Security Dispositif of Illiberal Governmentality," in *Governmentality: Current Issues and Future Challenges*, ed. Ulrich Bröckling, Susanne Krasmann, and Thomas Lemke (New York: Routledge, 2011).

119. Malthus, *Population*, 321.

120. Ibid., 367.

121. Ibid., 516.

122. Giorgio Agamben, *Homo Sacer: Sovereign Power and Bare Life* (Stanford, Calif.: Stanford University Press, 1998), 2.

123. Ibid., 83.

124. Giorgio Agamben, *Means Without End: Notes on Politics* (Minnesota: University of Minnesota Press, 2000), 133 and 33.

125. Agamben, *Homo Sacer*, 133.

126. It seems therefore unsurprising that his most recent work that addresses economy does not revolve around the biopolitical fracture. Instead, he adopts Foucault's understanding of liberal economy as governmentality and suggests extending its genealogy into the depths of Christian thought. Giorgio Agamben, "Ökonomische Theologie: Genealogie Eines Paradigmas," in *Theologie Und Politik: Walter Benjamin Und Ein Paradigma Der Moderne*, ed. Bernd Witte and Mauro Ponzi (Berlin: Erich Schmidt Verlag, 2005).

127. This is not to say that the economy is not also a juridical creature. Indeed, the question of how juridical measures and new "legalities" are invested today with creating economic spaces, points to an important field of research. Saskia Sassen, *Territory, Authority, Rights: From Medieval to Global Assemblages* (Princeton, N.J.: Princeton University Press, 2006). As Ronen Palan and Angus Cameron have argued, the offshore-economy, absolutely crucial to the creating of the global, is in essence a juridical construction. See Angus Cameron and Ronen Palan, *The Imagined Economies of Globalization* (London: Sage, 2004).

3. The Right to Live

1. Thomas Robert Malthus, *An Essay on the Principle of Population. Sixth Edition (1826) with Variant Readings from the Second Edition (1803)*, vol. 2 and 3 of *The Works of Thomas Robert Malthus*, ed. Edward Anthony Wrigley and David Souden (London: William Pickering, 1986), 697, 505, 333–334; see also 368.

2. Ibid., 554.

3. Karl Polanyi, *The Great Transformation: The Political and Economic Origins of Our Time* (Boston: Beacon, 1957), 139–40.

4. The system had its roots in the "systematization of parish charity" that had been in place since 1536. By 1572 the local justices were given the power to tax. For an extended discussion, see Joanna Innes, "The Distinctiveness of the English Poor Laws, 1750–1850," in *The Political Economy of British Historical Experience, 1688–1914*, ed. Donald Winch and Patrick O'Brien (Oxford: Oxford University Press, 2002), 381, 385.

5. Mitchell Dean, *The Constitution of Poverty: Toward a Genealogy of Liberal Governance* (London: Routledge, 1991), 68. Dean discussed in length the argument that counter this interpretation of the Malthusian influence on the poor laws on the grounds that the reform in 1834 did retain a right to relief and thus remained markedly different from Malthus's demands. As Dean plausibly argues, while the reforms were more limited, the "virtual elimination of relief to able-bodied males and those construed as their natural dependents" serves the same ends. Ibid., 104 and 95.

6. Polanyi, *The Great Transformation*, 77–79.

7. Dean, *Constitution of Poverty*, 99; and Innes, "English Poor Laws," 395.

8. Lisa Forman Cody, "The Politics of Illegitimacy in an Age of Reform: Women, Reproduction, and Political Economy in England's New Poor Law of 1834," *Journal of Women's History* 11, no. 4 (2000).

9. This analysis of the passions that create economic rationality resonates with the most recent research in sociology and political theory. Economic man is less "empirically descriptive" than "culturally performative." See, for example, Paul du Gay, "Which Is the 'Self' in 'Self-Interest'?," *Sociological Review* 53 (2005): 292; Alex Preda, *Framing Finance: The Boundaries of Markets and Modern Capitalism* (Chicago: University of Chicago Press, 2009); Emma Rothschild, *Economic Sentiments: Adam Smith, Condorcet, and the Enlightenment* (Cambridge, Mass.: Harvard University Press, 2001); Marieke de Goede, "Mastering 'Lady Credit,'" *International Feminist Journal of Politics* 2 (2000); Paul Langley, "Uncertain Subjects of Anglo-American Financialization," *Cultural Critique* 65 (2007); and Urs Stäheli, *Spektakuläre Spekulation: Das Populäre der Ökonomie* (Frankfurt am Main: Sukrkamp, 2007). More ethnographically and sociologically minded work has followed contemporary analysts and brokers into the "trading pit" and into the "city." It shows that these "rational actors" depend on their affective and technologically mediation for calculating the next move. See Caitlin Zaloom, *Out of the Pits: Traders and Technology from Chicago to London* (Chicago: University of Chicago Press,

2006). Rob Aitken discusses how economic investment is codified simultaneously as an act of political citizenship. Rob Aitken, *Performing Capital: Toward a Cultural Economy of Popular and Global Finance* (New York: Palgrave Macmillan, 2007). For a theoretical discussion, see Michel Callon, Yuval Millo, and Fabian Muniesa, eds., *Market Devices* (Oxford: Blackwell, 2007). Also see Michel Callon, "An Essay on Framing and Overflowing," in *The Laws of the Markets* (Oxford: Blackwell, 1998).

10. Michel Foucault, *The Birth of Biopolitics: Lectures at the Collège de France, 1978–79,* ed. Michel Sennellart (Basingstoke, U.K.: Palgrave Macmillan, 2008), 322.

11. Ibid., 45.

12. Michel Foucault, *Security, Territory, Population: Lectures at the Collège de France, 1977–78,* ed. Michel Sennellhart (Basingstoke, U.K.: Palgrave Macmillan, 2007), 72–73.

13. Nikolas Rose, "Government, Authority and Expertise in Advanced Liberalism," *Economy and Society* 22, no. 3 (1993): 285. For an extended discussion, see Mitchell Dean, *Governmentality: Power and Rule in Modern Society* (London: Sage Publications, 1999). Ulrich Bröckling has detailed how the entrepreneurial subject stands at the center of a neo-liberal paradigm of ruling, in which the imperative of self-activation has become ubiquitous. Ulrich Bröckling, *Das unternehmerische Selbst: Soziologie einer Subjektivierungsform* (Frankfurt am Main: Suhrkamp, 2007).

14. Dean, *Constitution of Poverty.*

15. Wendy Brown, "Neo-Liberalism and the End of Politics," *Theory & Event* 7, no. 1 (2003).

16. Gebhard Kirchgässner, *Homo oeconomicus: The Economic Model of Behaviour and Its Applications in Economics and Other Social Sciences* (New York: Springer, 2008), 1.

17. For a discussion of the history of economic man, see Mary S. Morgan, "Economic Man as Model Man: Ideal Types, Idealization and Caricatures," *Journal of the History of Economic Thought* 28, no. 1 (2006): 12 and 15. The account of economic man as a "pleasure machine" stems from the Irish economist Francis Edgeworth.

18. Frank Knight "worked out the details which allowed calculating man to play his full role in the formal neoclassical theory of the economy. . . . He argued that only by endowing calculating man with *full* information about everything in the economy (rather than limited information), and with *perfect* foresight about the future (rather than the uncertainty that Jevons had left out of his account), could the individual person make the necessary calculations that would allow him to judge accurately what actions to take in buying, selling, and consuming. And, only by assuming that there were infinitely many of him, and that each acted independently of the others, could neoclassical analysis depict the perfectly competitive economy necessary to arrive at an equilibrium outcome which maximized aggregate utility." Ibid., 14.

19. The caricature of economic man as a "walking computer" can be found in many textbooks but is still a distorted account of the more variegated interpretations of

rational economic man in economics, as Gebhard Kirchgässner points out. Kirchgässner, *Homo oeconomicus*, 15.

20. The most recent crisis has incited a discussion on how economic actors have been too greedy and too irrational. In part, this discussion rests on a moralizing critique on finance that has long historical antecedents. But it is also a discussion on how the market-efficiency hypothesis becomes implausible if one acknowledges the "animal spirits" of economic man. See George A. Akerlof and Robert J. Shiller, *Animal Spirits: How Human Psychology Drives the Economy, and Why It Matters for Global Capitalism* (Princeton, N.J.: Princeton University Press, 2009). The works that concentrate on this aspect take recourse to Keynesian critiques of economic man. See chapter 5 for a discussion on economic man in the twentieth century, especially the historicization of the "animal spirits."

21. Morgan, "Economic Man," 25.

22. Ibid., 4.

23. This statement requires a minor qualification: Philip Mirowski has explored how twentieth-century economics has failed to capitalize on how their computational metaphors, and cybernetic paradigms have actually undone the central role of economic man for modeling the economy. Modern economics fails to appreciate how its own paradigms have deconstructed the integrated self of neoclassical theory. Hence, economic man is kept alive after his own death: "The hot deliquescence of the *Homo Oeconomicus* is the dirty little secret of fin-de-siècle neoclassical economics." Philip Mirowski, *Machine Dreams: Economics Becomes a Cyborg Science* (Cambridge: Cambridge University Press, 2002), 536. For a similar argument on neoclassical economics as already working with a decentered notion of the subject, see David Ruccio and Jack Amariglio's contribution "From Unity to Dispersion: The Body in Neoclassical Economics" in *Postmodernism, Economics and Knowledge*, ed. Stephen Cullenberg, Jack Amariglio, and David F. Ruccio (London: Routledge, 2001), 143–65. They admit that neoclassical economists, "when pushed to defend the integrity and unity of their work . . . still resort to homo oeconomicus as the starting presupposition." Ibid., 165.

24. Foucault, *The Birth of Biopolitics*, 282. Friedrich von Hayek has made this argument most forcefully. Since economic man does not claim to know more than he can but decides based on his local knowledge and experience, the market contains all information available. In this argument, the market itself is the best of all possible orders insofar as it functions like an information-machine fed by the only viable knowledge accessible. See Friedrich A. Hayek, *Individualism and Economic Order* (Chicago: University of Chicago Press, 1948), 14; and Friedrich A. Hayek, "The Use of Knowledge in Society," *American Economic Review* 35, no. 4 (1945).

25. Max Weber, *The Protestant Ethic and the Spirit of Capitalism* (1930; repr. London: Routledge, 2001).

26. For a discussion of this anthropological empiricism, see Albert O. Hirschman, *The Passions and the Interests: Political Arguments for Capitalism Before Its Triumph* (Princeton, N.J.: Princeton University Press, 1997), 13–14. Also see Joseph Vogl,

Kalkül und Leidenschaft: Poetik des ökonomischen Menschen (Sequenzia: München, 2002), 35–49.

27. Hirschman, *Passions and Interests*, 48. Within this political tradition, economic interests are understood as belonging to the passions. But different from the passionate striving for glory or honor, the striving for economic gain is deemed to be calmer and steadier; it is thought of as more reflective and less destructive. The "rationally conducted acquisition of wealth" is endorsed as a "calm passion" that is both strong enough and "able to triumph over a variety of turbulent (yet weak) passions." Interest was understood as a "hybrid form of human action that was considered exempt from both the destructiveness of passion and the ineffectuality of reason." Ibid., 66 and 43–44.

28. Ibid., 100.

29. "The schema of an historical transition from a moral to an economic framework . . . is a chimerical one. . . . One discovers not the recession of ethical themes and concepts, but their emplacement in subordinate relations to what we might call the bioeconomic laws of population and subsistence." Dean, *The Constitution of Poverty*, 120; see also 111. Dean offers a reading that emphasizes both the novel plane of reality accorded to economy and the inextricable bonds that economic discourse maintained with such "moral" or political rationalities.

30. The recent discussions in social theory and cultural theory seek to distinguish the term "affect" from what is called "emotion." Affect is meant to address a form of intensity and attachment that has not yet coagulated within systems of meaning and psychological codes. Gilles Deleuze's attempt to distinguish a virtual level of "becoming" from the forms and terms of recognized subjectivity informs this division. Here, the term "affect" and the term "passion" are used equivocally. The question of how affects intersect below and beyond categories of experience and meaning is here part of a historicizing account: whereas Smith took the social coding of desire to be a building block of the economic order, Malthus assumed a bodily immediacy of attraction to lie at the heart of "savage life" that needed to be civilized. For a discussion of the Deleuzian notion of affect, see Brian Massumi, "The Autonomy of Affect," *Cultural Critique*, no. 31 (1995).

31. Morgan, "Economic Man," 3 and 4.

32. Nancy Folbre, *Greed, Lust and Gender: A History of Economic Ideas* (Oxford: Oxford University Press, 2009), 121.

33. The eighteenth century evaluated the passions differently from the seventeenth century—they lost an utterly destructive bent and became sentiments conducive to sociality instead of war. See Hirschman, *Passions and Interests*, 47.

34. Adam Smith, *An Inquiry into the Nature and Causes of the Wealth of Nations* (Oxford: Oxford University Press, 2008), 22.

35. Peter Minowitz, *Profits, Priests, and Princes: Adam Smith's Emancipation of Economics from Politics and Religion* (Stanford, Calif.: Stanford University Press, 1993), 65.

36. Smith, *Wealth of Nations*, 203.

37. Hirschman, *Passions and Interests*, 107; and Smith, *Wealth of Nations*, 203.

38. Rothschild, *Economic Sentiments*, 9; and Michael Shapiro, *Adam Smith: Desire, History, and Value*, in *International Political Economy and Poststructural Politics*, ed. Marieke de Goede, (Basingstoke, U.K.: Palgrave Macmillan, 2006).

39. Adam Smith, *The Theory of Moral Sentiment*, vol. 1 of *The Glasgow Edition of the Works and Correspondence of Adam Smith*, ed. Alec Lawrence Macfie and David Daiches Raphael (Indianapolis: Liberty Fund, 1982), 50.

40. Minowitz, *Profits, Priests, and Princes*, 69.

41. Adam Smith, *Lectures on Jurisprudence*, vol. 5 of *The Glasgow Edition of the Works and Correspondence of Adam Smith*, ed. Ronald Lindley Meek, David Daiches Raphael, and Peter Stein (Indianapolis: Liberty Classics, 1982), 352.

42. Minowitz, *Profits, Priests, and Princes*, 79.

43. Smith, *Wealth of Nations*, 203.

44. See Nancy Folbre's recent book on lust and greed as the "pursuit of self-interest beyond the virtuous bounds." The book traces "how cultural constraints on the pursuit of individual self-interest have been loosened in different ways for different grouped in different economic realms." Folbre, *Greed, Lust and Gender*, xxv. For Deidre McCloskey, this revelation of proper Smithian economics as having always been about an "ethos" of conduct that favors prudence, temperance, and justice leads the way to a new economics and a reinvigorated liberalism. It seems as if the diagnosed faults of "mechanistic" modeling of economic processes makes ethics appear as the solution to the old vices of this discipline. But recognizing that the economic subject is a socially codified and culturally defined subject, whose rationality and desires are not opposed to norms, but shaped by it, is first of all an analytical perspective. It is not the same as to find theoretical consolation in the fact that economic man has always been a moral being of sorts. Deirdre N. McCloskey, *The Vices of Economists, the Virtues of the Bourgeoisie* (Amsterdam: Amsterdam University Press, 1996), 125.

45. Smith, *Wealth of Nations*, 204.

46. Catherine Packham, "The Physiology of Political Economy: Vitalism and Adam Smith's Wealth of Nations," *Journal of the History of Ideas* 63, no. 3 (2002): 469.

47. Jennifer Pitts, *A Turn to Empire: The Rise of Imperial Liberalism in Britain and France* (Princeton, N.J.: Princeton University Press, 2005), 29.

48. For a discussion of the savage state in Smith, see David L. Blaney and Naeem Inayatullah, *Savage Economics: Wealth, Poverty, and the Temporal Walls of Capitalism* (Oxon: Routledge, 2010).

49. Pitts, *Turn to Empire*, 30.

50. Pitts argues that Smith does not subscribe to the depiction of the "Ignoble Savage" that Meek had identified as key to the narratives of progress in the eighteenth century.

51. Pitts, *Turn to Empire*, 36.

52. Rothschild, *Economic Sentiments*, 12.

53. This kind of universal applicability of the economic conception of modernity to different context, in which these explanatory models are not used, is itself an

epistemologically and culturally dubious move. As the anthropologist Stephen Gudeman has argued, the question is always "who gets to model whom." But in this context, withholding the universality of this model had its own racial and political subtext. See Stephen Gudeman, *Economics as Culture: Models and Metaphors of Livelihood* (London: Routledge, 1986), 157.

54. Thomas Robert Malthus, *Principles of Political Economy: Second Edition (1836) with Variant Readings from the First Edition (1820)*. Vol. 5 and 6 of *The Works of Thomas Robert Malthus*, ed. Edward Anthony Wrigley and David Souden (London: William Pickering, 1986), 283 and 281.

55. Malthus, *Population*, 446.

56. David Ricardo, *The Principle of Political Economy*, vol. 1 and 2 of *The Works and Correspondence of David Ricardo*, ed. Pierro Sraffa with M. H. Dobb (Cambridge: Cambridge University Press, 1951), 100.

57. M. J. D. Roberts, "The Concept of Luxury in British Political Economy: Adam Smith to Alfred Marshall," *History of the Human Sciences* 11, no. 1 (1998): 29.

58. Malthus, *Political Economy*, 278.

59. Nancy Folbre cites the first edition of Malthus's essay on population and discusses the role of desire in Malthus; see Folbre, *Greed, Lust and Gender*, 115.

60. Malthus, *Population*, 467 and 531.

61. Christopher Herbert, *Culture and Anomie: Ethnographic Imagination in the Nineteenth Century* (Chicago: University of Chicago Press, 1991), 117.

62. Ibid., 467–69.

63. Thomas Hobbes, *Leviathan* (Harmondsworth, U.K.: Penguin, 1985), 188.

64. Corey Robin, *Fear: The History of a Political Idea* (Oxford: Oxford University Press, 2004), 31, 33.

65. Ibid., 36. "Hobbes thus though about the fear of death and the dream of self-preservation not as a description of an already existing reality—of how human beings actually behaved in the world—but as a project of political and cultural reconstruction, requiring the creation of a new ethos and a new man." Ibid., 37–38.

66. As Robin puts it: "Fear lends the individual integrity and coherence, reminding him of that which matters to him most." Ibid., 41.

67. Ibid., 40–41. "The emblematic gesture of the fearful is thus not flight but exchange." Ibid 50. It is curious that this decidedly political theorist would come to define a political subject that is hard to distinguish from the economic subject. C. B. Macpherson had commented upon this long ago, claiming that Hobbes political theory is based on a possessive individualism which belongs to the emerging market order. Macpherson's reading is concerned with the question of how to found political obligation. The gist of his argument targets the assumption of "self-moving" individuals and "equal subordination" under a market regime as a quasi-ontology for Hobbes political theory. C. B. Macpherson, *The Political Theory of Possessive Individualism: Hobbes to Locke* (Oxford: Clarendon Press, 1962), 79, 87. He thus assumes what was not yet there for Hobbes's mind. For an extended discussion on the *homo oeconomicus* in relation to the *homo politicus*

see Wendy Brown, *The Undoing of the Demos: Neoliberalism's Stealth Revolution* (New York: Zone Books, 2015), ch. 3.

68. Malthus, *Population*, 331, 335; see also 454.
69. Ibid., 321 and 331; see also 567 and 342.
70. Both Condorcet and Smith are cited in Rothschild, *Economic Sentiments*, 13.
71. Malthus, *Political Economy*, 268.
72. Malthus, *Population*, 454.
73. Ibid.
74. Ibid., 370 and 571. Malthus translates the notion of the *vis medicatrix naturae* into a *vis medicatric republicae*. The former refers to the propensity of organisms to "intrinsically balance inner and outer forces." It holds that an organism, when experiencing "imbalances, . . . evince a natural tendency to restore harmony." Malthus uses this notion of medical and biological harmonization for his account of a political-cum-economic collective body. For a discussion, see Ed Cohen, *A Body Worth Defending: Immunity, Biopolitics, and the Apotheosis of the Modern Body* (Durham, N.C.: Duke University Press, 2009), 108.
75. Ibid., 333–34.
76. Rothschild, *Economic Sentiments*, 13–14.
77. Malthus, *Population*, 520.
78. Ibid., 59.
79. Hirokazu Miyazaki, "Economy of Dreams: Hope in Global Capitalism and Its Critiques," *Cultural Anthropology: Journal of the Society for Cultural Anthropology*. 21, no. 2 (2006): 149.
80. Malthus, *Political Economy*, 267.
81. Ibid., 283.
82. Malthus, *Population*, 566.
83. Ibid., 575; also cited and discussed in Folbre, *Greed, Lust and Gender*, 117.
84. Giovanna Procacci, "Social Economy and Government of Poverty," in *The Foucault Effect: Studies in Governmentality*, ed. Graham Burchell, Colin Gordon, and Peter Miller (Chicago: University of Chicago Press, 1991), 155.
85. Malthus, *Political Economy*, 184.
86. Cody, "The Politics of Illegitimacy," 132 and 136.
87. Dean, *Constitution of Poverty*, 85.
88. Malthus, *Population*, 519; also see 337.
89. Cody, "The Politics of Illegitimacy," 134.
90. Malthus, *Population*, 518.
91. This argument about how economic man is constitutively gendered adds an additional facet to the question of how gender is constitutive for economic thought. Feminist economists have argued that economic man is constitutively related to an excluded other half. Economic man has as his shadow a woman that is defined in all respects as the opposite to this figure and is given the role of ensuring the sociality and reproductive labor that economic man would always calculate not to do. Thus, the very characteristics of economic man are fashioned through an opposition to a private realm in which presupposed altruism, care,

and dependency reign. For an overview of feminist economics, see Marianne A. Ferber and Julie A. Nelson, *Feminist Economics Today: Beyond Economic Man* (Chicago: University of Chicago Press, 2003). For a discussion on how the neoliberal economic subject is gendered, see Wendy Brown, *Undoing the Demos*, 99–106.

92. For a contemporary analysis of how the shift from welfare to workfare is wound up with a project of sexual regulation that is characterized by racial and gendered profiling, patriarchal norms and commodification/objectification of intimate relations of especially those that suffer most from the cuts in social security, see Anna Marie Smith, *Welfare Reform and Sexual Regulation* (New York: Cambridge University Press, 2007).

93. Malthus, *Population*, 520.

94. Ibid., 237.

95. Ibid., 518–19, 336.

96. Ibid., 469.

97. Catherine Gallagher, *The Body Economic: Life, Death and Sensation in Political Economy and the Victorian Novel* (Princeton, N.J.: Princeton University Press, 2006), 42. Eric Heavner discusses the claims that Malthus should be understood in the perspective of his religious beliefs. The most prominent argument for such perspective is given by Donald Winch in his book *Riches and Poverty*, where he maintains that the transformation of Smith's science of political economy in the early nineteenth century cannot be interpreted without reference to Malthus's Christian beliefs and his natural theology. Heavner supports more the perspective taken here, asserting that the utilitarian origins of his theories give a more appropriate understanding of his thought. While Malthus is informed by the Anglican tradition, his religious principles are subjected to logic of analysis, which is secularized and utilitarian to its core. Eric Heavner, "Malthus and the Secularization of Political Ideology," *History of Political Thought* 17 (1996); and Donald Winch, *Riches and Poverty: An Intellectual History of Political Economy in Britain, 1750–1834* (Cambridge: Cambridge University Press, 1996), 411.

98. "It is clearly the duty of each individual not to marry till he has a prospect of supporting his children, but it is at the same time to be wished that he should retain undiminished his desire of marriage, in order that he may exert himself to realize this prospect, and be stimulated to make provision for the support of greater numbers." Malthus, *Population*, 472.

99. Ibid., 469; also see 476.

100. Malthus, *Population*, 476.

101. Cited in Sheldon Wolin, *Politics and Vision: Continuity and Innovation in Western Political Thought*, exp. ed. (Princeton, N.J.: Princeton University Press, 2004), 263, 291, and 293.

4. The Return of the Political and the Cultural Critique of Economy

1. Robert Colls, "Englishness and Political Culture," in *Englishness: Politics and Culture 1880–1920*, ed. Robert Colls and Philip Dodd (London: Croom Helm, 1986), 54.

2. Cited in Jed Esty, *Shrinking Island: Modernism and National Culture in England* (Princeton, N.J.: Princeton University Press, 2004), 95.

3. Richard Shannon, *The Crisis of Imperialism 1865–1915* (London: Hart-Davis, Mac-Gibbon, 1974), 109.

4. David Landes, *The Unbound Prometheus: Technological Change and Industrial Development in Western Europe from 1750 to the Present* (Cambridge: Cambridge University Press, 1969), 231. See also Shannon, *The Crisis of Liberalism*, 29–31.

5. Ronald Hyam, "The British Empire in the Edwardian Era," in *The Oxford History of the British Empire*, vol. 4, *The Twentieth Century*, ed. Judith M. Brown and William Roger Louis (Oxford: Oxford University Press, 1999), 49. For a discussion of the uncertainty regarding Empire, see also Esty, *A Shrinking Island*, 29.

6. Esty, *A Shrinking Island*, 25.

7. Hyam, "The British Empire in the Edwardian Era," 50.

8. Paul Peppis, *Literature, Politics, and the English Avant-garde: Nation and Empire, 1901–1918* (Cambridge: Cambridge University Press, 2000), 28.

9. Jose Harris, *Private Lives, Public Spirit: A Social History of Britain 1870–1914* (Oxford: Oxford University Press, 1993), 230; and Samuel Hynes, The Edwardian Turn of Mind (Princeton, N.J.: Princeton University Press, 1968), 54–56. The studies that made the poverty into an undeniable "social fact" prominently include *Life and Labour of the People of London* (1902/3) by Charles Booth; *Poverty: As Study of Town Life* (1901/2) by B. Seebohm Rowntree; Philip Snowden's *The Living Wage* (1912); and Sidney Webb and Beatrice Webb's *Minority Report of the Poor Law Commission* (1909). The rise of sociology as a science had considerable roots in reports like this and the concomitant aspiration for social administration and reform: it was deemed to offer necessary knowledge for effecting social progress and reform. See Stefan Collini, *Liberalism and Sociology: L. T. Hobhouse and Political Argument in England 1880–1914* (Cambridge: Cambridge University Press, 1979), 188. The institution of the Department of Social Science and Social Administration at the London School of Economics in 1912 was, among other things, responding to the needs of "obtain[ing] reliable contemporary social data." See Albert Henry Halsey, *History of Sociology: Science, Literature, and Society* (Oxford: Oxford University Press, 2004), 66 and 38f. As Hobson put it in a chapter entitled "The Need of a Sociology," "If our hopes of social progress rest more and more upon the capacity of societies for the conscious interpretation of social utility, the education of this consciousness through sociology is of supreme importance." Cited in Collini, *Liberalism and Sociology*, 192.

10. Daniel Pick, *Faces of Degeneration: A European Disorder, 1814–1918* (Cambridge: Cambridge University Press, 1989), 180. See also Harris, *Private Lives, Public Spirit*, 226.

11. Quoted and discussed in Rachel Potter, *Modernism and Democracy: Literary Culture 1900–1930* (Oxford: Oxford University Press, 2006), 7.

12. See Catherine Hall, Keith McClelland, and Jane Rendall, *Defining the Victorian Nation: Class, Race, Gender and the British Reform Act of 1867* (Cambridge: Cambridge University Press, 2000), 71. Also see Shannon, *Crisis of Imperialism*, 30 and 54.

13. Ute Frevert, *Die Zukunft der Geschlechterordnung: Diagnosen und Erwartungen an der Jahrhundertwende*, in *Das neue Jahrhundert: Europäische Zeitdiagnosen und Zukunftsentwürfe um 1900*, ed. Ute Frevert (Göttingen: Vandenhoeck und Ruprecht, 2000), 153. The Women's Franchise League was founded in 1889. The Women's Social and Political Union, founded in 1903, was the immediate predecessor of the militant suffragette movement. Ibid., 155.

14. Harris, *Private Lives, Public Spirit*, 27.

15. Jacques Rancière calls the "system of self-evident facts" the "distribution of the sensible," which he defines as an order of "sense perception that simultaneously discloses the existence of some-thing in common and the delimitations that define the respective parts and positions within it." Jacques Rancière, *The Politics of Aesthetics: The Distribution of the Sensible* (London: Continuum), 12. See the introduction to this book for a theoretical discussion.

16. Ann Banfield, *The Phantom Table: Woolf, Fry, Russell and the Epistemology of Modernism* (Cambridge: Cambridge University Press, 2000), 15 and 42. For helpful general account of the philosophical source and implications of modernism, see Michael Bell, "The Metaphysics of Modernism," in *The Cambridge Companion to Modernism*, ed. Michael Levenson (Cambridge: Cambridge University Press, 1999).

17. See George A. Akerlof and Robert J. Shiller, *Animal Spirits: How Human Psychology Drives the Economy, and Why It Matters for Global Capitalism* (Princeton, N.J.: Princeton University Press, 2009). The authors take recourse to Keynesian critiques of economic man. Previous models of the market are found wanting in how they account for the irrationality of economic conduct and thus for the irrationality of the market itself. Irrational affects, beliefs, narratives, passions, gut feeling, and contagious behavior are said to govern economic man, more than any concept of bounded rationality would admit.

18. Esty, *Shrinking Island*, 10.

19. Nietzsche was a major vantage point for the development of the sociology of Georg Simmel and Max Weber. See Klaus Lichtblau, *Kulturkrise und Soziologe um die Jahrhundertwende. Zur Genealogie der Kultursoziologie in Deutschland* (Frankfurt a.M.: Suhrkamp, 1996), 82.

20. Raymond Williams, *Keywords: A Vocabulary of Culture and Society* (London: Fontana, 1983).

21. See the introduction to this volume. For overviews, see du Gay and Pryke, *Cultural Economy*; and Pryke and du Gay, "Take an Issue." For the very early account of "economics as culture," see Escobar, *Encountering Development*, 61. The founding of the journal *Cultural Economy* provides a venue for these interdisciplinary

debates. For an up-to-date discussion of the field, see Best and Paterson, *Cultural Political Economy* (London: Routledge, 2010), 2–5.

22. Wolin, *Politics and Vision*, 454–55.

23. Keynes, *Social, Political and Literary Writings*, vol. 28 of *The Collected Writings of John Maynard Keynes*, ed. Donald Moggridge (London: Royal Economic Society, 1982), 42.

24. Esty, *Shrinking Island*, 16.

25. Robert C. Young has discussed this varied relationship between these terms. The claim that it is not one civilization but many, or the pitting of "national culture" against universal or mechanical civilization, has been a critical move that has been articulated since romanticism but achieves new prominence at this historical conjuncture; see Young, *Colonial Desires: Hybridity in Theory, Culture, and Race* (London: Routledge, 1995), ch. 2.

26. Quoted in Michael North, *Reading 1922: A Return to the Scene of the Modern* (Oxford: Oxford University Press, 1999), 53.

27. Esty, *A Shrinking Island*, 10.

28. Ritchie Robertson, "Primitivsm and Psychology: Niezsche, Freud, Thomas Mann," in *Modernism and the European Unconscious*, ed. Peter Collier and Judy Davies (Cambridge, Mass.: Polity Press, 1990), 80–83. See also Pick, *Faces of Degeneration*, 228.

29. See Derek Crabtree and A. P. Thirlwall, eds., *Keynes and the Bloomsbury Group* (London: Macmillan, 1980), 63. A book by Leonard Woolf published in 1939 was titled *Barbarians Within and Without*. For a discussion on civilization as key concern of Bloomsbury and the British thirties, see Christine Froula, *Virginia Woolf and the Bloomsbury Avant-Garde: War, Civilization, Modernity* (New York: Columbia University Press, 2005), 7–11. Also see Brian W. Shaffer, *The Blinding Torch: Modern British Fiction and the Discourse of Civilization* (Amherst: University of Massachusetts Press, 1993).

30. See Ann Stoler, "Making Empire Respectable: The Politics of Race and Sexual Morality in 20th-Century Colonial Cultures," *American Ethnologist* 16, no. 4 (1989): 646. The colonial politics of exclusion, Ann Stoler points out, was "contingent on constructing categories, legal and social classifications designating who was 'white,' who was 'native,' who could become a citizen rather than a subject, which children were legitimate progeny and which were not." The boundaries that separated colonizer from colonized were not self-evident or easily drawn and hence required the permanent purification of membership. Ibid., 635.

31. For an account of the critique of "insane imperialism," see Nicholas Owen, "Critics of Empire in Britain," in *The Oxford History of the British Empire. The Twentieth Century*, ed. Judith M. Brown and William Roger Louis (Oxford: Oxford University Press, 1999), 190. About the "sane imperialism" of political liberalism, see Colls, "Englishness and Political Culture," 49; and Dennis Smith, "Englishness and the Liberal Inheritance After 1886," in *Englishness: Politics and Culture 1880–1920*, ed. Robert Colls and Philip Dodd (London: Croom Helm, 1986), 262.

32. Hyam, *The British Empire in the Edwardian Era*, 51. The handbook *Scouting for Boys* from 1908 states the aim of countering the "deterioration of our race" explicitly: it claims to avert the alarming fall from standards of bodily strength. See Peppis, *Literature, Politics, and the English Avant-Garde*, 63.

33. Young, *Colonial Desires*, 53.

34. Ann Stoler refers for this account to Webster's *New World Dictionary* of 1972. See Stoler, "Making Empire Respectable," 643. David Spurr shows convincingly how this circular reference between moral and bodily categories is typical for colonial discourse. David Spurr, *The Rhetoric of Empire: Colonial Discourse in Journalism, Travel Writing and Imperial Administration* (Durham, N.C.: Duke University Press, 1994), 77. *Body and Will*, the title of a book by Henry Maudsley published toward the end of the nineteenth century, exemplarily shows that culture and biology intermeshed. Henry Maudsley, *Body and Will* (London: Kegan Paul, 1883). It was assumed that the "body is charged with stored virtue"—or, as most diagnoses of decay would have it, rotten through the lack of it. See Walter Bagehot, *Physics and Politics* (London: Kegan Paul Trench and Co., 1972), 6.

35. Quoted in Pick, *Faces of Degeneration*, 234.

36. See Harris, *Private Lives, Public Spirit*, 242–43, 214, and 236. See also Hynes, *Edwardian Turn of Mind*, 62.

37. Peppis, *Literature, Politics, and the English Avant-Garde*, 28. A liberal politician, who, after having outlined a program of social subsidies, said: "All this sounds terribly like rank Socialism. I'm afraid it is; but I am not in the least dismayed, because I know it also to be first rate Imperialism. Because I know Empire cannot be built on rickety and flat-chest citizens." See Ann Davin, "Imperialism and Motherhood," in *Patriotism: Making and Unmaking of British National Identity*, ed. Raphael Samuel (London: Routledge, 1989), 208. The debates around the Boer War thematized poverty in terms of the lack of fitness of the working class with respect to the need for military strength and health. See Anne Summers, "Edwardian Militarism," in *Patriotism: The Making and Unmaking of British National Identity*, ed. Raphael Samuel (London: Routledge, 1989), 242. Hobson argued that imperialism would not allow the proper "cultivation of oneself." See Esty, *Shrinking Island*, 26.

38. Pick, *Faces of Degeneration*, 186.

39. Ibid., 215.

40. North, *Reading 1922*, 70, 90, 94. See also 68–70 and 14.

41. George Bernard Shaw, *Man and Superman: A Comedy and a Philosophy* (Harmondsworth, U.K.: Penguin, 1903), 235 and 245–49. The anxieties about the "basis, value and effect of mass enfranchisement" can be found also in L. T. Hobhouse's *Democracy and Reaction (1904)* and C. F. G. Masterman's *The Condition of England (1909)*. See, for a discussion, David S. Thatcher, *Nietzsche in England 1890–1914* (Toronto: Toronto University Press, 1970), 205.

42. Collini shows that the notion of character implies a "mingling of ethical and physiological properties." It spurred the idea that "weakness of will, of which sentimentalism was a variety, could be walked or climbed out of the system." This "muscular

liberalism" was a dominant trait of Victorian culture toward the end of the nineteenth century. Stefan Collini, *Public Moralists: Political Thought and Intellectual Life in Britain 1850–1930* (Oxford: Clarendon Press, 1991), 113 and 93.

43. As long as imperialism would involve a moral obligation and not just a dedication to trade and power interests, it was supported. This became the position of the Fabian Society only after discussion and a split of the membership after a slight majority voted against declaring the Boer War as an act of imperialism. "In all of them there was the lingering image of a society of soldier-citizens who are rationally and collectively deployed against the anarchy of the free market." See Colls, "Englishness and Political Culture," 53. See also chapter 4 in Hynes, *Edwardian Turn of Mind*; and Pick, *Faces of Degeneration*, 218.

44. For a discussion on how such type of cultural critique and focus on modern individuality determined Max Weber's social theory, see Lichtblau, *Kulturkrise und Soziologe*, 151–55. For the discussion of Nietzsche in this respect, see Mark Warren, *Nietzsche and Political Thought* (Cambridge, Mass.: MIT Press, 1988), 9.

45. Quoted by Virginia Woolf from a letter of Roger Fry. See Virginia Woolf, *Roger Fry: A Biography* (Oxford: Blackwell Publishers, 1995), 272.

46. For an extended discussion of the adoption of mechanical analogies in neoclassical economic thought, see Philip Mirowski, *More Heat than Light: Economics as a Social Physics, Physics as Nature's Economics* (Cambridge: Cambridge University Press, 1989); and Irving Fisher, *Mathematical Investigations in the Theory of Value and Prices, and Appreciation and Interest* (New York: Cosimo Classics, 2007), 85.

47. Irving Fisher, *Elementary Principles of Economics* (New York: Macmillan, 1912), 404.

48. Irving Fisher, *National Vitality, Its Waste and Conservation*, Report of the National Conservation Commission, III, Senate Document 676, 60th Congress, 2nd Sess., reprinted version from the Princeton University Library (New York: Arno Press, 1976). See also the discussion of Fisher's eugenicist writings and activity's in Annie L. Cot, "Breed Out the Unfit and Breed in the Fit," *American Journal of Economics and Sociology* 64, no. 3 (2005). For a general discussion of "the Other" in classical and neoclassical economics, see Robert W. Dimand, "Economists and the Shadow of 'the Other' Before 1914," *American Journal of Economics and Sociology* 64, no. 3 (2005).

49. Quoted in Collini, *Public Moralists*, 92.

50. This quote stems from Marshall's main oeuvre *Principles of Economics*. It is cited in John Maynard Keynes, *The General Theory on Employment, Money and Interest*, vol. 7 of *The Collected Writings of John Maynard Keynes*, ed. Donald Moggridge (London: Royal Economic Society, 1973), 242.

51. John Maynard Keynes, *Essays in Persuasion*, vol. 9 of *The Collected Writings of John Maynard Keynes*, ed. Donald Edward Moggridge (London: Royal Economic Society, 1972), 330.

52. Ibid., 320.

53. "Of the maxims of orthodox finance none, surely, is more anti-social than the fetish of liquidity, the doctrine that it is a positive virtue on the part of investment institutions to concentrate their resources." Keynes, *General Theory on Employment*, 155.

54. Keynes, *Essays in Persuasion*, 329.

55. Keynes, *General Theory on Employment*, 240.

56. Georg Simmel, *The Philosophy of Money*, ed. David Frisby (London: Routledge, 2004), 212.

57. John Maynard Keynes, *The General Theory and After*, part II: *Defence and Development. Vol. 14 of The Collected Writings of John Maynard Keynes*, ed. Donald Edward Moggridge (London: Royal Economic Society, 1973), 116; and Keynes, *General Theory on Employment*, 167 and 174.

58. Keynes, *General Theory on Employment*, 242.

59. John Maynard Keynes, *Indian Currency and Finance*, vol. 1 of *The Collected Writings of John Maynard Keynes*, ed. Donald Moggridge (London: Macmillan for the Royal Society, 1971), 70 and 125–26.

60. Keynes, *Social, Political and Literary Writings*, 227.

61. See, for an extensive discussion, Hartmut Böhme, *Fetischismus und Kultur* (Reinbek: Rowohlt, 2006).

62. Keynes, *Essays in Persuasion*, 235.

63. Piero Mini, *Keynes, Bloomsbury and the General Theory* (New York: St. Martin's Press, 1991), 171.

64. Rossana Bonadei argues that Keynes and Freud share an interest for human character and for a critique of common sense, and share an understanding of their respective sciences not as systems but as working hypothesis. See Rossana Bonadei, "John Maynard Keynes: Contexts and Methods," in *John Maynard Keynes: Language and Method*, ed. Alessandra and Francesco Silva Marzola (London: Edward Elgar, 1994), 65–70. Ted Winslow sees the commonalities mainly in the psychological accounts of conventions that result from unconscious motives. See E. G. Winslow, "Keynes and Freud: Psychoanalysis in Keynes' account of the 'Animal Spirits' of Capitalism," *Social Research* 53, no. 4 (1986). R. M. O'Donnell contends that Freud's philosophical influence on Keynes seems minor, despite the Bloomsbury connection. See R. M. O'Donnell, *Keynes: Philosophy, Economics and Politics: The Philosophical Foundations of Keynes's Thought and their Influence on His Economics and Politics* (New York: St. Martin's Press, 1989), 47. Keynes himself did not take Freudian psychology to be a constitutive element of his argument, as the following account of the history of the gold standard indicates:

> Of late years the *auri sacra fames* has sought to envelop itself in a garment of respectability as densely respectable as was ever met with, even in the realms of sex and religion. Whether this was first put on as necessary armour to win the hard-won fight against bimetallism and is still worn, as the gold-advocates allege, because gold is the sole prophylactic against the plague of fiat moneys, or whether it is a furtive Freudian cloak, we need not be curious to inquire. But we may remind the reader of what he well knows—namely, that gold has become part of the apparatus of conservatism and is one of the matters which we cannot expect to see handled without prejudice. (Keynes, *Essays in Persuasion*, 162)

For other comments on Freud by Keynes, see Keynes, *Social, Political and Literary Writings*, 392; and Keynes, *Essays in Biography*, vol. 10 of *The Collected Writings of John Maynard Keynes*, ed. Donald Edward Moggridge (London: Macmillan for the Royal Economic Society, 1972), 448 and 442.

65. Keynes, *General Theory on Employment*, 202.

66. Adrian Stephen, Karin Stephen, and James Strachey had all studied with Freud in Vienna. James Strachey was the general editor of the *Standard Edition* of Freud in English and Leonard Woolf and Virginia Woolf's Hogarth Press was its publisher. For an account of the popularity of psychoanalysis at this time, see North, *Reading 1922*, 66–70.

67. Keynes, *General Theory on Employment*, 203.

68. Parallels in these discourses have been noticed before without being discussed in depth. Robert Skidelsky speaks of Keynes as having done for economics what Nietzsche did for morals. See Robert Skidelsky, *The Economist as Saviour 1920–1937*, vol. 2 of *John Maynard Keynes: A Biography* (London: Macmillan, 1992), 544. John Toye finds that the "parallelism of ideas is so close that it is hard to believe that Keynes was not deliberately alluding to the relevant section of Nietzsche's The Will to Power." John Toye, *Keynes on Population* (Oxford: Oxford University Press, 2000), 139. He refers in particular to the way in which Keynes posited the question of morality as a choice between altruistic concerns and the beauty of one's own life and to the "semitic founder" who introduced the "Negroid negro question into morality." The quote reads as follows:

> I wonder if in our heart of hears we would blame a man who chose the most splendid flights of passionate and mutual affection or who elected to [be] with Plato and Shakespeare in Paradise, rather than linger through eternity in a state of sordid and disgusting pain combined with the lowest and most degraded feelings and with the foulest and most malignant desires which are at the same time destined never to be satisfied—although, and this is necessary to complete the picture, the sacrifice were to lead to the enlightenment of two Negroid negroes from Central Africa and to their participation in the paradisiac supper party. Then came those dreadful stoics with their universal laws, their life in harmony with the universe and their semitic founder. It was they who introduced the Negroid negro question into morality. (John Maynard Keynes, "Egoism," in *The Papers of John Maynard Keynes*, File 26 of UA, *University Affairs* [Cambridge: King's College Archive, 1906], 5–6)

In general, Bloomsbury seemed to have a split reaction to Nietzsche. Rupert Brooke portrayed Nietzsche as "the Bible of modern man," while Leonard Woolf contends that he was mostly ignored in his circles. See Thatcher, *Nietzsche in England*, 268. With respect to Keynes, the reference to Nietzsche finds support in the collection of Nietzsche's books in Keynes' personal library. The following list has been put together by the very helpful archivist at the King's College Archive in Cambridge. The references in parenthesis refer to the signatures under which these books are classified in the King's College Library: *Die Geburt der Tragödie aus dem Geiste der Musik*, 8 Leipzig, 1872 (Keynes Cc.3.25); *Götzen-Dämmerung oder wie man mit dem Hammer philosophiert* 8 Leipzig, 1889 (Keynes Cc.3.24); *Jenseits von Gut und Böse. Vorspiel einer Philosophie der Zukunft* 8 Leipzig 1886 (Keynes Cc.3.23); *Menschliches, Allzumenschliches. Ein Buch für freie Geister* 8 Chemnitz 1878 (Keynes Cc.3.26); *Morgenröthe. Gedanken ueber die moralischen Vorurtheile* 8 Chemnitz 1881 (Keynes Cc.3.22); *Unzeitgemässe Betrachtungen. Drittes Stück: Schopenhauer als Erzieher* 8 Schloss Chemnitz 1874 (Keynes Cc.3.27); *Unzeitgemässe Betrachtungen. Viertes Stück: Richard Wagner in Bayreuth* 8 Schloss Chemnitz 1876 (Keynes Cc.3.28); and *Zur Genealogie der Moral. Eine Streitschrift* 8 Leipzig 1887 (Keynes Cc.3.21). These are all original editions.

69. Warren, *Nietzsche*, 48.
70. Ibid., 49 and 55.
71. Friedrich Nietzsche, *On the Genealogy of Morality*, ed. Keith Ansell-Pearson (Cambridge: Cambridge University Press, 1994), 7.
72. Peter Sedgwick, "Violence, Economy and Temporality: Plotting the Political Terrain of On the Genealogy of Morality," *Nietzsche-Studies* (2005): 166–67.
73. Nietzsche, *Genealogy of Morality*, 6.
74. Cowan states this clearly as he maintains,

> one should not conclude that Nietzsche was promoting a "pluralistic" understanding of subjectivity in any poststructuralist sense. Despite the illusory nature of the willing subject's identification only with the commanding part of himself, Nietzsche still holds up this configuration as a model for the correct functioning of a healthy will. . . . Nietzsche is still thoroughly convinced of the need for gaining a unity of goal and direction through the hierarchical coordination of organic and psychological forces. (Michael Cowan, "'Nichts ist so sehr zeitgemäss als Willensschwäche': Nietzsche and the Psychology of the Will," *Nietzsche-Studien* [2005]: 52)

75. Keynes, *General Theory on Employment*, 151.
76. Ibid., 145 and 150.
77. Keynes, *Essays in Persuasion*, 287.
78. Keynes, *General Theory on Employment*, 162. The account of the animal spirits continues as follows: "Only a little more than an expedition to the South Pole, is it based on an exact calculation of benefits to come. Thus if the animal spirits are dimmed and the spontaneous optimism falters, leaving us to depend on nothing but a mathematical expectation, enterprise will fade and die." Ibid.
79. Cowan, "Nietzsche and Psychology of Will," 53.
80. Keynes, *General Theory on Employment*, 162–63.
81. Keynes, *General Theory and After*, part II, 113.
82. Ibid., 124. The phrase "dark night of uncertainty" stems from Fitzgibbons. It is here adopted from a discussion about uncertainty and probability that Skidelsky has summarized in the biography of Keynes. See Skidelsky, *Economist as Saviour*, 87.
83. Keynes, *General Theory on Employment*, 162.

84. Ibid., 154.

85. Cowan, "Nietzsche and Psychology of Will," 55.

86. Friedrich Nietzsche, *Nachgelassene Fragment 1887–1889*, vol. 13 of *Friedrich Nietzsche. Sämtliche Werke*, ed. Giorgio Colli and Mazzino Montinari (München: Deutscher Taschenbuchverlag dtv, 1999), 113.

87. Friedrich Nietzsche, *Jenseits von Gut und Böse: Zur Genealogie der Moral*, vol. 5 of *Friedrich Nietzsche: Sämtliche Werke*, ed. Giorgio Colli and Mazzino Montinari (München: Deutscher Taschenbuch Verlag dtv, 1999), 164, my translation; and Keynes, *Social, Political and Literary Writings*, 104.

88. Quoted in O'Donnell, *Keynes*, 248.

89. Keynes's *Treatise on Probability* confirms this view as he tries to prove the validity of arguments that are "rational but not conclusive" or "reasonable but not certain." Keynes, *General Theory and After*, part II, 106. "Without perfect foresight, all one can do is act in the most rational way possible on the data and abilities available. One tries and sees, errors being corrected and new strategies essayed." Strongly opposed to understanding probability as a matter of calculated frequencies that can be reduced to numbers, then computed and weighed, probability is to Keynes a logical relation of inference between knowledge and expectation. Cited in O'Donnell, *Keynes*, 28, 30, and 44. See, for further discussion, Sheila Dow and John Hillard, *Keynes, Knowledge and Uncertainty* (Aldershot, U.K.: Edward Elgar, 1995).

90. O'Donnell, *Keynes*, 78.

91. Anna Carabelli and Nicolo De vecchi, "On Hayek and Keynes Once Again: A Reply to Butos & Koppl," *Review of Political Economy* 16, no. 2 (2004): 281.

92. John Maynard Keynes, *The "General Theory" and After: A Supplement*, vol. 29 of *Collected Writings of John Maynard Keynes*, ed. Donald Moggridge (London: Macmillan for the Royal Economic Society, 1979), 294.

93. Keynes, *General Theory on Employment*, 152.

94. Ibid.

95. Ibid., 153.

96. Ibid., 154, 152.

97. Keynes, *General Theory*, part II, 114.

98. Keynes, *General Theory on Employment*, 158.

99. Keynes, *Social, Political and Literary Writings*, 299.

100. The quote continues as follows: "There is a great deal of it rather tiresome and absurd once you begin to look into it, yet nevertheless is an essential bulwark against overwhelming wickedness. . . . It called in even certain aesthetic elements to its aid, and the precise form of Treasury draft was one of the real weapons in its armoury. Things could only be done in a certain way, and that made a great many things impossible, which was the object aimed at." John Maynard Keynes, "The State and Finance. Lecture Given to Society of Civil Servants on 10 December," in *The Papers of John Maynard Keynes*, File 2 of PS, *Speeches and Lectures Given Outside Cambridge University 1905–1946* (Cambridge: King's College, 1920).

101. John Maynard Keynes, "Modern Civilization," in *The Papers of John Maynard Keynes*, File 22 of UA, *University Affairs* (Cambridge: King's College Archive, 1905), 2.

102. Keynes, *General Theory on Employment*, 204.

103. Keynes, *Social, Political, and Literary Writings*, 76.

104. O'Donnell, *Keynes*, 109.

105. Keynes, *Essays in Biography*, 445.

106. Skidelsky, *Economist as Saviour*, 58.

107. Lorraine Daston and Peter Galison, *Objectivity* (New York: Zone Books, 2007), 255.

108. Anna Carabelli and Nicolo De Vecchi, "Hayek and Keynes: From a Common Critique of Economic Method to Different Theories of Expectations," *Review of Political Economy* 13, no. 3 (2001): 271, 275.

109. Ibid., 278. For a discussion of Hayek's notion of the "invisibility" of the market and the limited sight of the subject as being part of a political philosophy in the tradition of Edmund Burke, see Emma Rothschild's very convincing history of the "invisible hand" in liberalism. Emma Rothschild, *Economic Sentiments: Adam Smith, Condorcet, and the Enlightenment* (Cambridge, Mass.: Harvard University Press, 2001), ch. 5.

110. Keynes, *Essays in Biography*, 446–47.

111. Keynes, "Modern Civilization," 7–8.

112. John Maynard Keynes, "The Political Doctrines of Edmund Burke," in *The Papers of John Maynard Keynes*, File 20/3 of UA, *University Affairs* (Cambridge King's College Archive, 1904), 4. See, for an extended discussion of Keynes's political philosophy, O'Donnell, *Keynes*. Keynes himself qualifies his judgment on democracy in following words: "Democracy is still on trial, but so far it has not disgraced itself. . . . The temper . . . maybe better restrained and modified by a means of expression, that by confinement under an authority, however will-intentioned." Keynes, "The Political Doctrines of Edmund Burke," 62.

113. Keynes, *Essays in Persuasion*, 295–96.

114. Keynes, *A Treatise on Money: The Applied Theory of Money*, vol. 6 of *Collected Works of John Maynard Keynes*, ed. Donald Moggridge (London: MacMillan St. Martin's Press, 1971), 323.

115. Keynes, *General Theory on Employment*, 154.

116. John Maynard Keynes, *Economic Articles and Correspondence: Investment and Editorial*, vol. 12 of *The Collected Writings of John Maynard Keynes*, ed. Donald Edward Moggridge (London: Macmillan for the Royal Economic Society, 1983), 238.

117. Keynes, *General Theory on Employment*, 157 and 155.

118. Keynes, *Essays in Persuasion*, 295, 300, 296.

119. Keynes, *General Theory on Employment*, 158–59.

120. For all Bloomsberries, "contempt for the stupidity of the dominant sectors of the ruling class was a point of longstanding convergence between them." Crabtree and Thirlwall, *Keynes and the Bloomsbury Group*, 48. See also Robert Skidelsky,

John Maynard Keynes, 1883–1946: Economist, Philosopher, Statesman (London: Macmillan, 2003), 174.

121. Keynes, *Essays in Persuasion*, 287, 156, 192–93, 187. He spells out the consequences of this marriage with gold in equally moral and social terms: The "financial fashion plates" also

> remind the intending bridegroom that matrimony means heavy burdens from which he is now free; that it is for better, for worse, that it will be for him to honour and obey; that the happy days, when he could have the prices and the bank rate which suited the housekeeping of his bachelor establishment, will be over—though of course, he will be asked out more when he is married; that Miss G. happens to be an American shop that in future the prices of grapefruit and popcorn are likely to be more important to him that those of eggs and bacon. (Ibid., 192–93)

122. Ibid., 200, 225, 158.

123. *The Economic Consequences of Peace* became "an international bestseller and, over the coming month and years, one of the most influential books of the twentieth century." Skidelsky, *John Maynard Keynes*, 237. It introduced Keynes as a public intellectual. His first fame resulted from this political commentary, not from any economic expertise.

124. Keynes entertains "a little envy, perhaps, for his undoubting conviction that frontiers, races, patriotisms, even wars need be, are ultimate verities for mankind, which lends for him [Churchill] a kind of dignity and even nobility to events, which for others are only a nightmare interlude, something to be permanently avoided." Keynes, *Essays in Persuasion*, 57.

125. As Keynes presented the argument, he gave much weight to these studies of characters. After having outlined that no substantial conflict of interest stood between the Fourteen Points of Wilson and the British demands, he turned toward the "intimate workings of the heart and character," taking place as the "the president, the Tiger and the Welsh which were shut up in a room together for six months and the Treaty was what came out." See Keynes, *Essays in Biography*, 11 and 22.

5. The Economic Unbound

1. Cited in Timothy Mitchell, "Fixing the Economy," *Cultural Studies* 12, no. 1 (1998): 85.

2. John Maynard Keynes, *Essays in Persuasion*, vol. 9 of *The Collected Writings of John Maynard Keynes*, ed. Donald Edward Moggridge (London: Royal Economic Society, 1972), 238, 148, and 239.

3. Ibid., 232; and John Maynard Keynes, *The General Theory on Employment, Money and Interest*, vol. 7 of *The Collected Writings of John Maynard Keynes*, ed. Donald Moggridge (London: Royal Economic Society, 1973), 131.

4. Keynes did not advocate a turn toward unqualified public expenditure: he made a distinction between "current" and "capital" spending and wanted the capital budget to fluctuate with employment. The investment programs were to be treated as "off-budget" but still subjected to the sense of "what things cost," to "sound accounting in order to measure efficiency and maintain economy." See Robert Skidelsky, *John Maynard Keynes, 1883–1946: Economist, Philosopher, Statesman* (London: Macmillan, 2003), 160. Keynes distinguished between economy, or "cheapness," which was due to skill and efficiency in production, and cheapness "which means [to] ruin the producer." The latter he declared to be a "greatest economic disaster." Keynes, *Essays in Biography*, 136.

5. Max Weber, *The Protestant Ethic and the Spirit of Capitalism* (1930; repr. London: Routledge, 2001); Marcel Mauss, *The Gift: Form and Reason for Exchange in Archaic Societies* (London: Routledge, 2001); Georg Simmel, *The Philosophy of Money*, ed. David Frisby (London: Routledge, 2004); and Joseph Schumpeter, *The Theory of Economic Development* (Cambridge, Mass.: Harvard University Press, 1934). As Jean Baudrillard has pointed out, Georges Bataille's critique of economy does take recourse to a naturalized notion of expenditure and mirrors the economy of scarcity by merely reversing its tenets as it is "flip-side of accumulation." Jean Baudrillard, *When Bataille Attacked the Metaphysical Principle of Economy*, in *Bataille: A Critical Reader*, ed. Fred Botting and Scott Wilson (Oxford: Blackwell, 1998), 193. But Bataille's inquiry also commences to outline a notion of the whole that cannot be grasped in terms of a totality closed upon itself, as Jacques Derrida has argued, even if his attempt to think differently potentially reunites with the economic tradition. See Jacques Derrida, *From Restricted to General Economy: A Hegelianism Without Reserve*, in *Writing and Difference*, trans. Alan Bass (London: Routledge, 1978). The limits of Bataille's thought expose themselves in the very moment that he has to admit that for the perspective of living beings, anguish and scarcity remain the defining pillars of economy. The general economy of expenditure and the individual economy of scarcity remain in place. Georges Bataille, *The Accursed Share: An Essay on General Economy* (New York: Zone Books, 1988), 119. Bataille himself refers to Keynes several times in his writings, implicitly or explicitly.

6. George L. S. Shackle, *Keynesian Kaleidics: The Evolution of a General Political Economy* (Edinburgh: Edinburgh University Press, 1974), 81.

7. Hannah Arendt is credited by Ernst Vollrath, as Oliver Marchart points out, to have discovered "in contradistinction to the Heiddegerian 'ontological difference,' the 'political difference,' that is the difference between politically authentic politics and politically perverted politics." Oliver Marchart, *Post-Foundational Political Thought: Political Difference in Nancy, Lefort, Badiou and Laclau* (Edinburgh: Edinburgh University Press, 2007), 38. The notion of the political has a historical trajectory that commenced in "German debates in the early years of the twentieth century to Post-World War II France, and only during the last years spilled over from French thought into the Anglo-American debates." Ibid., 55. Carl Schmitt's book *The Concept of the Political* already signals with his title that

differentia specifica of politics is at stake. See Carl Schmitt, *The Concept of the Political* (Chicago: Chicago University Press, 1996).

8. John Maynard Keynes, *Essays in Persuasion*, vol. 9 of *The Collected Writings of John Maynard Keynes*, ed. Donald Edward Moggridge (London: Royal Economic Society, 1972), 11 and 59.

9. Karl Polanyi, *The Great Transformation: The Political and Economic Origins of Our Time* (Boston: Beacon, 1957), 24.

10. Cited in Bernd Widdig, *Culture and Inflation in Weimar Germany* (Berkeley: University of California Press, 2001), 10.

11. Keynes, *Essays in Persuasion*, 162.

12. Polanyi, *The Great Transformation*, 232.

13. Before writing *General Theory*, Keynes had written extensively on monetary theory. As a young clerk at the India Office, he was concerned with the management of the gold standard of India. He financed his return to scholarly life in Cambridge through his lectures on monetary theory. Thus, biographical and historical circumstances favored money as a choice of subject matter. The two books on money before the *General Theory* were *The Tract on Monetary Reform* (1923) and *A Treatise on Money* (Vol. I: *The Pure Theory of Money*; Vol. II: *The Applied Theory of Money*; 1930). The editors describe the difference between Keynes's early and later writings as follows:

> In his *Tract on Monetary Reform* . . . Keynes stood well within the limits of the Cambridge orthodoxy of his day . . . although his policy goals of price stability, erring if necessary towards slight inflation, his preference for national management and changes in exchange rates, and his emphasis on the short run were all at odds with the tempers of Marshall and Pigou. It was in his movement from the position of the Tract that he was to break new ground. (Introduction to *The General Theory and After: Preparation*, part I, vol. 13 of *The Collected Writings of John Maynard Keynes*, ed. Donald Moggridge [London: Macmillan for the Royal Society, 1973], 15)

Also see John Maynard Keynes, *The General Theory on Employment, Money and Interest*. Vol. 7 of *The Collected Writings of John Maynard Keynes*, ed. Donald Moggridge (London: Royal Economic Society, 1973), vii. In general, one can say that Keynes always granted money and bank policies a paramount influence for either interrupting or smoothing the system. He locates the determining role of money in the gap that exists between the motivations to invest and the motivations to consume. According to Keynes, these motivations are not aligned mechanically, so that the one would rise when the other falls or vice versa. See Keynes, *General Theory and After*, part I, 93. For an overview, see Skidelsky, *John Maynard Keynes*, 25, 49, 60, 160.

14. Paul Davidson, "Keynes and Money," in *A Handbook of Alternative Monetary Theory*, ed. Philip and Malcom Sawyer Arestis (Cheltenham, U.K.: Edward Elgar, 2006), 149. For the Post-Keynesians, money mattered very much, even more than for the monetarist, who thought that there exists a long-run neutrality of

money. For this discussion, see John Edward King, *A History of Post-Keynesian Economics Since 1936* (Cheltenham, U.K.: Edward Elgar, 2002).

15. It is not uncommon that money becomes the primordial entry point for those who seek a different perspective on matters economic. Within social theory many who are most uncompromising in respect to the discipline of economics commence with money—notably, Niklas Luhmann, *Die Wirtschaft der Gesellschaft* (Frankfurt a.M.: Suhrkamp, 1994); and Jacques Derrida, *Given Time: I. Counterfeit Money* (Chicago: Chicago University Press, 1992). For a discussion on the sociology of money, see Nigel Dodd, *The Sociology of Money: Economics, Reason & Contemporary Society* (New York: Continuum, 1994).

16. See the introduction to this work for a discussion and presentation of these different strands of Keynesianism.

17. Quoted in Roger Backhouse and Bradley Bateman, "The Keynesian Revolution," in *The Cambridge Companion to Keynes*, ed. Roger and Bradley Bateman Backhouse (Cambridge: Cambridge University Press, 1996), 167. For a discussion of this introduction of money and time in terms of uncertainty that befalls the economic subject, see Michel Verdon, *Keynes and the 'Classics': A Study in Language, Epistemology and Mistaken Identities* (London: Routledge, 1996), 118–24.

18. The phrase "expectational time" stems from George Shackle. It shows that the question of time was mostly tied to the subject as a decision maker; see Fernando Carvalho, "On the Concept of Time in Shacklean and Sraffian Economics," in *Joan Robinson (1903–1983) and George Shackle (1903–1992)*, ed. Mark Blaug (Aldershot, U.K.: Edward Elgar, 1992), 58. The notion of "economic objectivity" is used by David Woodruff in his book about Russia's monetary reforms. He shows very convincingly that monetary politics shapes conventions and institutions that design a form of objectivity "in which modes of valuing create the reality of economic facts." David Woodruff, *Money Unmade. Barter and the Fate of Russian Capitalism* (Ithaca, N.Y.: Cornell University Press, 1999), 202. The notion of economic objectivity has been taken up for this work. See the introduction to this book for further discussion.

19. As Geoffrey Ingham elucidates, there were of course differing, minor strands of monetary theory that cannot be subsumed under the following presentation—among them, those of Sir James Steuart and the Banking and Currency Schools around 1830. But they did not define the most hegemonic account of money that came to shape nineteenth-century policies and debates. For this argument, it is less important to record the history of monetary thought in all its shades than to highlight an important conceptual difference in thinking about money at the beginning of the twentieth century. See Geoffrey Ingham, *The Nature of Money* (Cambridge: Polity, 2004), 39–45.

20. Cited in Keynes, *General Theory and After*, part I, 254.

21. Ingham puts this emphasis very lucidly: "Traditional economic definitions of money have largely revolved around the four main functions that money is said to perform: a store of value; a means of exchange; a method of payment; and a unit of account. Economists usually focus on that money which is said to perform

these four functions at once, that is 'modern' money, usually some kind of token currency, not valuable in and of itself, which has conventionally been issued by the state. Despite the number of functions attributed to it, however, economists tend to attend only to money's ability to act as a medium of exchange, with it being taken for granted that the other functions will necessarily ensue." Ingham, *The Nature of Money*, 17. Also see Emily Gilbert, "Common Cents: Situating Money in Time and Space," *Economy and Society* 34, no. 3 (2005): 358. Keynes made rather explicit that money thought about as a medium of exchange is "a convenience which is devoid of significance or real influence." John Maynard Keynes, *The General Theory and After*, part II: *Defence and Development*, vol. 14 of *The Collected Writings of John Maynard Keynes*, ed. Donald Edward Moggridge (London: Macmillan for the Royal Society, 1973), 115.

22. Joseph Schumpeter, *A History of Economic Analysis* (London: Routledge, 1987), 277.

23. Carl Menger, *Principles of Economics* (New York: New York University Press, 1981), 260.

24. Paul Samuelson, *Economics: An Introductory Analysis* (New York: McGraw-Hill, 1967), 55. See, again, Joseph Schumpeter for an account of the real side of economy vis-à-vis the veil of money: "Real analysis proceeds from the principle that all the essential phenomena of economic life are capable of being described in terms of goods and services, of decisions about them, and of relations between them. . . . Thus money has been called a 'garb' or 'veil' of the things that really matter." Schumpeter, *History of Economic Analysis*, 277.

25. Ingham, *The Nature of Money*, 17.

26. Walter Benn Michaels, "The Gold Standard and the Logic of Naturalism," *Representations* 9, Special Issue: *American Culture Between the Civil War and World War I* (1985): 183.

27. Marc Shell, "The Issue of Representation," in *The New Economic Criticism: Studies at the Intersection of Literature and Economics*, ed. Martha Woodmansee and Mark Osteen (London: Routledge, 1999), 57.

28. Cited in Bill Carruthers and Sarah Babb, "The Colour of Money and the Nature of Value: Greenbacks and Gold in Postbellum America," *American Journal of Sociology* 101, no. 6 (1996): 1568.

29. The notion of "honest money" stems from Friedrich von Hayek. Even though Hayek does not subscribe to the notion that money is neutral per se, he argues for monetary policies that strive for such neutrality or honesty. See Friedrich A. von Hayek, *Denationalisation of Money: An Analysis of the Theory and Practice of Concurrent Currencies*. (London: Institute of Economic Affairs, 1976), 23.

30. See Nadja Gernalzick's discussion of Keynes and Derrida. She elucidates the parallel moves within philosophy and economics, drawing out unexpected similarities between the economist of the 1930s and the philosopher of the 1960s. See her "From Classical Dichotomy to Differential Contract: The Derridean Integration of Monetary Theory," in *Critical Studies: Metaphors of Economy*, ed. Nicole Bracker and Stefan Herbrechter, (Amsterdam: Rodopi, 2005).

31. For the rise of credit theories of money, see Ingham, *The Nature of Money*, 47–52.

32. Mauss, *Gift*, 46.

33. John Maynard Keynes, *Social, Political and Literary Writings*, vol. 28 of *Collected Writings of John Maynard Keynes*, ed. Donald Moggridge (London: Macmillan for the Royal Society, 1982), 255.

34. The remainder of the quote introduces the technical term of "money of account," which is central to monetary theory. In order to not make the philosophical argument more difficult than it needs to be, I have omitted the rest of the explanation. For the sake of completion and for the interested reader, the quote continues as follows:

> or (3) if it is used as the term in which prices are expressed, or (4) if it is used as an habitual medium of exchange. In the first three cases the article in question is the term in a money-of-account, in the fourth case it is used as actual money. Now for most important social and economic purposes what matters is the money of account; for it is the money of account, which is the subject of contract and of customary obligation. The currency reforms, which matter, are those which change the money of account. (Keynes, *Social, Political, and Literary Writings*, 252–53)

35. Ibid., 254.

36. Schumpeter, *History of Economic Analysis*, 718.

37. Augusto Graziani, *The Theory of the Monetary Circuit*, in *Concepts of Money: Interdisciplinary Perspectives from Economics, Sociology and Political Science*, ed. Geoffrey Ingham (Cheltenham, U.K.: Edward Elgar, 2005). For this argument, see also Dodd, *Sociology of Money*; Ingham, *Nature of Money*.

38. Keynes, *General Theory on Employment*, 294.

39. Ibid., 294; emphasis in original.

40. Keynes, *Social, Political and Literary Writings*, 226; and Keynes, *General Theory on Employment*, 294. Regarding the act of coinage, the difference between a representational account of money and the shift to a temporal frame becomes palpable. Within a representational framing of money, coinage *does* capture the essence of money, whereas the expression of obligation for contractual relations does not. For those who understand money in terms of a representation, the emergence of money as a standard for expressing obligations is therefore decidedly not the moment that a social order becomes a monetary order because it is neither an instrument of circulation or medium of payment. "The existence, as for example in Egypt, of a standard of values already fulfilling the role of measures of values . . . does not yet constitute the criterion of a monetary economy—far from it—for the standard is neither an instrument of circulation (symbolic function) nor a medium of payment (real function)." Jean-Joseph Goux, *Symbolic Economies: After Marx and Freud* (Ithaca, N.Y.: Cornell University Press, 1990), 66. This quote requires some explanation. It stems from Jean-Joseph Goux, a philosopher and literary scholar who has studied the analogy of money and language. He criticizes the assumption that money (or language) could ever function as a neutral medium of representation. "The connection between signifier and signified

is as fragile, random and arbitrary as the one that endows a piece of base metal or a rectangle of paper with market value." Ibid., 102. At the same time, this critique of the neutrality of representation remains tied to a representationalist framework for thinking about money.

41. "First of all, credit money 'brackets' time since a period of the future is reserved or 'colonised' as a stream of obligations." Andrew Leyshon and Nigel Thrift, *Moneyspace: Geographies of Monetary Transformation* (London: Routledge, 1997), 293.

42. Keynes, *Social, Political and Literary Writings*, 255–56.

43. Ibid., 258.

44. Keynes, *General Theory on Employment*, 240.

45. Ibid., 239.

46. Ibid.

47. These different relations of adequation or substitution exist between a certain monetary unit and its standard—be it gold or a different standard managed by a political authority—and between a monetary unit and the quantity of goods "which a unit of money will purchase." John Maynard Keynes, *A Treatise on Money: The Pure Theory of Money*, vol. 5 of *The Collected Writings of John Maynard Keynes*, ed. Donald Moggridge (London: Macmillan St. Martin's Press, 1971), 47–55, 72, 76–77. See also Keynes, *Essays in Persuasion*, 59.

48. Keynes, *Pure Theory of Money*, 4.

49. Ibid., 6. Keynes specifies: "To regard representative money, even when it conforms to an objective standard, as being still a debt will suggest false analogies." Ibid.

50. "Time is money. He that can earn ten shillings a day by his labour, and goes abroad, or sits idle, one half of that day, though he spends but sixpence during his diversion or idleness, ought not to reckon that the only expense; he has really spent, or rather thrown away, five shillings besides." Benjamin Franklin, *Advice to a Young Tradesman, Written by an Old One* (New Haven, Conn.: Yale University Press, 1961), 306.

51. Ingham refers to James Buchan for this rendering of money. Ingham, *The Nature of Money*, 4.

52. Keynes, *General Theory and After*, part I, 115–116.

53. Karl Marx, *Grundrisse* (New York: Vintage, 1973), 254.

54. Keynes, *General Theory and After*, part I, 116; and Keynes, *General Theory and After*, part II, 101.

55. In her book on time, the social theorist Helga Nowotny describes this form of drawing on the future with the notion of an "extended present": "The future is disposed of as if it were the present and an extended present is thereby produced." Helga Nowotny, *Time: The Modern and Postmodern Experience* (Cambridge: Polity Press, 1994), 52.

56. Quoted in Robert Skidelsky, *The Economist as Saviour, 1920–1937*, vol. 2 of *John Maynard Keynes: A Biography* (London: Macmillan, 1992), 276.

57. Keynes, *General Theory and After*, part II, 210. "Finance is essentially a revolving fund. It employs no savings. It is, for the community as a whole, only a bookkeeping transaction. As soon as it is 'used' in the sense of being expended, the lack of liquidity is automatically made good." Ibid., 219.

58. John Maynard Keynes, *A Treatise on Money: The Applied Theory of Money*, vol. 6 of *The Collected Writings of John Maynard Keynes*, ed. Donald Moggridge (London: Macmillan St. Martin's Press, 1971), 134, 139, esp. 140; and Keynes, *Essays on Biography*, 324.

59. Marx, *Grundrisse*, 515 and 458.

60. Leyshon and Thrift, *Moneyspace*, 293.

61. Keynes, *General Theory and After*, part II, 101.

62. Moreover, as Todd Lowry has argued in an archaeology of the circulation concept, the "great wheel of circulation" reaches back to mathematical and theological models of rational order in ancient philosophy and the Renaissance: "It should be noted that by the time of the Renaissance the reinforcement of a long Pythagorean and mathematical-theological background had elevated circulation analysis to the status of a universal explanatory essence of all process." Todd Lowry, "The Archaeology of the Circulation Concept in Economic Theory," *Journal of the History of Ideas* 35, no. 3 (1974): 430.

63. Schumpeter, *History of Economic Analysis*, 243.

64. Fernand Braudel, *The Wheels of Commerce*, vol. 2 of *Civilization and Capitalism 15th–18th Century* (Berkeley: University of California Press, 1992), 144; Karl Marx, *Capital: A Critique of Political Economy* (London: Penguin, 1990), 249 and 256; and Derrida, *Given Time*, 246. Marx also likens this circulation to the "metabolic process." Marx, *Capital*, 228.

65. Keynes, *General Theory on Employment*, 241 and 239.

66. Ibid., 164 and 293–94.

67. Ibid., 294.

68. In terms of the measurement of temporality, "interest rate" is the economic term that articulates such practical link between "today and tomorrow" as it defines the difference that is due after time has passed. Ibid., 222.

69. A. C. Pigou suggested early on that "Einstein did for Physics what Mr. Keynes believes himself to have done for Economics." Teodore Togati and James Galbraith have each suggested a reading of why this comparison is plausible. Galbraith explicitly mentions that the collapse of the separation between space and time in Einstein's theory has its equivalent in the account of monetary production in Keynes: "the marriage of conceptual domains previously held to be distinct." But he does not specifically refer to the question of temporality and measurement. James K. Galbraith, "Keynes, Einstein and Scientific Revolution," in *Keynes, Money and the Open Economy: Essays*, vol. 1 of *Essays in Honour of Paul Davidson*, ed. by Philip Arestis (Cheltenham, U.K.: Edward Elgar Publishing, 1998). Togati also picks up the question of time, its constitutive nature for Einstein and for Keynes, but does not elaborate on temporality in this way either. See Teodore Dario Togati, "Keynes as the Einstein of Economic Theory," *History of Political Economy* 33, no. 1 (2001): 128.

70. Stephen Kern, *The Culture of Time and Space 1880–1918* (Cambridge, Mass.: Harvard University Press, 1983), 19.

71. John Maynard Keynes, "Essay on Time," in *The Papers of John Maynard Keynes*, File 17 of UA, *University Affairs* (Cambridge: King's College, 1903), 3 and 7.

72. Ibid., 9.

73. Ibid., 5.

74. Keynes, *General Theory on Employment*, 215 and 146.

75. Ibid., 225.

76. Ibid., 223; and Keynes, *General Theory and After*, part II, 102.

77. "In this respect I consider that the difference between myself and the classical [school] lies in the fact that they regard the rate of interest as a non-monetary phenomenon." Keynes, *General Theory and After*, part II, 80.

78. Ibid., 103.

79. Athol Fitzgibbons, *Keynes's Vision: A New Political Economy* (Oxford: Clarendon, 1988), 113.

80. Barry Eichengreen, *Golden Fetters: The Gold Standard and the Great Depression 1919–1939* (Oxford: Oxford University Press, 1992), 3.

81. Of course, Marx's thought on money should not be reduced to this short-handed comparison. What makes his account different from the liberal understanding of money is the emphasis on money as a medium that turns the "value form" into a tangible abstraction. Hence, even though he declared money to be insubstantial, he also draws attention to the materialization of abstraction that money fashions. See Marx, *Grundrisse*, 138. For a discussion of the commodity theory of money to which Marx adhered, see Steve Fleetwood, *A Marxist Theory of Commodity Money revisited*, in *What Is Money*, ed. John Smithin (London: Routledge, 2000). For a recent social theoretical use to think about money on the basis of Marx, see Ben Fine and Costas Lapavitsas, "Markets and Money in Social Theory: What Role for Economics?," *Economy and Society* 29, no. 3 (2000).

82. Polanyi, *The Great Transformation*, 25.

83. See, for this discussion, Richard Timberlake, "Gold Standard Policy and Limited Government," in *Money and the Nation State: The Financial Revolution. Government and the World Monetary System*, ed. Kevin Dowd and Richard Timberlake (New Brunswick, N.J.: Transaction Publishers, 1998).

84. As many have pointed out, the gold standard required all along management and cooperation of central banks. For a classical account, see Polanyi, *Great Transformation*. See also Eichengreen, *Golden Fetters*, 3.

85. "The creation of new wealth wholly depends on the prospective yield of the new wealth reaching the standard set by the current rate of interest." Keynes, *General Theory on Employment*, 212.

86. Ibid., 203.

87. The technical description runs as follows: "It seems then that the *rate of interest on money* plays a peculiar part in setting a limit to the level of employment, since it sets a standard to which the marginal efficiency of a capital asset must attain if it is to be newly produced" the reason being: "It is that asset's rate of interest which declines most slowly as the stock of assets in general increases, which eventually knocks out the profitable production of each of the other." Ibid., 222, 229.

88. Ibid., 131.

89. Ibid., 204.

90. The vantage point is the observation of a state that does not "follow from logical necessity." Ibid., 250, 254. Already in his *Tract on Monetary Reform*, usually considered to be rooted in the orthodoxy of classical political economy, Keynes argued for a standard of value that is "subject of deliberate decision": "We can no longer afford to leave it in the category of which the distinguishing characteristics are possessed in different degrees by the weather, the birth rate and the Constitution, matters which are settled by natural causes, or are the resultant of the separate action of many individuals acting independently, or require a revolution to change them." Keynes, *A Tract on Monetary Reform*, vol. 4 of *The Collected Writings of John Maynard Keynes*, ed. Donald Moggridge (London: Royal Economic Society, 1971), 36.

91. Keynes, *General Theory on Employment*, 203.

92. Keynes, *Essays in Persuasion*, 193, 202.

93. Ibid., 223.

94. Ibid., 224.

95. Gilles Deleuze, *Foucault* (London: Continuum, 2006), 41.

96. Keynes, *General Theory on Employment*, 235; and Keynes, *General Theory and After*, part I, 489.

6. The Archipolitics of Macroeconomics

1. This coinage of words is taken from Ian Hacking, *Representing and Intervening: Introductory Topics in the Philosophy of Natural Science* (1983; repr. Cambridge: Cambridge University Press, 1994).

2. Richard P. Adelstein, "'The Nation as an Economic Unit': Keynes, Roosevelt, and the Managerial Ideal," *Journal of American History* 78, no. 1 (1991): 171. See, for a general discussion, Timothy Mitchell, "Fixing the Economy," *Cultural Studies* 12, no. 1 (1998). Also see Daniel Breslau, "Economics Invents the Economy: Mathematics, Statistics, and Models in the Work of Irving Fisher and Wesley Mitchell," *Theory and Society* 32, no. 3 (2003): 382.

3. Mary Morgan and Marcel Boumans have unearthed and discussed this model in depth. It was constructed by Bill Philips in the late 1940s in the attempt to directly link "the economic ideas with hydraulic ones": "Philips' faith in the ability of his machine to produce comprehension out of confusion proved correct. The machine as a large 'physical inscription' created 'optical consistency' in the sense Bruno Latour has defined: all the theoretical elements and institutional arrangements were made homogenous in space in such a way 'that allows you to change scale, to make them presentable and to combine them at will.'" Mary S. Morgan and Marcel Boumans, "Secrets Hidden by Two-Dimensionality: The Economy as a Hydraulic Machine," in *Models: The Third Dimension of Science*, ed. Soyara de Chadarevian and Nick Hopwood (Stanford, Calif.: Stanford University Press, 2004), 374 and 391.

4. Tomo Suzuki, "The Epistemology of Macroeconomic Reality: The Keynesian Revolution from an Accounting Point of View," *Accounting, Organizations and Society* 28, no. 5 (2003): 476. As Michael Bernstein puts the relevance of Keynes for the emergence of the statistical construct of macroeconomy, "Hardly the first to approach the analysis of economic performance from an aggregate perspective, John Maynard Keynes nevertheless provided, in the 1936 publication of his General Theory, a theoretical apparatus by which to array the constituent parts of a macroeconomic system in a discrete framework that aided the compilation of data." Michael Bernstein, *A Perilous Progress: Economists and Public Purpose in Twentieth-Century America* (Princeton, N.J.: Princeton University Press, 2004), 78.

5. Much has been written about Keynes's own attitude toward these models. On the one hand, the distance between the wider horizon of his thought and these models has been emphasized by Keynes himself, who used numbers and models only in pragmatic ways. The story of his encounter with Jan Tinbergen, who had been employed at the League of Nations for furthering the statistical modeling of the economy, is often told in this respect. On presenting statistical figures that supported Keynes, he is reported to have answered: "How nice for you to have found the correct figure." Yuval Yonay, *The Struggle Over the Soul of Economics: Institutionalist and Neoclassical Economists in America Between the Wars* (Princeton, N.J.: Princeton University Press, 1998), 191. Keynes explains his understanding of economic knowledge and economic models as follows: "It seems to me that economics is a branch of logic, a way of thinking; . . . it is of the essence of a model that one does not fill in real values for the variable functions. To do so would make it useless as a model." John Maynard Keynes, *The General Theory and After*, part II, *Defence and Development*, vol. 14 of *The Collected Writings of John Maynard Keynes*, ed. Donald Edward Moggridge (London: Royal Economic Society, 1973), 296–97. At the same time, Keynes never repudiated these models. On the contrary, he endorsed them warmly. "I have found it instructive and illuminating and I really have no criticisms. I think that you have re-orientated the argument beautifully." Ibid., 84. For an exemplary discussion, see Sheila Dow and John Hillard, *Keynes, Knowledge and Uncertainty* (Aldershot, U.K.: Edward Elgar, 1995).

6. Yonay, *Soul of Economics*, 192.

7. Quoted in Suzuki, "Epistemology," 502.

8. Peter Clarke, *The Keynesian Revolution in the Making, 1924–1936* (Oxford: Oxford University Press, 1988), 315.

9. Jim Tomlinson, "Managing the Economy, Managing the People: Britain c. 1931–70," *Economic History Review* 58, no. 3 (2005): 557. As Saskia Sassen, among others, has highlighted, one should be wary of depicting the rise and demise of the "national economy" as an indicator of the rise or demise of the role of politics and the state vis-à-vis the economy in general. See Saskia Sassen, *Territory, Authority, Rights: From Medieval to Global Assemblages.* (Princeton, N.J.: Princeton University Press, 2006).

10. Andrew Barry, "The Anti-Political Economy," *Economy and Society* 31, no. 2 (2002).

11. William Walters, "Anti-Political Economy: Cartographies of 'Illegal Immigration' and the Displacement of the Economy," in *Cultural Economy*, ed. Jacqueline Best and Matthew Patterson (New York: Routledge, 2010), 116.

12. As Jacqueline Best has pointed out, Keynesianism hopes to deal with economy in an "essential apolitical" way, "seeking to supersede political contestation through economic expertise, either domestic or international." Jacqueline Best, *The Limits of Transparency: Ambiguity and the History of International Finance*, Cornell Studies in Money (Ithaca, N.Y.: Cornell University Press, 2005), 49.

13. Jacques Rancière, *Dissensus: On Politics and Aesthetics* (London: Continuum, 2010), 69 and 92. See the introduction to this book for a more extended discussion.

14. For a kindred take on the construction of the "national economy" and its attendant understanding of technocratic government, see Colin Danby, "Contested States, Transnational Subjects: Toward a Post Keynesianism Without Modernity," in *Postcolonialism Meets Economics*, ed. Eiman O. Zein-Elabdin and S. Charusheela (London: Routledge, 2004), 254.

15. The question of population in Keynesian economics has rarely been the object of discussion. Toye's *Keynes and Population* is a notable exception to this silence. John Toye, *Keynes and Population* (Oxford: Oxford University Press, 2000). In his comprehensive study, Toye mentions that only two scholars extensively discuss the issue of population in Keynes. But their work does not yet take into account the unpublished lectures on population by Keynes into account. Ibid., 7. Attending to the issue of population and its accompanying themes of eugenics sheds an often unwanted light on Keynes. It is interesting that Toye felt the need to preface his book on Keynes and population with a defense that "there is no intention, even if it were possible, to deny what already stands to his eternal credit, or to snatch away the laurels long since won." "Keynes's high achievements," Toye assures, "should never be forgotten." He presents the reaction to his first article in 1997 as "causing a passing storm. The article received extensive national newspaper coverage. . . . On the one hand, there was outrage that I dared to say such a thing about a cultural icon like Keynes. . . . On the other hand, there were elaborate expressions of indifference . . . since in those days everybody who was anybody was racially prejudiced." Ibid., 4.

16. Suzuki, "Epistemology"; Bernstein, *Perilous Progress*; Alain Desrosières, *The Politics of Large Numbers: A History of Statistical Reasoning* (Cambridge, Mass.: Harvard University Press, 1998), 279; Theodore M. Porter, "Economics and the History of Measurement," *History of Political Economy* 33, no. 1 (2001); Peter Miller, "Accounting for Progress—National Accounting and Planning in France: A Review Essay," *Accounting, Organizations and Society* 11, no. 1 (1986); and Breslau, "Economics."

17. Suzuki, "Epistemology," 507, 490, and 493.

18. Porter, "Measurement," 19.

19. Manu Goswami, *Producing India: From Colonial Economy to National Space* (Chicago: University of Chicago Press, 2004), 220.

20. Mitchell, "Fixing the Economy," 89.

21. Jed Esty, *A Shrinking Island: Modernism and National Culture in England* (Princeton, N.J.: Princeton University Press, 2004), 176. See also Nathaniel Berman, who suggested a similar perspective on the forging of these new realities that are at once "normative concepts," entailing a "historically specific form of faith." Nathaniel Berman, "Economic Consequences, Nationalist Passions: Keynes, Crisis, Culture and Policy," *American University Journal of International Law and Policy* 10, no. 2 (1996): 627.

22. For an account of anticolonial struggles and discourses that took recourse to the understanding of the national economy, see Goswami, *Producing India*. See also Arturo Escobar, *Encountering Development: The Making and Unmaking of the Third World* (Princeton, N.J.: Princeton University Press, 1995); and Timothy Mitchell, *The Rule of Experts: Egypt, Techno-Politics and Modernity* (Berkeley: University of California Press, 2002). Both authors have unpacked the relations of power that are ingrained in the models of national development as tied to the understanding of Third World in the twentieth century.

23. As Uma Kalpagam has pointed out, not only the trade discourses of the East India Company but also the economists at the India Office were preoccupied "with sorting the 'profits' and 'losses' of India framed as an economic unity." Uma Kalpagam, "Colonial Governmentality and the 'Economy,'" *Economy and Society* 29, no. 3 (2000): 422. Manu Goswami's account of the "political economy of nationalism" takes up this thread and elaborates how the subsequent shift from the mercantile form of colonialism under the company toward a territorial form of colonial power under state directives furthered such macroeconomic "intelligibility of the colonial economy as temporally dynamic and territorial distinct entity." The colonial economy was cast as distinct body politic that required a distinct understanding of profitability—based "not of necessity to the Government as capitalists, *but to the entire body politic of the State*," as an official report on public works in India put it. Goswami, *Producing India*, 79. The colonial account of India as an economic unit later became reemployed in the struggles against colonial dependence. The conceptualization of India as an economic unit turned into a tool against the colonial regime. Because the colonial regime was depicted as a "drain of the nation," the "ideal of independent nationality was articulated not to the least on the basis of an economic argument," as Partha Chatterjee, *inter alia*, has shown. Partha Chatterjee, *The Nation and Its Fragments: Colonial and Postcolonial Histories* (Princeton, N.J.: Princeton University Press, 1993), 203. Timothy Mitchell has furnished a substantial argument on how "the economy" emerged within the colonial and postcolonial government of the economy in Egypt. Mitchell, *Rule of Experts*.

24. It is interesting to note that U.S. and U.K. national accounts were developed quite independently of each other. Jim Tomlinson, "Why Was There Never a 'Keynesian Revolution' in Economic Policy?," *Economy and Society* 10, no. 1 (1981): 82.

25. "How to Pay for the War" is a piece written by Keynes. See John Maynard Keynes, *Activities 1939–1945: Internal War Finance*, vol. 22 of *The Collected Writings*

of John Maynard Keynes, ed. Donald Moggridge and Elizabeth Johnson (London: Royal Economic Society, 1978).

26. "The support of most American economists in intervention preceded the Great Depression," as Yuval Yonay points out: "The experience of a managed economy during World War I strengthened the belief of many economists that coordination and planning could increase economic productivity." Yonay, *Soul of Economics*, 4. See also Bernstein, *Perilous Progress*, 34, 36, 42.

27. Breslau, "Economics," 405.

28. Bernstein, *Perilous Progress*, 82, 79.

29. Suzuki, "Epistemology," 484.

30. Bernstein, *Perilous Progress*, 81. In the words of John Hicks, "social accounting . . . is nothing else but the accounting of the whole community or nation" just as "private accounting is the accounting of the individual firm." cited in Suzuki, "Epistemology," 480.

31. "Under the supervision of Keynes, then at the treasury, Meade and Stone established the first official national accounting system." Suzuki, "Epistemology," 480. See also Gilles Dostaler, *Keynes and His Battles* (Cheltenham, U.K.: Edward Elgar, 2007), 201.

32. Suzuki, "Epistemology," 484.

33. Bernstein, *Perilous Progress*, 78.

34. Adelstein, "'Nation as Economic Unit,'" 161. "The phrase 'nation as an economic unit' appears in the announcement of the award of the 1984 Nobel Memorial Prize in economics to Sir Richard Stone, an assistant to John Maynard Keynes in the British Treasury during World War II where they began to develop the modern system of national income accounts." Ibid., n162.

35. Ibid., 172–74.

36. Adelstein, "'Nation as Economic Unit,'" 186, 162.

37. Esty, *Shrinking Island*, 167.

38. John Maynard Keynes, *Essays in Persuasion*, vol. 9 of *The Collected Writings of John Maynard Keynes*, ed. Donald Edward Moggridge (London: Royal Economic Society, 1972), 19. This recuperative nationalism, to be sure, did not envision a world without hierarchies, centers, or larger economic units. On the contrary, Keynes's vision for postwar reconstruction did assume some form of continuation of the "British Empire" that "will actually possess overseas enormous stocks of food and materials." John Maynard Keynes, *Activities 1940–1944. Shaping the Post-War World: The Clearing Union*, vol. 25 of *The Collected Works of John Maynard Keynes*, ed. Donald Edward Moggridge (London: Royal Economic Society, 1980), 13 and 56.

39. Keynes, *Activities 1940–1944*, 55.

40. Keynes's article on national self-sufficiency can be found in the *Activities 1931–1939. World crisis and policies in Britain and America*, vol. 21 of *Collected Writings of John Maynard Keynes*, ed. Donald Moggridge (Cambridge: Macmillan for Royal Economic Society, 1982). For a discussion of the latter forms of embedded liberalism that sought to combine national and international development, see

Jonathan Kirshner, "Keynes, Capital Mobility and the Crisis of Embedded Liberalism," *Review of International Political Economy* 6, no. 3 (1999); and Don Markwell, *John Maynard Keynes and International Relations: Economic Paths to War and Peace* (Oxford: Oxford University Press, 2006).

41. Keynes, *Activities 1940–1944*, 55.

42. John Maynard Keynes, "Notes on the Prolegomena to a New Socialism," in *The Papers of John Maynard Keynes*, File 24 of L, *Letters* (Cambridge: Kings College Archive, 1924), 46.

43. John Maynard Keynes, *Activities 1922–1929: The Return to Gold and Industrial Policy*, part I, vol. 19 of *The Collected Writings of John Maynard Keynes*, ed. Donald Edward Moggridge (London: Royal Economic Society, 1981), 437.

44. Ibid., 441.

45. Keynes, *Essays in Persuasion*, 292.

46. John Maynard Keynes, "Toast 'Malthus in Piam Memoriam' given at 50th anniversary dinner of the Malthusian League," in *The Papers of John Maynard Keynes*, File 3 of PS, *Speeches and Lectures Given Outside Cambridge* (Cambridge: King's College Archive, 1927), 113.

47. Keynes, "Typescript for Presentation of Galton gold medal by Eugenics Society," in *The Papers of John Maynard Keynes*, File 7 of PS, *Speeches and Lectures Given Outside of Cambridge* (Cambridge: Kings College Archive, 1946), 531.

48. Keynes, *Activities 1922–1929*, 120.

49. Toye, *Keynes on Population*, 29. Keynes's writings on population begin early on with the manuscript on population in 1912 and conclude with the Galton Lecture in 1937, including a lecture on population in 1914, remarks in parts of *Economic Consequences of Peace*, and a paper on Malthus published in the *Essays in Biography*. The lecture of 1914 is not published in the *Collected Works*. In his book on Keynes, Toye offers a transcript of this lecture, otherwise only accessible in the King's College Archive. The Galton Lecture, given to the Eugenics Society in 1937, is reprinted in Keynes, *General Theory and After*, part II.

50. Edmund Ramsden has explored how population functions in these debates about eugenics and demography as a "loose boundary concept" within a scientific field. Edmund Ramsden, "Carving Up Population Science: Eugenics, Demography and the Controversy over the 'Biological Law' of Population Growth," *Social Studies of Science* 32, no. 5–6 (2002). The notion of "boundary-work" stems from Thomas Gieryn, "Boundary-Work and the Demarcation of Science from Non-Science: Strains and Interests in Professional Ideologies of Scientists," *American Sociological Review* 48, no. 6 (1983). Ramsden borrows the notion of "loose boundary concepts" from Llana Löwy, "The Strength of Loose Concepts—Boundary Concepts, Federative Experimental Strategies and Disciplinary Growth: The Case of Immunology," *History of Science* 30 (1992). The conception of "boundary objects" stems from Susan Leigh Star and James R. Griesemer, "Institutional Ecology, 'Translations' and Boundary Objects: Amateurs and Professionals in Berkeley's Museum of Vertebrate Zoology, 1907–39," *Social Studies of Science* 19, no. 3 (1989).

51. For a discussion of population, eugenics, and demography in the twentieth century, see Ramsden, "Population Science"; Marc Frey, "Experten, Stiftungen und Politik: Zur Genese des globalen Diskurses über Bevölkerung seit 1945," *Zeithistorische Forschungen* [*Studies in Contemporary History*] 4, no. 1–2 (2007); Alison Bashford, "Population, Geopolitics, and International Organizations in the Mid-Twentieth Century," *Journal of World History* 19, no. 3 (2008); and Matthew Connelly, "To Inherit the Earth: Imagining World Population, from the Yellow Peril to the Population Bomb," *Journal of Global History* 1, no. 3 (2006).

52. Frey, "Experten, Stiftungen und Politik."

53. For an account of the World Population Conference in Geneva and the international organizations concerned with population, see Alison Bashford, "Nation, Empire, Globe: The Spaces of Population Debate in the Interwar Years," *Comparative Studies in Society and History* 49, no. 1 (2007).

54. Quoted in Toye, *Keynes on Population*, 387.

55. Connelly, "Inherit the Earth," 303.

56. Cited in Toye, *Keynes on Population*, 141.

57. It remains a curious circumstance that the lecture on population has not been published in the *Collected Writings of John Maynard Keynes*. "Keynes' manuscript on 'Population,' the basis of a lecture he delivered on 2 May 1914, was not finally published in any form until 1993, and then only as one small part of the archive of Keynes' papers that was made available by King's college." See Toye, *Keynes on Population*, 44–47. He points out that the lecture notes were not published in the omissions, while others, such as the much less substantial preface to the 1922 Cambridge economic handbook on population, were. Given that the lecture of 1914 has no parallel in other writings of Keynes, Toye finds the omission unintelligible. He refrains from any imputation of editorial intent, concluding only that "there is still work to do for the editors." Ibid.

58. John Maynard Keynes, "Population: Lecture delivered to the Political Philosophy and Science Club," in *The Papers of John Maynard Keynes*, file 1 of SS, *Special Subjects* (Cambridge: King's College Archive, 1914), 27.

59. Ibid., 34–35.

60. Keynes, *Essays in Persuasion*, 57.

61. Giorgio Agamben takes the stance that the biopolitical paradigm of politics constitutes the Western political tradition at its core. It produces inevitably zones in which rights are suspended and sovereign violence reigns. See Giorgio Agamben, *Homo Sacer: Sovereign Power and Bare Life* (Stanford, Calif.: Stanford University Press, 1998). Michel Foucault adopts a more historicizing perspective that allows for a more fine-grained differentiation of what biopolitics amounts to. To him, Nazism is a return of sovereign logics of power within a biopolitical paradigm. Michel Foucault, *The History of Sexuality: An Introduction*, vol. 1 (New York: Vintage Books, 1990). It marks thus a specific historical conjunction. Etienne Balibar suspects that the links between the articulation of a national community and the racisms that divide the universal hierarchies of "species life" are

indelible. Etienne Balibar, *Masses, Classes, Ideas: Studies on Politics and Philosophy Before and After Marx* (New York: Routledge, 1994), 202.

62. He suggests that a logic of immunization accounts for this intimate yet conditioned link between biopolitics and thanatopolitics. See ch. 2 and 3 in his book *Bios: Biopolitics and Philosophy* for a discussion of how to conceptualize this complex link between a politics of life and a politics of death Roberto Esposito, *Bios: Biopolitics and Philosophy* (Minneapolis: University of Minnesota Press, 2008).

63. In the case of Keynes personally, the commitment to some fundamental tenets of political liberalism seems to hold against this biopolitical discourse that undermines these political rights. In the case of his pronounced anti-Semitism, Keynes himself wrote to his wife, Lydia: "I made my usual conversation about the Jews in the Combination Room last night, and then immediately afterwards signed a petition for a great Mansion House Meeting to be called in their favour." Donald Moggridge, *Maynard Keynes: An Economist's Biography* (London: Routledge, 1992), 609. He supported the emigration of Jews from Germany to England. Likewise, in the context of the discussion on coercive eugenic measures, Keynes apparently withdrew support. Toye only finds a letter in which Keynes replies to a request by his mother for support of coercive measures: "I seem to have a liking for the not quite dotty." See Toye, *Keynes on Population*, 144.

64. Keynes, *General Theory and After*, part II, 85.

65. Keynes, "Population," 15.

66. John Maynard Keynes, *Activities 1920–1922. Treaty Reversion and Reconstruction*, vol. 17 of *The Collected Writings of John Maynard Keynes*, ed. Donald Moggridge (London: Royal Economic Society, 1977), 270.

67. Keynes, *General Theory on Employment*, 242.

68. Keynes, *General Theory and After*, part II, 131–33.

69. John Maynard Keynes, *Essays in Biography*, vol. 10 of *The Collected Writings of John Maynard Keynes*, ed. Donald Edward Moggridge (London: Royal Economic Society, 1972), 107.

70. John Maynard Keynes, *The General Theory and After: Preparation*, part I, vol. 13 of *The Collected Writings of John Maynard Keynes*, ed. Donald Moggridge (London: Macmillan for the Royal Society, 1973), 488.

71. Keynes, *General Theory on Employment*, 32.

72. Thomas Robert Malthus, *An Essay on the Principle of Population. Sixth Edition (1826) with Variant Readings from the Second Edition (1803)*, vol. 2 and 3 of *The Works of Thomas Robert Malthus*, ed. Edward Anthony Wrigley and David Souden (London: William Pickering, 1986), 575.

73. Michel Foucault, *The Order of Things: An Archaeology of the Human Sciences* (New York: Vintage Books, 1994), 259.

74. For this point, see Toye, *Keynes on Population*, 145.

75. Keynes, "Toast," 113.

76. Keynes, *General Theory on Employment*, 129.

77. John Maynard Keynes, "A Survey of the Present Position of Socialism: Speech given to the Society for Socialist Inquiry and Propaganda" in *The Papers of John Maynard Keynes,* File 5 of PS, *Speeches and Lectures Given Outside Cambridge University 1905–1946* (Cambridge: King's College, 1931), 105. The variables for tuning what is sound are the following: "It will be essential, either that we alter our institution and the distribution of wealth in a way which causes a smaller proportion of income to be saved, or that we reduce the rate of interest sufficiently to make profitable very large changes in technique or in the direction of consumption which involve a much larger use of capital in proportion to output." Keynes, *General Theory and After,* part II, 131.

78. Following statements indicate this balancing of reasons. The argument for more postponement and saving is directed at the economist Hobson, who argued that underconsumption is at the heart of the economic problem. While Hobson preferred to distribute and release resources for consumption, Keynes pressed the need for more "materialized" capital goods: "I think that the community can still benefit greatly from an increased stock of capital goods." Keynes, *General Theory and After,* part I, 334. But depending on the degree of population decline or growth, Keynes finds more equality in distribution and consumption advisable, since a "stationary population needs more consumption." Keynes, *General Theory and After,* part II, 132. "With a stationary population we shall, I argue, be absolutely dependent for the maintenance of prosperity and civil peace on policies of increasing consumption by a more equal distribution of incomes and of forcing down the rate of interest so as to make profitable a substantial change in the length of the period of production." Ibid.

79. Keynes, "Population," 21–23 and 35. According to Toye, Keynes did not substantially recant this argument and sustained the racial (and anti-Semitic) differentiation throughout. Toye, *Keynes on Population,* 149–55.

80. Mitchell, *Rule of Experts,* 212.

81. Escobar, *Encountering Development,* 35 and 47.

82. John Maynard Keynes, *Social, Political and Literary Writings,* vol. 28 of *The Collected Writings of John Maynard Keynes,* ed. Donald Moggridge (London: Royal Economic Society, 1982), 345.

83. Ibid., 344.

84. Keynes, *Activities 1940–1944,* 55.

85. Keynes, *Essays in Persuasion,* 326.

86. Ibid., 331.

87. Giorgio Agamben, *Ökonomische Theologie: Genealogie eines Paradigmas,* in *Theologie und Politik: Walter Benjamin und ein Paradigma der Moderne,* ed. Bernd Witte and Mauro Ponzi (Berlin: Erich Schmidt Verlag, 2005), 28.

88. Keynes, *General Theory on Employment,* 221.

89. There might be indeed a Nietzschean resonance in all of this—as I argue in chapter 4, the Nietzschean understanding of culture, subjectivity, and temporality is an illuminating frame for understanding the kind of Keynesian critique of economy and its governmental vision. Just as in the case of Nietzsche, the deconstruction of

inherited modes of framing economy and the disturbing affirmation of old hierarchies and racial distinctions is closer than one wishes for. For a very lucid discussion of the deeply ingrained "parasitic logic" in Nietzsche's thought, see Janet Ward, "Nietzsche's Transvaluation of Jewish Parasitism," *Journal of Nietzsche Studies* 24 (2002).

90. Keynes, *Essays in Biography*, 383. On Keynes's anti-Semitism, see Toye, *Keynes on Population*, 149.

91. Keynes, *Essays in Biography*, 383

92. Cited in Robert Skidelsky, *John Maynard Keynes, 1883–1946: Economist, Philosopher, Statesman* (London: Macmillan, 2003), 589.

93. Keynes, *General Theory on Employment*, 129 and 340.

94. Keynes, *Essays in Persuasion*, 336.

95. Keynes, *Social, Political and Literary Writings*, 342.

96. Jacques Derrida, *Given Time: I. Counterfeit Money* (Chicago: Chicago University Press, 1992), 6.

97. This elaboration stems from Carl Schmitt, *Der Nomos der Erde im Jus Publicum Europaeum* (Berlin: Duncker & Humblot, 1997), 44. Referring here to Schmitt does not intend to imply a similarity of political position. Especially in respect to the unwavering commitment to political principles of liberalism in the tradition of John Stuart Mill, *inter alia*, these thinkers diverge fundamentally. Drawing attention to this question of *nomos* and measure only aims at illuminating how a question about the "right measure" had appeared in political and economic discourse alike in the very moment that more deterministic and neutral accounts of these spheres were questioned.

98. Keynes, *Essays in Biography*, 174.

99. Jacques Donzelot, "The Promotion of the Social," *Economy and Society* 17, no. 3 (1988): 415–25.

100. Keynes, *Essays in Persuasion*, 295.

101. Ibid., 285. In his lecture series on *Security, Territory, Population*, Michel Foucault traced the pastoral political rationality from its ancient sources to the political-theological reflections of Christianity to its remnants within the liberal tradition. Michel Foucault, *Security, Territory, Population: Lectures at the Collège de France, 1977–1978*, ed. Michel Sennellart (Basingstoke: Palgrave Macmillan, 2007). According to Foucault, it is the Christian tradition that adds to the pastorate the themes of obedience and subjection, while the Greek model of politics is a rebuttal to the pastoral scheme. Ibid., 146. The pastoral elements in Keynes's writings clearly relate to the ancient sources of pastoral care, as the following paragraph will show.

102. Keynes, *Essays in Persuasion*, 285.

103. Keynes, *Social, Political and Literary Writings*, 32.

104. John Maynard Keynes, *The General Theory and After. A Supplement*, vol. 29 of *The Collected Writings of John Maynard Keynes*, ed. Donald Moggridge (London: Royal Economic Society, 1979), 241.

105. A reference to Plato is also dominant in the biographical essay "My Early Beliefs," in Keynes, *Essays in Biography*. There is also a reference to Plato in Keynes's essay

"Modern Civilization," 10. In both cases, the question of individual judgment and the institution of the political order are at stake.

106. Jacques Rancière, *The Philosopher and His Poor* (Durham, N.C.: Duke University Press, 2003), 3. There seems to be a fondness for Plato among economists. Apparently, Alfred Marshall had planned to write a book on Plato's republic, trying to imagine what kind of Republic Plato would wish for had he lived in Marshall's time. See Keynes, *Essays in Biography*, 231.

107. Keynes, *Social, Political and Literary Writings*, 31.

108. The relation between a vision of pending conflict and a new knowledge or new vision that would dim these struggles is also stated in a piece named "Trotsky on England." Against Trotsky, he maintains most clearly that the lack of proper vision is the root of the political question, not force:

> He [Trotsky] assumes that the moral and intellectual problems of the transformation of society have been already solved—that a plan exists, and that nothing remains except to put it into operation. . . . Trotsky's book must confirm us in our conviction of the uselessness, the empty-headedness of force at the present stage of human affairs. Force would settle nothing—no more in the class war than in the wars of nations or in the wars of religion. An understanding of the historical process, to which Trotsky is so fond of appealing, declares not for, but against, force at this juncture of things. We lack more than usual a coherent scheme of progress, a tangible ideal. . . . The next move is with the head, and fists must wait. (Keynes, *Essays in Biography*, 66–67)

109. Keynes, *Social, Political and Literary Writings*, 31.

110. Keynes, *Essays in Persuasion*, 332.

111. As Peter Galison and Lorraine Daston have elucidated in their history of objectivity, this ideal of objectivity relies, *inter alia*, on mechanical methodologies in order to ensure the elimination of individual judgment and theoretical frames. Lorraine Daston and Peter Galison, "The Image of Objectivity," *Representations* 40, no. Special Issue Autumn (1992): 82.

112. Lorraine Daston and Peter Galison, *Objectivity* (New York: Zone Books, 2007), 255.

113. Keynes, *General Theory on Employment*, 297.

114. Ibid., 247.

115. Keynes, *General Theory and After*, part II, 296–97.

116. Ibid., 300.

117. Keynes, *Essays in Biography*, 262.

118. The liberal tradition Keynes situates himself in combined "the conservative individualism of Locke, Hume, Johnson, and Burke with the socialism and democratic egalitarianism of Rousseau, Paley, Bentham and Godwin." Keynes, *Essays in Persuasion*, 274–80. Robert Colls gives a good overview of this deeply held assumption that it was "the good fortune of the English to have the idealist-historicist mix deep within themselves. Self-help and the freedom it engendered might indeed be a universal quality, but it also had to be quintessentially English.

Freedom . . . has in all times been a marked feature in the English character, and furnishes the true measure of our power as a nation." Robert Colls "Englishness and Political Culture," in *Englishness: Politics and Culture 1880–1920*, ed. Robert Colls and Philip Dodd (London: Croom Helm, 1986), 35.

119. O'Donnell, *Keynes*, 277.

120. John Maynard Keynes, "The Political Doctrines of Edmund Burke," in *The Papers of John Maynard Keynes*, File 20/3 of UA, *University Affairs* (Cambridge King's College Archive, 1904), 4.

121. Ibid.

122. Ibid., 55.

123. Ibid., 9, 84.

124. Ibid., 42.

125. Ibid., 29.

126. John Maynard Keynes, "Agenda and Report of a Meeting of Economists, Civil Servants and Politicians at King's College," in *The Papers of John Maynard Keynes*, File 4 of FI, *International Finance and German Reparations 1919–1923* (Cambridge: King's College, 1919), 9.

127. Keynes, *Social, Political and Literary Writings*, 334.

128. Miller and Rose, "Governing Economic Life," 8.

129. Foucault, *The Birth of Biopolitics*, 271.

130. Adelstein, "'Nation as Economic Unit,'" 197. This reading qualifies Michel Foucault's perspective on Keynesianism. Foucault himself never considered Keynesianism as a variation of the specific liberal governmentality. He juxtaposed the search for a "new" or "neo-liberal" agenda from the 1930s onward, to the forms of "non-liberalism" that "interventionist policies, whether in the form of Keynesian style economics, planning, or economic and social programs" implied. The New Deal wrongly remained for Foucault the reference point for characterizing Keynesianism as a "non-liberal" mode of planning. Reading Keynesianism as a type of liberal governmentality not only excavate the political rationalities that animate this form of economic government, but also add a new, hitherto neglected, facet of the genealogies of liberal governmentality. Foucault, *The Birth of Biopolitics*, 218. As Miller and Rose put it, the "governing of the economy" after the Second World War is ill-understood if only cast as interventionism or central management tout court. See Miller and Rose, "Governing Economic Life," 8.

131. John Maynard Keynes, "Current Monetary Problems: Lecture Given to the Institute of Bankers," in *The Papers of John Maynard Keynes*, File 2 of PS, *Speeches and Lectures Given Outside Cambridge University 1905–1946* (Cambridge: King's College, 1922), 236.

132. Keynes, *General Theory and After*, part II, 116.

133. Keynes, *Essays in Persuasion*, 225.

134. Ibid., 335.

135. Keynes, *General Theory on Employment*, 316 and 322.

136. Ibid., 104, 160.

137. Ibid., 322.

138. Keynes, *General Theory on Employment*, 348. Keynes argues that "the desire of the individual to augment his personal wealth by abstaining from consumption has usually been stronger than the inducement of the entrepreneur to augment the national wealth by employing labour on the construction of durable assets." Ibid.

139. Ibid., 201.

140. Ibid.

141. Ibid., 234. Keynes devotes considerable care to dissect what he deems to be a kernel of truth in the work of Silvio Gesell. The term "carrying costs" refers to the wear and tear that any material object is subject to. Money, as an object, is created and governed as to not have these "carrying costs." Gesell sought to change this.

142. Ibid., 167.

143. Ibid., 14.

144. Ibid., 120.

145. Jacqueline Best summarizes the Keynesian program of governing money: "Capital movements would be limited, protecting states from volatility and insulating them from the short-term demands of the market, so that they could pursue their own macroeconomic stabilizing measures. Exchange rates would be fixed, limiting the scope for currency speculation. International credit would become increasingly public in nature reducing the influence of Wall Street and the Coty on the terms of international economic development. The 'euthanasia' of the rentier, as Keynes described in in his General Theory, was to be complemented with the euthanasia of the speculator, and perhaps even of the international banker." Best, *The Limits of Transparency*, 48.

146. Keynes, *Essays in Persuasion*, 355. The following quote states the logic of this revolving fund clearly: "But if the banking system chooses to make the finance available and the investment projected by the new issues actually takes place, the appropriate level of incomes will be generated out of which there will necessarily remain over an amount of saving exactly sufficient to take care of the new investment." Keynes, *General Theory and After*, part II, 210. It is crucial to note the warped temporality of back from the future that is at work in this account: The savings needed from the beginning will have been made if they can be used at the moment.

147. Keynes, *General Theory and After*, part II, 219.

148. Keynes, *Social, Political and Literary Writings*, 34.

149. Keynes, *General Theory on Employment*, 173, 207.

150. Ibid., 317.

151. Ibid., 320.

152. Keynes, *Essays in Persuasion*, 26.

153. Ibid.

154. Keynes, *Activities 1940–1944*, 57.

155. Markwell, *Keynes and International*, 244.

156. Keynes, *Activities 1940–1944*, 28–30.

157. Keynes, *Activities 1931–1939*, 240–41.

Epilogue

1. Nitasha Kaul, *Writing Economic Theory an Other Way*, in *Postcolonialism Meets Economics*, ed. Eiman O. Zein-Elabdin and S. Charusheela (London: Routledge, 2004), 189.

2. The full quote is: "Economy of time, to this all economy ultimately reduces itself." Karl Marx, *Grundrisse* (New York: Vintage, 1973), 173. Max Weber quotes Benjamin Franklin's dictum that "time is money" in order to explicate the spirit of capitalism. Max Weber, *The Protestant Ethic and the Spirit of Capitalism* (1930; repr. London: Routledge, 2001), 14–16. For a comprehensive study of modern acceleration see Hartmut Rosa, *Social Acceleration: A New Theory of Modernity* (New York: Columbia University Press, 2015).

3. For an argument about how derivatives allow different currencies to retain their moneyness in a context of flexible exchange rates, see Dick Bryan and Michael Rafferty, "Financial Derivatives and the Theory of Money," *Economy and Society* 36, no 1 (2007).

4. For an interesting discussion of the polymorphous meaning of measure in ancient Greece that seems to have interesting resonances with the definition given above, see Michel Foucault, *Lectures on the Will to Know: Lectures at the College de France 1970–1971 and Oedipal Knowledge*, ed. Daniel Defert (London: Palgrave Macmillan, 2013), 133–46.

5. See the discussion on cultural economy and the references given in the introduction to this book. An overview, specifically about the debate concerning "the market" can be found in the introductory chapter of Koray Calsikan's *Market Threads: How Cotton Farmers and Traders Create a Global Commodity* (Princeton, N.J.: Princeton University Press, 2010).

6. J. K. Gibson-Graham, *The End of Capitalism (as We Knew It): A Feminist Critique of Political Economy* (Cambridge, Mass.: Blackwell, 1996), 4 and 17.

7. Bruno Latour, *Reassembling the Social: An Introduction to Actor-Network Theory* (Oxford: Oxford University Press, 2005), 178.

8. Koray Caliskan and Michel Callon, "Economization, Part 1: Shifting Attention from the Economy Towards Processes of Economization," *Economy and Society* 38, no. 3 (2009): 378.

9. See Judith Butler's discussion about the "performativity thesis" in studying the market. Judith Butler, "Performative Agency," *Journal of Cultural Economy* 3, no. 2 (2010): 152 and 154.

10. Fernand Braudel, *Capitalism and Material Life 1400–1800* (New York: Harper & Row, 1967), xiii.

11. Fernand Braudel, *The Perspective of the World*, vol. 3 of *Civilization and Capitalism 15th–18th Century* (Berkeley: University of California Press, 1992), 239.

12. There are resonances to be explored between the anthropology of exchange as, for example, furthered Marcel Mauss's work on gift exchange. As known, Mauss argues that gift exchange has an uncertain economic status: it hovers between a gift and an exchange, and is structured by obligations, rivalry, political concerns

about peace, *inter alia*. Interestingly, the time that passes between receiving and returning a gift is introduced as what modulates the economic character of the exchange. Again, not exchange per se but its specific articulation defines its economic character. Hence, one can read Mauss's work from the vantage point of "the economic," whose malleability he exposes in relations of exchange. Marcel Mauss, *The Gift: Form and Reason for Exchange in Archaic Societies*. London: Routledge, 2001.

13. Hans Blumenberg, "Geld oder Leben: Eine metaphorologische Studie zur Konsistenz der Philosophe Georg Simmels," in *Ästhetik und Soziologie um die Jahrhundertwende: Georg Simmel*, ed. Hannes Böhringer and Karlfried Gründer (Frankfurt/M: Klostermann 1976), 122.

14. Jacques Rancière, *The Philosopher and His Poor* (Durham, N.C.: Duke University Press, 2003), 3. For his discussion of time as the very "agent" that fashions the exclusion of politics, see p. 6.

15. Marie-José Mondzain, *Image, Icon, Economy: The Byzantine Origins of the Contemporary Imaginary* (Stanford, Calif.: Stanford University Press, 2005), 40 and 22. See also Agamben's etymology of the word "*oikonomia*" in early Christian texts. Giorgio Agamben, "Ökonomische Theologie: Genealogie eines Paradigmas," in *Theologie und Politik. Walter Benjamin und ein Paradigma der Moderne*, ed. Bernd Witte and Mauro Ponzi (Berlin: Erich Schmidt Verlag, 2005). For a discussion of the semantic history of the notion of economy, see Theo Stemmler, *Oekonomie. Sprachliche und Literarische Aspekte eines 2000 Jahre Alten Begriffs* (Tübingen: Gunter Narr Verlag, 1985), 32 and 57.

16. Jacques Derrida, *Given Time: I. Counterfeit Money* (Chicago: Chicago University Press, 1992), 16.

17. Ann Laura Stoler, *Race and the Edicuation of Desire: Foucault's History of Sexuality and the Colonial Order of Things* (Durham: Duke University Press, 1995), 107 and 178.

Bibliography

Abbott, Andrew. "The Problem of Excess." *Sociological Theory* 32, no. 1 (2014): 1–26.

Adelstein, Richard P. "'The Nation as an Economic Unit': Keynes, Roosevelt, and the Managerial Ideal." *Journal of American History* 78, no. 1 (1991): 160–87.

Agamben, Giorgio. *Homo Sacer: Sovereign Power and Bare Life*. Stanford, Calif.: Stanford University Press, 1998.

——. *Means Without End: Notes on Politics*. Minnesota: University of Minnesota Press, 2000.

——. "Ökonomische Theologie: Genealogie Eines Paradigmas." In *Theologie Und Politik: Walter Benjamin und ein Paradigma der Moderne*, ed. Bernd Witte and Mauro Ponzi, 20–31. Berlin: Erich Schmidt Verlag, 2005.

Aitken, Rob. *Performing Capital: Toward a Cultural Economy of Popular and Global Finance*. New York: Palgrave Macmillan, 2007.

Akerlof, George A., and Robert J. Shiller. *Animal Spirits: How Human Psychology Drives the Economy, and Why It Matters for Global Capitalism*. Princeton, N.J.: Princeton University Press, 2009.

Arendt, Hannah. *On Revolution*. New York: Viking Press, 1963.

Arestis, Philip. *The Post-Keynesian Approach to Economics*. Aldershot, U.K.: Edward Elgar, 1992.

Armitage, David. *The Ideological Origins of the British Empire*. Cambridge: Cambridge University Press, 2000.

Avery, John. *Progress, Poverty, and Population: Re-Reading Condorcet, Godwin, and Malthus*. London: F. Cass, 1997.

Backhouse, Roger, and Bradley Bateman. "The Keynesian Revolution." In *The Cambridge Companion to Keynes*, ed. Roger and Bradley Bateman Backhouse, 19–38. Cambridge: Cambridge University Press, 1996.

Bagehot, Walter. *Physics and Politics*. London: Kegan Paul Trench and Co., 1972.

Baker, Keith Michael. "The Early History of the Term 'Social Science.'" *Annals of Science* 20, no. 3 (1964): 211–26.

———. "The Idea of a Declaration of Rights." In *The French Idea of Freedom: The Old Regime and the Declaration of Rights of 1789*, ed. Dale Van Kley, 154–98. Stanford, Calif.: Stanford University Press, 1994.

Balibar, Etienne. *Masses, Classes, Ideas: Studies on Politics and Philosophy Before and After Marx*. New York: Routledge, 1994.

Banerjee, Prathama. "Debt, Time and Extravagance: Money and the Making of 'Primitives' in Colonial Bengal." *Indian Economic and Social History Review* 37, no. 4 (2000): 423–45.

Banfield, Ann. *The Phantom Table: Woolf, Fry, Russell and the Epistemology of Modernism*. Cambridge: Cambridge University Press, 2000.

Barker, Francis, ed., *1789, Reading, Writing Revolution: Proceedings of the Essex Conference on the Sociology of Literature*. Colchester, U.K.: University of Essex, 1982.

Barry, Andrew. "The Anti-Political Economy." *Economy and Society* 31, no. 2 (2002): 268–84.

Bashford, Alison. *Global Population. History, Geopolitics, and Life on Earth*. New York: Columbia University Press, 2014.

———. "Nation, Empire, Globe: The Spaces of Population Debate in the Interwar Years." *Comparative Studies in Society and History* 49, no. 1 (2007): 170–201.

———. "Population, Geopolitics, and International Organizations in the Mid-Twentieth Century." *Journal of World History* 19, no. 3 (2008): 327–47.

Bataille, Georges. *The Accursed Share: An Essay on General Economy*. New York: Zone Books, 1988.

Baudrillard, Jean. "When Bataille Attacked the Metaphysical Principle of Economy." In *Bataille. A Critical Reader*, ed. Fred Botting and Scott Wilson, 191–95. Oxford: Blackwell, 1998.

Bell, Michael. "The Metaphysics of Modernism." In *The Cambridge Companion to Modernism*, ed. Michael Levenson, 9–32. Cambridge: Cambridge University Press, 1999.

Berland, Nicolas, and Eve Chiapello. "Criticisms of Capitalism, Budgeting and the Double Enrolment: Budgetary Control Rhetoric and Social Reform in France in the 1930s and 1950s." *Accounting, Organizations and Society* 34, no. 1 (2009): 28–57.

Berman, Nathaniel. "Economic Consequences, Nationalist Passions: Keynes, Crisis, Culture and Policy." *American University Journal of International Law and Policy* 10, no. 2 (1996): 619–70.

Bernstein, Michael. *A Perilous Progress: Economists and Public Purpose in Twentieth-Century America*. Princeton, N.J.: Princeton University Press, 2004.

Best, Jacqueline. *The Limits of Transparency: Ambiguity and the History of International Finance*. Cornell Studies in Money. Ithaca, N.Y.: Cornell University Press, 2005.

———. "Why Economy Is Often the Exception to Politics as Usual." *Theory, Culture & Society* 24, no. 4 (2007): 87–109.

Best, Jacqueline, and Matthew Paterson, eds., *Cultural Political Economy*. London: Routledge, 2010.

Blaney, David L., and Naeem Inayatullah. *Savage Economics: Wealth, Poverty, and the Temporal Walls of Capitalism*. New York: Routledge, 2010.

Blumenberg, Hans. "Geld oder Leben: Eine metaphorologische Studie zur Konsistenz der Philosophe Georg Simmels," in *Ästhetik und Soziologie um die Jahrhundertwende: Georg Simmel*, ed. Hannes Böhringer and Karlfried Gründer, 121–34. Frankfurt/ M: Klostermann 1976.

Böhme, Hartmut. *Fetischismus und Kultur*. Reinbek: Rowohlt, 2006.

Boltanski, Luc, and Ève Chiapello. *The New Spirit of Capitalism*. London: Verso, 2005.

Boltanski, Luc, and Laurent Thévenot. *On Justification: Economies of Worth*. Princeton, N.J.: Princeton University Press, 2006.

Bonadei, Rossana. "John Maynard Keynes: Contexts and Methods." In *John Maynard Keynes: Language and Method*, ed. Alessandra and Francesco Silva Marzola, 13–75. London: Edward Elgar, 1994.

Bonar, James. *Malthus and His Work*. London: Routledge, 2014.

Braudel, Fernand. *Capitalism and Material Life 1400–1800*. New York: Harper & Row, 1967.

——. *The Perspective of the World*. Vol. 3 of *Civilization and Capitalism 15th–18th Century*. Berkeley: University of California Press, 1992.

——. *The Wheels of Commerce*. Vol. 2 of *Civilization and Capitalism 15th–18th Century*. Berkeley: University of California Press, 1992.

Breslau, Daniel. "Economics Invents the Economy: Mathematics, Statistics, and Models in the Work of Irving Fisher and Wesley Mitchell." *Theory and Society* 32, no. 3 (2003): 379–411.

Bröckling, Ulrich. *Das unternehmerische Selbst: Soziologie einer Subjektivierungsform*. Frankfurt am Main: Suhrkamp, 2007.

——. "Human Economy, Human Capital: A Critique of Biopolitical Economy." In *Governmentality: Current Issues and Future Challenges*, ed. Ulrich Bröckling, Susanne Krasmann, and Thomas Lemke. 247–68. New York: Routledge, 2011.

Bröckling, Ulrich, Susanne Krasmann, and Thomas Lemke. "From Foucault's Lectures at the College de France to Studies of Governmentality: An Introduction." In *Governmentality: Current Issues and Future Challenges*, ed. Ulrich Bröckling, Susanne Krasmann, and Thomas Lemke, 1–33. New York: Routledge, 2011.

Brown, Vivienne. *Adam Smith's Discourse: Canonicity, Commerce, and Conscience*. London: Routledge, 1994.

Brown, Wendy. "Neo-Liberalism and the End of Politics." *Theory & Event* 7, no. 1 (2003).

——. *The Undoing of the Demos: Neoliberalism's Stealth Revolution*. New York: Zone Books, 2015.

Bryan, Dick, and Michael Rafferty. "Financial Derivatives and the Theory of Money." *Economy and Society* 36, no. 1 (2007): 134–58.

Buchan, Bruce. "The Empire of Political Thought: Civilization, Savagery and Perceptions of Indigenous Government." *History of the Human Sciences* 18, no. 2 (2005): 1–22.

Buck-Morss, Susan. "Envisioning Capital: Political Economy on Display." *Critical Inquiry* 21 (1995): 434–67.

——. "Hegel and Haiti." *Critical Inquiry* 26, no. 4 (2000): 821–65.

———. *Hegel, Haiti and Universal History*. Pittsburgh: University of Pittsburgh Press, 2009.

Burke, Edmund. *The Portable Edmund Burke*, ed. Isaac Kramnick. New York: Penguin Books, 1999.

———. *Revolutionary Writings: Reflections on the Revolution in France and the First Letter on a Regicide Peace*, ed. Iain Hampsher-Monk. Cambridge: Cambridge University Press, 2014.

Butler, Judith. *Bodies That Matter: On the Discursive Limits of "Sex."* New York: Routledge, 1993.

———. "Performative Agency." *Journal of Cultural Economy* 3, no. 2 (2010): 147–61.

Caliskan, Koray. *Market Threads: How Cotton Farmers and Traders Create a Global Commodity*. Princeton, N.J.: Princeton University Press, 2010.

Caliskan, Koray, and Michel Callon. "Economization, Part 1: Shifting Attention from the Economy Towards Processes of Economization." *Economy and Society* 38, no. 3 (2009): 369–98.

Callari, Antonio. "Economics as the Postcolonial Other." In *Postcolonialism Meets Economics*, ed. Eiman O. and S. Charusheela Zein-Elabni, 113–29. London: Routledge, 2004.

Callon, Michel. *The Laws of the Markets*. Oxford: Blackwell, 1998.

———. "Performativity, Misfires and Politics." *Journal of Cultural Economy* 3, no. 2 (2010): 163–69.

Callon, Michel, Yuval Millo, and Fabian Muniesa, eds., *Market Devices*. Oxford: Blackwell, 2007.

Cameron, Angus, and Ronen Palan. *The Imagined Economies of Globalization*. London: Sage, 2004.

Carabelli, Anna. *On Keynes's Method*. London: Macmillan, 1988.

———. "Uncertainty and Measurement in Keynes: Probability and Organicness." In *Kenyes, Knowledge and Uncertainty*, ed. Sheila and John Hillard Dow, 137–60. Aldershot, U.K.: Edward Elgar, 1995.

Carabelli, Anna, and Nicolo De Vecchi. "Hayek and Keynes: From a Common Critique of Economic Method to Different Theories of Expectations." *Review of Political Economy* 13, no. 3 (2001): 269–285.

———. "On Hayek and Keynes Once Again: A Reply to Butos & Koppl." *Review of Political Economy* 16, no. 2 (2004): 249–56.

Carruthers, Bill, and Sarah Babb. "The Colour of Money and the Nature of Value: Greenbacks and Gold in Postbellum America." *American Journal of Sociology* 101, no. 6 (1996): 1556–91.

Carvalho, Fernando. "On the Concept of Time in Shacklean and Sraffian Economics." In *Joan Robinson (1903–1983) and George Shackle (1903–1992)*, ed. Mark Blaug, 55–70. Aldershot, U.K.: Edward Elgar, 1992.

Castel, Robert. *From Manual Workers to Wage Laborers: Transformation of the Social Question*. New Brunswick, N.J.: Transaction Publishers, 2003.

Chakrabarty, Dipesh. *Provincializing Europe: Postcolonial Thought and Historical Difference*. Princeton, N.J.: Princeton University Press, 2000.

Chatterjee, Partha. *The Nation and Its Fragments: Colonial and Postcolonial Histories.* Princeton, N.J.: Princeton University Press, 1993.

Chowers, Eyal. 2002. "The Physiology of the Citizen: The Present-Centered Body and Its Political Exile." *Political Theory* 30:649–76.

Christie, Jan. "Conservatism and Stability in British Society." In *The French Revolution and British Popular Politics*, ed. Mark Philp. Cambridge: Cambridge University Press, 1991.

Claassen, Rutger. "Scarcity." In *Handbook of Economics and Ethics*, ed. Jan Peil and Irene van Staveren, 470–77. Cheltenham, UK: Edward Elgar, 2009.

Claeys, Gregory. *French Revolution Debate in Britain: The Origins of Modern Politics.* New York: Palgrave Macmillan, 2007.

——. "The Origins of the Rights of Labor: Republicanism, Commerce, and the Construction of Modern Social Theory in Britain, 1796–1805." *Journal of Modern History* 66 (1994): 249–90.

Claeys, Gregory, and Christine Lattekt. "Radicalism, Republicanism and Revolutionism." In *The Cambridge History of Nineteenth-Century Political Thought*, ed. Gareth Stedman Jones and Gregory Claeys, 200–254. Cambridge: Cambridge University Press, 2011.

Clarke, Peter. *The Keynesian Revolution in the Making, 1924–1936.* Oxford: Oxford University Press, 1988.

Cody, Lisa Forman. "The Politics of Illegitimacy in an Age of Reform: Women, Reproduction, and Political Economy in England's New Poor Law of 1834." *Journal of Women's History* 11, no. 4 (2000): 131–56.

Cohen, Isaac Bernard. "The Scientific Revolution and the Social Sciences." In *The Natural Sciences and the Social Sciences*, ed. Isaac Bernard Cohen, 153–204. Dordrecht: Kluwer, 1994.

Colander, David, Robert E. Prasch, and Falguni A. Sheth, ed., *Race, Liberalism, and Economics.* Ann Arbor: University of Michigan Press, 2004.

Collier, Stephen. "Topologies of Power. Foucault's Analysis of Political Government Beyond 'Governmentality.'" *Theory, Culture and Society* 26, no. 6 (2009): 78–108.

Collini, Stefan. *Liberalism and Sociology: L. T. Hobhouse and Political Argument in England 1880–1914.* Cambridge: Cambridge University Press, 1979.

——. *Public Moralists: Political Thought and Intellectual Life in Britain 1850–1930.* Oxford: Clarendon Press, 1991.

Colls, Robert. "Englishness and Political Culture." In *Englishness: Politics and Culture 1880–1920*, ed. Robert Colls and Philip Dodd, 29–61. London: Croom Helm, 1986.

Colls, Robert, and Philip Dodd. *Englishness: Politics and Culture 1880–1920.* London: Croom Helm, 1986.

Condorcet, Marquis de, Jean-Antoine-Nicolas. *Sketch for a Historical Picture of the Progress of the Human Mind.* New York: Noonday Press, 1955.

Connelly, Matthew. *Fatal Misconception.* Cambridge: Harvard University Press, 2008.

——. "To Inherit the Earth: Imagining World Population: From the Yellow Peril to the Population Bomb." *Journal of Global History* 1, no. 3 (2006): 299–319.

Connolly, William. *The Fragility of Things: Self-Organizing Processes, Neoliberal Fantasies, and Democratic Activism.* Durham, N.C.: Duke University Press, 2013.

Cooper, Melinda. *Life as Surplus: Biotechnology and Capitalism in the Neoliberal Era.* Seattle: University of Washington Press, 2008.

Cope, Kevin Lee, and Rüdiger Ahrens. *Talking Forward, Talking Back: Critical Dialogues with the Enlightenment.* New York: AMS Press, 2002.

Cot, Annie L. "Breed out the Unfit and Breed in the Fit." *American Journal of Economics and Sociology* 64, no. 3 (2005): 793–826.

Cowan, Michael. "'Nichts Ist So Sehr Zeitgemäss Als Willensschwäche': Nietzsche and the Psychology of the Will." *Nietzsche-Studien* (2005): 48–74.

Crabtree, Derek, and A. P. Thirlwall, eds., *Keynes and the Bloomsbury Group.* London: Macmillan, 1980.

Danby, Colin. "Contested States, Transnational Subjects: Toward a Post Keynesianism Without Modernity." In *Postcolonialism Meets Economics,* ed. Eiman O. Zein-Elabdin and S. Charusheela, 253–70. London: Routledge, 2004.

Daston, Lorraine. "Condorcet and the Meaning of Enlightenment." *Proceedings of the British Academy* 151 (2007): 113–34.

——. "Mathematics and the Moral Sciences: The Rise and Fall of the Probability of Judgments, 1785–1840." In *Epistemological and Social Problems of the Sciences in the Early Nineteenth Century,* ed. Hans Niels Jahnke and Michael Otte, 287–309. Dordrecht: Springer Netherlands, 1981.

Daston, Lorraine, and Peter Galison. "The Image of Objectivity." *Representations* 40, Special Issue Autumn (1992): 81–128.

——. *Objectivity.* New York: Zone Books, 2007.

Davidson, Paul. "Keynes and Money." In *A Handbook of Alternative Monetary Theory,* ed. Philip Arestis and Malcom Sawyer, 139–53. Cheltenham, U.K.: Edward Elgar, 2006.

Davies, William. *The Limits of Neoliberalism: Authority, Sovereignty and the Logic of Competition.* London: Sage, 2014.

Davin, Ann. "Imperialism and Motherhood." In *Patriotism: Making and Unmaking of British National Identity,* ed. Raphael Samuel. London: Routledge, 1989.

de Goede, Marieke. *International Political Economy and Poststructural Politics.* New York: Palgrave Macmillan, 2006.

——. "Mastering 'Lady Credit.'" *International Feminist Journal of Politics* 2 (2000): 58–81.

——. "Repoliticizing Financial Risk," *Economy and Society* 33, no. 2 (2004): 197–217.

——. *Virtue, Fortune and Faith: A Genealogy of Finance.* Minneapolis: University of Minnesota Press, 2005.

Dean, Mitchell. *The Constitution of Poverty: Toward a Genealogy of Liberal Governance.* London: Routledge, 1991.

——. *Governmentality: Power and Rule in Modern Society.* London: Sage Publications, 1999.

——. "Liberal Government and Authoritarianism." *Economy and Society* 31, no. 1 (2002): 37–61.

——. "A Political Mythology of World Order: Carl Schmitt's Nomos." *Theory Culture and Society* 23, no. 5 (2006): 1–22.

Deleuze, Gilles. *Foucault*. London: Continuum, 2006.

Derrida, Jacques. *From Restricted to General Economy: A Hegelianism Without Reserve*. In *Writing and Difference*, trans. Alan Bass. London: Routledge, 1978.

——. *Given Time: I. Counterfeit Money*. Chicago: Chicago University Press, 1992.

Desrosières, Alain. *The Politics of Large Numbers: A History of Statistical Reasoning*. Cambridge, Mass.: Harvard University Press, 1998.

Dickinson, Harry Thomas. *British Radicalism and the French Revolution, 1789–1815*. Oxford: Blackwell, 1985.

Dillon, Michael, and Luis Lobo-Guerrero. "The Biopolitical Imaginary of Species-Being." *Theory, Culture and Society* 26, no. 1 (2009): 1–23.

Dimand, Robert W. "Classical Political Economy and Orientalism: Nassau Senior's Eastern Tours." In *Postcolonialism Meets Economics*, ed. Eiman O. Zein-Elabdin and S. Charusheela, 73–90. London: Routledge, 2004.

——. "Economists and the Shadow of 'the Other' before 1914." *American Journal of Economics and Sociology* 64, no. 3 (2005): 827–50.

Dinwiddy, John. "Interpretations of Anti-Jacobinism." In *The French Revolution and British Popular Politics*, ed. Mark Philp, 38–49. Cambridge: Cambridge University Press, 1991.

Dodd, Nigel. *The Sociology of Money: Economics, Reason & Contemporary Society*. New York: Continuum, 1994.

Donzelot, Jacques. "The Promotion of the Social." *Economy and Society* 17, no. 3 (1988): 394–427.

Dostaler, Gilles. *Keynes and His Battles*. Cheltenham, U.K.: Edward Elgar, 2007.

Dow, Sheila, and John Hillard. *Keynes, Knowledge and Uncertainty*. Aldershot, U.K.: Edward Elgar, 1995.

du Gay, Paul. "Which Is the 'Self' in 'Self-Interest'?" *Sociological Review* 53 (2005): 391–411.

du Gay, Paul, and Michael Pryke, eds., *Cultural Economy: Cultural Analysis and Commercial Life*. Thousand Oaks, Calif.: Sage, 2002.

Duden, Barbara. "Population." In *The Development Dictionary: A Guide to Knowledge and Power*, ed. Wolfgang Sachs, 146–57. London: Zed Books, 1999.

Ehrlich, Paul R. *The Population Bomb*. New York: Ballantine Books, 1968.

Eichengreen, Barry. *Golden Fetters: The Gold Standard and the Great Depression 1919–1939*. Oxford: Oxford University Press, 1992.

Escobar, Arturo. *Encountering Development: The Making and Unmaking of the Third World*. Princeton, N.J.: Princeton University Press, 1995.

Esposito, Roberto. *Bios: Biopolitics and Philosophy*. Minneapolis: University of Minnesota Press, 2008.

Esty, Jed. *A Shrinking Island: Modernism and National Culture in England*. Princeton, N.J.: Princeton University Press, 2004.

Ferber, Marianne A., and Julie A. Nelson. *Feminist Economics Today: Beyond Economic Man*. Chicago: University of Chicago Press, 2003.

Ferguson, James. *The Anti-Politics Machine: "Development," Depoliticization, and Bureaucratic Power in Lesotho*. Cambridge: Cambridge University Press, 1990.

Financial Crisis Inquiry Commission. *Financial Crisis Inquiry Report: Final Report of the National Commission on the Causes of the Financial and Economic Crisis in the United States.* Public Affairs, 2011.

Fine, Ben, and Costas Lapavitsas. "Markets and Money in Social Theory: What Role for Economics?" *Economy and Society* 29, no. 3 (2000): 357–82.

Fisher, Irving. *Elementary Principles of Economics.* New York: Macmillan, 1912.

——. *Mathematical Investigations in the Theory of Value and Prices, and Appreciation and Interest.* New York: Cosimo Classics, 2007.

——. *National Vitality, Its Waste and Conservation.* Report of the National Conservation Commission, III, Senate Document 676, 60th Congress, 2nd Sess., Reprinted Version from the Princeton University Library. New York: Arno Press, 1976.

Fitzgibbons, Athol. *Keynes's Vision: A New Political Economy.* Oxford: Clarendon, 1988.

Fleetwood, Steve. "A Marxist Theory of Commodity Money Revisited." In *What Is Money*, ed. John Smithin, 174–93. London: Routledge, 2000.

Folbre, Nancy. *Greed, Lust and Gender: A History of Economic Ideas.* Oxford: Oxford University Press, 2009.

Foot, Michael, and Isaac Kramnick. "Editor's Introduction: The Life, Ideology and Legacy of Thomas Paine." In *Thomas Paine Reader*, ed. Michael Foot and Isaac Kramnick, 7–38. Harmondsworth; New York: Penguin Books, 1987.

Foucault, Michel. *Archaeology of Knowledge.* London: Routledge, 2002.

——. *The Birth of Biopolitics: Lectures at the Collège de France, 1978–79*, ed. Michel Sennellart. Basingstoke, U.K.: Palgrave Macmillan, 2008.

——. *The History of Sexuality: An Introduction.* Vol. 1. New York: Vintage Books, 1990.

——. *Lectures on the Will to Know: Lectures at the College de France 1970–1971 and Oedipal Knowledge*, ed. Daniel Defert. London: Palgrave Macmillan, 2013.

——. "Methodologie pour la connaissance du monde: Comment se debarrasser du Marxisme." In *Foucault: Dits et écrits 1954–1988*, vol. 2, *1954–1988*, ed. Daniel Defert and Francois Ewald, 595–618. Paris: Gallimard, 2008.

——. *Nietzsche, Genealogy, History*, in *Language, Counter-Memory, Practice: Selected Essays and Interviews by Michel Foucault*, ed. Donald F. Bouchard. Ithaca, N.Y.: Cornell University Press, 1977.

——. *The Order of Things: An Archaeology of the Human Sciences.* New York: Vintage Books, 1994.

——. *Security, Territory, Population: Lectures at the Collège De France, 1977–78*, ed. Michel Sennellart. Basingstoke: Palgrave Macmillan, 2007.

——. *Society Must Be Defended: Lectures at the Collège De France, 1975–76*, ed. Mauro Bertani, Alessandro Fontana, François Ewald, and David Macey. New York: Picador, 2003.

Franklin, Benjamin. "Advice to a Young Tradesman, Written by an Old One." In Vol. 3 of *The Papers of Benjamin Franklin*, ed. Leonard Labaree. New Haven, Conn.: Yale University Press, 1961.

Frevert, Ute. "Die Zukunft der Geschlechterordnung. Diagnosen und Erwartungen an der Jahrhundertwende." In *Das Neue Jahrhundert: Europäische Zeitdiagnosen Und*

Zukunftsentwürfe Um 1900, ed. Ute Frevert, 146–84. Göttingen: Vandenhoeck und Ruprecht, 2000.

Frey, Marc. "Experten, Stiftungen und Politik: Zur Genese des Globalen Diskurses über Bevölkerung seit 1945." *Zeithistorische Forschungen* [*Studies in Contemporary History*] 4, no. 1–2 (2007): 137–59.

Froula, Christine. *Virginia Woolf and the Bloomsbury Avant-Garde: War, Civilization, Modernity*. New York: Columbia University Press, 2005.

Galbraith, James K. "Keynes, Einstein and Scientific Revolution." In *Keynes, Money and the Open Economy: Essays*. Vol. 1 of *Essays in Honour of Paul Davidson*, ed. Philip Arestis, 14–21. Cheltenham, U.K.: Edward Elgar Publishing, 1998.

Gallagher, Catherine. *The Body Economic: Life, Death and Sensation in Political Economy and the Victorian Novel*. Princeton, N.J.: Princeton University Press, 2006.

——. "The Body Versus the Social Body in the Works of Thomas Malthus and Henry Mayhew." *Representations* 14 (1986): 83–106.

Gay, Peter. *The Enlightenment: An Interpretation: The Science of Freedom*. New York: W. W. Norton, 1996.

Gernalzick, Nadja. "From Classical Dichotomy to Differential Contract: The Derridean Integration of Monetary Theory." In *Critical Studies: Metaphors of Economy*, ed. Nicole Bracker and Stefan Herbrechter, 55–68. Amsterdam: Rodopi, 2005.

Gibson-Graham, J. K. *The End of Capitalism (as We Knew It): A Feminist Critique of Political Economy*. Cambridge, Mass.: Blackwell, 1996.

Gieryn, Thomas. "Boundary-Work and the Demarcation of Science from Non-Science: Strains and Interests in Professional Ideologies of Scientists." *American Sociological Review* 48, no. 6 (1983): 781–95.

Gilbert, Emily. "Common Cents: Situating Money in Time and Space." *Economy and Society* 34, no. 3 (2005): 356–87.

Gilbert, Geoffrey. *World Population: A Reference Handbook*. Santa Barbara, Calif.: ABC-CLIO, 2001.

Godwin, William. *An Enquiry Concerning Political Justice*. Vol 3 of *Political and Philosophical Writings*, ed. Mark Philp and Austin Gee. London: W. Pickering, 1993.

Goswami, Manu. *Producing India: From Colonial Economy to National Space*. Chicago: University of Chicago Press, 2004.

Goux, Jean-Joseph. *Symbolic Economies: After Marx and Freud*. Ithaca, N.Y.: Cornell University Press, 1990.

Graziani, Augusto. "The Theory of the Monetary Circuit." In *Concepts of Money: Interdisciplinary Perspectives from Economics, Sociology and Political Science*, ed. Geoffrey Ingham. Cheltenham, U.K.: Edward Elgar, 2005.

Gudeman, Stephen. *Economics as Culture: Models and Metaphors of Livelihood*. London: Routledge, 1986.

Gupta, Akhil. "Imagining Nations." In *A Companion to the Anthropology of Politics*, ed. David and Joan Vincent Nugent, 267–81. Malden, Mass.: Blackwell, 2004.

Hacking, Ian. *Historical Ontology*. Cambridge, Mass.: Harvard University Press, 2004.

——. *Representing and Intervening: Introductory Topics in the Philosophy of Natural Science*. 1983. Reprint, Cambridge: Cambridge University Press, 1994.

Halévy, Elie. *The Growth of Philosophic Radicalism*. Boston: Beacon Press, 1966.

———. *L'Evolution de la doctrine utilitaire de 1789 À 1815*. Vol. 2 of *La Formation du radicalisme philosophique*. Paris: Presses Universitaires de France, 1995.

———. *Le Radicalism philosophique*. Vol. 3 of *La Formation du radicalisme philosophique*. Paris: Les Presses Universitaires de France, 1995.

Hall, Catherine, Keith McClelland, and Jane Rendall. *Defining the Victorian Nation: Class, Race, Gender and the British Reform Act of 1867*. Cambridge: Cambridge University Press, 2000.

Halsey, Albert Henry. *A History of Sociology in Britain: Science, Literature, and Society*. Oxford: Oxford University Press, 2004.

Hardt, Michael, and Antonio Negri. *Empire*. Cambridge, Mass.: Harvard University Press, 2000.

Harris, Jose. *Private Lives, Public Spirit: A Social History of Britain 1870–1914*. Oxford: Oxford University Press, 1993.

Hayek, Friedrich A. von. *Denationalisation of Money: An Analysis of the Theory and Practice of Concurrent Currencies*. London: Institute of Economic Affairs, 1976.

———. *The Fatal Conceit: The Errors of Socialism*. Chicago: University of Chicago Press, 1989.

———. *Individualism and Economic Order*. Chicago: University of Chicago Press, 1948.

———. "The Use of Knowledge in Society." *American Economic Review* 35, no. 4 (1945): 519–30.

Heavner, Eric. "Malthus and the Secularization of Political Ideology." *History of Political Thought* 17 (1996): 408–30.

Heilbron, Johan. *The Rise of Social Theory*. Minneapolis: University of Minnesota Press, 1995.

Herbert, Christopher. *Culture and Anomie: Ethnographic Imagination in the Nineteenth Century*. Chicago: University of Chicago Press, 1991.

Hess, Jonathan M. *Reconstructing the Body Politic: Enlightenment, Public Culture and the Invention of Aesthetic Autonomy*. Detroit, Mich.: Wayne State University Press, 1999.

Hirschman, Albert O. *The Passions and the Interests: Political Arguments for Capitalism Before Its Triumph*. Princeton, N.J.: Princeton University Press, 1997.

Ho, Karen. *Liquidated: An Ethnography of Wall Street*. Durham, N.C.: Duke University Press, 2009.

Hobbes, Thomas. *Leviathan*, ed. C. B. Macpherson. Harmondsworth, U.K.: Penguin, 1985.

Hollander, Samuel. *The Economics of Thomas Robert Malthus*. Toronto: University of Toronto Press, 1997.

Honig, Bonnie. *Political Theory and the Displacement of Politics*. Ithaca, N.Y.: Cornell University Press, 1993.

Hont, Ivstan, and Michael Ignatieff, eds. *Wealth and Virtue: The Shaping of Political Economy in the Scottish Enlightenment*. Cambridge: Cambridge University Press, 1983.

Hufton, Olwen H. *Women and the Limits of Citizenship in the French Revolution*. Toronto: University of Toronto Press, 1992.

Hume, David. *David Hume: Writings on Economics*, ed. Eugene Rotwein. London: Thomas Nelson, 1955.

——. *Hume's Moral and Political Philosophy*, ed. Henry D. Aiken. New York: Hafner, 1948.

Hyam, Ronald. "The British Empire in the Edwardian Era." In *The Oxford History of the British Empire*. Vol. 4, *The Twentieth Century*, ed. Judith M. Brown and William Roger Louis, 47–63. Oxford: Oxford University Press, 1999.

Hynes, Samuel. *The Edwardian Turn of Mind*. Princeton, N.J.: Princeton University Press, 1968.

Ingham, Geoffrey. *The Nature of Money*. Cambridge: Polity, 2004.

Ingram, James. "The Politics of Claude Lefort's Political: Between Liberalism and Radical Democracy." *Thesis Eleven* 87, no. 1 (2006): 33–50.

Innes, Joanna. "The Distinctiveness of the English Poor Laws, 1750–1850." In *The Political Economy of British Historical Experience, 1688–1914*, ed. Donald Winch and Patrick O'Brien, 381–407. Oxford: Oxford University Press, 2002.

James, Patricia. *Population Malthus: His Life and Times*. London: Routledge, 1979.

Jones, Gareth Stedman. *An End to Poverty? A Historical Debate*. London: Profile Books, 2004.

Kadish, Alon, and Keith Tribe. "Introduction: The Supply of and Demand for Economics in Late Victorian Britain." In *The Market for Political Economy: The Advent of Economics in British University Culture, 1850–1905*, ed. A. Kadish and K. Tribe, 1–19. London: Routledge, 1993.

Kalpagam, Uma. "Colonial Governmentality and the 'Economy.'" *Economy and Society* 29, no. 3 (2000): 418–38.

Kant, Immanuel. "The Contest of Faculties." In *Political Writings*, ed. Hans Reiss, 176–90. Cambridge: Cambridge University Press, 1991.

——. *Critique of Pure Reason*, ed. Paul Guyer and Allen W. Wood. Cambridge: Cambridge University Press, 1998.

——. "Perpetual Peace: A Philosophical Sketch." In *Political Writings*, ed. Hans Reiss, 93–115. Cambridge: Cambridge University Press, 1991.

Kaul, Nitasha. "Writing Economic Theory an Other Way." In *Postcolonialism Meets Economics*, ed. Eiman O. Zein-Elabdin and S. Charusheela, 183–200. London: Routledge, 2004.

Kern, Stephen. *The Culture of Time and Space 1880–1918*. Cambridge, Mass.: Harvard University Press, 1983.

Keynes, John Maynard. *Activities 1920–1922: Treaty Reversion and Reconstruction*. Vol. 17 of *The Collected Writings of John Maynard Keynes*, ed. Donald Moggridge. London: Royal Economic Society, 1978.

——. *Activities 1922–1929: The Return to Gold and Industrial Policy*. Part I. Vol. 19 of *The Collected Writings of John Maynard Keynes*, ed. Donald Edward Moggridge. London: Royal Economic Society, 1981.

——. *Activities 1931–1939: World Crisis and Policies in Britain and America*. Vol. 21 of *The Collected Writings of John Maynard Keynes*, ed. Donald Moggridge. Cambridge: Royal Economic Society, 1982.

——. *Activities 1939–1945: Internal War Finance*. Vol. 22 of *The Collected Writings of John Maynard Keynes*, ed. Donald Moggridge and Elizabeth Johnson. London: Royal Economic Society, 1978.

——. *Activities 1940–1944. Shaping the Post-War World: The Clearing Union*. Vol. 25 of *The Collected Writings of John Maynard Keynes*, ed. Donald Edward Moggridge. London: Royal Economic Society, 1980.

——. "Agenda and Report of a Meeting of Economists, Civil Servants and Politicians at King's College." In *The Papers of John Maynard Keynes*, File 4 of FI, *International Finance and German Reparations 1919–1923*. Cambridge: King's College, 1919.

——. "Current Monetary Problems: Lecture Given to the Institute of Bankers." In *The Papers of John Maynard Keynes*, File 2 of PS, *Speeches and Lectures Given Outside Cambridge University 1905–1946*. Cambridge: King's College, 1922.

——. *Economic Articles and Correspondence: Academic*. Vol. 11 of *The Collected Writings of John Maynard Keynes*, ed. Donald Edward Moggridge. London: Royal Economic Society, 1983.

——. *Economic Articles and Correspondence: Investment and Editorial*, Vol. 12 of *The Collected Writings of John Maynard Keynes*, ed. Donald Edward Moggridge. London: Royal Economic Society, 1983.

——. "Egoism." In *The Papers of John Maynard Keynes*, File 26 of UA, *University Affairs*. Cambridge: King's College Archive, 1906.

——. "Essay on Time." In *The Papers of John Maynard Keynes*. File 17 of UA, *University Affairs*. Cambridge: King's College, 1903.

——. *Essays in Biography*. Vol. 10 of *The Collected Writings of John Maynard Keynes*, ed. Donald Edward Moggridge. London: Royal Economic Society, 1972.

——. *Essays in Persuasion*. Vol. 9 of *The Collected Writings of John Maynard Keynes*, ed. Donald Edward Moggridge. London: Royal Economic Society, 1972.

——. *The 'General Theory' and After. A Supplement*. Vol. 29 of *The Collected Writings of John Maynard Keynes*, ed. Donald Moggridge. London: Royal Economic Society, 1979.

——. *The General Theory and After. Part I: Preparation*. Vol. 13 of *The Collected Writings of John Maynard Keynes*, ed. Donald Moggridge. London: Royal Economic Society, 1973.

——. *The General Theory and After. Part II: Defence and Development*. Vol. 14 of *The Collected Writings of John Maynard Keynes*, ed. Donald Edward Moggridge. London: Royal Economic Society, 1973.

——. *The General Theory on Employment, Money and Interest*. Vol. 7 of *The Collected Writings of John Maynard Keynes*, ed. Donald Moggridge. London: Royal Economic Society, 1973.

——. *Indian Currency and Finance*. Vol. 1 of *The Collected Writings of John Maynard Keynes*, ed. Donald Moggridge. London: Royal Economic Society, 1971.

——. "Modern Civilization." In *The Papers of John Maynard Keynes*, File 22 of UA, *University Affairs*. Cambridge: King's College Archive, 1905.

——. "Notes on the Prolegomena to a New Socialism." In *The Papers of John Maynard Keynes,* File 24 of L, *Letters*. Cambridge: Kings College Archive, 1924.

——. "The Political Doctrines of Edmund Burke." In *The Papers of John Maynard Keynes*, File 20/3 of UA, *University Affairs*. Cambridge King's College Archive, 1904.

———. "Population: Lecture Delivered to the Political Philosophy and Science Club." In *The Papers of John Maynard Keynes*, File 1 of SS, *Special Subjects*. Cambridge: King's College Archive, 1914.

———. *Social, Political and Literary Writings*. Vol. 28 of *The Collected Writings of John Maynard Keynes*, ed. Donald Moggridge. London: Royal Economic Society, 1982.

———. "The State and Finance: Lecture Given to Society of Civil Servants on 10 December." In *The Papers of John Maynard Keynes*, File 2 of PS, *Speeches and Lectures Given Outside Cambridge University 1905–1946*. Cambridge: King's College, 1920.

———. "A Survey of the Present Position of Socialism: Speech Given to the Society for Socialist Inquiry and Propaganda." In *The Papers of John Maynard Keynes*, File 5 of PS, *Speeches and Lectures Given Outside Cambridge University 1905–1946*. Cambridge: King's College, 1931.

———. "Toast 'Malthus in Piam Memoriam' Given at 50th Anniversary Dinner of the Malthusian League." In *The Papers of John Maynard Keynes*, File 3 of PS, *Speeches and Lectures Given Outside Cambridge*. Cambridge: King's College Archive, 1927.

———. *A Tract on Monetary Reform*. Vol. 4 of *The Collected Writings of John Maynard Keynes*, ed. Donald Moggridge. London: Royal Economic Society, 1971.

———. *A Treatise on Money: The Applied Theory of Money*. Vol. 6 of *The Collected Writings of John Maynard Keynes*, ed. Donald Moggridge. London: Royal Economic Society, 1971.

———. *A Treatise on Money: The Pure Theory of Money*. Vol. 5 of *The Collected Writings of John Maynard Keynes*, ed. Donald Moggridge. London: Royal Economic Society, 1971.

———. "Typescript for Presentation of Galton Gold Medal by Eugenics Society." In *The Papers of John Maynard Keynes*, File 7 of PS, *Speeches and Lectures given outside Cambridge*. Cambridge: King's College Archive, 1946.

King, John Edward. *A History of Post-Keynesian Economics Since 1936*. Cheltenham, U.K.: Edward Elgar, 2002.

Kirchgässner, Gebhard. *Homo oeconomicus: The Economic Model of Behaviour and Its Applications in Economics and Other Social Sciences*. New York: Springer, 2008.

Kirshner, Jonathan. "Keynes, Capital Mobility and the Crisis of Embedded Liberalism." *Review of International Political Economy* 6, no. 3 (1999): 313–37.

———. "Money Is Politics." *Review of International Political Economy* 10, no. 4 (2003): 645–60.

———. "The Political Economy of Low Inflation." *Journal of Economic Survey* 15, no. 1 (2001): 41–70.

Kramnick, Isaac. *The Rage of Edmund Burke: Portrait of an Ambivalent Conservative*. New York: Basic Books, 1977.

Krippner, Greta. *Capitalizing on Crisis: The Political Origins of the Rise of Finance*. Cambridge, Mass.: Harvard University Press, 2011.

Krugman, Paul and Robin Wells. *Macroeconomics*. New York: Worth, 2009.

Landes, David. *The Unbound Prometheus: Technological Change and Industrial Development in Western Europe from 1750 to the Present*. Cambridge: Cambridge University Press, 1969.

Langley, Paul. "Uncertain Subjects of Anglo-American Financialization." *Cultural Critique* 65, no. 1 (2007): 67–91.

———. *Liquidity Lost: The Governance of the Global Financial Crisis*. Oxford: Oxford University Press, 2015.

Latour, Bruno. "Postmodern? No, Simply Amodern! Steps Towards an Anthropology of Science." *Studies in History and Philosophy of Science Part A* 21, no. 1 (1990): 145–71.

——. *Reassembling the Social: An Introduction to Actor-Network Theory.* Oxford: Oxford University Press, 2005.

——. *We Have Never Been Modern.* Cambridge, Mass.: Harvard University Press, 1993.

Lawrence, Christopher. "The Nervous System and Society in the Scottish Enlightenment." In *Natural Order: Historical Studies of Scientific Culture,* ed. Barry Barnes and Steven Shapin. Beverly Hills, Calif.: Sage Publications, 1979.

Lee, Roger, Andrew Leyshon, and Adrian Smith. "Rethinking Economies/Economic Geographies." *Geoforum* 39, no. 3 (2008): 1111–15.

LeMahieu, D. L. "Malthus and the Theology of Scarcity." *Journal of the History of Ideas* 40, no. 3 (1979): 467–74.

Lemke, Thomas. *Biopolitics: An Advanced Introduction.* New York: New York University Press, 2011.

Levine, Philippa. "States of Undress: Nakedness and the Colonial Imagination." *Victorian Studies* 50, no. 2 (2008): 189–219.

Levy, Davis M., and Sandra Peart. "The Negro Science of Exchange: Classical Economics and Its Chicago Revival." In *Race, Liberalism, and Economics,* ed. David Colander, Robert E. Prasch and Falguni A. Sheth. 56–84. Ann Arbor: University of Michigan Press, 2004.

Leyshon, Andrew, and Nigel Thrift. *Moneyspace: Geographies of Monetary Transformation.* London: Routledge, 1997.

Lichtblau, Klaus. *Kulturkrise und Soziologe um die Jahrhundertwende. Zur Genealogie der Kultursoziologie in Deutschland.* Frankfurt a.M.: Suhrkamp, 1996.

Locke, John. *Two Treatises of Government,* ed. Peter Laslett. Cambridge: Cambridge University Press, 1988.

Lowry, Todd. "The Archaeology of the Circulation Concept in Economic Theory." *Journal of the History of Ideas* 35, no. 3 (1974): 429–44.

Löwy, Llana "The Strength of Loose Concepts—Boundary Concepts, Federative Experimental Strategies and Disciplinary Growth: The Case of Immunology." *History of Science* 30 (1992): 371–96.

Luhmann, Niklas. *Die Wirtschaft der Gesellschaft.* Frankfurt a.M.: Suhrkamp, 1994.

MacKenzie, Donald A., Fabian Muniesa, and Lucia Siu. *Do Economists Make Markets? On the Performativity of Economics.* Princeton, N.J.: Princeton University Press, 2007.

Macpherson, C. B. *The Political Theory of Possessive Individualism: Hobbes to Locke.* Oxford: Clarendon Press, 1962.

Malthus, Thomas Robert *An Essay on the Principle of Population: The First Edition (1798) with Introduction and Bibliography.* Vol. 1 of *The Works of Thomas Robert Malthus,* ed. Edward Anthony Wrigley and David Souden. London: William Pickering, 1986.

——. *An Essay on the Principle of Population. Sixth Edition (1826) with Variant Readings from the Second Edition (1803).* Vol. 2 and 3 of *The Works of Thomas Robert Malthus,* ed. Edward Anthony Wrigley and David Souden. London: William Pickering, 1986.

———. *Principles of Political Economy: Second Edition (1836) with Variant Readings from the First Edition (1820).* Vol. 5 and 6 of *The Works of Thomas Robert Malthus,* ed. Edward Anthony Wrigley and David Souden. London: William Pickering, 1986.

Marchart, Oliver. *Post-Foundational Political Thought: Political Difference in Nancy, Lefort, Badiou and Laclau.* Edinburgh: Edinburgh University Press, 2007.

Markwell, Don. *John Maynard Keynes and International Relations: Economic Paths to War and Peace.* Oxford: Oxford University Press, 2006.

Marouby, Christian. "Adam Smith and the Anthropology of the Enlightenment: The 'Ethnographic' Sources of Economic Progress." In *The Anthropology of the Enlightenment,* ed. Larry Wolff and Marco Cipolloni, 85–102. Stanford, Calif.: University of Stanford Press, 2007.

Marx, Karl. *Capital: A Critique of Political Economy.* London: Penguin Books, 1990.

———. *Grundrisse.* Harmondsworth, U.K.: Penguin, 1973.

Marzola, Alessandra. "Rhetoric and Imagination in the Economic and Political Writings of J. M. Keynes." In *John Maynard Keynes. Language and Method,* ed. Alessandra Marzola and Francesco Silva, 192–223. Aldershot, U.K.: Edward Elgar, 1994.

Massumi, Brian. "The Autonomy of Affect." *Cultural Critique,* no. 31 (1995): 83–109.

Maudsley, Henry. *Body and Will.* London: Kegan Paul, 1883.

Mauss, Marcel. *The Gift: Form and Reason for Exchange in Archaic Societies.* London: Routledge, 2001.

McCloskey, Deirdre N. *The Vices of Economists, the Virtues of the Bourgeoisie.* Amsterdam: Amsterdam University Press, 1996.

McClure, Kirstie. *Judging Rights: Lockean Politics and the Limits of Consent.* Ithaca, N.Y.: Cornell University Press, 1996.

McNally, David. "Political Economy to the Fore: Burke, Malthus and the Whig Response to Popular Radicalism in the Age of the French Revolution." *History of Political Thought* 21, no. 3 (2000): 427–47.

Meadows, Donella H. *The Limits to Growth: A Report for the Club of Rome's Project on the Predicament of Mankind.* New York: Universe Books, 1972.

Menger, Carl. *Principles of Economics.* New York: New York University Press, 1981.

Metha, Uday Singh. *Liberalism and Empire: A Study in Nineteenth-Century British Liberal Thought.* Chicago: Chicago University Press, 1999.

Meuret, Denis. "A Political Genealogy of Political Economy." *Economy and Society* 17, no. 2 (1988): 225–50.

Michaels, Walter Benn. "The Gold Standard and the Logic of Naturalism." *Representations* 9, Special Issue: *American Culture Between the Civil War and World War I* (1985): 105–32.

Milgate, Murray, and Shannon Stimson. *After Adam Smith: A Century of Transformation in Politics and Political Economy.* Princeton, N.J.: Princeton University Press, 2009.

Mill, John Stuart. *Principles of Political Economy with Some of their Applications to Social Philosophy.* Vol. 3 of *The Collected Works of John Stuart Mill,* ed. John M Robson. Toronto: University of Toronto Press, 1965.

Miller, Peter. "Accounting for Progress—National Accounting and Planning in France: A Review Essay." *Accounting, Organizations and Society* 11, no. 1 (1986): 83–104.

Miller, Peter, and Nikolas Rose. "Governing Economic Life." *Economy and Society* 19, no. 1 (1990): 1–31.

Mini, Piero. *Keynes, Bloomsbury and the General Theory.* New York: St. Martin's Press, 1991.

Minowitz, Peter. *Profits, Priests, and Princes: Adam Smith's Emancipation of Economics from Politics and Religion.* Stanford, Calif.: Stanford University Press, 1993.

Mirowski, Philip. *Machine Dreams: Economics Becomes a Cyborg Science.* Cambridge: Cambridge University Press, 2002.

——. *More Heat Than Light: Economics as a Social Physics, Physics as Nature's Economics.* Cambridge: Cambridge University Press, 1989.

——, ed. *Natural Images in Economic Thought: "Markets Read in Tooth & Claw."* Cambridge: Cambridge University Press, 1994.

——. *Never Let a Serious Crisis Go to Waste: How Neoliberalism Survived the Financial Meltdown.* London: Verso, 2013.

Mirowski, Philip, and Edward Nik-Khah. "Command Performance: Exploring What STS Thinks It Takes to Build a Market." In *Living in a Material World. Economic Sociology Meets Science and Technology Studies,* ed. Trevor Pinch and Richard Swedberg, 89–130. Cambridge, Mass.: MIT Press, 2008.

Mitchell, Timothy. *Carbon Democracy: Political Power in the Age of Oil.* London: Verso Books, 2011.

——. "Fixing the Economy." *Cultural Studies* 12, no. 1 (1998): 82–101.

——. *The Rule of Experts: Egypt, Techno-Politics and Modernity.* Berkeley: University of California Press, 2002.

Miyazaki, Hirokazu. "Economy of Dreams: Hope in Global Capitalism and Its Critiques." *Cultural Anthropology: Journal of the Society for Cultural Anthropology* 21, no. 2 (2006): 147–72.

Moggridge, Donald. *Maynard Keynes: An Economist's Biography.* London: Routledge, 1992.

Mondzain, Marie-José. *Image, Icon, Economy: The Byzantine Origins of the Contemporary Imaginary.* Stanford, Calif.: Stanford University Press, 2005.

Morgan, Mary S. "Economic Man as Model Man: Ideal Types, Idealization and Caricatures." *Journal of the History of Economic Thought* 28, no. 1 (2006): 1–27.

Morgan, Mary S., and Marcel Boumans. "Secrets Hidden by Two-Dimensionality: The Economy as a Hydraulic Machine." In *Models: The Third Dimension of Science,* ed. Soyara de Chadarevian and Nick Hopwood, 369–401. Stanford, Calif.: Stanford University Press, 2004.

Mouffe, Chantal. *On the Political.* London: Routledge, 2005.

Myrdal, Gunnar. *The Political Element in the Development of Economic Theory.* Cambridge, Mass.: Harvard University Press, 1954.

Nietzsche, Friedrich. *Jenseits Von Gut Und Böse: Zur Genealogie der Moral.* Vol. 5 of *Friedrich Nietzsche: Sämtliche Werke,* ed. Giorgio Colli and Mazzino Montinari. München: Deutscher Taschenbuch Verlag dtv, 1999.

——. *Nachgelassene Fragment 1887–1889.* Vol. 13 of *Friedrich Nietzsche. Sämtliche Werke,* ed. Giorgio Colli and Mazzino Montinari. München: Deutscher Taschenbuchverlag dtv, 1999.

——. *On the Genealogy of Morality*, ed. Keith Ansell-Pearson. Cambridge: Cambridge University Press, 1994.

North, Michael. *Reading 1922: A Return to the Scene of the Modern*. Oxford: Oxford University Press, 1999.

Nowotny, Helga. *Time: The Modern and Postmodern Experience*. Cambridge: Polity Press, 1994.

O'Donnell, R. M. *Keynes: Philosophy, Economics and Politics: The Philosophical Foundations of Keynes's Thought and Their Influence on His Economics and Politics*. New York: St. Martin's Press, 1989.

Okin, Susan Moller. "Gender, the Public, and the Private." In *Political Theory Today*, ed. David Held, 67–90. Oxford: Blackwell Polity Press, 1991.

Opitz, Sven. "Government Unlimited: The Security Dispositif of Illiberal Governmentality." In *Governmentality: Current Issues and Future Challenges*, ed. Ulrich Bröckling, Susanne Krasmann, and Thomas Lemke, 93–114. New York: Routledge, 2011.

Owen, Nicholas. "Critics of Empire in Britain." In *The Oxford History of the British Empire. The Twentieth Century*, ed. Judith M. Brown and William Roger Louis, 188–211. Oxford: Oxford University Press, 1999.

Packham, Catherine. "The Physiology of Political Economy: Vitalism and Adam Smith's Wealth of Nations." *Journal of the History of Ideas* 63, no. 3 (2002): 465–81.

Pagden, Anthony. "Human Rights, Natural Rights, and Europe's Imperial Legacy." *Political Theory* 31 (2003): 171–99.

Paine, Thomas. *Rights of Man, Common Sense, and Other Writings*, ed. Mark Philp. Oxford: Oxford University Press, 1995.

Parekh, Bhikhu. "Liberalism and Colonialism." In *The Decolonization of Imagination: Culture, Knowledge and Power*, ed. Jan Nederveen Peiterse and Bhikhu Parekh, 81–98. London: Zed Books, 1995.

Peart, Sandra. *The Economics of W. S. Jevons*. London: Routledge, 1996.

Peppis, Paul. *Literature, Politics, and the English Avant-Garde: Nation and Empire, 1901–1918*. Cambridge: Cambridge University Press, 2000.

Philp, Mark, eds., *The French Revolution and British Popular Politics*. Cambridge: Cambridge University Press, 1991.

——. *Reforming Ideas in Britain: Politics and Language in the Shadow of the French Revolution, 1789–1815*. Cambridge: Cambridge University Press, 2014.

Pick, Daniel. *Faces of Degeneration: A European Disorder, 1814–1918*. Cambridge: Cambridge University Press, 1989.

Pitkin, Hanna. *The Attack of the Blob: Hannah Arendt's Concept of the Social*. Chicago: University of Chicago Press, 1998.

Pitts, Jennifer. *A Turn to Empire: The Rise of Imperial Liberalism in Britain and France*. Princeton, N.J.: Princeton University Press, 2005.

Pocock, J. G. A. "Cambridge Paradigms and Scotch Philosophers: A Study of the Relations between the Civic Humanist and the Civil Jurisprudential Interpretation of Eighteenth-Century Social Thought." In *Wealth and Virtue: The Shaping of Political Economy in the Scottish Enlightenment*, ed. Ivstan Hont and Michael Ignatieff, 235–52. Cambridge: Cambridge University Press, 1983.

Polanyi, Karl. *The Great Transformation: The Political and Economic Origins of Our Time.* Boston: Beacon, 1957.

——. *Trade and Market in the Early Empires: Economies in History and Theory.* Glencoe, Ill.: Free Press, 1957.

Poovey, Mary. *A History of the Modern Fact: Problems of Knowledge in the Sciences of Wealth and Society.* Chicago: Chicago University Press, 1998.

Porter, Theodore M. "Economics and the History of Measurement." *History of Political Economy* 33, no. 1 (2001): 4–22.

Potter, Rachel. *Modernism and Democracy: Literary Culture 1900–1930.* Oxford: Oxford University Press, 2006.

Preda, Alex. *Framing Finance: The Boundaries of Markets and Modern Capitalism.* Chicago: University of Chicago Press, 2009.

Procacci, Giovanna. "Social Economy and Government of Poverty." In *The Foucault Effect: Studies in Governmentality,* ed. Graham Burchell, Colin Gordon and Peter Miller, 151–68. Chicago: University of Chicago Press, 1991.

Pryke, Michael, and Paul du Gay. "Take an Issue: Cultural Economy and Finance." *Economy and Society* 36, no. 3 (2007): 339–54.

Ramsden, Edmund. "Carving Up Population Science: Eugenics, Demography and the Controversy Over the 'Biological Law' of Population Growth." *Social Studies of Science* 32, no. 5–6 (2002): 857–99.

Rancière, Jacques. "Democracy, Republic, Representation." *Constellations* 13, no. 3 (2006): 297–307.

——. *Disagreement: Politics and Philosophy.* Minneapolis: University of Minnesota Press, 1998.

——. *Dissensus: On Politics and Aesthetics.* London: Continuum, 2010.

——. *On the Shores of Politics.* London: Verso, 1995.

——. *The Philosopher and His Poor.* Durham, N.C.: Duke University Press, 2003.

——. *The Politics of Aesthetics: The Distribution of the Sensible.* London: Continuum.

——. "Ten Thesis on Politics." *Theory & Event* 5 (2001): 1–17.

Rao, Mohan. *From Population Control to Reproductive Health: Malthusian Arithmetic.* London: Sage, 2004.

Redman, Deborah A. *The Rise of Political Economy as a Science: Methodology and the Classical Economists.* Cambridge, Mass.: MIT Press, 1997.

Robbins, Lionel. *The Nature and Significance of Economic Science.* London: Macmillan, 1932.

Roberts, M. J. D. "The Concept of Luxury in British Political Economy: Adam Smith to Alfred Marshall." *History of the Human Sciences.* 11, no. 1 (1998): 23–47.

Robertson, Ritchie. "Primitivsm and Psychology: Niezsche, Freud, Thomas Mann." In *Modernism and the European Unconscious,* ed. Peter Collier and Judy Davies. Cambridge, Mass.: Polity Press, 1990.

Robin, Corey. *Fear: The History of a Political Idea.* Oxford: Oxford University Press, 2004.

Robinson, Joan. "An Open Letter from a Keynesian to a Marxist." In Vol. 4 of the *Collected Economic Papers.* Oxford: Basil Blackwell, 1973.

——. "What Has Become of the Keynesian Revolution?" In *Essays on John Maynard Keynes*, ed. Milo Keynes, 123–31. Cambridge: Cambridge University Press, 1975.

Roitman, Janet. *Anti-Crisis*. Durham, N.C.: Duke University Press, 2014.

Rosa, Hartmut. *Social Acceleration: A New Theory of Modernity*. New York: Columbia University Press, 2015.

Rose, Nikolas. "Government, Authority and Expertise in Advanced Liberalism." *Economy and Society* 22, no. 3 (1993): 283–99.

——. *Politics of Life Itself: Biomedicine, Power, and Subjectivity in the Twenty-First Century*. Princeton, N.J.: Princeton University Press, 2007.

Rosen, Frederick. "The Principle of Population as Political Theory: Godwin's of Population and the Malthusian Controversy." *Journal of the History of Ideas* 31, no. 1 (1970): 33–48.

Rothschild, Emma. *Economic Sentiments: Adam Smith, Condorcet, and the Enlightenment*. Cambridge, Mass.: Harvard University Press, 2001.

——. "Political Economy." In *The Cambridge History of Nineteenth-Century Political Thought*, ed. Gareth Stedman Jones and Gregory Claeys, 748–79. Cambridge: Cambridge University Press, 2011.

Royle, Edward, and James Walvin. *English Radicals and Reformers, 1760–1848*. Lexington: University Press of Kentucky, 1982.

Ruccio, David, and Jack Amariglio. "From Unity to Dispersion: The Body in Neoclassical Economics." In *Postmodernism, Economics and Knowledge*, ed. Stephen Cullenberg, Jack Amariglio, and David F. Ruccio, 143–65. London: Routledge, 2001.

Rudé, George F. E. *The Crowd in the French Revolution*. Oxford: Clarendon Press, 1959.

Sahlins, Marshall David. *Stone Age Economics*. Chicago: Aldine-Atherton, 1972.

Samuelson, Paul. *Economics: An Introductory Analysis*. New York: McGraw-Hill, 1967.

Sassen, Saskia. *Territory, Authority, Rights: From Medieval to Global Assemblages*. Princeton, N.J.: Princeton University Press., 2006.

Schabas, Margaret. "British Economic Theory from Locke to Marshall." In *The Cambridge History of Science*, ed. Theodore Porter, 171–82. Cambridge: Cambridge University Press, 2003.

——. *The Natural Origins of Economics*. Chicago: University of Chicago Press, 2005.

Schabas, Margaret, and Neil De Marchi. *Oeconomies in the Age of Newton*. Durham, N.C.: Duke University Press, 2003.

Schmitt, Carl. *The Concept of the Political*. Chicago: Chicago University Press, 1996.

——. *Der Nomos Der Erde im Jus Publicum Europaeum*. Berlin: Duncker & Humblot, 1997.

Schumpeter, Joseph. *A History of Economic Analysis*. London: Routledge, 1987.

——. *The Theory of Economic Development*. Cambridge, Mass.: Harvard University Press, 1934.

Sedgwick, Peter. "Violence, Economy and Temporality. Plotting the Political Terrain of on the Genealogy of Morality." *Nietzsche-Studien* (2005): 163–85.

Shackle, George L. S. *Keynesian Kaleidics: The Evolution of a General Political Economy*. Edinburgh: Edinburgh University Press, 1974.

Shaffer, Brian W. *The Blinding Torch: Modern British Fiction and the Discourse of Civilization*. Amherst: University of Massachusetts Press, 1993.

Shannon, Richard. *The Crisis of Imperialism, 1865–1915*. London: Hart-Davis, MacGibbon, 1974.

Shapiro, Michael. "Adam Smith: Desire, History, and Value." In *International Political Economy and Poststructural Politics*, ed. Marieke de Goede. Basingstoke, U.K.: Palgrave Macmillan, 2006.

Shaw, George Bernard. *Man and Superman: A Comedy and a Philosophy*. Harmondsworth, U.K.: Penguin, 1903.

Shell, Marc. "The Issue of Representation." In *The New Economic Criticism: Studies at the Intersection of Literature and Economics*, ed. Martha Woodmansee and Mark Osteen, 53–74. London: Routledge, 1999.

Shone, Richard. "A General Account of the Bloomsbury Group." In *Keynes and the Bloomsbury Group*, ed. Derek Crabtree and A. P. Thirlwall. London: Macmillan, 1980.

Simmel, Georg. *The Philosophy of Money*, ed. David Frisby. London: Routledge, 2004.

Skidelsky, Robert. *John Maynard Keynes, 1883–1946: Economist, Philosopher, Statesman*. London: Macmillan, 2003.

——. *Hopes Betrayed 1883–1920*. Vol. 1 of *John Maynard Keynes: A Biography*. London: Macmillan, 1983.

——. *The Economist as Saviour, 1920–1937*. Vol. 2 of *John Maynard Keynes: A Biography*. London: Macmillan, 1992.

Smith, Adam. *An Inquiry into the Nature and Causes of the Wealth of Nations*, ed. Kathryn Sutherland. Oxford: Oxford University Press, 2008.

——. *Lectures on Jurisprudence*. Vol. 5 of *The Glasgow Edition of the Works and Correspondence of Adam Smith*, ed. Ronald Lindley Meek, David Daiches Raphael, and Peter Stein. Oxford: Clarendon Press, 1978.

——. *The Theory of Moral Sentiment*. Vol. 1 of *The Glasgow Edition of the Works and Correspondence of Adam Smith*, ed. Alec Lawrence Macfie and David Daiches Raphael. Indianapolis: Liberty Classics, 1982.

Smith, Anna Marie. *Welfare Reform and Sexual Regulation*. New York: Cambridge University Press, 2007.

Smith, Dennis. "Englishness and the Liberal Inheritance After 1886." In *Englishness: Politics and Culture 1880–1920*, ed. Robert Colls and Philip Dodd, 254–82. London: Croom Helm, 1986.

Smith, Olivia. *The Politics of Language 1791–1819*. Oxford: Clarendon Press, 1984.

Snowdon, Brian, Howard Vande, and Peter Wynarczyk. *A Modern Guide of Macroeconomics*. Cheltenham, U.K.: Edward Elgar Publishing, 1994.

Spivak, Gayatri Chakravorty. "Scattered Speculations on the Question of Value." *Diacritics*, Winter 1985, 73–93.

Spurr, David. *The Rhetoric of Empire: Colonial Discourse in Journalism, Travel Writing and Imperial Administration*. Durham, N.C.: Duke University Press, 1994.

Stäheli, Urs. "The Rhythm of the Stock Exchange. A Case Study on the Stock Ticker and Its Effects on Inclusion." *Zeitschrift für Soziologie* 33, no. 3 (2004): 245–62.

——. *Spektakuläre Spekulation: Das Populäre Der Ökonomie*. Frankfurt am Main: Sukrkamp, 2007.

Star, Susan Leigh, and James R. Griesemer. "Institutional Ecology, 'Translations' and Boundary Objects: Amateurs and Professionals in Berkeley's Museum of Vertebrate Zoology, 1907–39." *Social Studies of Science* 19, no. 3 (1989): 387–420.

Stemmler, Theo. *Oekonomie. Sprachliche und Literarische Aspekte eines 2000 Jahre Alten Begriffs*. Tübingen: Gunter Narr Verlag, 1985.

Stoler, Ann Laura. "Making Empire Respectable: The Politics of Race and Sexual Morality in 20th-Century Colonial Cultures." *American Ethnologist* 16, no. 4 (1989): 634–60.

——. *Race and the Education of Desire: Foucault's History of Sexuality and the Colonial Order of Things*. Durham, N.C.: Duke University Press, 1995.

Summers, Anne. "Edwardian Militarism." In *Patriotism: The Making and Unmaking of British National Identity*, ed. Raphael Samuel, 126–258. London: Routledge, 1989.

Sunder Rajan, Kaushik. *Biocapital: The Constitution of Postgenomic Life*. Durham, N.C.: Duke University Press, 2006.

Suzuki, Tomo. "The Epistemology of Macroeconomic Reality: The Keynesian Revolution from an Accounting Point of View." *Accounting, Organizations and Society* 28, no. 5 (2003): 471–517.

Taylor, Charles. *Modern Social Imaginaries*. Durham, N.C.: Duke University Press, 2004.

Tellmann, Ute. "Catastrophic Populations and the Fear of the Future: Malthus and the Genealogy of Liberal Economy." Theory, Culture & Society 30, no. 2 (2013): 135–55.

——. "The Economic Beyond Governmentality. The Limits of Conduct." In *Governmentality. Current Issues and Future Challenges*, ed. Ulrich Bröckling, Susanne Krasmann and Thomas Lemke, 285–303. New York: Routledge, 2011.

——. "Foucault and the Invisible Economy." *Foucault Studies*, no. 6 (2009): 5–24.

Thatcher, David S. *Nietzsche in England 1890–1914*. Toronto: Toronto University Press, 1970.

Thompson, E. P. *The Making of the English Working Class*. New York: Vintage, 1966.

Timberlake, Richard. "Gold Standard Policy and Limited Government." In *Money and the Nation State: The Financial Revolution. Government and the World Monetary System*, ed. Kevin Dowd and Richard Timberlake. New Brunswick, N.J.: Transaction Publishers, 1998, 167–91.

Togati, Teodore Dario. "Keynes as the Einstein of Economic Theory." *History of Political Economy* 33, no. 1 (2001): 117–38.

Tomlinson, Jim. "Managing the Economy, Managing the People: Britain c. 1931–70." *Economic History Review* 58, no. 3 (2005): 555–85.

——. "Why Was There Never a 'Keynesian Revolution' in Economic Policy?" *Economy and Society* 10, no. 1 (1981): 72–87.

Toye, John. *Keynes on Population*. Oxford: Oxford University Press, 2000.

Tribe, Keith. *Land, Labour and Economic Discourse*. London: Routledge and Kegan Paul, 1978.

Tuite, Clara. "Frankenstein's Monster and Malthus' 'Jaundiced Eye': Population, Body Politics, and the Monstrous Sublime." *Eighteenth-Century Life* 22, no. 1 (1998): 141–55.

Vaihinger, Hans. *The Philosophy of as If: A System of the Theoretical, Practical and Religious Fictions of Mankind.* London: Kegan Paul, 1924.

Verdon, Michel. *Keynes and the 'Classics': A Study in Language, Epistemology and Mistaken Identities.* London: Routledge, 1996.

Vogl, Joseph. *Kalkül und Leidenschaft: Poetik des ökonomischen Menschen.* München: Sequenzia, 2002.

Waldby, Cathy, and Robert Mitchell. *Tissue Economies: Blood, Organs, and Cell Lines in Late Capitalism.* Durham, N.C.: Duke University Press, 2006

Walker, R. B. J. "Conclusion: Cultural, Political, Economy." In *Cultural Political Economy,* ed. Jacqueline Best and Matthew Patterson, 225–33. New York: Routledge, 2010.

Walters, William. "Anti-Political Economy: Cartographies of 'Illegal Immigration' and the Displacement of the Economy." In *Cultural Economy,* ed. Jacqueline Best and Matthew Patterson, 113–38. New York: Routledge, 2010.

——. "Decentring the Economy." *Economy and Society* 28, no. 2 (1999): 312–23.

Walzer, Arthur E. "Logic and Rhetoric in Malthus's 'Essay on the Principle of Population, 1798.'" *Quarterly Journal of Speech* 73, no. 1 (1987): 1–17.

Ward, Janet. "Nietzsche's Transvaluation of Jewish Parasitism." *Journal of Nietzsche Studien* 24 (2002): 54–83.

Warren, Mark. *Nietzsche and Political Thought.* Cambridge, Mass.: MIT Press, 1988.

Waterman, Anthony Michael. *Revolution, Economics and Religion: Christian Political Economy, 1789–1833.* Cambridge: Cambridge University Press, 1991.

Weber, Max. *Gesammelte Aufsätze zur Soziologie und Sozialpolitik.* Tübingen: Mohr, 1988.

——. *The Protestant Ethic and the Spirit of Capitalism.* 1930. Reprint, London: Routledge, 2001.

Welch, Cheryl B. "Social Science from the French Revolution to Positivism." In *The Cambridge History of Nineteenth-Century Political Thought,* ed. Gareth Stedman Jones and Gregory Claeys, 171–99. Cambridge: Cambridge University Press, 2011.

Wells, Roger A. E. *Insurrection: The British Experience, 1795–1803.* Gloucester: A. Sutton, 1983.

Wicke, Jennifer. "Mrs. Dalloway Goes to Market: Woolf, Keynes, and Modern Markets." *NOVEL: A Forum for Fiction* 28, no. 1 (1994): 5–23.

Widdig, Bernd. *Culture and Inflation in Weimar Germany.* Berkeley: University of California Press, 2001.

Williams, David. *Condorcet and Modernity.* Cambridge: Cambridge University Press, 2004.

Williams, Elizabeth A. *The Physical and the Moral: Anthropology, Physiology, and Philosophical Medicine in France, 1750–1850.* Cambridge: Cambridge University Press, 1994.

Williams, Raymond. *Keywords: A Vocabulary of Culture and Society.* London: Fontana, 1983.

——. "The Significance of 'Bloomsbury' as a Social and Cultural Group." In *Keynes and the Bloomsbury Group,* ed. Derek Crabtree and A. P. Thirlwall, 40–67. London: Macmillan, 1980.

Winch, Donald. *Malthus.* Oxford: Oxford University Press, 1987.

——. "Malthus Versus Condorcet Revisited." *European Journal of the History of Economic Thought* 3, no. 1 (1996): 44–60.

——. *Riches and Poverty: An Intellectual History of Political Economy in Britain, 1750–1834.* Cambridge: Cambridge University Press, 1996.

——. "Robert Malthus: Christian Moral Scientist, Arch-Demoralizer or Implicit Secular Utilitarian?," *Utilitas* 5, no. 2 (1993): 239–53.

——. "Science and the Legislator: Adam Smith and After." *Economic Journal* 93, no. 371 (1983): 501–20.

Winslow, E. G. "Keynes and Freud: Psychoanalysis in Keynes' Account of the 'Animal Spirits' of Capitalism." *Social Research* 53, no. 4 (1986): 549–78.

Wolin, Sheldon. *Politics and Vision: Continuity and Innovation in Western Political Thought.* Exp. ed. Princeton, N.J.: Princeton University Press, 2004.

Woodruff, David. *Money Unmade: Barter and the Fate of Russian Capitalism.* Ithaca, N.Y.: Cornell University Press, 1999.

Woolf, Virginia. *Roger Fry: A Biography.* Oxford: Blackwell Publishers, 1995.

Xenos, Nicholas. "Liberalism and the Postulate of Scarcity." *Political Theory* 15, no. 2 (1987): 225–43.

——. *Scarcity and Modernity.* London: Routledge, 1990.

Yonay, Yuval. *The Struggle Over the Soul of Economics: Institutionalist and Neoclassical Economists in America Between the Wars.* Princeton, N.J.: Princeton University Press, 1998.

Young, Robert C. *Colonial Desires: Hybridity in Theory, Culture, and Race.* London: Routledge, 1995.

Zaloom, Caitlin. *Out of the Pits: Traders and Technology from Chicago to London.* Chicago: University of Chicago Press, 2006.

Zein-Elabdin, Eiman O., and S. Charusheela. *Postcolonialism Meets Economics.* London: Routledge, 2004.

Index

cultural critique); and degeneration, 122–23, 252n34 (*see also* degeneration, tropes of); and the fear of savage life, 107 (*see also* "savage life" concept); Freudian analysis of, 120; hierarchies of, 85, 95, 100–101, 106, 239n112, 245n50 (*see also* colonialism; "savage life" concept); immediate vs. delayed gratification and, 101–2, 106, 109–10; meaning of, 120, 121, 124, 251n25; population as political-cultural community on the path of civilization, 177–78, 179–80; and the role of fear or hope, 105–6; universal civilization vs. multiple/national cultures, 120, 251n25

civil society, 210n26

classical economy/economics: genealogy of, 16; Keynes's challenge to, 22–23, 215n63, 216n68 (*see also* Keynes, John Maynard); Smith's political economy vs., 15. *See also* liberal economic thought; liberal economy; *and specific topics and individuals*

classical liberalism: anti-political impulses of, 6; and the gold standard, 161; Keynes's critique of, 12, 20–22 (*see also* Keynes, John Maynard); and monetary interest, 160–61, 267n77; neutrality of money in, 19, 145, 212nn39–40, 260–61n7. *See also specific topics and individuals*

Clemenceau, Georges, 139

coinage, 149, 264–65n40

Collini, Stefan, 124, 252n42

Colls, Robert, 115, 278–79n118

colonialism: colonial-racial hierarchies and the history of liberal economics, 67–68, 70–75, 203, 235n43, 236n48; colonial-racial hierarchies and the love of money, 70–72, 101–2, 127–28; cultural critique and, 121; and the emergence of national economy, 170, 271n23; European disgust at native living conditions, 70–71, 234n37; politics of exclusion, 251n30; and the "savage life" concept, 9, 67–68, 69, 70–75, 127–28, 235n43 (*see also* primitivism; "savage life" concept). *See also* British Empire and British imperialism; civilization

common, the, 28, 30

Condorcet, Marquis de: differences between Malthus and, 49, 227n79; on fear, 104, 105; on French revolutionary fervor, 43; Malthus on, 49, 52, 53, 227n90; openness and indeterminacy of liberal socioeconomics in, 49–51, 58; on political subjectivity, 226n79; on scarcity, 78; "sentient being" as starting point for, 47; social mathematics of, 50, 226n70; on the social sciences, 226n66

conformity, 133–34

Connelly, Matthew, 234n37

consumption: balancing, 177–78, 276n77; immediate or savage consumption, 102 (*see also* immediacy); Keynesianism on underconsumption, 290n78 (*see also* Hobson, John A.); vs. saving, 110 (*see also* gratification, immediate vs. delayed; saving)

contingency, notion of, 26, 217n77

contracts, 149

conventions: convention theory, 27–28, 129–30; economy as convention in Keynes, 129–36; judgment and, 136–40

Cook, James, 70, 234n29

Cowan, Michael, 256n74

credit theory of money, 149–50, 265n41. *See also* money: credit and debt

crises. *See* economic crises; liberalism: crises within

cultural critique: and colonialism and imperial policy, 121, 251n30, 251–52n32; defining, 120; the economy as convention, 130–36; indeterminate frontiers of politics and economy, 136–40; in Keynes's writings, 119, 125–29, 130–33, 134–41 (*see also* Keynes, John Maynard); limits of, 8, 140–41; and the meaning of civilization, 118, 120–21 (*see also* civilization); and the question of economy generally, 8–9, 118, 119; rise of, 120–24. *See also* degeneration, tropes of

cultural economy, 24–26, 119

culture: cultural forms/conventions, in Nietzsche's thought, 129–30; cultural-racial hierarchies and "savage life," culture (*continued*)

67–68, 70–72 (*see also* "savage life" concept); defining as term, 119, 120; double role of concept, 121–22; economy as, 24–25; political-cultural communities on the path of civilization, 177–78, 179–80; as term of debate, 118. *See also* cultural critique; cultural economy

currency crises, 144. *See also* gold standard; money

Dangerfield, George, 117
Daston, Lorraine, 50, 67, 79, 135
Davidson, Paul, 145
Davies, William, 1
Dean, Mitchell, 95, 98, 210n23, 219n91, 230n6, 241n5, 244n29
death, fear of, 103–4. *See also* fear
debt. *See* money: credit and debt; war debt
degeneration, tropes of, 118, 122–24, 125–26, 174, 251–52n32, 252n34
Deleuze, Gilles, 165, 244n30
democracy, 136–38, 258n112. *See also* suffrage
Derrida, Jacques, 156, 182, 260n5
developmentalism, national, 170. *See also* specific countries
Dickinson, Harry Thomas, 45, 224n43
Dillon, Michael, 238–39n98
dissensus, liberal (late 1700s–early 1800s), 43–46, 58, 223n27, 223n33
distribution of the sensible, Rancière's notion of, 218n86, 250n15
division of labor, 72, 236n48
Dodd, Nigel, 212n40
"double constitution," as term, 10, 208–9n13
Douglas, C. H., 176
du Gay, Paul, 217n77

East India College, 42, 72, 222n20
East India Company. *See* British East India Company
ecological system, 15, 66–67
economic (self-)interest, 94–99, 106–7, 108, 147. *See also* economic man; rationality
economic, the (notion of): and the analysis of forms/patterns of economic temporality, 199–200 (*see also* temporality); benefits of studying, 200–202; defined by time, measure, and circularity, 159–60 (*see also* temporality: and money); definition and use of term, 4–5, 143–44, 208n9; disentangling from the notion of economy, 6–7, 34–35, 195–96; dissecting from liberal economy, 81–82; distinction between the ontic and the ontological, 208n8; double movement between internal openness and fixation, 28–29; essential ambiguities, 167–68; (exploring the) malleability of, 4, 9, 282n12; fate of, 164–65; gold standard and, 162–63; malleability fixed/constrained/displaced, 5, 10, 11–12, 196, 202 (*see also* archipolitics; boundaries between economics and politics; Keynesianism; Malthus, Robert Thomas); money as entry point for exploring, 145, 262n15; parallel conceptualization of "the political" and, 5–6; political languages and, 192–94; as quasi-ontological, 5, 196–97; question both opened and closed by Keynes, 203; and the question of temporality in Keynes, 146, 150–51, 197–99 (*see also* temporality); reasons for introducing concept, 28–30; role of temporality in understanding, 197–99 (*see also* futurity; temporality); scarcity viewed from the perspective of, 67, 76–82; strategy for unpacking/examining, 9, 12–13, 26. *See also* economy; genealogy of the economic
Economic Consequences of Peace, The (Keynes), 139, 193–94, 259n123. *See also* Keynes, John Maynard
economic crises: financial crisis of 2008, 1–2, 10, 24, 199; Keynes on currency crises, 144; at the turn of the 19th century, 115–16
economic development, 24–25, 170
economic futurity. *See* futurity
economic man (*homo oeconomicus*): "animal spirits" of, 118, 133; and fear, hope, and the making of economic order, 11–12, 95, 103–7, 110, 246nn65–67; Foucault on, 30; Halévy on, 49; history of, and the politics of affect, 95–99, 110–11, 242nn17–19,

Escobar, Arturo, 271n22

Esposito, Roberto, 175, 275n62

Essay on the Principle of Population
(Malthus): context, 42, 43–46; on
economic man, 98–99; editions, 221n14;
indeterminacy a dominant theme in,
42–43, 52–57; link between population
and scarcity established, 65, 67–68; on
the need for uniform, universal laws,
55–57, 228n104; "savage life" concept in,
70–75 (*see also* "savage life" concept);
success and influence of, 16–17, 41–42,
176, 211n32, 221n14, 222n16, 233n21.
See also Malthus, Robert Thomas

Esty, Jed, 119, 215n59

eugenics, 122–24, 173, 174–75, 270n15, 276n63.
See also population; racism

euthanasia of the rentier, 180, 190, 280n145

exchange rate, 189, 280n145

Fabian Society, 123, 124, 253n43

fear: of death, 103–4; in the entrepreneurial
subject, 188–89; Hobbes on, 103; and the
making of economic man/economic
order, 11–12, 95, 103–7, 110, 246nn65–67;
of want, 104–5. *See also* futurity; "savage
life" concept

Financial Crisis Inquiry Commission, 1

financial crisis of 2008, 1–2, 10, 24, 199

First World War. *See* World War I

Fisher, Irving, 125, 212n40

Folbre, Nancy, 245n44

foresight. *See* futurity

Foucault, Michel: on the advent of
naturalism in economic thought, 14;
bioeconomic necessity omitted, 210n23,
230n6; on biopolitics, 69, 83–86, 87,
209n16, 240n115, 274n61; and the
biopolitics debate, 68–69, 82, 83,
238–39n98; on discourse analysis, 33,
219n98; on economic man, 30, 97;
genealogical analysis defined/described,
32; on the "history of scarcity"
formulated by liberal economics, 74, 177,
230n6; importance of, in writing a
genealogy of the economic, 31–33; on an
impoverished political imagination,
34–35; on Keynesianism, 279n130; on

late-18th-century politicization of life,
40; on liberal governmentality, 31, 83–85,
94, 111; on the "naturality" of the
population, 84; on the pastoral political
rationality, 277n101; on the political
dimension of economics, 30–31; on
population and liberalism, 63–64; on the
problem of the Enlightenment, 53; on
society and the social, 47

France, 39, 225n61; French Revolution, 39,
40, 43–44, 45, 59–60, 90

franchise, the. *See* suffrage

Franklin, Benjamin, 153, 156, 197, 265n50

Freud, Sigmund, 120, 128, 254n64, 255n66

frugality, 100. *See also* saving

Fry, Roger, 21, 124, 141, 214n54

futurity (economic): capital and, 80;
cultural-racial hierarchies and, 125;
drawing on the future, 154–55, 265n55;
economic man and future hopes/fears,
11–12, 95, 109, 110–11, 125 (*see also* fear;
hope); importance of question, for
specifying the economic, 197–98; and
the investment/saving cycle, 280n146;
Keynesian critique of economic man
and, 126–27, 130, 197–98 (*see also*
economic man); meaning of changed by
financial crisis, 199; money as
potentiality, 127, 153–54; as
preoccupation of Nietzsche, 130; "savage
life" lacking sense of, 74–75, 78–79,
237n85 (*see also* "savage life" concept);
scarcity as producer of, 9–10, 79, 177, 197
(*see also* scarcity). *See also* gratification,
immediate vs. delayed; saving

Galbraith, James, 266n69

Galison, Peter, 67, 79, 135

Gallagher, Catherine, 73

genealogy of the economic: concept
explained, 3, 33, 195–96, 219n98;
Foucault's work and, 31–33, 94;
methodology, 32–35; reading Keynes
from the perspective of, 21–24, 145,
197–98, 203 (*see also* Keynes, John
Maynard); reading Malthus from the
perspective of, 18–19, 197, 203 (*see also*
Malthus, Robert Thomas); and

improvement, desire for, 99–102, 104–5
Inayatullah, Naeem, 235n43, 236n48
India, 128, 178, 271n23
individual, the: cultural critique and
  modern subjectivity, 124, 252n42;
  individual judgement, 57–58, 134–35,
  136–37; Keynes on individual investor/
  businessman, 130–31, 133–34; and money
  as medium of exchange, 147; in
  neoclassical economics, 125. *See also*
  economic man; entrepreneurs and the
  entrepreneurial subject
indolence, Malthus on, 101–2
inflation, 144, 154
Ingham, Geoffrey, 153, 262n19, 262–63n21
interest (concern, self-interest), 94–99, 104,
  106–7, 111. *See also* economic man;
  rationality
interest rates: as conventional phenomenon,
  128–29; and the creation of new wealth,
  267n85; and employment, 267n87; and
  the gold standard, 162–63; Keynes on,
  134, 158, 160–61, 267n77; Keynes's interest
  in, 160; monetary policy re the interest
  rate, 189–90, 280n145; as non-monetary
  phenomenon, 267n77; rate sustained by
  unwillingness to wait, 126; Simmel on,
  127; temporality of, 156, 158, 266n68.
  See also money: credit and debt
International Conference on World
  Population (Geneva, 1927), 174
international monetary system, 193–94
international order, Keynes's views on, 172,
  193–94, 272n38
investment, 132, 260n4. *See also* interest
  rates; stock market
Ireland and the Irish, 74–75, 101, 236–37n61
irrationality, 123, 132–33, 250n17. *See also*
  economic man; rationality
island metaphor(s), 77

James, Patricia, 222n20
Jameson, Frederic, 215n59
Jevons, Stanley, 65–66, 232n13
judgment, individual: as concern of cultural
  critique, 141; faults and corruption of,
  136–40, 258n112, 258n120, 259n121;
  Keynes on, 134–35; of leaders, 138–40,

258n120; liberal skepticism regarding,
  57–58, 136–37; poor judgment, 136–38.
  See also masses, the; rationality

Kalpagam, Uma, 271n23
Kant, Immanuel, 42, 43, 57, 79
Kern, Stephen, 159
Keynes, John Maynard: about, 20–21; on
  "animal spirits," 131, 133, 256n78;
  antidemocratic skepticism of, 136–37,
  258n112; anti-Semitism of, 180–81,
  276n63; on art and the state, 179; on
  bankers and the treasury, 138–39,
  259n121; on Burke, 184–86; on choosing/
  applying models, 23, 216n69; on
  choosing a standard of value, 268n90;
  conceptual map of the national economy
  developed, 171, 272n31, 272n34 (*see also*
  macroeconomics); in the context of
  modernism, 21–23, 215nn58–59,
  215nn62–63; cultural critique in Keynes's
  writings, 119, 125–41; on currency crises,
  144; on distribution and consumption,
  178, 276n78; economic man, critique of,
  125–33 (*see also* economic man); on
  economics as science of thinking in
  terms of models, 184; as the Einstein of
  economics, 22, 158–59, 215n63, 266n69;
  on the end of economy, 180; on finance
  as a revolving fund, 191, 280n146; on
  futurity (postponed gratification),
  126–27, 197–98; Gernalzick's discussion
  of, 263n30; on the gold standard, 161–64,
  254n64; historical relevance of, 23–24;
  and the hydraulic conception of national
  economy, 23, 166–68, 183, 203–4,
  269nn4–5 (*see also* national economy); on
  interest rates, 267n75, 267n85, 267n87,
  276n77; on the liberal tradition, 278n118;
  on liquidity, 127, 253n53; on love of
  money, 127–28; on Malthus, 173, 175,
  238n93; on monetary interest, 134, 158,
  160–61, 267n77; on monetary policy,
  188–91, 280n141, 280n146; on money as a
  medium of exchange, 263n21; money in
  Keynes's thought (generally), 10, 11–12,
  23–24 (*see also* money); on morality, 134,
  135–36, 255n68, 257n100; parallels

liberalism: crises within, 20, 33, 116–17, 118, 212–13n46; and the development of economy as a a concept/domain, 8; division between politics and economy in, 5–6; economic necessity invented for, 3 (*see also* economic necessity); embedded liberalism, 166 (*see also* economic policy; macroeconomics; national economy); in Foucault's thought, 30, 63–64, 94; indeterminate meaning of, at the turn of the 18th century, 46–52, 226–27n79, 227n80, 227n82, 227n90 (*see also* Condorcet, Marquis de); Keynesian settlement of, 11–12, 20–21 (*see also* Keynes, John Maynard); liberal dissensus (late 1700s–early 1800s), 43–46, 58, 223n27, 223n33; liberal governmental technologies, 187–88 (*see also* governmentality, liberal: governing [through] money); Malthusian settlement of, 11 (*see also* Malthus, Robert Thomas); neutrality of money, for classical liberalism, 19, 145, 212nn39–40, 260–61n7 (*see also* money: as representation); new/Progressive liberalism, 123, 252n37; studying the hybrid entanglement of politics and economy within, 204–5; at the turn of the 19th century, 115. *See also* classical liberalism; governmentality, liberal; liberal economic thought; liberal economy; neoliberalism; *and specific individuals and schools of thought*

Liberal Party (Great Britain), 121

liberal skepticism, 57–58

life: "calculation of lives," 85–87, 240n115; division between politics and, 87–89; as political question, 39–41. *See also* biopolitics; "savage life" concept

Lippmann, Walter, 123

liquidity, 127–28, 130, 151–52, 176, 198, 253n53. *See also* money

Lloyd George, David, 139

Lobo-Guerrero, Luis, 238–39n98

Locke, John, 57–58, 57–58, 234n28

Lowry, Todd, 266n62

Löwy, Ilana, 273n50

Machiavelli, Niccolò, 97

MacPherson, C. B., 231n10, 246n67

macroeconomics: as blueprint for managing economy, 21; boundaries purified by, 167; economist as expert and statesman, 181–86; hydraulic Keynesianism, 23, 166–68, 183, 203–4, 268n3, 269nn4–5; Keynes's role in the development of, 166–67, 269nn4–5; *nomos* in, 182, 277n97; as part of wider vision for Europe, 172; role of population in, 168; statistical rendering constitutively important in, 168–69. *See also* Keynes, John Maynard; Keynesianism; national economy

Malinowski, Bronislaw, 120

Malthus, Robert Thomas: about, 16; alarmed by increasing political contestation, 43–44, 46, 54–55; on the body as social problem, 70–75 (*see also* "savage life" concept); and the boundary between economy and politics, 11; "calculation of lives" discussed, 86–87; capital in Malthus's thought, 80–82, 238n93; on Condorcet, 49, 52, 53, 227n90; and economic man, 93–94, 98–99, 101–7, 244n30 (*see also* economic man); on education, 57; on fear and the making of economic order, 103–7; fear of indeterminacy (lack of limits/foundations), 52, 53–57; on the French Revolution, 43; on generalizing from observations, 54; impact and influence of, 3, 17, 41–42, 92–93, 211n34, 221n14, 222n16, 222n19, 233n21, 241n5; on the Irish and potatoes, 74–75, 236–37n61; island metaphor used, 77; Keynes on, 173, 175, 238n93; malleability of the economic in Malthus's thought, 12; on the need for uniform, universal laws, 55–57, 228n104; new epistemology of scientific objectivity, 53–55; on the oscillation between scarcity and abundance, 73, 236n52; on Owen, 221n14; on Paine's *Rights of Man*, 52; political views, 54–55, 57, 86; politicization of life feared, 11, 54–55, 58–59; and poor law reforms, 11, 17, 41–42, 86, 92–94, 107–9, 241n5 (*see also* Poor Laws); population linked with scarcity, 65, 67–68, 176–77 (*see also* population; scarcity); reading Arendt alongside, 59; right to live declared nonexistent, 11, 16–17, 90–91, 203; role in this book, and author's approach, 7, 9, 13, 18–19, 34, 42; "savage life" in Malthus's thought, 11, 70–75, 78–79, 86–87, 101–2, 105–6, 176–77, 197 (*see also* "savage life" concept); scarcity in Malthus's thought, 76–82, 176–77, 197 (*see also* scarcity); theological underpinnings, 17–18, 211n35, 248n97; as transitional figure, 17–19; views on education, 228n108; on *vis medicatrix republicae*, 105, 247n74; on women, marriage, and sexual morality, 107–10, 248nn97–98. See also *Essay on the Principle of Population*; population; *Principle of Effect Demand, The*

Mann, Thomas, 144
Marchart, Oliver, 207–8n7
market: all information contained by, 243n24; drawbacks of viewing as machine, 200; economic man and, 95–96; emergence of the self-regulated market, 91; global market, 204; market equilibrium, 20–21, 23, 125, 145–46, 182, 213n53; market order and population, in Hayek's thought, 66

marriage, economic man and, 93–94, 108–10, 248nn97–98. See also women
Marshall, Alfred, 125–26, 174, 278n106
Marx, Karl: on all economy as an economy of time, 197, 281n2; Arendt on, 60–61, 229n30; on capital, 155, 156; on the gold standard, 161, 162; Keynes on, 176; on misers, 154; on money, 267n81

Marxism, 6, 13
masses, the, 123–24, 136–38. See also degeneration, tropes of; poor, the
mass psychology, 123
Maudsley, Henry, 252n34
Mauss, Marcel, 143, 149, 156, 281–82n12
McCloskey, Deirdre, 245n44
McNally, David, 211n32, 211n34
Meadows report, 66
measure, politics as act of giving, 168, 182
Menger, Carl, 147

methodology, 32–35
Meuret, Denis, 219n93
Mill, John Stuart, 147, 162, 212n39, 277n97
Miller, Peter, 187
Millo, Yuval, 208n9
Mini, Piero, 128
Mirowski, Philip, 216n72, 243n23
Mitchell, Timothy, 209n22, 271nn22–23
Mitchell, Wesley, 170–71
modernism, Keynes in the context of, 21–23, 215nn58–59, 215nn62–63
Modigliani, Franco, 213n53
money: as central theme for critique of liberal economy, 144; choosing a standard of value, 268n90; circular movement of, 156, 266n62; contractual origins of, 264n34; credit and debt, 149–50, 152–53, 155–56, 191, 265n41, 265n49; currency crises (1880s–1920s), 144–45; determining role of, in Keynes's thought, 261n13; early 20th-century monetary disorder, 19–20; as entry point for exploring the economic, 145, 262n15; future value of, 154; gold as, 150, 152, 259n121 (*see also* gold standard); as governing tool/medium, 11–12, 187–92, 203–4, 280nn145–46; "honest" money, 148, 162, 263n29; inflation, 144, 154; international monetary system, 193–94; and the invention of the managed economy, 19–24 (*see also* national economy); liquidity, 127–28, 130, 151–52, 176, 198, 253n53; as main lever for Keynesian critique, 4; and materiality, 157–59; as measure of relative value, 151–52, 265n47; as medium of exchange, 147–48, 262–63n21; monetary vs. nonmonetary assets, 151–52; "money of account," 264n34; origins of, 149, 151–52, 264–65n40; paper money debates, 148; as potentiality, 127, 153–54; purchasing power, 152–53; quantity theory of, 212n40; real and monetary economy linked, 157–59; as representation (neutrality of money), 19, 145, 147–49, 152, 162, 212nn39–40, 260–61n7, 261n14, 262n19, 262–63n21, 264–65n40, 265n49 (*see also* gold standard); saving, 110,

Rudé, Georg, 224n43
rules, obedience to, 135. *See also* morality:
  Keynes on
Russell, Bertrand, 21, 214n54
Russia, 116, 186

Sahlin, Marshall, 231–32n10
Said, Edward, 69
Samuelson, Paul, 147
Sassen, Saskia, 269n9
"savage life" concept: civilization and the
  fear of, 107; cultural-racial hierarchies
  and, 67–68, 70–72; defined and
  explained, 67–68, 74; Keynesian "savage"
  passions contrasted with, 188–89; in
  Malthus's thought, 11, 70–75, 78–79,
  86–87, 101–2, 105–6, 176–77, 197; the poor
  as degenerate savages, 122–23 (*see also*
  degeneration, tropes of); and the
  reframing of liberal economy, 11, 67–68,
  70–75, 111, 235n43, 236n48; savage
  immediacy, 102, 105, 109–10; savage vs.
  civilized state in Smith's thought, 72,
  100–101, 234n27, 236n48, 245n50; and
  scarcity, 9–10, 78–79, 89, 176–77; sense of
  futurity lacking, 74–75, 78–79, 237n85.
  See also civilization
saving (money), 110, 126–27, 142–43,
  153–55, 188–89, 265n57, 276n78. *See also*
  futurity; gratification, immediate vs.
  delayed
Say, Jean-Baptiste, 238n93
scarcity: in Bataille's thought, 260n5;
  biopolitics and, 86; and the "calculation
  of lives," 85–87; central to economics,
  65–66; ecological limits and, 66–67; as
  epistemic virtue, 79–80, 81; as the
  epistemology of the future, 76–82;
  formalist understanding of, 14–15;
  Foucault on, 230n6; island metaphor, 77;
  in Jevons's work, 65–66, 232n13; in liberal
  economic thought, 14–15, 16–17, 65–66,
  231–32n10; in Malthus's thought, 9, 17,
  41, 65, 176–77, 197, 203 (*see also* Malthus,
  Robert Thomas; "savage life" concept);
  objectivity of, 67, 79; oscillation between
  abundance and, 73–74, 76, 236n52;
  paradox of absolute limits, 77–78;

population and, 9, 64–68, 73–74, 77–81,
  176–77, 236n52 (*see also* population);
  realism linked to, 76–77; and the right to
  live, 90; and "savage life," 9–10, 78–79,
  89, 176–77; Smith on, 14. *See also*
  population
"scene," definition and use of, 32–33, 219n97
Schabas, Margaret, 65
Schmitt, Carl, 144, 260–61n7, 277n97
Schumpeter, Joseph, 143, 156, 263n24
Scottish Enlightenment, 47, 50–51, 65,
  225n56
Second World War. *See* World War II
Security, Territoriality, Population
  (Foucault), 83, 277n101. *See also* Foucault,
  Michel
security dispositif, 64, 230n6
self-interest: economic man and, 97–98,
  99–101, 107 (*see also* economic man;
  rationality); Malthus and the rhetoric of,
  98–99
sentient being, and the study of sensibility,
  47, 225n56
sexuality: colonial fascination with native
  nakedness, 71; Malthus on sexual
  morality, regulation, and marriage,
  107–10, 248nn97–98. *See also* women
Shackle, George, 132, 146, 262n18
Shiller, Robert J., 250n17
Shone, Richard, 214n54
Simmel, Georg, 127, 143, 250n19
skepticism, liberal, 57–58
Skidelsky, Robert, 215(62), 255n68, 256n82
slavery question, 235n44, 235nn43–44
Smith, Adam: and civilizational
  hierarchies, 100–101, 245n50; civil society
  in Smith's thought, 210n26; economic
  justification for the pursuit of self-
  interest, 97–98; on economic man, 93,
  96, 98, 99–101, 105, 106, 244n30; on fear
  as instrument of government, 104; and
  the notion of scarcity, 14, 231n10;
  political economy in Smith's thought, 15;
  on politics as 'folly of man,' 51; and the
  "savage state" (state of nature), 72,
  100–101, 234n27, 236n48; sentient being
  as starting point for, 47
Smith, Olivia, 45

Williams, Raymond, 21
Wilson, Woodrow, 139, 259n125
Winch, Donald, 57, 210n24, 227n79, 248n97
Winslow, Ted, 254n64
Wolin, Sheldon, 6, 120, 120
women: and economic man, 93–94, 107–10, 247n91, 248nn97–98; single mothers, 11, 107–9; Women's March on Versailles (1789), 39; women's suffrage, 117, 250n13
Woodruff, David, 262n18
Woolf, Leonard, 21, 121, 214n54, 255n66, 255n68
Woolf, Virginia, 21, 115, 121, 214n54, 255n66

working class, 123, 252n37. *See also* poor, the
World Bank, 66
World War I: and political and economic planning, 170–71, 272n26; Versailles peace conferences, 139, 259n125; war debt following, 193–94
World War II, and the emergence of national economy, 169–72

Xenos, Nicholas, 231n10

Yonay, Yuval, 272n26
Young, Robert, 121–22